Peter Francis Kornicki and Ian James McMullen have put together a remarkable collection of essays on different aspects of religion in Japan by an international team of contributors. Their subjects range from the new religions of post-war Japan to beliefs about fox possession in the Heian period, and from French missionaries in Okinawa in the mid-nineteenth century to the Ainu bear festival in Hokkaidō. Other chapters examine the religious life of Minamoto no Yoritomo, the founder of the first shogunate in the late twelfth century, and the role of pilgrimage in Japanese religion. The essays offer fresh insights into the rich religious traditions of Japan, many of which have been previously neglected in the English-language writing on Japan. They are dedicated to Carmen Blacker, a leading scholar on Japanese religion and folklore.

University of Cambridge Oriental Publications 50

Religion in Japan

A series list is shown at the back of the book

Carmen Blacker

Religion in Japan

Arrows to heaven and earth

Edited by
P. F. KORNICKI
University of Cambridge
and
I. J. MCMULLEN
University of Oxford

CAMBRIDGE
UNIVERSITY PRESS

PUBLISHED BY THE PRESS SYNDICATE OF THE UNIVERSITY OF CAMBRIDGE
The Pitt Building, Trumpington Street, Cambridge, United Kingdom

CAMBRIDGE UNIVERSITY PRESS
The Edinburgh Building, Cambridge CB2 2RU, UK   http://www.cup.cam.ac.uk
40 West 20th Street, New York, NY 10011–4211, USA   http://www.cup.org
10 Stamford Road, Oakleigh, Melbourne 3166, Australia
Ruiz de Alarcón 13, 28014 Madrid, Spain

First published 1996
Reprinted 1999

Printed in the United Kingdom at the University Press, Cambridge

A catalogue record for this book is available from the British Library

Library of Congress Cataloguing in Publication data
Religion in Japan: arrows to heaven and earth / edited by
P. F. Kornicki and I. J. McMullen.
p.   cm. – (University of Cambridge oriental publications:
[no.] 50)
Includes index.
ISBN 0 521 55028 9
1. Japan – Religious life and customs. I. Kornicki, Peter F.
(Peter Francis) II. McMullen, James, 1939– . III. Series.
BL2210.RA28 1995
200'.952 – dc20   95–13011   CIP

ISBN 0 521 55028 9 hardback

TO CARMEN BLACKER
TEACHER, COLLEAGUE, AND FRIEND

CONTENTS

ILLUSTRATIONS

The illustrations, which accompany Fosco Maraini's contribution to this volume, depict the Ainu iyomande ritual held at Kotan in 1954. The photographs were all taken by Professor Maraini himself and have not been published before.

NOTES ON CONTRIBUTORS

PATRICK BEILLEVAIRE is chargé de recherche at the Centre National de la Recherche Scientifique (Paris) and a member of the Centre de Recherche sur le Japon Contemporaine of the Ecole des Hautes Etudes en Sciences Sociales. His main areas of interest are Okinawan traditional culture and society, the diffusion of knowledge about Okinawa in eighteenth- and nineteenth-century Europe, and theoretical representations of Japanese society and social behaviour. His previous works include *Le Japon en langue française* (1993) and 'Au seuil du Japon: le mémoire du P. Gaubil sur les Ryûkyû et ses lecteurs', in *L'Ethnographie* LXXXVI-2 (1990).

JOHN BREEN is lecturer in Japanese in the East Asian Department at the School of Oriental and African Studies, University of London. His main research interest is the intellectual history of the late Tokugawa and early Meiji periods. His recent publications include 'Shintoists in Restoration Japan', *Modern Asian Studies* (1990); and his 'Beyond prohibition–Christianity in Restoration Japan' is forthcoming in John Breen and Mark Williams, eds, *Christianity in Japan: a dialogue between cultures*. He is currently preparing his PhD thesis, 'Emperor, state and religion in Restoration Japan', for publication.

MARTIN COLLCUTT is professor of East Asian studies and history at Princeton University. Interested in medieval Japanese society and religion, he is currently working on a series of studies of the religous interests and policies of the Kamakura shōgunate. His previous publications include *Five Mountains: the Rinzai Zen monastic institution in medieval Japan* (1981) and *A cultural atlas of Japan* (with Isao Kumakura and Marius B. Jansen, 1988).

HELEN HARDACRE is now professor of Japanese studies at the Edwin O. Reischauer Institute of Japanese Studies, Harvard University; she has previously taught at Princeton University and Griffith University, in Queensland, Australia. Her main field of interest is religion in modern and contemporary Japan, and she is the author of *Kurozumikyō and the new religions of Japan* (1986) and *Shinto and the state, 1868–1988* (1989).

ELIZABETH G. HARRISON is assistant professor of East Asian studies at the University of Arizona. Her main areas of interest are religion and intellectual history in pre-modern and modern Japan. Her previous works include a dissertation entitled 'Encountering Amida: Jōdo Shinshū sermons in eighteenth-century Japan' (1992) and translations of two articles on religion and modernization in *Ethnological Studies* 29 (1990).

JOY HENDRY is professor of social anthropology at Oxford Brookes University. Her current areas of interest are politeness and other forms of indirect communication in contemporary Japan. Her most recent books are *Understanding Japanese society* (1987), which is soon to appear in a new edition, and *Wrapping culture: politeness, presentation and power in Japan and other societies* (1993).

PETER KORNICKI is university lecturer in Japanese at Cambridge University and a fellow of Robinson College. His main research field is Japanese cultural history. His previous publications include *The reform of fiction in Meiji Japan* (1982) and *Early Japanese books in Cambridge University Library* (1991; with N. Hayashi).

JAMES McMULLEN is university lecturer in Japanese at Oxford University and TEPCO tutorial fellow in Japanese at Pembroke College. His main research field is Japanese Confucianism and intellectual history of pre-Restoration Japan. His previous publications include 'Rulers or fathers? A casuistical problem in early modern Japanese thought', in *Past and Present* 116 (1987) and *Genji gaiden: the origins of Kumazawa Banzan's commentary on The Tale of Genji* (1992).

FOSCO MARAINI is now retired, but for many years was professor of Japanese at the Università degli Studi di Firenze in Italy. His first contacts with the Ainu took place in 1938–41, when he worked in the University of Hokkaidō with Professor S. Kodama. Since then he has visited the Ainu many times, most recently in 1993. His *Gli Iku-bashui degli Ainu* (1942) is now being translated into Japanese, and amongst his other works he published *Segreto Tibet* in 1951 (translated into English in 1952 as *Secret Tibet)*. He has given a collection of nearly 500 Ainu artifacts to the Anthropological Museum of the University of Florence.

MIYAKE HITOSHI is a professor in the Faculty of Letters at Keiō University and a well-known specialist on shugendō and the folk religions of Japan. He is the author of numerous books and articles on shugendō, amongst them *Shugendō shisō no kenkyū* 修験道思想の研究 (1985) and *Kumano shugen* 熊野修験 (1992).

PETER NOSCO is professor of East Asian languages and cultures, and history, at the University of Southern California. His principal areas of research are the intellectual and social history of the Tokugawa period. His previous works include *Remembering paradise: nativism and nostalgia in eighteenth-century Japan* (1990) and *Confucianism and Tokugawa culture* (edited, 1984).

IAN READER is senior lecturer in Japanese studies at the University of Stirling. His main areas of interest are the study of popular religion in contemporary Japan, religious consumerism, and the comparative study of pilgrimage. His recent publications include *Pilgrimage in popular culture* (1993), which he edited with Tony Walter, and *Religion in contemporary Japan* (1991).

IVO SMITS has recently completed a doctorate at Leiden University with a thesis entitled 'The pursuit of loneliness: Chinese and Japanese nature poetry in medieval Japan' and is now a Research Fellow with the Royal Netherlands Academy of Sciences. His main area of interest is Japanese literature, both classical and modern. He has published 'Unusual expressions: Minamoto no Toshiyori and poetic innovation in medieval Japan' in *The Transactions of the Asiatic Society of Japan* in 1993, and forthcoming in 1995 are a Dutch translation of *Izumi shikibu nikki*, and *The pursuit of loneliness: Chinese and Japanese nature poetry in medieval Japan, ca.1050–1150.*

DAVID WATERHOUSE is a professor in the Department of East Asian Studies at the University of Toronto. He worked in the Department of Oriental Antiquities in the British Museum and the Center for Asian Arts at the University of Washington before moving to Toronto in 1966. He has wide-ranging interests in Asian arts and thought and is the author of a number of books and catalogues, including *Harunobu and his age: the development of colour printing in Japan* (1964) and *Early Japanese prints in the Philadelphia Museum of Art* (1983).

CARMEN BLACKER

During a long career, for most of which she has been based at the University of Cambridge, Carmen Blacker has become established as an eminent scholarly authority on Japanese religion and folklore, and a compelling figure in the world of Japanese studies. Her contributions as a scholar and teacher, however, have been richer and more varied than this characterisation might suggest.

Carmen's full-time commitment to Japanese might be dated symbolically from the moment when, at the age of eighteen, like many of the generation of scholars of Japan that was to dominate the field in the post-war decades, she joined the war effort. War service, however, merely made decisive an inclination that she had felt since her school-days. Reading in world mythology, she had become intrigued by the long names of Japanese divinities. Her parents supported what was thought an eccentric interest at the time. After an exhaustive search for some sort of textbook, her mother discovered a copy of a nineteenth-century Japanese grammar by Baba Tatsui (1850–88) in Great Russell Street, and her father found a correspondence course in the language. As a pupil at Benenden, she made Japanese part of her secret life. There, she encountered Juliet Piggott, a fellow pupil who had been to Japan. Though in different school houses, the two girls were able to arrange meetings. Juliet's father, the Japanophile Major-General F. S. G. Piggott (1883–1966), whom Carmen was later to commemorate in an article, had been military attaché in Tokyo, and, on his return to England, offered to teach Carmen the language during school holidays. She cycled nine miles each way from her family home in Surrey to attend his lessons, which consisted partly of study of old *tokuhon* (school readers). The General was an excellent speaker and teacher of Japanese, and her interest intensified. She left school early, and joined twice-weekly sessions of a course in Japanese at the School of Oriental and African Studies in the University of London. From there, she was recruited to the Government Communications Headquarters at Bletchley Park, the centre of the immensely successful British research into enemy communications and codes.

At Bletchley, she worked compiling a list of Japanese nouns of potential strategic relevance from 'pinches' (captured enemy documents) for a sub-section of the naval section. Her work, unlike its counterpart in German, was never consulted for operational purposes. In a recent memoir, Carmen has written of her sense of the futility of this task and her feelings of frustration.[1]

---

1 'Recollection of *temps perdu* at Bletchley Park', in F. H. Hinsley and Alan Stripp, eds., *Code breakers: the inside story of Bletchley Park* (Oxford: Oxford

Before the end of the war, she was transferred back to the School of Oriental and African Studies of the University of London as a Special Lecturer, where she both taught Japanese to military personnel and studied for a degree. She graduated with First Class Honours in 1947. Her fellow graduate was Ronald Dore, and one of her examiners was Arthur Waley. No instruction had been provided in history. The details of a candidate's performance on particular papers were normally strictly confidential, but, after the examination, Waley, with the lofty disregard for conventions for which he was known, summoned Carmen to Gordon Square and informed her of certain 'rather silly mistakes' in her history paper. From SOAS, she went in 1947 to Somerville College, Oxford, to read Philosophy, Politics, and Economics. It was her enjoyment of eighteenth- and nineteenth-century European political and moral thought that set her wondering how these ideas, particularly the concept of natural science, could have been assimilated into Japan in the nineteenth century. This interest determined the direction of her first research interest in Japan and led to her University of London doctoral dissertation on Fukuzawa Yukichi (1835–1901). Research for this took her abroad, first as a Henry Fellow to the Harvard–Yenching Institute (1950–1) and then as Treasury Student to Keiō (1951–3), where she was the only foreign student, but was welcomed, she recalls, with great hospitality. It was during this first stay in Japan that, having learnt of his writings on Fukuzawa, she met the prominent intellectual historian and political scientist Maruyama Masao, who gave her invaluable advice and encouragement.

The dissertation was published as *The Japanese enlightenment: a study of the writings of Fukuzawa Yukichi* (1964). This study set new standards in Meiji intellectual history. Drawing on a knowledge of both the Japanese tradition of Chinese learning and early European influences on Tokugawa thought on the one hand, and on her knowledge of the Western tradition on the other, as well as on the work of Maruyama, Carmen surveyed the revolution in thinking worked by Fukuzawa in a number of different fields: world view, ethics, the family, history, politics and international relations. The book is marked by the lucidity and elegance of structure and style that have characterised her writing. All seemed set for a research career in this important field. Indeed, Carmen followed up her work on Fukuzawa with an article on his conservative contemporary, Ōhashi Totsuan (1816–62), who rejected Western science with something of the vehemence with which Fukuzawa had embraced it, but did so, she showed, with coherence and clarity. This article was the first in a series of sympathetic studies of neglected or minor figures, some of whom have now become fashionable, that Carmen has published throughout her career. This series includes, as well as Totsuan, the historian Rai San'yō (1780–1832); Yoshio Markino (Makino Yoshio), the Japanese expatriate artist who worked in London between the wars; Minakata Kumagusu (1867–1941), the folklorist and polymath; Sir Francis Taylor Piggott

---

University Press, 1994), pp. 300–5.

(1852–1925), an advisor on the Meiji Constitution of 1889, and his son Major-General F. S. G. Piggott, Carmen's old tutor; Marie Stopes (1880–1958), the palaeobotanist and pioneer of birth control, who visited Japan in 1907–9 in the former capacity, and others. Nor did Carmen abandon her interest in intellectual history with her work on Fukuzawa, Ōhashi Totsuan, and Rai San'yō. She has taught the subject throughout her teaching career, at Cambridge and also as a course of lectures at Columbia, where she was Visiting Professor in 1965–6.

In 1955, Carmen was appointed Assistant Lecturer, and from 1958, University Lecturer, in Japanese Studies in the Faculty of Oriental Studies, University of Cambridge, and this has been her main academic home since then. Her colleagues at Cambridge included Eric B. Ceadel, bibliographer and specialist in waka and later University Librarian; Charles D. Sheldon, the economic historian, author of *The rise of the merchant class in Tokugawa Japan* (1958); and Douglas E. Mills, specialist in medieval literature and author of *A collection of tales from Uji* (1970). Among the lectors (instructors in Japanese) in the early years were Itasaka Gen, editor of the Kôdansha *Encyclopedia of Japan,* Ishibashi Hiro, now Principal of Ueno Gakuen University, and Torigoe Bunzō, the well-known Waseda University scholar of Japanese theatre.

At Cambridge, the long vacations could be used for visits to Japan, then still relatively cheap if one took the ten-day route through Russia, and Carmen was able to develop her long-standing interest in Japanese religion, particularly Buddhism, by direct observation and practice. On these visits, she would often enjoy the hospitality of the novelist Osaragi Jirō, staying in the tea-house of his home in Kamakura. There, she visited the Zuisenji, made the acquaintance of the *rōshi* (Zen master) at the Engakuji, and, with assiduity as she recalls, practised *zazen* for several years. These experiences inspired her to make Japanese religion her main field of research, a switch from intellectual history of which, she feels, Fukuzawa himself would have heartily disapproved. She became increasingly aware of the subtle interconnectedness of the phenomena of Japanese religious life, ranging from conventional practices to the new religions, then still regarded with scorn by educated people. Through an interest in the Shugendō, she embarked on the sustained study of Japanese shamanism. An important source of help and information was Hori Ichirō of the University of Tokyo, and she would call on him on successive summer visits to Japan.

During the sixties, Carmen collected the material that forms the basis of her best-known work, *The catalpa bow: a study of shamanistic practices in Japan* (1975). This book rapidly and deservedly attained the status of a classic. It achieves what all scholars of Japan want for their writing, but very few manage: recognition as work of value in its own right, beyond the parochial boundaries of Japanese studies. Moreover, it embodies Carmen's strengths as a scholar: wide reading in primary historical sources and in the Japanese scholarly literature, vigorous field work, sympathy for ordinary people, and clarity and elegance in presentation. She covered spectacular territory, literally as well as metaphorically. The book is based on countless visits to sacred places, mountains, lakes, temples, and shrines, and interviews with monks, priests, shamans, pilgrims, aspirants, and members of the Japanese public. Carmen performed the *kaihōgyō*, an arduous ritual circumambulation of Mt Hiei, failure at which was said to require suicide. She participated in the week long *akinomine* austerity on Mt. Haguro in Yamagata Prefecture. Three times she ascended Ontake, the sacred volcano that straddles the border between Nagano and Gifu prefectures. Her accounts of these exertions, however, do not alone account for the book's success. The prose seems, on occasion, to have absorbed something of the numinous quality of its subject matter, and there are passages of vividly evocative scenic description and of narrative skill. Pervading the book is a deeply felt poignancy, deriving in part from the fortitude of many of its subjects, often driven by adversity to seek shamanic help, and in part from its documentation of a fragile, vanishing world.

Since *The catalpa bow,* Carmen has produced a series of articles, papers, and addresses on Japanese religion and folklore. These have covered a variety of subjects, including animal witchcraft, pilgrims in Japanese history, healing, Shintō mythology, the Daijōsai (enthronement) ceremony. She has also collaborated with the distinguished Cambridge historian of Han China, Michael Loewe, on editing two volumes of essays which reflect their shared interest in cosmology and divination. Meanwhile, Japanese religion still retains its fascination, not least because, as Carmen expresses it, 'the old constantly appears in a new guise'. Some traditional themes, the power of trance and the role of the *miko,* for instance, reappear in the 'new–new religions'. Carmen has now conducted the basic research for another study, on the folkloric figure of the *ijin* (outsider) in Japan. From 1977 until his death in 1994, she was given invaluable guidance in her work by Professor Gorai Shigeru, a scholar of folklore, whom she describes as possessed of phenomenally wide reading, extraordinary energy, and imaginative insight into the inner workings of Japanese religion. Through him, she also met his remarkable French pupil, Dr Anne Bouchy. Much of her more recent research has also been pursued travelling in the company of her friend the Ryūgū Otohime (Princess of the Dragon Palace), founder of the Ryūgū Kazoku religion, a figure whom Carmen sees as re-enacting in a modern context many of the basic themes of traditional Japanese religion.

In addition to Columbia, Carmen has held Visiting Professorships in the Department of Religion at Princeton (1979) and the Department of East Asian Studies of the University of Toronto (1992). She has been Visiting Fellow at the Research Institute for Humanistic Studies, University of Kyoto (1986), and for some years has taught annually at the Ueno Gakuen University, Tokyo, where she has been appointed to the position of Professor. Carmen has been elected Honorary Member of the Folklore Society (1988), of which she was also President in 1983; Fellow of the British Academy (1989); Honorary Fellow of Somerville College, Oxford (1991); and Fellow Emeritus of Clare Hall, Cambridge (1992), where she had been a Fellow while in post as University Lecturer in Japanese. The Japanese Government appointed her a member of the Order of the Precious Crown for services to Japanese Studies in 1988. She retired from her Cambridge teaching post in 1992, and lives in the village of Grantchester, to the south of Cambridge.

In the more than four decades since her first visits, Japan has changed considerably. With the massive rise in economic prosperity, much of the old way of life has disappeared. On her first visit, Carmen recalls, life was hard for Japanese as well as for foreign visitors. In the fifties, she had felt it necessary to conceal the financial value of her scholarship grant, as it embarrassingly exceeded the salaries of her professors. Conditions were harsh; she would need five sweaters as well as two futon to stay warm on winter nights in her six-mat room. But there was a whole world to explore. Every walk encountered something interesting; every excursion yielded a new acquaintance, or afforded a vivid glimpse of the past. She quotes an expression of which D. T. Suzuki was fond, '*enzan mugen sōsō*' (the distant hills, unbounded, blue-green, layer on layer). Forty years on, Japan's new-found material wealth has dimmed that bright perspective. However, Carmen believes, Shintō, Buddhism, and the values of the older Japanese culture can still teach us, in these days of ecological peril, that nature is potentially holy and shares the same existential ground as ourselves, our Buddha Nature; this is a lesson that we must learn, if life on our planet is to survive.

PRINCIPAL PUBLICATIONS OF CARMEN BLACKER

1953 'The *Kyūhanjō* of Fukuzawa Yukichi', *Monumenta Nipponica*, 9: 304–29.

1959 'Ōhashi Totsuan: a study in anti-Western thought', *Transactions of the Asiatic Society of Japan*, Third Series, 7: 147–68.

1961 'Japanese historical writing in the Tokugawa period (1603–1868)', with W. G. Beasley, in W. G. Beasley and E. Pulleyblank, eds., *Historians of China and Japan*, (Oxford: Oxford University Press), pp. 245–63.

1963 'Initiation in the Shugendo: the passage through Ten States of Existence', in C. J. Bleeker, ed., *Initiation*, Studies in the History of Religions (Supplement to *Numen*) 10 (Leiden: E. J. Brill), pp. 96–111.

1963 'The divine boy in Japanese Buddhism', *Asian Folklore Studies*, 22: 77–88.

1964 *The Japanese enlightenment: a study of the writings of Fukuzawa Yukichi*, University of Cambridge Oriental Publications 10 (Cambridge: Cambridge University Press).

1967 'Supernatural abductions in Japanese folklore', *Asian Folklore Studies*, 26.ii: 111–148.

1969 'Intent of courtesy', in Ivan Morris, ed., *Madly singing in the mountains: an appreciation and anthology of Arthur Waley* (London: George Allen and Unwin), pp. 21–28.

1971 'Millenarian aspects of the New Religions in Japan', in Donald Shively, ed., *Tradition and modernization in Japanese culture* (Princeton: Princeton University Press), pp. 563–600.

1971 'The religions of Japan', in C. J. Bleeker and G. Widengren, eds., *Historia religionum: handbook for the history of religions* (Leiden: E. J. Brill), pp. 516–49.

1973 'Animal witchcraft in Japan', in Venetia Newall, ed., *The witch figure: folklore essays by a group of scholars in England honouring the 75th birthday of Katharine Briggs* (London: Routledge and Kegan Paul), pp. 1–20.

1975 *Ancient cosmologies*, edited with Michael Loewe (London: George Allen and Unwin).

1975 *The catalpa bow: a study of shamanistic practices in Japan* (London: George Allen and Unwin).

1978   'The snake woman in Japanese myth and legend', in J. R. Porter and W. M. S. Russell, eds., *Animals in folklore* (Cambridge: D. S. Brewer for the Folklore Society), pp. 113–25.

1979   『梓弓』 (Tokyo: Iwanami Shoten) (a translation of *The catalpa bow* into Japanese by Akiyama Satoka).

1981   *Divination and oracles*, edited with Michael Loewe (London: George Allen and Unwin).

1981   'The angry ghost in Japan', in H. R. E. Davidson and W. M. S. Russell, eds., *The folklore of ghosts* (Cambridge: D. S. Brewer for the Folklore Society), pp. 95–105.

1983   'Minakata Kumagusu, a neglected Japanese genius', *Folklore*, 94: 139–52. (Presidential address to the Folklore Society, March 1983.)

1984   'The exiled warrior and the hidden village', *Folklore*, 95: 139–50.

1984   'The religious traveller in the Edo period', *Modern Asian Studies*, 18: 593–608.

1985   'A room with a gourd: recollections of Osaragi Jiro', *Cambridge Review*, 2286 (1985): 84–85.

1986   *The catalpa bow: a study of shamanistic practices in Japan*, second edition (London: George Allen and Unwin).

1986   'The dark flower', *Temenos*, 7: 298–303.

1988   'Two Shinto myths: the Golden Age and the Chosen People', in Sue Henney and Jean-Pierre Lehmann, eds., *Themes and theories in modern Japanese history: essays in memory of Richard Storry* (London: Athlone Press), pp. 64–77.

1989   'The seer as a healer in Japan', in H. R. E. Davidson, ed., *The seer in Celtic and other traditions* (Edinburgh: John Donald Publishing), pp. 116–23.

1990   'Rethinking the study of Japanese religion', in Adriana Boscaro, Franco Gatti and Massimo Raveri, eds., *Rethinking Japan* (Folkestone: Japan Library Limited), pp. 237–41.

1990   'The Shinza or God-seat in the Daijōsai: throne, bed, or incubation couch?', *Japanese Journal of Religious Studies*, 17: 179–97.

1990   'Yoshio Markino: a recollection', in *The Japan Society Proceedings*, 115: 27–40.

1990   「日本人にとって『異人』とは何か」, *Chūō kōron* 1259: 122–35.

1991   'Two Piggotts: Sir Francis Taylor Piggott (1852–1925) and Major General F. S. G. Piggott (1883–1966)', in Sir Hugh Cortazzi and Gordon Daniels, eds., *Britain and Japan 1859–1991: themes and personalities* (London: Routledge), pp. 118–27.

1991   'Marie Stopes (1907–1958) and Japan', in Sir Hugh Cortazzi and Gordon Daniels, eds., *Britain and Japan 1859–1991: themes and personalities* (London: Routledge), pp.157–65.

1994   'Recollections of *temps perdu* at Bletchley Park', in F. H. Hinsley and Alan Stripp, eds., *Code breakers: the inside story of Bletchley Park* (Oxford: Oxford University Press, 1994), pp. 300–5.

ACKNOWLEDGEMENTS

This volume of essays honours Carmen Blacker, the eminent scholar of Japanese religion and folklore, who retired from her teaching post at the University of Cambridge in 1992. The book grew out of an international workshop, entitled 'Rethinking the study of Japanese religion', convened by Carmen Blacker herself and Peter Kornicki. It was held at Newnham College, Cambridge, from 3 to 7 April 1991, and was partly funded by the Erasmus Programme of the European Community, under the auspices of the Leiden Group of Japanese Studies. The editors wish to express their thanks to all who contributed to the success of that occasion, not all of whom are represented by a paper in this book, as well as to the Erasmus Programme and the Great Britain Sasakawa Foundation, which made it possible to invite scholars from Japan, Australia, and North America. In addition to chapters by participants at the workshop, this book also contains contributions from other former students and colleagues of Carmen Blacker, and the editors thank them all for their patience during the process of editing their manuscripts for publication. Thanks are also due to the Japan Foundation Endowment Committee for a grant to assist with editorial expenses and to the Publications Committee of the Faculty of Oriental Studies at Cambridge for meeting other expenses associated with publication. Ms Joanne Bennett-Murray provided invaluable secretarial assistance.

The subtitle of the volume is intended as an *engo* on *The catalpa bow*, Carmen Blacker's best-known work. It was suggested by a directive for the Yabusame (archery rite), according to which the leader of the ritual points a drawn bow to heaven and to earth for peace between these two realms. The editors are deeply grateful to Ms Naoko Matsubara for the fine original woodblock print illustrating this theme which she created for the dust-jacket.

1

Notes on the *kuji*

David Waterhouse

INTRODUCTION

In *The catalpa bow*, Carmen Blacker alludes in two places to the *kuji* 九字, 'nine syllables', as used by a female ascetic to heal a headache,[1] and by ascetics on Mt Ontake:

> One pair, poised on the edge of a precipitous slope down to the lake, was particularly remarkable. The *maeza* stood close to the medium, twisting his hands with ferocious intensity into the nine mudras known as *kuji*, repeating as he did so the nine accompanying magic syllables:
> *Rin-byō-tō-sha-kai-jin-retsu-zai-ZEN!*
> At the last syllable his voice rose to a sharp yell, while with two fingers stiffly outstretched he made the nine strokes of the gate, four vertical, five horizontal, through which no evil influences may pass. He then thrust his fingers fiercely forwards towards the medium's stomach in the pointed sword mudra, shouting meanwhile in sharp grunting tones the syllables 'A-UN-A-UN!'. These, the first and last letters of the Sanscrit alphabet, are believed to encompass between them the entire universe ...[2]

It is unnecessary here to describe the rest of the proceedings, which seem to vary from case to case. The purpose is sometimes to heal, sometimes to exorcise evil influences, sometimes to obtain advice from the spirit world; the medium commonly enters a trance; the *Heart sūtra* (*Hannya shingyō* 般若心經) is frequently recited as well; and always the ritual is either practised by *yamabushi* 山伏, mountain ascetics, or inspired by the *yamabushi* tradition. Blacker herself adds a footnote:

---

1 Carmen Blacker, *The catalpa bow: a study of shamanistic practices in Japan*, second edition (London: Unwin Hyman, 1986), p. 244.
2 *Ibid.*, p. 289.

1

> The *kuji* is a spell of Taoist, not Buddhist origin, which at some
> time was adopted by the *shugendō* and assigned its nine mudras.[3]

As authority she cites a short article in *Mikkyō daijiten*, which sheds some
further light on the matter.[4] Putting this together with information from
other sources, including the history of *ninjutsu* 忍術 and other Japanese
martial arts, it is possible to give a fuller account of the *kuji*. There are
additional associations in Japanese religious thought between the *kuji*, the
gorin 五輪 ('five *cakras*') and the *godai* 五大 ('five greats', or five 'elements',
in Tantric Buddhist theory); but these will not be discussed here. What follows,
if unavoidably technical in places, is no more than a summary account of a
vast subject, about which my curiosity was stimulated not only by Blacker's
brief reference but also by encountering survivals of these things in certain
kinds of martial arts practice.

CHINESE ORIGINS: GE HONG AND TANLUAN

The *kuji* are indeed Taoist in origin, and are given differing interpretations in
Taoism and in *shugendō* 修験道, the 'path of experience through askēsis', as
the religion of the *yamabushi* is more formally called. The normal formula
for the *kuji* is in fact quoted first in a well-known Taoist text, the *Neipian* 內
篇 of Ge Hong 葛洪 (*c.*280–*c.*340 AD; also known as Baopuzi 抱朴子), in a
chapter entitled 'Into mountains, over streams' (Deng-she 登涉).[5] This chapter
describes, with a wealth of fascinating practical detail, how to live in the
mountains, and what precautions to take there. Ge Hong introduces the nine-
character formula as a secret prayer to the Six Jia (Liu Jia 六甲), ancient
Taoist gods; and he says that it must be constantly recited in secret, when one
enters the mountains. It actually forms a grammatical Chinese sentence (*lin
bing dou zhe jie chen lie zai qian* 臨兵鬪者皆陳列在前), which can be
translated, 'May those who preside over warriors all be my vanguard!' Other
literal translations are possible; and there are also esoteric interpretations,
especially in Japanese sources. Ge Hong himself explains that it is a prayer to
avert evil influences and to ensure that things will proceed without difficulty.

The method of 'cutting the nine characters' (*kuji o kiru* 九字を切る), as
practitioners of *shugendō* describe it, is used by them quite correctly, as a

---

3 *Ibid.*, p. 353.
4 Mikkyō jiten hensankai 密教辞典編纂会, ed., *Mikkyō daijiten* 密教大辞典,
revised and enlarged edition, 6 vols. (Kyōto: Hōzōkan, 1970), vol. II, p. 332.
5 James R. Ware, *Alchemy, medicine and religion in the China of a.d. 320: the Nei
p'ien of Ko Hung* (Cambridge, Mass.: MIT Press, 1966), p. 279f.

2

preparatory ritual of protection, to cut off demonic influences and their *inki* (Ch. *yinqi* 陰気), 'vital substance': influences that proceed from the 'shady side' of life or indeed of the mountains themselves. As several Japanese authors point out, in connection with the *kuji*, nine is the perfect number for *yang* 陽, the 'bright side'.[6] It is so interpreted, for example, when determining the individual hexagram lines for fate-calculation according to the *Yijing* 易經, the 'Classic of Changes'.[7]

The *kuji* are next cited in a canonical Chinese Buddhist text, the *Wangsheng lunzhu* 往生論註, by Tanluan 曇鸞 (476?–542?). Tanluan was a native of Yenmen 雁門 in Shanxi 山西 province, and was no doubt inspired by the example of Huiyuan 慧遠 (334–416), who also came from Yenmen and is credited among other things with having founded a Pure Land Society as early as 402.[8] After entering the Buddhist order (on Wutaishan 五台山), Tanluan concentrated on studying the 'four treatises', texts of Mādhyamika philosophy, which are attributed to Nāgārjuna (third century AD) or his disciple Āryadeva and had been translated into Chinese by Huiyuan's friend Kumārajīva (350–409?).[9] Attracted by the Three Treatises School, Tanluan practised meditation on Emptiness, as recommended by Nāgārjuna; but, while attempting to make an annotated translation of the *Dafangdeng dajijing* 大方等大集經, an important *sūtra* of the Vaipulya class, he was taken ill.[10] Recovering soon

6 Mochizuki Shinkō 望月信亨 (1954): *(Mochizuki) Bukkyō daijiten* (望月) 佛教大辭典, enlarged edition, 10 vols. (Sekai Seiten Kankō Kyōkai, 1954), vol. I, p. 661; Miyake Hitoshi 宮家準, *Shugendō girei no kenkyū* 修験道儀礼の研究 (Shunjūsha, 1971), p. 479; Murayama Shūichi 村山修一, *Nihon on'yōdō shi sōsetsu* 日本陰陽道史総説 (Hanawa Shobō, 1981), p. 406.
7 Miyazaki Ichisada 宮崎市定, 'Le développement de l'idée de divination en Chine', in *Mélanges de Sinologie offerts à Monsieur Paul Demiéville*, vol. I (Bibliothèque de l'Institut des Hautes Etudes Chinoises, vol. XX) (Paris: Presses Universitaires de France, 1966), p. 165.
8 Kenneth K. S. Ch'en, *Buddhism in China: a historical survey* (Princeton: Princeton University Press, 1964), p. 343.
9 The 'four treatises' (*silun* 四論) were: (1) *Zhonglun* 中論 (4 rolls; T.1564: strictly = *Mādhyamakaśāstra*, but known under other Sanskrit names also); (2) *Shinimenlun* 十二門論 (1 roll; T.1568: = *Dvādaśanikāyaśāstra*?); (3) *Dazhidulun* 大智度論 (100 rolls; T.1509: = *Mahāprajñāpāramitopadeśa*); and (4) *Bolun* 百論 (2 rolls; T.1569: = *Śata[ka]śāstra*?). Nos. (1), (2) and (4) were later taken as the canonical texts of the *Sanlunzong* 三論宗 (Jap. *Sanronshū*), the 'Three Treatises School'. No. (4) is by Āryadeva, the other three by Nāgārjuna. *Cf.* Paul Demiéville et al., *Répertoire du canon bouddhique sino-japonais*, 2nd edition, revised and enlarged (Fascicule annexe du Hōbōgirin; Paris: Librairie d'Amérique et d'Orient, Adrien Maisonneuve; and Tōkyō: Maison Franco-Japonaise, 1978) s.v.; Fujita Kōtatsu 藤田宏達, *Zenson* 善導, Jinrui no chiteki isan 18 人類の知的遺産 18 (Kōdansha, 1985), p. 73.
10 On the Vaipulya sūtras and their transmission to China, *cf.* Lokesh Chandra,

afterwards, he resolved that he would pursue methods of defeating old age and of attaining immortality; and he went south across the Yangzi river, to the court of emperor Wudi 武帝 (r.502–49) of Liang 梁. At some date between 527 and 529 he encountered the famous Taoist sage Tao Hongjing 陶弘景 (456–536), from whom he received the Classic of Immortals (*Xianjing* 仙經), in ten rolls: a text (or group of texts) which cannot now be identified. On the way home with this, however, he met Bodhiruci I, the Indian scholar and translator of Buddhist texts.[11] The story goes that Bodhiruci spat on the ground on hearing about the *Xianjing*, and made a contemptuous remark about it. He then presented to Tanluan a copy of the *Guanjing* 観經, in which, he maintained, was given the method for gaining immortality. Tanluan immediately burnt the *Xianjing*, and devoted the rest of his life to studying and preaching about the Pure Land. If the date of his birth is given correctly as 476, he would have been 54 or 55 at the time.[12]

The *Guanjing*, 'Sūtra on visualisation', was apparently the *Guan wuliangshou jing* 観無量寿經, 'Sūtra on visualising immeasurable life' (T.365). The Sanskrit title of this text has been reconstructed as *Amitāyurbuddhānusmṛtīsūtra*,[13] but it does not exist in Sanskrit or Tibetan, and is known only from the Chinese version and a Uighur translation. Demiéville suggests it may be apocryphal (and therefore a Chinese forgery?): but Fujita, who has studied the structure of the text with great care, makes the best case he can for regarding it as authentic.[14]

Iranian elements in the formation of Tantric Buddhism, presented to the symposium on 'The Silk Route and the Diamond Path' held on 7, 8 November 1982 at the Frederick S. Wight Art Gallery, University of California, Los Angeles. Typescript, 80 pp. (New Delhi: the author, 1982), pp. 14–40.

11 Bodhiruci I (not to be confused with Bodhiruci II) came from central India, and arrived in Luoyang 洛陽 in about 508. He worked there until about 534–7; and then in Ye, in Western Henan 河南: Demiéville et al., *Répertoire du canon bouddhique sino-japonais*, p. 237a.

12 The main source for Tanluan's life is the *Xu Gaosengzhuan* 続高僧伝 (T.2060), compiled by Daoxuan 道宣 (596–667). The account presented here is based in the first instance on Fujita, *Zenson*, pp. 73–5, but has been supplemented from several other Japanese sources, e.g. Kyōdai Tōyōshi Jiten Hensankai 京大東洋史辞典編纂会, ed., (*Shinpen*) *Tōyōshi jiten* (新編) 東洋史辞典 (Tōkyō: Sōgensha, 1980), p. 648. Afterwards, Tanluan lived at the Dayansi 大巌寺 in Bingzhou 并州 (modern Taiyuan 大原), Shanxi Province; and in his last years at Xuanzhongsi 玄中寺 in Fenzhou 汾州, south-west of there. According to one account he was the founder of this monastery; but other sources place its foundation in 472: (*Shinpen*) *Tōyōshi jiten*, p. 258. In addition to the *Wangsheng lunzhu*, Tanluan was the author of the *Zan Amituofo ji* 讃阿彌陀佛偈 (T.1978) and the *Lüelun anle jingtu yi* 略論案楽浄土義 (T.1957).

13 Demiéville et al., *Répertoire du canon bouddhique sino-japonais*, p. 46.

14 Fujita Kōtatsu 藤田宏達, *Kan muryōju kyō kōkyū* 観無量寿経講究 (Kyōto:

4

The full title of Tanluan's *Wangsheng lunzhu* is *Wuliangshou jing youpotishe yuansheng ji zhu* 無量寿經優婆堤舍願生偈註, 'Commentary on the discourse (*upadeśa*) about the Sūtra on immeasurable life, and on the verses (*gāthā*) about the vow to be reborn [in the Pure Land]' (T.1819). The text on which Tanluan writes his commentary is ascribed to Vasubandhu, and was translated into Chinese by none other than Bodhiruci I (T.1524).[15] The name *Wuliangshou jing*, 'Sūtra on immeasurable life', was borrowed by him from one of the old translations of the *Larger Sukhāvatīvyūha*, describing the Paradise of Amitābha: either that by the Parthian An Shigao 安世高 (at Luoyang *c.*148–170), or that by the Sogdian monk Kang Sengkai 康僧鎧 (Saṃghavarman? Active at Luoyang from 252).[16] Tanluan begins by distinguishing the 'Easy' and 'Difficult' Paths, previously identified in the *Shizhu piposha lun* 十住毘婆沙論 (T.1521), a work which, like the *Guan wuliangshou jing*, does not exist in Sanskrit or Tibetan, but is known from its Chinese translation.[17] The text is, however, credited to Nāgārjuna; and the translation was made in the early fifth century by Kumārajīva (350–409?), aided by the Kashmiri monk Buddhayaśas (who arrived in Chang-an 長安 in 408 and worked there till 412). There is no reason to doubt its authenticity; and, since Tanluan had previously made a particular study of Nāgārjuna's thought, it is natural enough that he would cite him.

For Tanluan, the Easy Path is *tali* 他力 (Jap. *tariki*), 'the strength of another', a term which strictly renders Sanskrit *paratantra*, and is described both by Vasubandhu and in the *Laṅkāvatāra sūtra* as one of the three types of *svabhāva*, 'own-nature': in this case, meaning 'dependent on something else'. Vasubandhu also gave currency to the term *vīrya*, which is, among

Shinshū Ōtani-ha Shūmusho Shuppanbu, 1985), *passim*; Fujita Kōtatsu, *Zenson*, pp. 74–5, 125–6.

15 The full title in Chinese is *Wuliangshou jing youpotishe yuansheng ji* 無量寿經優波堤舍願生偈. This is customarily abbreviated as *Wuliangshou jing lun* 無量寿経論, as *Jingtu lun* 浄土論 or as *Wangsheng lun* 往生論. The Sanskrit title has been reconstructed as *Sukhāvatīvyūhopadeśa*.

16 An Shigao's translation is listed in the catalogue *Gujin yijing tuji* 古今譯經圖紀 (T.2151), compiled by Jingmai 靖邁 in 664–5; *cf.* Bunyiu Nanjio, *A catalogue of the Chinese translation of the Buddhist Tripitaka, the sacred canon of the Buddhists in China and Japan* (Oxford: Clarendon Press, 1883) p.10b, n.1. It is now lost. Saṃghavarman apparently borrowed the name from this source for his translation (T.360). Another early equivalent was *Wuliang qingjing pingdengjiao* 無量清浄平等覺, 'Immeasurably clean and pure and of universal perception', as chosen by Shi Loujiachen 支婁迦讖 (Lokakṣema(?): active at Luoyang 167?–*c.*186), a monk from the nomadic Yuezhi 月氏 people (T.361). Altogether, twelve Chinese translations of the sūtra were made, of which five survive.

17 The Sanskrit title has been reconstructed as *Dāśabhūmi-kavībhāṣā*: Demiéville et al., *Répertoire du canon bouddhique sino-japonais*, s.v.

other things, the second of 'five faculties' (*pañca-indriya*), to be cultivated by all followers of Buddhism; and which means 'spiritual vigour, valour'. In Chinese it became *zili* 自力 (Jap. *jiriki*), 'own strength'; and the contrast between *tali* and *zili* became central not only to Tanluan but also in all later Pure Land thought, notably in Japan.

It happens that Bodhiruci I had also translated the *Laṅkāvatāra sūtra* into Chinese (T.671), in 513: so that his influence on Tanluan, and on the introduction of Pure Land thought into China, should not be underestimated. However, apart from his translation of the *Wuliangshou jing lun*, Bodhiruci is not known to have had any direct connection with Pure Land teaching, although he translated works by Vasubandhu on other aspects of Buddhist thought. It seems rather that Tanluan picked up ideas about the Pure Land which had been current in China since at least the time of Huiyüan; and, with the stimulus provided by Bodhiruci, as well as his own prior studies of Mādhyamika philosophy, took them in a new direction. His discussion of the name of Amitābha, for example, with its distinction between different kinds of name, seems to be indebted to the latter source.

Corless goes further, questioning the whole story of Tanluan's meeting with Bodhiruci and of his burning the *Xuanjing* (whatever it was), and doubting whether the *Guanjing* should be identified as the *Guan wuliangshou jing*.[18] Without going as far as this, we may agree that the *Xu Gaosengzhuan* account, like so many of its kind, smacks of hagiography. Moreover, as both Corless and Japanese commentators agree, Taoism remained important for Tanluan, either because he continued to believe in it, or because it was expedient at the time to present Pure Land teachings in a Taoist guise. The story about his early illness suggests that he was more interested in prolonging the life of his physical body, than in becoming an Immortal in the spiritual sense; and indeed Tao Hongjing was renowned for his pharmaceutical skills.[19] In the end, Tanluan seems to have combined the practice of Taoist alchemy with Buddhist beliefs in the Pure Land; and his *Wangsheng lunzhu* contains many examples of protective spells and cures, drawn from Baopuzi or other sources. It is in this light that we must regard his commendation of the *kuji*.[20]

18 Roger J. Corless, 'T'an-luan: Taoist sage and Buddhist Bodhisattva', in David W. Chappell, ed., *Buddhist and Taoist practice in medieval Chinese society*, Buddhist and Taoist Studies II (Honolulu: University of Hawaii Press, 1987), p. 42 and p. 43, n.6.
19 *Cf.* Michel Strickmann, 'On the alchemy of T'ao Hung-ching', in Holmes Welch and Anna Seidel, eds, *Facets of Taoism: essays in Chinese religion* (New Haven and London: Yale University Press, 1979), *passim*.
20 Corless, following the Japanese scholar Michibata Ryōshū 道端良秀, questions whether Tanluan even knew the *Neipian* at first hand, since it may have been handed down orally: 'T'an-luan: Taoist sage and Buddhist Bodhisattva', p. 44, n. 22. This

TRANSMISSION TO JAPAN: KAKUBAN, SHINRAN AND OTHERS

The *kuji* played a very minor role in Tanluan's thought and practice. He has been discussed at some length here only because of the importance which *kuji* came to have in Japan, and the strong possibility that the *Wangsheng lunzhu* had a role in their transmission there. Meditation on the name of Amida-butsu 阿彌陀佛 was introduced to Enryakuji by Ennin 圓仁 (794–864), who had learnt it during his stay on Wutai shan.[21] Interest in rebirth in the Pure Land quickened as a result of the belief that the period of *mappō* 末法, the 'coming end of the dharma', had started in 1052, the Japanese calculation of this date placing it exactly 500 years later than the Chinese one. In addition, of course, the teaching of Genshin 源信 (942–1017), Hōnen 法然 (1133–1212) and Shinran 親鸞 (1173–1262) helped to disseminate Pure Land teaching. It is significant that all three men were learned clerics who began their careers by studying on Hieizan 比叡山; and Shinran in particular displays familiarity with Tanluan's writings. Indeed Shinran, whose religious name uses the same second character as the name Tanluan, quotes from the *Wangsheng lunzhu*,[22] and refers to Tanluan deferentially as the first Chinese master of Pure Land teachings. Shinran distinguished seven patriarchs of the Pure Land Sect: among whom Nāgārjuna and Vasubandhu represented India; Genshin and Hōnen represented Japan; and Tanluan, Daochuo 道綽 (562–645) and Shandao 善導 (618–81) represented China. At least seven separate paintings of the Seven Patriarchs, executed between 1477 and 1608, have survived in Japanese monastery collections.[23]

Even before this, however, Hōnen's disciple Shunjōbō Chōgen 俊乘房 重源 (1121–1206), who accompanied Eisai 榮西 (1141–1215) on his first visit to China in 1168 and who later took the name Namu Amidabutsu 南無 阿彌陀佛, had brought back a Chinese painting of Five Chinese Patriarchs of the Pure Land Sect, in which pride of place was given to Tanluan himself. This Southern Song painting, or a thirteenth-century copy of it, survives at Nison-in 二尊院, Kyōto; it served as the basis for a set of five paintings from

seems to be an extreme point of view, since Tanluan would have had access to ample written sources.

21 Edward Kamens, *The three jewels: a study and translation of Minamoto Tamenori's Sanbōe* (Ann Arbor: Center for Japanese Studies, The University of Michigan, 1988), pp. 342–3.

22 Takamichi Takahatake, *Young man Shinran: a reappraisal of Shinran's life*, SR Supplements, vol. 18 (Waterloo, Ont.: Wilfrid Laurier University Press, 1987), pp. 65–6.

23 Ishida Mosaku 石田茂作, *Bukkyō bijutsu no kihon* 仏教美術の基本 (Tōkyō Bijutsu, 1967), p. 328, gives the dates and locations of these paintings.

the Muromachi period, preserved at the Mandaraji 曼荼羅寺, in Kōnan-shi 江南市, Aichi-ken 愛知県; and it probably inspired a handscroll painting of the deeds of the five men, which is datable to the Kamakura period and is preserved at the Kōmyōji 光明寺 in Kamakura.[24] According to the official life of Hōnen (compiled 1307–p.1317), Hōnen himself selected the 'five Chinese patriarchs', and instructed Chōgen to seek out the painting of them while he was in China.[25]

In all this, we find no mention of the *kuji*; and modern Japanese reference works, while mentioning the *Neipian* and the *Wangsheng lunzhu*, associate the spread of *kuji* in Japan with *mikkyō* 密教, the 'secret teachings', of Shingon and Tendai Buddhism, rather than with Pure Land. They may be correct in this assumption; but it seems impossible to document it for the early centuries of *mikkyō* in Japan; and there is a *prima facie* case for suspecting an initial transmission via Pure Land teaching. It may also be that the *kuji* entered Japanese religious practice, specifically that of early *shugendō*, in part through a direct Taoist transmission, whether oral or written; but, again, it is impossible to prove this.

In the frequent incendiary fires at Tendai and Shingon monasteries, early texts which would throw light on the matter have probably been lost. An important clue is provided, however, by a surviving text, *Gorin kuji myō himitsu shaku* 五輪九字明秘密釋, by the Shingon monk Kakuban 覺鑁 (1095–1143), posthumously known as Kōgyō Daishi 興教大師. After early studies at Ninnaji 仁和寺, and at Kōfukuji 興福寺 in Nara, Kakuban entered Kōyasan 高野山 in 1114. Returning to Ninnaji the following year, he received ritual consecrations not only there, but also at Daigoji 醍醐寺 and at the Tendai monastery of Miidera 三井寺. Having undergone this varied training, he put together a syncretic teaching which included not only elements of Tendai and Shingon *mikkyō* but also Pure Land Buddhism. Equating Dainichi Nyorai 大日如來 and Amida Nyorai 阿彌陀如來, he emphasised the 'Pure Land adorned with mystery' (*mitsugon jōdo* 密嚴浄土), of Dainichi Nyorai; a Shingon version of the invocation to Amida (the *nenbutsu* 念佛); and

24 The Nison-in painting is illustrated in several convenient places: Sawa Ryūken 佐和隆研, *Butsuzō zuten* 仏像図典 (Yoshikawa Kōbunkan, 1962), p.189; Ishida, *Bukkyō bijutsu no kihon*, p. 329; Jōji Okazaki, *Pure Land Buddhist painting*, translated and edited by Elizabeth ten Grotenhuis (Kōdansha International Ltd & Shibundō, 1977), p. 17. In the light of this evidence, it is too strong to say that Tanluan was 'picked up, dusted off, and enthroned as the first teacher of Sukhāvatī Buddhism by Shinran Shōnin': Corless, 'T'an-luan: Taoist sage and Buddhist Bodhisattva', p. 42.
25 Harper Havelock Coates and Ryugaku Ishizuka, *Hōnen the Buddhist saint: his life and teaching*, 5 vols. (Kyōto: The Society for the Publication of Sacred Books of the World, 1949), p. 190. The same source repeats the story of Tanluan's meeting with Bodhiruci (p. 568).

visualisation of the syllable 'A' (*Ajikan* 阿字觀).

After an audience with the retired emperor Toba 鳥羽 (1103–56; r.1107–28), Kakuban received authority for the rebuilding of Kōyasan; and, having first established his Denpōin 傳法院 in the Kii 紀伊 peninsula (modern Wakayama-ken 和歌山県), he re-established it on Kōyasan in 1131, as Dai Dempōin 大傳法院. By 1135, with further imperial support, he had become Abbot (*zasu* 座主) of Kongōbuji 金剛峯寺, the main monastery on Kōyasan; but, because of a violent feud between rival factions on the mountain, he was obliged to resign the following year, and secluded himself at the Mitsugon-in 密嚴院 to practise austerities. In 1140 another violent quarrel erupted between Kongōbuji and Dai Dempōin, concerning the boundaries of the monastic estates; the Mitsugon-in was attacked; and Kakuban and his followers fled to Negorosan 根來山, where he founded a new monastery, Enmyōji 圓明寺, and died peacefully only three years later.[26]

From its title, *Gorin kuji myō himitsu shaku* would appear to be about the *gorin*, the 'five *cakras*' and how they are associated in some way with the *kuji*. When one examines the actual text, however, this expectation is not entirely borne out.[27] Kakuban wrote many short ritual texts and commentaries for his followers; but *Gorin kuji hishaku*, as it is commonly known for short, is a more extended work. Starting from the point of view that Dainichi is really Amida, it first explains the secret meaning of the 'seed characters' (*shuji* 種字) for the *gorin*, which in Shingon thought came to be correlated with the *godai*, 'five great [elements]', as well as with five superposed geometrical shapes, the *gorin-tō* 五輪塔, '*stūpa* of the five *cakras*'. This *stūpa*, familiar as a grave marker throughout Japan, appears to be a native invention,[28] and, though secondary sources are not clear on this point, its

26 These details are extracted from Ōno Tatsunosuke 大野達之助, ed., *Nihon bukkyō shi jiten* 日本仏教史辞典 (Tōkyōdō Shuppan, 1979), p. 76; and Nakamura Hajime 中村元 et al., eds, (*Iwanami*) *Bukkyō jiten* (岩波) 仏教辞典 (Iwanami Shoten, 1989), p. 114. The chief source for Kakuban's life is the *Denpōin Hongan Kakuban Shōnin engi* 傳法院本願覺鑁上人縁起; and there is a collection of his writings, *Kōgyō Daishi zenshū* 興教大師全集 (1909). I have not consulted either of these for purposes of the present study; but many of Kakuban's works are included in Suzuki Gakujutsu Zaidan 鈴木学術財団, ed., (*Zōho kaitei*) *Nihon Daizōkyō* (増補改訂) 日本大蔵經, 100 vols. (Kōdansha, 1978), and in the convenient compilation by Nagamatsu Shunkyō 長松峻恭, *Shingon-shū seiten* 真言宗聖典, 22nd reprint (Kyōto: Heirakuji Shoten, 1966).

27 A *kambun kundoku* 漢文訓讀 version of the text is included in Nagamatsu, *Shingon-shū seiten*, pp. 1366–1414.

28 However, the shape also appears in Korean art as early as the eleventh or twelfth century: *cf.* a miniature glass stūpa (and silver cover) of the Koryŏ period, preserved in the National Museum of Korea: illustrated in Evelyn McCune, *The arts of Korea:*

dissemination may be due to Kakuban's text, which includes a diagram of it. In the writings of Kūkai 空海 (774–835), however, the *godai*, or rather the *rokudai* 六大, 'six great [elements]' (including consciousness), correspond to the 'universal of essence or substance' (*taidai* 體大), which is coextensive with the Body of Dainichi Nyorai, and hence with the Dharma Body (*dharmakāya*; Jap. *hosshin* 法身) of the entire universe. The doctrine of *sokushin jōbutsu* 即身成佛, 'achievement of Buddhahood in this very body', is closely associated with this by Kūkai, as part of a cluster of mutually supportive teachings.

Kakuban expounds the meaning of the *gorin* under ten 'gates' (*mon* 門), concluding with a hymn in praise of the *sokushin jōbutsu* teaching. He then passes on to the *kuji*; but these turn out to be not the old Taoist spell, but a nine-character *dhāraṇī* invocation to Amida, written in *siddham* (Jap. *shittan* 悉曇), and reading *On-a-miri-ta-tei-sei-ka-ra-un*! These syllables are correlated with the 'nine categories of rebirth' (*kubon ōjō* 九品往生) which are distinguished in Pure Land Buddhism; and the mystic significance of each syllable is explained in detail, as a further series of 'gates'. Just as the *gorin* are the gates to the Dharma Body of the 'five forms of knowledge' possessed by Dainichi Nyorai, so these *kuji* are the gates to the Body of bliss (*sambhogakāya*; Jap. *hōshin* 報身) of the 'nine categories'.[29] Entry to the Pure Land, whether it be construed as being of Dainichi Nyorai or of Amida Nyorai, may be attained in this life, through appropriate practices based on the *gorin* or on the *kuji*, respectively. The Pure Land is actually everywhere, not some distant paradise. In the second half of *Gorin kuji hishaku*, Kakuban comments in detail on each of his *kuji*.[30]

This attractive but heterodox teaching may have been partly responsible for the struggles in which Kakuban found himself embroiled. After his untimely death on Negorosan, his interpretations were given greater currency by Raiyu 頼瑜 (1226–1304), who in 1288 re-established the Dai Denpōin and the Mitsugon-in on Negoro-san;[31] and by another successor, Shōken 聖憲 (1307–92); and Kakuban came to be recognised as founder of the 'New Rite' Shingon school (Shingi Shingon-shū 新儀真言宗), as opposed to the 'Old Rite' Shingon school (Kogi Shingon-shū 古儀真言宗) on Kōyasan. By the

---

an illustrated history (Rutland, Vt., & Tokyo: Charles E. Tuttle Company, 1962), pl. 139; it is found also in later Tibetan art, albeit in a slightly different form (apparently deriving independently from later Indian antecedents).

29 Nagamatsu, *Shingon-shū seiten*, p. 1371. A *shugendō kuji* ritual which uses Kakuban's formula is included in the *Shugen jinpi gyōhō fuju shū* (discussed below), No. 81; (*Zōho kaitei*) *Nihon Daizōkyō*, vol. 94, p. 46.

30 Nagamatsu, *Shingon-shū seiten*, pp. 1391f.

31 Ōno, *Nihon bukkyō shi jiten*, p. 479.

late sixteenth century Negorosan had become the site of a large complex of monasteries, whose warrior-monks (*sōhei* 僧兵) were renowned for their prowess, intrigued in politics, and threatened the city of Ōsaka, in much the same way as the warrior-monks of Hieizan had threatened Kyōto. Consequently, in 1585 Toyotomi Hideyoshi 豊富秀吉 (1536–98) attacked and destroyed all the buildings on the mountain, with the exception of the main *stūpa* (built 1480–1547) and the Daishidō 大師堂 (1391). It was not until the time of Tokugawa Tsunayoshi 德川綱吉 (1646–1709), the fifth Tokugawa *shōgun*, that a programme of rebuilding could be initiated. Meanwhile, Shingi Shingon-shū had divided into two branches, Buzan-ha 豊山派 and Chizan-ha 智山派.[32]

These later developments, and the doctrinal and ritual changes associated with them, need not concern us. On the other hand, although Kakuban does not mention the Taoist *kuji*, we can safely assume that he would know of them from Tanluan; and that they influenced him in devising his own set of *kuji*. Moreover, it may well be that he was indirectly responsible for the importation of the Taoist *kuji* into both *shugendō* and the martial arts. After all, Negorosan (in modern Naka-gun 那賀郡) is not far from Yoshinoyama 吉野山 and the *shugendō* headquarters at Ōmine 大峰, all in modern Wakayama-ken.

Kakuban may have been the first to adapt the *kuji* for Japanese Buddhist use; but he was followed in 1730 by Nichiei 日榮, of Kyōto, a monk of the Nichiren school, who compiled a useful treatise on *shugendō*, entitled *Shugen koji benran* 修験故事便覧. In this, he recommends using a sequence of nine characters drawn from the *Lotus Sūtra* (the chief text of Nichiren-shū 日蓮宗).[33] This prayer is: *Ryō-hyaku-yu-jun-nai-mu-sho-sui-gen* 令百由旬内無諸衰患, 'Cause all enfeebling sicknesses to be naught for a distance of a hundred yojanas!' According to Nichiei, this is a quotation from ch. 1, 'Introduction', of the *Lotus sūtra*; but he is in error. It is in fact from ch. 26, 'Dhāraṇī' (in Kumārajīva's Chinese version), where it is uttered by the *deva* king Vaiśravaṇa (Jap. *Bishamon-ten* 毘沙門天) as a guarantee of protection for holders of the *Lotus sūtra* itself.[34]

---

32 Ōno, *Nihon bukkyō shi jiten*, pp. 271, 326; Nakamura et al., (*Iwanami*) *Bukkyō jiten*, p. 647. For the story of Hideyoshi's campaign, *cf.* G. Renondeau, 'Histoire des moines guerriers du Japon', in *Mélanges publiés par l'Institut des Hautes Études Chinoises*, tome premier (Bibliothèque de l'Institut des Hautes Études Chinoises, vol. XI; Paris: Presses Universitaires de France, 1957), pp. 296–9.

33 It is reprinted in (*Zōho kaitei*) *Nihon Daizōkyō*, vol. 96; for the passage in question, see p. 318.

34 *Cf.* the English translation by Leon Hurvitz, *Scripture of the lotus blossom of the fine dharma (The Lotus sūtra)* (New York: Columbia University Press, 1976) pp. 321–2). Nichiei's mistake seems to have been missed by modern Japanese

Even earlier, in Jōdo Shinshū 浄土真宗, the sect founded by Shinran, there was a cult of nine other characters, which form an invocation to Amida, and read *Namu fukashigi-kō Nyorai* 南無不可思議光如來, 'Homage to the Tathāgata of Inconceivable Light!' It was the custom to display this as the centrepiece in a trio of hanging scrolls. The right-hand scroll was inscribed with the familiar six-character formula *Namu Amida-butsu* 南無阿彌陀佛; and the left-hand scroll with a ten-character formula, also an invocation to Amida: *Kimyō jinjippō mugekō Nyorai* 歸命盡十方無礙光如來, 'Homage to the Tathāgata whose light shines without obstruction universally in the ten directions!' It is not clear when this custom originated; but the expressions *fukashigi-kō Nyorai* and *namu fukashigi-kō* both occur in writings of Shinran himself.[35] Bukkōji 佛光寺, one of the chief monasteries in Kyōto of Jōdo Shinshū, seems to be especially associated with the cult, and owns a hanging scroll inscribed with the nine characters by emperor Go-Mizunoo 後水尾 (1596–1680).[36] At any rate, the use of a nine-character formula in Jōdo Shinshū recalls Shinran's interest in Tanluan; and the ten-character formula too may be connected with another Taoist formula, also of ten characters.[37]

commentators: e.g. *Mikkyō daijiten*, p. 332; Murayama, *Nihon on'yōdō shi sōsetsu*, p. 406. Nichiei goes on to claim (p. 319) that the Taoist *kuji* formula too comes from the Lotus *sūtra*!

35   The word *fukashigi*, translating Skt. *acintya*, is apparently taken from the *Sukhāvatīvyūha*, though it occurs in other relevant texts. Shinran's expressions come from his *Kyōgyō shinshō* 教行信證 and *Shōshin nembutsu ge* 正信念佛偈 respectively. *Cf.* Numa Hōryō 沼法量 and Kozuka Yoshikuni 小塚義国, eds., *Shinshū koji seigo jiten* 真宗故事成語辞典 (Kyōto: Hōzōkan, 1982), pp. 306–8.

36   Bukkōji was probably founded in 1324, though one dubious legend credits it to Shinran himself, in 1222: Ōno, *Nihon bukkyō shi jiten*, p. 416. The scroll by emperor Go-Mizunoo is illustrated in Shibudani Yūkyō 澁谷有教, ed., *Bukkōji jiten* 佛光寺辞典 (Kyōto: Honzan Bukkōji, 1984), p. 99.

37   The Taoist ten-character formula is: *Ten-ryū-ko-ō-shō-ze-myō-ki-sui-dai* 天龍虎王勝是命鬼水大. If one traces this on the palm of the hand with one's finger, and clenches one's fist, evil influences are swept away, and good fortune ensues: Kindaichi Kyōsuke 金田一京助, *Jikai* 辞海 (Sanseidō, 1954), p. 571. Slightly different versions of this text appear in other sources: e.g. in two of the rituals included in *Fuju shū*: (*Zōho kaitei*) *Nihon Daizōkyō*, vol. 94, pp. 96–7. According to Numa and Kozuka, p. 308, there is a saying, that 'one cuts the nine characters [i.e. with the sword *mudrā*], but not the ten characters' (*kuji wa kitte mo jūji wa kirenu*). They explain this as due to the influence of the Taoist *kuji* (which they slightly misquote). As we shall see, the *kuji* and the *jūji* were often used together in *shugendō* rituals; but a detailed examination of the *jūji* is beyond the scope of the present essay. *Cf.* the passages about *jūji* quoted below.

KUJI RITUALS IN *SHUGENDŌ*

Although there are loose ends in the argument, the evidence presented so far indicates that the *kuji* entered Japanese thought and practice first via Pure Land Buddhism. However, the silence of the sources suggests that, even if they were known to some *shugendō* ascetics, they must have played a rather minor role prior to about 1500. *Shugendō* can trace its origins back to the eighth century, and to the teaching of such charismatic though shadowy figures as En no Ozunu 役小角 on Mt Katsuragi 葛城, Shin-ei 神叡 on Mt Yoshino, Rōben 良弁 on Mt Ōmine, Shōdō 勝道 on Nikkō 日光, Taichō 泰澄 on Hakusan 白山, Hōren 法蓮 on Hikosan 彦山, and so on. Most of these men were students of the *Lotus sūtra*, and their prayers or *dhāraṇī* were dedicated above all to Kujaku Myōō 孔雀明王, Kokūzō Bosatsu 虚空藏菩薩, Kannon Bosatsu 觀音菩薩 and Yakushi Nyorai 藥師如來.[38] Their influence was felt from the beginning in both Tendai-shū 天臺宗 and Shingon-shū 真言宗; and it is impossible to recount the early history of these two schools in Japan without taking account of *shugendō*.

Despite this, the earliest texts detailing *shugendō* rituals and doctrines were apparently compiled in the Muromachi period, by such men as Akyūbō Sokuden 阿吸房即傳 (*fl. c.*1509–*c.*1558), an ascetic from Hikosan.[39] For periods prior to this, information about *shugendō* practice can be extracted from various of the texts of *engi* 縁起, the legendary histories of individual mountains, shrines and monasteries, as well as from some early chronicles, and from surviving early icons of such supernatural beings as Zaō Gongen 蔵王権現. For our purposes, however, the most directly relevant texts are collections of rituals made during the Edo and Meiji periods. Certain of these undoubtedly incorporate far older material; but it is usually impossible to attribute individual rituals to an earlier period, particularly one before 1600. The *shugendō* texts assembled in *Nihon Daizōkyō*, vols. 92–96, include many rituals which incorporate some version of the *kuji*; and several of these are cited below. Such sources often indicate the *mudrās* and the divine symbolism associated with each character, and may give other esoteric information; but we do not learn how or when these correlations came into existence.[40] In the circumstances, the following notes can be no more than tentative.

38 Miyake Hitoshi 宮家準, *Shugendō: yamabushi no rekishi to shisō* 修験道ー山伏の歴史と思想 (Kyōikusha, 1978), pp. 13–14, 25–9.
39 For further information on these early collections, see Miyake Hitoshi, *Shugendō shisō no kenkyū* 修験道思想の研究 (Shunjūsha, 1985), pp. 87–98.
40 A table summarising the associations is provided by Miyake, in both of his big books on *shugendō* (*Shugendō girei no kenkyū*, p. 507; *Shugendō shisō no kenkyū*, p. 402); but he does not consider in any detail questions of origin and dating.

The largest and most significant collection of *shugendō* rituals is *Shugen jinpi gyōhō fuju shū* 修驗深秘行法符咒集, edited in its present form by Nakano Tatsue 中野達慧 (1871–1934). The name of the original compiler is unknown; but in ten volumes and under 376 headings it gives details of 440 rituals.[41] A continuation, *Shugen jinpi gyōhō fuju zokushū* 修驗深秘行法符珠咒續集, in two volumes, was also edited by Nakano Tatsue, and adds a further 47 rituals. The *Fuju shū*, as it may be called for short, represents the practice of Tōzan-ha 當山派, which is one of the two main lineages of *shugendō*, and derives from a grouping in the Heian period of 36 monasteries in the Yamato region. In the Muromachi period Tōzan-ha came under the administrative control of the Sambōin 三寶院 at Daigoji; and the core of the Fuju shū seems to be a collection made by Gien 義演 (1558–1626), a monk of the Sambōin. However, it also incorporates earlier collections, including one by In-yū 印融 (1435–1519), of Kōyasan; and one said to have been made by the mysterious Ninkan 仁寬 (fl. early twelfth century). Ninkan, a Shingon monk associated with Daigoji, was exiled in 1113 to the Izu 伊豆 peninsula in eastern Japan; but subsequently taught *mikkyō* to specialists in *yin-yang* 陰陽 and *Yijing* divination in the Musashi 武蔵 region, and is regarded as the founder of Tachikawa-ryū 立川流, a heretical Shingon sect. Ninkan's teaching was systematised only in the fourteenth century, by Kōshin 弘真 (1278–1357) at Daigoji, and by Yūkai 宥快 (1345–1416) on Kōyasan.[42] Whether or not they can be credited to Ninkan himself, the Taoist elements in the *Fuju shū* rituals are plain to see, and would appear to date from at least early Muromachi times.[43]

At least 26 rituals in the *Fuju shū* and its continuation include the *kuji*.[44] Sometimes the details of the ritual are not spelled out; and it is not always clear if one is meant to conclude by 'cutting' the characters. Often, however, the grid for cutting is illustrated. The strokes are made with alternately horizontal and vertical strokes: five horizontal and four vertical to protect a

41 It is reprinted in (*Zōho kaitei*) *Nihon Daizōkyō*, vol. 94, pp. 11–166. The *Zokushū* is in the same volume, pp. 167–93.
42 The foregoing notes are based on the commentary in (*Zōho kaitei*) *Nihon Daizōkyō*, vol. 99, pp. 323–4; on Ōno, *Nihon bukkyō shi jiten*, pp. 333, 397, 471–2; and on Miyake, *Shugendō: yamabushi no rekishi to shisō*, pp. 15–16.
43 Another collection of ritual texts, *Shugenshū shintō jinja injin* 修驗宗神道神社印信, in (*Zōho kaitei*) *Nihon Daizōkyō* vol. 92, pp. 338–54, is also in the lineage descending from Ninkan; and it may be significant that it too includes *kuji* rituals (pp. 340, 343). However, the postface of this collection is dated 1771, so it may include Edo-period additions.
44 Those which I have noted, in the numbering of the *Nihon Daizōkyō* edition, are, in *Fuju shū*: 59; 60; 73; 80; 81; 127; 194; 195; 196; 197; 198; 199; 200; 201; 202; 221; 229; 230; 243; 245; 253; 293; 318; and, in the *Zokushū*: 5; 9; 32.

man, and four horizontal and five vertical to protect a woman. Sometimes the grid alone is given; but we must presume that the syllables themselves were uttered.

The largest number of *kuji* rituals appear in volumes 6 and 7 of the *Fuju shū*, which are concerned above all with the protection of military equipment and the expulsion of evil spirits, respectively. However, the *kuji* ritual might be used for other purposes, such as to protect the teeth. Sometimes the *kuji* is followed by a *jūji* ritual;[45] and volume 6 includes a separate small group of *jūji* rituals.

One of the most interesting aspects of the *kuji* is the series of symbolic associations between each syllable and various *mudrās*, *shuji*, Buddhist super-natural beings, heavenly bodies and even Shintō deities. The correlations given in the *Fuju shū* texts and in other sources are not entirely consistent with one another; but that is hardly surprising, since the *kuji* rituals spring from folk tradition as much as from esoteric learning. Even in the case of the *mudrās* and the Buddhist equivalences, apparently no canonical list is being followed; and I have not been able to pinpoint the origin of particular sets of correlations beyond the ritual texts themselves. Probably much of the evidence has been lost. From internal evidence, however, it is possible to explain some of them, and to formulate hypotheses about their history.

THE *KUJI* AND BUDDHIST SUPERNATURAL BEINGS

The Buddhist honji 本地, 'original ground', for each of the *kuji* is given in two successive rituals in the *Fuju shū*, volume 6. These are No. 199, *Kuji hon-i* 九字本位, and No. 200, *Kuji no daiji* 九字大事. The information is laid out for comparison in Table 1:

45 E.g. Nos. 80; 81; 243; 293; 318. For the *jūji*, *cf.* n.37 above.

Table 1

Kuji syllable		Fuju shū 199	Fuju shū 200
Rin	臨	Tamonten 多門天	Bishamon 毘沙門
Byō	兵	Gōsanze 降三世	Jūichimen 十一面
Tō	鬪	Jikokuten 持國天	Nyoirin 如意輪
Sha	者	Kongōyasha 金剛夜叉	Fudōson 不動尊
Kai	皆	Fudō 不動	Aizen Myōō 愛染明王
Jin	陳	Gundari 軍荼利	Shō Kannon 正觀音
Retsu	列	Kōmokuten 廣目天	Amida 阿彌陀
Zai	在	Daiitoku 大威德	Miroku 彌勒
Zen	前	Zōchōten 增長天	Monju 文殊

Tamonten and Bishamon are names for the same figure; but in other respects the two lists are quite different, and it is curious that Fudō, the only other figure who is common to both, appears in two different places. The correlations given in No. 200 appear to be the more familiar today;[46] but those of No. 199 carry an authenticity of their own. The list has more internal logic, being made up of the five great Vidyārājas (Jap. Godai Myōō 五大明王) and the four Deva kings (Jap. Shitennō 四天王), all of them fierce or military in appearance. In this arrangement, Fudō Myōō 不動明王 takes his proper place at the centre, with the other figures arranged symmetrically round him.[47] The scheme thus constitutes a simple but powerful protective maṇḍala, as illustrated in Table 2 (together with the Sanskrit names of all the figures). I do not know if this configuration is actually found in association with kuji practice, but it is certainly implied. The conclusion to be drawn is both that No. 199 originated in strict Shingon tradition and that it addresses the concerns

---

46 They are quoted without comment in, for example, Mikkyō daijiten, p. 332; and in the useful if non-scholarly compilation by Ono Kiyohide 小野清秀, Kaji kitō himitsu taizen 加持祈祷秘密大全 (Ōsaka: Daibunkan Shoten, 1968), pp. 365–6.

47 The same list of nine figures arranged in a different order (the Shitennō followed by the Godai Myōō, with Fudō Myōō last) appears in another kuji ritual, No. 5 in the Zokushū ((Zōho kaitei) Nihon Daizōkyō, vol. 94, p. 168), but the standard sequence of mudrās remains the same. Detailed discussion of the history and iconography of these figures and their groupings is beyond the scope of this paper. Briefly, Fudō Myōō is the kyōryō rinshin 教令輪身, 'wheel body who imposes the [Buddhist] teaching', of Dainichi Nyorai (Mahāvairocana). The cult of the Five Vidyārājas, 'kings of knowledge', was probably introduced to China by the Indian missionary and translator Amoghavajra (705–74). It was then brought to Japan in the ninth century by Kūkai. The cult of the Four Deva Kings, divine protectors of Buddhism who occupy a mountain with four peaks lying half-way up Mt Sumeru, goes back in Japan to the seventh century.

of bushi 武士 and others likely to be exposed to real physical danger, in, for example, the Muromachi period.

Table 2

E
Jikokuten (Dhṛtarāṣṭra)
Gōsanze (Trailokyavijaya)

N		C		S
Tamonten (Vaiśravaṇa)	Kongōyasha (Vajrayakṣa)	Fudō (Acalanātha)	Gundari (Kuṇḍali)	Zōchōten (Virūḍhaka)

Daiitoku (Yamāntaka)
Kōmokuten (Virūpākṣa)

S

No. 200, on the other hand, is eclectic in its choice of supernatural beings, and it is at first hard to discern any symmetry or pattern in it. However, the presence of Aizen Myōō is noteworthy. This figure, whose name means 'The knowledge king dyed with [the red colour of] love', is the Sanskrit Rāgarāja. His cult was introduced into Japan by Kūkai, and some impressive sculptures and paintings of him have survived from the twelfth and thirteenth centuries.[48] Such images depict him with a strong red complexion, with a fierce aspect and usually with six arms. In addition, there is a two-headed form, Ryōzu Aizen 両頭愛染, in which one head personifies the masculine aspect, and the other is feminine, personifying love (*ai*). From this point of view Aizen may be paired (as here) with Fudō. The main canonical text for all this was translated into Chinese by Vajrabodhi, the teacher of Amoghavajra, in the earlier eighth century;[49] but the cult acquired a more local character in

48 Ishida, *Bukkyō bijutsu no kihon*, pp. 224, 226, gives a convenient list of examples in Japanese collections; though for good illustrations of the pieces, and for pieces in Western collections, one must turn elsewhere.

49 The Chinese title of the *sūtra* is *Jingangfeng louge yiqie yuqie yuqijing* 金剛峯

17

Japan, where it had a particular appeal to followers of Tachikawa-ryū. In another unorthodox branch of Shingon, Ono-ryū 小野流, which traces its ancestry to Ningai 仁海 (951–1046), which had special connections with Daigoji, and which was at its height in the thirteenth and fourteenth centuries, Aizen Myōō was actually the principal icon.[50]

On these grounds alone we should be justified in seeing the influence of Tachikawa-ryū or Ono-ryū in the formation of *Fuju shū* No. 200. Moreover, it also includes Shō Kannon, Jūichimen and Nyoirin, three of the six Avalokiteśvaras (Jap. *Roku Kannon* 六観音), a list which was introduced to Japan through the voluminous writings of Ningai himself. Lokesh Chandra postulates that this list, not to be confused with the separate list of thirty-three Avalokiteśvaras (Jap. *Sanjūsan Kannon* 三十三観音), emerged in China at the beginning of the eighth century.[51] Ningai connects them with the Six Paths of Existence (ṣaḍgati; Jap. *rokudō* 六道): of those included in *Fuju shū* No. 200, Shō Kannon is associated with the inhabitants of hell (*jigoku* 地獄), Jūichimen Kannon with the *asuras* (Jap. *ashura* 阿修羅), and Nyoirin Kannon with the gods, or *devas* (Jap. *ten* 天). The concept of the Six Paths entered Japan in the tenth century, and became influential in art and culture from the eleventh century onwards. Both as an intellectual doctrine and in popular religious practice it is closely related to the worship of Amida: the six forms of Kannon, his chief lieutenant and the most compassionate of bodhisattvas, operate on his behalf in each of the six paths of existence to rescue sentient beings from the chains of causation.[52] Thus *Fuju shū* No. 200 reflects also the influence of Pure Land teaching.

Of the two last figures in the list, Miroku is of course Maitreya, the Future Buddha; and in the later Heian period Kinpusen 金峰山, the region lying between Yoshinoyama and the peak of Mt Ōmine, came to be regarded as both the Pure Land of Miroku and the Pure Land of Amida. These were the most significant of an elaborate series of correspondences involving Kinpusen, Yoshino-yama and neighbouring regions; and they were given

---

樓閣一切瑜伽瑜祇經 (T.867). For Aizen Myōō, see further Sylvain Lévi, J. Takakusu, and Paul Demiéville, eds., *Hōbōgirin: dictionnaire encyclopédique du Bouddhisme d'après les sources chinoises et japonaises*, premier fascicule (Tōkyō: Maison Franco-Japonaise, 1929), pp. 15–17; Sawa, *Butsuzō zuten*, pp. 119–20; *Mikkyō daijiten*, pp. 3–7, 2280.

50 For further information on Ono-ryū and Ningai, *cf. Mikkyō daijiten*, pp. 188–91, 1768–9. The connection with Daigoji dates from the time of Gihan 義範 (1023–88), a pupil of Ningai.

51 Lokesh Chandra, *The thousand-armed Avalokiteśvara* (New Delhi: Indira Gandhi National Centre for the Arts and Abhinav Publications, 1988), p. 44.

52 For a convenient short article on this huge topic, see (*Iwanami*) *Bukkyō jiten*, pp. 848–9, s.v. *rokudō*.

18

impetus not only by the prevailing belief in *mappō* but also directly by
Fujiwara no Michinaga 藤原道長 (966–1027), who both promoted the *rokudō*
teaching of Ningai and presented scrolls of the *Sukhāvatīvyūha* to Kinpusenji
金峰山寺, following his ascent of the mountain.[53] Lastly, Monju (Mañjuśrī),
one of the most important of the celestial bodhisattvas, has special
associations with Mt Katsuragi; and there are several *shugendō*
rituals dedicated to him, including two in the *Fuju shū* (Nos. 41 and 42).[54]

THE *KUJI*, THE NINE AND THE SEVEN HEAVENLY BODIES

Fuju shū No. 197, *Kujisuijaku* 九字垂迹, and No. 198, *Kujihonji* 九字本地,
are paired rituals which provide further sets of correlations for the *kuji*,
although the text of these rituals is not entirely reliable. The purpose of the
rituals is to obtain protection for particular age-groups, as well as longevity;
and the correlations are with various *hoshi* 星, heavenly bodies (or 'stars').
In the first ritual (No. 197), one faced south, intoned the *kuji* nine times and
clenched the teeth nine times. This destroyed the baleful influence which a
star might be exerting at that time on a person in a particular age-group,
immediately converting it into a good star. Sundry other evil influences were
dissipated too. In the second ritual (No. 198), one faced north, again intoned
the *kuji* nine times, and clenched the teeth nine times. This ensured protection
and long life to the age of 81 (9 x 9); and the ritual is also recommended for
protecting arrow shafts and sword points, and for use by practitioners on
many other occasions, ranging from situations of danger, sickness and so on,
to the practice of music.[55]

The heavenly bodies for No. 197 correspond to the Indian *navagraha*,
'nine seizers' (Jap. *kushū* 九執), which influence the destinies of mankind,
for better or worse. Among them, only the Sun is a star, strictly speaking;
while Rāhu and Ketu, the ascending and descending nodes, are variously
explained in Indian myth and do not correspond to any regular heavenly
body. In simple terms, Rāhu is the cause of eclipses, a dragon's head; while
Ketu is a comet or meteor, symbolised by a dragon's tail.[56] The Japanese
and Indian names, with their English identifications, are given in Table 3(a),
together with the age-groups corresponding to each. However, the age groups

53 *Cf.* Miyake, *Shugendō shisō no kenkyū*, pp. 270–3.
54 Miyake, *Shugendō girei no kenkyū*, pp. 401–2.
55 For the text of these rituals, see (*Zōho kaitei*) *Nihon Daizōkyō*, vol. 94, pp. 92–4.
56 For further information, see John Dowson, *A classical dictionary of Hindu
mythology and religion, geography, history, and literature* (Calcutta, etc.: Rupa &
Co., 1982; reprint of 1878 edition), pp. 252–3, s.v. *Rāhu*; p. 157, s.v. *Ketu*.

have been corrected in three cases according to another source, which indicates further that for higher age-groups one keeps adding nine (so that the next higher age-groups influenced by Keitosei, for example, would be 16, 25, 34 and so on).[57]

Table 3(a)

South

Kuji syllable	Kuyōsei九曜星	Navagraha	Identity	Age(+9's)
Rin	Keitosei 計都星	Ketu	'Descending Node'	7
Byō	Nichiyōsei 日曜星	Rāvi (or Sūrya)	Sun	5
Tō	Mokuyōsei 木曜星	Bṛhaspati	Jupiter	9
Sha	Kayōsei 火曜星	Maṅgala	Mars	6
Kai	Ragosei 羅 候星	Rāhu	"Ascending Node"	1
Jin	Doyōsei 土曜星	Śani	Saturn	2
Retsu	Getsuyōsei 月曜星	Candra	Moon	8
Zai	Kin-yōsei 金曜星	Śukra	Venus	4
Zen	Suiyōsei 水曜星	Budha	Mercury	3

The stars for No. 198 are the 'seven stars of the Northern Dipper' (Jap. hokuto shichishō 北斗七星), that is, of Ursa Major. The Sino-Japanese Buddhist names for these stars are of obscure origin; but they must correspond somehow to one of several Indian lists of the Seven Sages (Skt. saptarṣi).[58] Plainly the text of No. 198, as printed, is corrupt. The first two kuji, as well as the names of the first two stars, are missing; although two devas, Gatten and Nitten, have been supplied to accompany the final two kuji.[59] (This last detail may be authentic.) For three of the stars, correlations for individuals born under symbolic animals of the twelve earthly branches (Jap. jūnishi 十二支) have been added; but the listings are garbled. In addition, three characters are incorrectly written. In Table 3(b), an attempt has been made to correct

57 Cf. Miyake, Shugendō girei no kenkyū, pp. 267–8. The discrepancies in the Fuju shū text are for Ragosei, where it has 'ages 10 and 11'; and for Nichiyōsei and Getsuyōsei, where 5 and 8 are reversed. Miyake strangely passes over the latter in silence.

58 For the various Indian names, see Dowson, A classical dictionary of Hindu mythology and religion, p. 268. For a discussion of the Sino-Japanese names, see Nojiri Hōei 野尻抱影, Hoshi to tōhō bijutsu 星と東方美術 (Kōseikaku, 1971), pp. 83–4. Also see Mikkyō daijiten, p. 2041.

59 Gatten is simply the Moon Goddess, Candra (or Soma); while Nitten is the Sun God, Sūrya (or Āditya).

these errors, and to supply the missing *jūnishi*.[60] (It will be noticed that there are no *jūnishi* for Gatten and Nitten.)

Table 3(b)

	North	
Kuji syllable	Hokuto shichishō	Jūnishi
Rin	[Donrōshō 貪狼星]	ne 子
Byō	[Komonshō 巨門星]	ushi 丑
Tō	Rokuzonshō 祿存星	tora 寅, i 亥
Sha	Monkokushō 文曲星	u 卯, inu 戌
Kai	Renjōshō 廉貞星	tatsu 辰, tori 酉
Jin	Mukokushō 武曲星	mi 巳, saru 申
Retsu	Hagunshō 破軍星	uma 午, hitsuji 未
Zai	Gatten 月天	
Zen	Nitten 日天	

There has been considerable discussion of the place of the Nine and the Seven heavenly bodies in Japanese religious practice. In *yin-yang* theory (and in Chinese astrology) the Nine Heavenly Bodies are associated with the five agents (*gogyō* 五行), with various colours, with compass directions, with the twelve earthly branches and their symbolic animals, with numbers from one to nine, and so on.[61] It is unclear how much of this is relevant to the *shugendō* equation between the *kuji* and the *kuyōsei*. However, Kūkai himself took *yin-yang* theory seriously; and in the tenth and eleventh centuries a succession of Shingon masters interested themselves in esoteric rain-making and other rituals based partly on *yin-yang* thought. Among these men, the most well-known was Ningai himself (who thereby acquired the nickname Ame Sōjō 雨層正, 'Abbot of Rain').

The Seven Stars too are closely associated with *yin-yang* thought and stellar divination; and it would take us far afield to discuss the various

60 In making these corrections to the *jūnishi*, I have partly based myself on a table in Miyake, *Shugendō girei no kenkyū*, p. 267; also on Nojiri, *Hoshi to tōhō bijutsu*, pp. 80–3.

61 For details, see *Mikkyō daijiten*, p. 333; Yoshino Hiroko 吉野裕子, *On'yō gogyō shisō kara mita Nihon no matsuri – Ise Jingū saishi, daijōsai o chūshin to shite* 陰陽五行思想からみた日本の祭一伊勢神宮祭記.大嘗祭を中心として (Kōbundō, 1978), pp. 37–41; Murayama, *Nihon on'yōdō shi sōsetsu*, pp. 201f.; Yoshino Hiroko, *Eki to Nihon no saishi: shintō e no isshiten* 易と日本の祭記一神道への一視点 (Kyōto: Jinbun Shoin, 1984), pp. 41–2.

ramifications of the theory.[62] From late Heian times, the Nine and the Seven Heavenly Bodies, as well as other supernatural entities, began to be combined in *hoshi mandara* 星曼茶羅, 'star maṇḍala' paintings, of which the earliest surviving example, on silk, is preserved at Hōryūji 法隆寺, Nara, and belongs to the late Fujiwara period (twelfth century). Another, different in composition but also containing the Nine and the Seven heavenly bodies, is at Kumedadera 久米田寺, Ōsaka, and is of much the same date or slightly later. These paintings, and some similar examples from the Kamakura and Muromachi periods, possess a mysterious haunting beauty as works of art, apart from their function in esoteric ritual.[63]

In the *hoshi mandara* the central figure is Ichiji Kinrin Butchō 一字金輪 佛頂, the Indian Ekākṣara-buddhoṣṇīṣa-cakra (or, more simply, Ekākṣa-roṣṇīṣa-cakra). Ichiji Kinrin personifies the supreme virtue located in the protuberance on the crown of a Buddha's head (his *uṣṇīṣa*); and is thus another way of denoting Dainichi Nyorai himself. Kinrin, 'Golden Wheel', is supreme among four *cakravartīrājas* (Jap. *tenrinjōō* 轉輪聖王), 'sage-kings who turn their wheels', and whose power is unbounded. The Ichiji, 'one character', is the Sanskrit syllable *bhrūṃ* (Jap. *boron*); the merits of all Buddhas and Bodhisattvas, and their whole spiritual practice, are based on this one object of worship, which thereby assumes the highest significance and power, and which is the focus of several *kuji* rituals in *shugendō*.[64]

A prayer based on the *hoshi mandara* was devised in 1131 for the retired emperor Toba by the Shingon monk Kanshin 寛信 (1084–1153). Kanshin, who was closely associated with Kanjuji 觀修寺 in Kyōto, was apparently at that time at Gangōji 元興寺 in Nara. He is credited with synthesising Shingon

---

62 For some further information, see Yoshino, *On'yō gogyō shisō kara mita Nihon no matsuri*, pp. 112–13; Murayama, *Nihon on'yōdō shi sōsetsu*, pp. 117–18, 212–131; Yoshino, *Eki to Nihon no saishi*, pp. 192–4.

63 The Hōryūji and Kumedadera paintings are illustrated and discussed by Nojiri, *Hoshi to tōhō bijutsu*, pp. 71–5. Both are classified as Important Cultural Art Objects (*jūyō bijutsu hin* 重要美術品). Other *hoshi mandara* are illustrated by him and by Sawa, *Butsuzō zuten*, pp. 162–3. Another example, datable to the Muromachi period, is in the Royal Ontario Museum, Toronto. *Cf.* also *Mikkyō daijiten*, pp. 2043–4. There has apparently been little sustained examination of these maṇḍalas.

64 For Ichiji Kinrin, see (*Iwanami*) *Bukkyō jiten*, p. 30, s.v. The other *cakravartīrājas* are associated with Silver, Copper and Iron Wheels. For some *kuji* rituals using the syllable *boron*, see (*Zōho kaitei*) *Nihon Daizōkyō*, vol. 94, pp. 63, 95, 102, 103, 130, 140, 170, 178. In such rituals it is associated with the *ura* 裏, 'rear'. In Shingon Buddhism, Ichiji Kinrin dwells with the Dainichi Nyorai of the Diamond World maṇḍala; in the Matrix World maṇḍala his counterpart is Butsugen Butsumo 佛眼佛 母, or Buddhalocanī-buddhomātṛī: see Adrian Snodgrass, *The Matrix and Diamond World mandalas in Shingon Buddhism*, 2 vols. (New Delhi: Aditya Prakashan, 1988), vol. 1, p. 258; (*Iwanami*) *Bukkyō jiten*, pp. 696–7, s.v.

and Hossō 法相 teachings, but was also initiated into Ono-ryū. Another long offertory prayer to the stars from Ono-ryū is unattributed, but is datable to the middle Heian period. Its text refers not only to the stars of the Northern Dipper but to various other Taoist deities as well.[65]

From this material, and that cited earlier, we are justified in concluding that the transmission of stellar symbolism to *shugendō* was partly due to Ono-ryū. However, another source may have been Jōdo Shinshū, since the Shin-shū monk Kakuzen 覺禪 (1143–?) refers to it in his *Kakuzenshō* 覺禪 鈔 (compiled over a period of more than thirty years, down to 1217). As for Taoism itself, there was interest in the subject at the Japanese court from the earliest days of contact with China; and in the ninth century the courtier Tokinao Kawabito 刀伎直川人 (later known as Jigaku Sanjin 滋岳山人) compiled several texts on it, including *Rokkō rokujō* 六甲六帖, which was commissioned by the emperor himself in 871. Kakuzen seems to have been influenced by this in his explanation of the Seven Heavenly Bodies; and, in the *hoshi mandara*, the next outer circle to that of the Nine and the Seven Heavenly Bodies houses Twelve Divine Generals, according to a list first set out in the *Kakuzenshō*.[66]

Fuju shū No. 198 begins with a list of 40 miscellaneous supernatural figures, variously associated with each of the *kuji*. The correlations in this list are frequently at variance with those of Nos. 199 and 200; they are not consistent internally, in that the same name occurs more than once; and they do not form an overall pattern, though there are some pairs. It is clear that the list was put together from several sources; and in the absence of further evidence, discussion of it would be speculative. In its present form it appears to be later than the rest of the ritual. An overall view of Nos. 197 and 198 suggests that even if the esoteric symbolism of the Nine and the Seven heavenly bodies can be traced back to the Heian period, these *shugendō* rituals, like Nos. 199 and 200, belong to a later phase of Japanese religious practice, probably in the Muromachi period.

.

---

65 Murayama, *Nihon on'yōdō shi sōsetsu*, pp. 210f. For Kanshin, Ōno, *Nihon bukkyō shi jiten*, pp. 91–2, *s.v.*
66 Sawa, *Butsuzō zuten*, pp. 162–3; Murayama, *Nihon on-yōdō shi sōsetsu*, pp. 208–10. Rokkō is also the name of a mountain region near Kōbe. Murayama indicates that the Japanese military title shōgun 將軍 derives originally from the names of certain of these Twelve Divine Generals. Presumably this was at the end of the eighth century, since the earliest references to it, or rather to the full title *seii tai shōgun* 征 夷大將軍, are for 794 (in the *Nihongi ryaku* 日本紀略, compiled in the late Heian period) and 811 (in the *Nihon kōki* 日本後紀, completed in 840).

THE *KUJI* AND *MUDRĀS*

Fuju shū No. 200 is one among several rituals which include another important set of correlations for the *kuji*: that with *mudrās* (Jap. *in* 印), hand-signs of the kind which are used throughout the Buddhist and Hindu world in Asia, and not only in religious practice but also in dance, theatre, martial arts and so on. This topic is fraught with difficulty, not least because so often the transmission of the signs has been secret and is often unrecorded. It is therefore possible to give only a fragmented account of the subject.[67] Moreover, within Shingon tradition alone there are hundreds of *mudrās*, and variant names for many of them; the same supernatural being may be symbolised (or invoked) by more than one *mudrā*; and the interpretation of individual *mudrās* may differ slightly between different teachers and monasteries. Table 4 gives the *mudrās* according to the list in *Mikkyō daijiten*;[68] but there are minor discrepancies with the lists to be found in other secondary sources[69] and in the *Fuju shū*, *Zokushū*[70] and other primary sources.

Table 4

Kuji syllable	*Mudrā*
Rin	kongōshin-in 金剛針印 (dokko-in 獨股印)
Byō	daikongōrin-in 大金剛輪印
Tō	gejishi-in 外獅子印
Sha	naijishi-in 內獅子印
Kai	gebaku-in 外縛印
Jin	naibaku-in 內縛印
Retsu	chiken-in 智拳印
Zai	nichirin-in 日輪印
Zen	hōbyō-in 寶瓶印

67 The well-known study of Japanese *mudrā* by E. Dale Saunders, *Mudrā: a study of symbolic gestures in Japanese Buddhist sculpture* (London: Routledge & Kegan Paul, 1960), barely scratches the surface of the subject for English readers. Hand-signs have also been used in many cultures as a form of musical notation: see Edith Gerson-Kiwi, 'Cheironomy', in Stanley Sadie, ed., *The new Grove dictionary of music and musicians* (London: Macmillan Publishers Limited, 1980), vol. 4, pp. 191–6. The earliest evidence for such 'cheironomy' comes from Pharaonic Egypt.
68 *Mikkyō daijiten*, p. 332.
69 E.g. Ono, *Kaji kitō himitsu taizen*, pp. 365–6; Miyake Hitoshi, *Shugendō jiten* 修驗道辞典 (Tōkyōdō, 1986), p. 92.
70 *Cf. Fuju shū* Nos. 94, 95; *Zokushū* Nos. 5, 32.

The differences mostly involve the first and the last syllables. Kongōshin is Vajrasūci, the Diamond Needle Bodhisattva, an important figure in the Ākāśagarbha Mansion of the Matrix World maṇḍala;[71] while the *dokko-in* is a *mudrā* associated with Bishamon-ten, at least in Shingon Buddhism.[72] The latter therefore fits the identification of the first *kuji* syllable with Bishamon-ten; but *hōbyō-in*, the 'treasure vase' *mudrā*, is either the symbol of Samantabhadra (Jap. Fugen 普賢) in the Central Mansion of the Matrix World maṇḍala, rather than of Mañjuśrī (Monju); or, more likely, it is here the symbol of Ichiji Kinrin.[73] In some sources (e.g. *Fuju shū* No. 201), the last syllable is represented by *ongyō-in* 隱形印, which is a *mudrā* for Marishi-ten 摩利支天 (see below).[74] Ono identifies the first *mudrā* as Fugen Sanmaiya 普賢三昧耶; but his drawing of it appears to be identical to one for Daikongōrin大金剛輪.[75] In that the *kuji* ritual has been used for many purposes, it is easy to see that the first and last *mudrās*, occupying the most significant positions, could have various meanings attached to them. Nevertheless, the standard *mudrās* for the *kuji* do reveal a structural pattern. They flow one into another; symbolically, the first and last *mudrās* complement one another, whatever their precise interpretation; and there are two internal pairs (*gejishi* and *naijishi*; *gebaku* and *naibaku*), formed with fingers laced to face outwards, then inwards. The *mudrās*, like other aspects of the *kuji*, may sometimes have been understood as alternately *yin* and *yang*.

OTHER CORRELATIONS

Three other types of correlation for the *kuji* syllables deserve brief mention. Many of the *shugendō* rituals include portions written in *siddham* script. Kakuban's formula for the *kuji*, quoted earlier, is so written; and at least one of the *kuji* rituals (*Zokushū*, No. 5) includes a set of nine *shuji* syllables corresponding to each of the *kuji* syllables. However, the sounds of these syllables are not the same as those of the *kuji* themselves; nor are they the regular *shuji* for the supernatural beings and *mudrās* listed below each of

71 Snodgrass, *The Matrix and Diamond World mandalas in Shingon Buddhism*, pp. 424–5.
72 Miyano Yūchi 宮野宥智 and Mizuhara Gyōei 水原堯栄, eds., *(Shingon) Mikkyō zuin shū* (真言) 密教圖印集, 2 vols. reprinted as 1 vol. (Kōyasan: Matsumoto Nisshindō Shoten, 1971), vol. 2, fol. 27b.
73 Kokusho Kankōkai 国書刊行会, ed., *(Kaitei) Zuin taikan* (改訂)圖印大鑑, 2nd edition (Kokusho Kankōkai, 1987), p. 25.
74 *Mikkyō daijiten*, pp. 2088, 2089.
75 Ono, *Kaji kitō himitsu taizen*, p. 365; *cf.* Miyano and Mizuhara, *(Shingon) Mikkyō zuin shū*, vol. 1, sect. 1, fol. 3a.

them. In the absence of further evidence no conclusions can be drawn. The *shuji* may be read as follows: *Ri(n)-na(n)-tan-sha-ku-chirin-raku-rau-ron*! These are Japanese readings, which may or may not represent a Sanskrit *mantra*.[76]

The same ritual goes on to give a set of correlations with Taoist deities. A similar, but significantly different, list appears in another collection of rituals, *Shugen jōyō hihō shū* 修驗常用秘法集, compiled by Sonkai 尊海 (1826–92).[77] The ritual in question is of uncertain age, being the last of several additions to an 1822 manuscript on which the collection is for the most part based. For convenience, the two sets of correlations are set out together in Table 5, as lists A and B respectively.

Table 5

Kuji syllable	Taoist deities (A)	Taoist deities (B)
Rin	Taishi 太子	Seiryū 青龍
Byō	Shujaku 朱雀	Bunnō 分王
Tō	Bunnō 文王	Shujaku 朱雀
Sha	Genbu 玄武	Jodō 除道
Kai	Santei 三諦	Genbu 玄武
Jin	Byakko 白虎	Sanmyō 三妙
Retsu	Gyokujo 玉女	Hyakko 百狐
Zai	Kyūchin 九陣	Gyokujo 玉女
Zen	Seiryū 青龍	Rikugō 六合

Clearly, there is a connection between the two lists: but without entering into a lengthy discussion, we are entitled to suspect list B of being a later version, altered through oral transmission. Bunnō in both lists is surely the same personage (the founder of the Zhou 周 dynasty), though the name is written differently in list B; and Hyakko is perhaps meant to be Byakko. In both lists, Seiryū should strictly be Sōryū 蒼龍, to round out the set of Four Constellations (with Byakko, Genbu and Shujaku).

Lastly, in the Edo period, versions of the *kuji* were practised in various schools of Shintō;[78] and sets of correlations developed between the *kuji* and

76 *Cf.* note 47 above. Another set of nine *shuji* syllables, which definitely represents a Sanskrit *mantra*, is discussed below, note 102.

77 The collection is printed in (*Zōho kaitei*) *Nihon Daizōkyō*, vol. 92, pp. 229–50. For the ritual in question, see pp. 249–50.

78 Shimonaka Yasaburō 下中彌三郎, ed., *Shintō daijiten* 神道大辭典, 3 vols. (Heibonsha, 1937–40), vol. 1, p. 437. It is perhaps needless to add that the forms of Shintō divination known as *kuji* 籤 (or *mikuji* 御籤 or *omikuji* 御御籤) have no

deities from the Shintō pantheon. One such set is given in Table 6;[79] but it is not the only one, and seems specific to one school or locale in the Yamato region. Again, in the absence of further documentation it would be premature to draw conclusions.

Table 6

Kuji syllable	Shintō deity
Rin	Tenshōkō Daijingū 天照皇太神宮
Byō	Shō Hachiman Daijin 正八幡大神
Tō	Kasuga Daimyōjin 春日大明神
Sha	Kamo Daimyōjin 加茂大明神
Kai	Inari Daimyōjin 稲荷大明神
Jin	Sumiyoshi Daimyōjin 住吉大明神
Retsu	Tanyū Daimyōjin 丹生大明神
Zai	Nittenshi 日天子
Zen	Marishi-ten 摩利支天

MARISHI-TEN AND THE *KUJI* IN JAPANESE MARTIAL ARTS

It will be seen that in Table 6 the correlation given for the last *kuji* is Marishi-ten, who is not a Shintō deity at all. In fact many of the *shugendō* rituals, including not a few of the *kuji* rituals themselves, are dedicated to this deity, who corresponds to the Indian goddess of the dawn, Mārīcī, and is ultimately an emanation of Mahāvairocana himself. Mārīcī, like the sun-god Sūrya, rides across the sky in a chariot; but whereas his is drawn by horses, that of Mārīcī is drawn by seven pigs. The *Sādhanamālā* (twelfth century) and other iconographic texts describe six emanations of the goddess, varying in the number of their faces and arms; but one of her regular attributes is a needle and string, with which she sews up the mouths and eyes of the wicked. In Hinduism her cult is evidently old; but in the later Buddhist art of India, Tibet and China, Mārīcī is above all a Tantric deity, depicted riding in her chariot or simply enthroned, with one (or two) faces like that of a sow (probably by confusion with Vajravārāhī, 'Diamond Sow', another emanation of Mahāvairocana).[80]

connection with this.

79 After Ono, *Kaji kitō himitsu taizen*, pp. 365–6.

80 Antoinette K. Gordon, *The iconography of Tibetan Lamaism*, 2nd edition, reprint (Rutland, Vt., & Tokyo: Charles E. Tuttle Company, Inc., for Paragon Book Reprint Corp., New York. 1972), p. 74; Benoytosh Bhattacharyya, *The Indian Buddhist*

Mārīcī, whose name means 'shimmering', is technically a *deva*, but is ranked as a bodhisattva in Sino-Japanese Buddhism, according to the indications of canonical texts about her. The latter include works translated by Amoghavajra (705–74?) and Devaśānti (d.1000).[81] A *dhāraṇī* text on Mārīcī, translated by Amoghavajra, was brought to Japan by Kūkai, by Ennin and by Enchin 圓珍 (814–91).[82] Marishi-ten started to receive attention in Japanese texts of the twelfth to fourteenth centuries. These include the following:

> *Besson zakki* 別尊雑記, by Shinkaku 心覺 (d.1180);
> *Kakuzenshō* 覺禅鈔, by Kakuzen 覺禅 (1143–?);
> *Zuzōshō* 圖像抄, by Ejū 惠什 (*fl. c.*1135);
> *Byakuhō kushō* 白寶口鈔, by Ryōson 亮尊 (recording the sayings of his teacher Ryōzen 亮禅, 1258–1341);
> *Hishō mondō shō* 秘鈔問答抄, by Raiyu 賴瑜 (1226–1304);
> *Gyōrinshō* 行林抄, by Jōnen 靜然 (*fl. c.*1154);
> *Asaba shō* 阿娑縛抄, by Shōchō 承澄 (1205–82).[83]

Of these, *Gyōrin shō* and *Asaba shō* represent Tendai *mikkyō*; the remainder are by Shingon monks. Despite this plenitude of references, images of Marishi-ten are uncommon in Japanese art; but the cult was apparently taken into *shugendō* during the Muromachi period, perhaps in the sixteenth century. The canonical texts prescribe for the goddess *ongyō-in*, the '*mudrā* which conceals its form'; and this may have contributed to her appeal among the traditionally secretive *yamabushi*. However, Marishi-ten was also taken up among the *bushi* 武士, and most notably in certain lineages of martial arts.

We have seen above that many *kuji* rituals are military in purpose. In fact, several of them include in their title the word *heihō* 兵法, which was the normal sixteenth-century word for martial arts.[84] (It is so used, for example, in the celebrated *Gorin no sho* 五輪書, 'Book of five rings [literally, five *cakras*]', by Miyamoto Musashi 宮本武蔵 (1584–1645). The earliest reference

iconography, second edition, (Calcutta: Firma K. L. Mukhopadhyay, 1968), pp. 207–14; (*Iwanami*) *Bukkyō jiten*, p. 761. *Kuji* rituals specifically dedicated to Marishi-ten include *Fuju shū* Nos. 59, 60 & 202; and *Zokushū* No. 9; also *Shugen jōyō hihō shū*, the first ritual: (*Zōho kaitei*) *Nihon Daizōkyō*, vol. 92, pp. 229–30. For useful short discussions of these and other *shugendō* rituals dedicated to Marishi-ten, see Miyake, *Shugendō girei no kenkyū*, pp. 410–11, 487–9, 499–500.
81 T.1254–59. *Cf.* Demiéville et al., *Répertoire du canon bouddhique sino-japonais*, p.111; also Sawa, *Butsuzō zuten*, pp. 154–5.
82 T.1255(a). See *Mikkyō daijiten*, p. 2089, *s.v.*
83 This list is based on one in *Mikkyō daijiten*, p. 2089, *s.v. Marishiten*.
84 For example, *Fuju shū*, Nos. 194, 195, 196; *Zokushū*, No. 5.

I have discovered to the use of *kuji* on the battlefield occurs in a somewhat unlikely place. In *Taigenshō* 體原鈔, an important long text on court music, compiled by the Kyōto musician and poet Toyohara Muneaki 豊原統秋 (1450–1524) between 1511 and 1512, there is a description of an intricate *kuji* ritual, to be used by a general when preparing to do battle. The details of the ceremony include diagrams of trays to be laid with salted plums, seaweed, pickled vegetables, radishes and so on, for each of the nine syllables; and an explanation is provided also of the meaning and effect of the prayer. At the end is a date corresponding to the tenth month, 1363; and a colophon stating that this ritual dates from the time when Minamoto no Yoriyoshi 源頼義 (988–1075) was subjugating Abe no Sadatō 安部貞任 (1019–62) and his younger brother Munetō 宗任 (dates unknown).[85]

This last comment refers to the 'Former Nine Years' Campaign' (*Zen kunen no eki* 前九年の役), a war of some twelve years' duration (from 1051 to 1062).[86] It may have been added by Muneaki himself, and can be discounted: but the location of the campaign, in Mutsu 陸奥 (the extreme north of Honshū), and the connection with Yoriyoshi, founder of a shrine to Hachiman 八幡 near Kamakura, may be significant, as indications of what had come to be believed by the sixteenth century about the military use of *kuji*. Yoriyoshi and his son Yoshiie 義家 (1039–1106) in fact laid the foundations of the Minamoto cult of Hachiman, and the redefinition of this ancient deity as God of War. In 1180 the Tsurugaoka Hachimangū 鶴岡八幡宮 was founded at Kamakura by the greatest Minamoto of all, Yoritomo 頼朝 (1147–99).[87]

In writing about the *kuji* ritual, Muneaki seems to have been transcribing from a manuscript in his possession; and perhaps he had no personal knowledge of the practice. While particular significance attaches to the date, it is also noteworthy that before the *kuji* are repeated the general's troops make symbolic formations before or between him and the altar, according to particular stars and Buddhist or Shintō supernatural beings; that the ritual may have added to it a visualisation of the *jūji* too; and that it concludes with an invocation of Marishi-ten.

Ōmori Nobumasa has indicated recently that the popularity of Marishi-ten

85 The section on *kuji* is in ch. 12, *jō* 上: Masamune Atsuo 正宗敦夫 et al., eds, *Taigenshō* 體源鈔, 4 vols. (Nihon Koten Zenshū Kankōkai, 1933), vol. 4, pp. 1561–71. For *Taigenshō* and its author, see Shimonaka Kunihiko 下中邦彦, ed., *Ongaku jiten* 音楽事典, 5 vols. (Heibonsha, 1959–60), vol. 3, pp. 1714a–1715a; 2085a. The name Muneaki 統秋 is sometimes read Sumiaki; but this is probably an error.

86 For a concise summary of this campaign, see George Sansom, *A history of Japan to 1334* (London: The Cresset Press, 1958), pp. 249–51.

87 See further Christine Guth Kanda, *Shinzō: Hachiman imagery and its development* (Cambridge, Mass., & London: Harvard University Press, 1985), p. 44.

in martial arts circles may have been due to a mysterious lone warrior of the fourteenth century, Jion 慈恩, also known as Nen-ami 念阿彌; and it is likely that Jion also practised the *kuji* ritual.[88] If the date transcribed by Toyohara Muneaki is reliable, the connection between the *kuji*, Marishi-ten and the martial arts cannot have originated with Jion; but we may conclude that it became stronger during or after his lifetime, that he may have had a hand in spreading the practice associated with it, and that Kamakura, or even northern Japan, was an early centre.

Unfortunately, the sources for Jion's life are so confusing that it is hard to be certain of some of the most basic facts concerning him.[89] He may nevertheless be regarded as a pioneer of what has come to be called *musha shugyō* 武者修行, 'askēsis of military men': a cultural phenomenon which is not unique to Japan, but which acquired its own special flavour there and reached something of a climax in the sixteenth century in the life and career of Miyamoto Musashi. It seems that Jion was originally from Sōma 相馬, in Mutsu. This could imply the village of Sōma in modern Aomori-ken 青森県, but is more likely at this period to refer to the city or district of Sōma in modern Miyagi-ken 宮城県. At any rate, when Jion was still small, his father was killed, and his mother took him for safety south to what is now part of the city of Yokohama. At the age of seven (by Japanese reckoning) he became a disciple of one Yūgyō Shōnin 遊行上人 of Fujisawa in Sagami Province (Sōshū Fujisawa 相州藤澤), in modern Kanagawa-ken 神奈川県; and he adopted the religious name Nen-ami (his original secular name was Yoshimoto 義元).

Jion took up swordsmanship (*kenpō* 劍法) in order to avenge his father's death; and at the age of ten is said to have been initiated into mysterious arts on Kurama-san 鞍馬山 (near Kyōto), where the young Minamoto no Yoshitsune 源義經 (1159–89) had studied martial arts with goblins. The source does not explain how Jion had got to this distant place at such a tender age, unless his mother took him. When he was 16, Jion received a 'secret transmission' (*hiden* 秘傳) from the monk Jinsō Eiyū 神僧榮祐, of Jufukuji 壽福寺, a Rinzai 臨濟 Zen monastery in Kamakura, not far from Fujisawa. Jufukuji, founded in 1200 by Myōan Eisai (or Yōsai) 明庵榮西 (1141–1215),

---

88 Ōmori Nobumasa 大森宣昌, *Bujutsu densho no kenkyū: kinsei budō shi e no apurōchi* 武術伝書の研究―近世武道史へのアプローチ (Jijinkan, 1991), pp. 174–86.

89 In what follows, I have relied on accounts by Watatani Kiyoshi 綿谷雪 and Yamada Tadashi 山田忠史, (*Zōho dai kaitei*) *Bugei ryūha daijiten* (増補大改訂) 武芸流派大事典 (Tōkyō Kopī Shuppanbu, 1978), pp. 683–5, and by Sasama Yoshihiko 笹間良彦, (*Zusetsu*) *Nihon budō jiten* (図説) 日本武道辞典 (Kashiwa Shobō, 1982), pp. 550–1.

was the first Zen monastery in Kamakura; and it was associated with several famous Zen masters, including the Chinese teacher Lanqi Daolong 蘭渓道隆 (1213–78) and Mujū Ichien 無住一圓 (1226–1312), author of *Shasekishū* 沙石集, an important collection of Buddhist tales.[90] In 1368, aged either 18 or at least 20 (according to some sources), Jion was in Kyūshū, where he mastered further secrets of swordsmanship at Anra*kuji* 安樂寺, in Tsukushi 筑紫. This monastery, which no longer exists, was attached to the Dazaifu Temmangū 大宰府天満宮 (in modern Fukuoka-ken 福岡県), the ancient Shintō shrine established at the grave of Sugawara no Michizane 菅原道真 (845–903).

After this, Jion returned home, and reverted to secular life, taking the name Sōma Shirō Yoshimoto 相馬四郎義元. This was presumably so that he could avenge himself on his father's enemies without violating Buddhist vows. Subsequently he entered the Zen order, taking the name Jion; and during the remainder of his life he practised and taught in various provinces. In 1408 he founded a monastery called Chōfukuji 長福寺, at Namiai 波合, in Shinano Province (Shinano no kuni 信濃國), corresponding to the village of Namiai in modern Nagano-ken 長野県. It happens that the great Takeda Shingen 武田信玄 (1521–73), a Zen warrior of a later generation, died in this place: an indication that the martial legacy of Jion may have lived on in Shinano. In any case, Jion installed an image of Marishi-ten at Chōfukuji; and, even if direct evidence is lacking, there is good reason to suppose that he and his followers incorporated the *kuji* into their practice.[91] By 1408, Jion was calling himself Nendai Oshō 念大和尚. It is uncertain how much longer he lived; but in 1793 a memorial stone to him under this name was erected in Namiai, and it is still preserved there.

From the sources, it is clear that Jion taught swordsmanship as well as Zen; and his name has been invoked in connection with several lineages in martial arts, including not only swordsmanship but also *sōjutsu* 槍術 ('spear art'); *shuhaku* 手搏 (a kind of unarmed defence against sword attacks); and *maho* 魔法 ('sorcery'). This last implies arts of both deception (*tonkōjutsu* 遁甲術) and casting spells (*jujutsu* 呪術): for example, by the use of *kuji*. It has been suggested further that he may have taught a general system of *bujutsu* 武術 ('martial arts'); and the Katori Shintō-ryū 香取神道流 of Iizasa Chōisai 飯篠長威齋 (1387?–1487/8), which is also a composite system, may

---

90 There is an English translation and study of this work by Robert E. Morrell, *Sand and pebbles (Shasekishū): the tales of Mujū Ichien, a voice for pluralism in Kamakura Buddhism* (Albany, N.Y.: State University of New York Press, 1985).

91 Chōfukuji is known today as Gyōōin 尭翁院; and belongs to the Sōtō 曹洞 school of Zen. *Nen-ryū shōhō heihō miraiki mokuroku* 念流正法兵法未來記目録 (1596), a detailed text from the martial arts lineage which claims Jion as its founder, includes *kuji* (and *jūji*) rituals.

owe something to his example. It is significant that Katori Shintō-ryū is one surviving school of martial arts in which the *kuji* are still used.[92]

Jion's school is most commonly referred to as Nen-ryū 念流; but we also encounter the names Jion-ryū 慈恩流 and Okuyama Nen-ryū 奥山念流, Okuyama apparently being yet another name which he sometimes used. The names of his fourteen most distinguished pupils, in Kyōto as well as in eastern Japan, are given in two of the sources. One of the schools most closely connected with him is Chūjō-ryū 中条流, which traces its lineage back to Chūjō Nagahide 中条長秀 (d.1384). The problem of disentangling sources for Jion's life is complicated by the fact that there was apparently more than one person of this name. One legend, which has him experiencing a vision about swordsmanship in a rock cave at Udo 鵜戸, in Hyūga Province (Hyūga no kuni 日向國), in modern Miyazaki-ken 宮崎県, is obviously far-fetched, and seems to be due to confusion with another legend.

According to the late Imai Fukuzan 今井福山, 'Warrior Zen began with the samurai who came to Eisai at Jufukuji in Kamakura, from 1215'.[93] Although Jion trained at Jufukuji somewhat later than this, he may be regarded as a significant figure in the history of Japanese martial arts, for several reasons. There were undoubtedly lone samurai before him; but he was one of the first among them who combined the practice of martial arts with the practice of Zen. Moreover, he communicated his skills to others, and so helped to lay foundations for the later system of *ryūgi* 流儀, the 'method for lineages (*ryūha* 流派)', a mode of artistic transmission seen not only in martial arts but also in painting, music, dance, theatre and other art-forms, from the fifteenth century onwards. Thirdly, after a long personal odyssey, Jion seems to have arrived at a technical and spiritual synthesis of several martial arts, in a manner which was to become ever more refined from the sixteenth century onwards.

My information about the use of *kuji* in the martial arts traditions is incomplete. In addition to Nen-ryū and Katori Shintō-ryū, they have a place in Masaki-ryū 正木流 (a school of fighting with the *naginata* 薙刀 glaive

92 Convenient descriptions of Katori Shintō-ryū may be found in works by the late Donn Draeger, though he is guilty of some historical exaggeration: e.g., *Classical bujutsu* and *Classical budo*, The Martial Arts and Ways of Japan, vols 1 and 2 (New York and Tokyo: Weatherhill, 1973). A less accessible publication, which reproduces some early documents of the school, is Ryūso Seitan Roppyakunen Kinensai Jikkō Iinkai 流祖生誕六百年記念祭実行委員会 et al., eds., *Tenshin Shōden Katori Shintō-ryū kinen shi* 天真正伝香取神道流記念誌. (Sawara-shi: Ryūso Iizasa Chōisai Ienao Kai, 1987): I am obliged to my student Mr Bill Sutherland for making this available to me.

93 Quoted by Trevor Leggett, *The warrior kōans: early Zen in Japan* (London: Arkana, 1985), p. 10.

and other weapons) and in Chigen Imagawa-ryū 智元今川流 (a school of swordsmanship and other weapons systems). Imagawa-ryū and some other schools further use a *jūji* ritual; and some schools, such as Shindō Musō-ryū 神道無雙流 and Jikishinkage-ryū 直心影流 (swordsmanship and other arts, including *jūjutsu* 柔術 unarmed combat) use the syllables *A-Un* 阿吽, as in *shugendō* rituals involving *kuji*.[94]

In all cases, the *kuji* or other short incantation serves two purposes above all: to protect the practitioner, at least in the imagination, against malevolent forces, particularly from the spirit world; and to concentrate his or her own mental and physical energy. The aptness of the *kuji* formula is indicated by the literal meaning of the Chinese sentence which it embodies. In his autobiography, the *Baopuzi waibian* 抱朴子外篇, Ge Hong himself, while disparaging such skills, boasts that as a young man he himself studied archery, swordsmanship and the use of the seven-foot staff; and that he successfully led in battle a unit of several hundred men.[95]

From a psychological point of view, we may consider that the *kuji* work as a kind of mild self-hypnosis; or that they act as 'anchors' (I borrow this term from the American system known as 'neuro-linguistic programming'), enabling the practitioner to access a desired state of mind for whatever he or she wishes to do next. The human organism apparently responds to signs, symbols and metaphors, regardless of their reality; and so the ancient magic may yet work.

THE CASE OF *NINJUTSU*

One other martial art in which *kuji* play a part is *ninjutsu* 忍術, the Japanese art of stealth. In the hierarchy of *bujutsu*, *ninjutsu* has inevitably remained on

---

94 In the last case, it is not clear from the information available to me whether a *kuji* ritual too is performed. Other martial arts traditions, including Taisha-ryū タイ捨流, Mikami-ryū 三神流, Araki-ryū 荒木流 and Mubyōshi-ryū 無拍子流, have incorporated elements of Shingon ritual into their practice, most of these schools being of swordsmanship. See David A. Hall, 'Bujutsu and the esoteric tradition', *Hoplos* (A newsletter publication of the International Hoplological Research Center), 1.5 (1979):1–4 and 1.6 (1979): 2–5; Donn F. Draeger, 'Esoteric Buddhism in Japanese warriorship', in *The Draeger lectures at the University of Hawaii* (Unpublished typescript, [1976–8]); Osano Jun 小佐野淳, *Nihon dentō bujutsu shintai* 日本伝統武術真諦 (Airyūdō, 1989), pp. 239–41; Minoru Kiyota, 'Buddhist thought in kendō and bushidō: the Tenshin Shōden school of swordsmanship', in M. Kiyota and H. Kinoshita, eds, *Japanese martial arts and American sports: cross-cultural perspectives on means to personal growth* (Nihon University, 1990), pp. 17–28.
95 Ware, *Alchemy, medicine and religion in the China of a.d. 320*, p. 19.

the fringe, if not literally in the shadows, striving for respectability but never quite achieving it. It is likely that it has nevertheless preserved a number of archaic features. The earliest record of *shinobi* 忍び stealth techniques is in the famous legend of Yamato Takeru no Mikoto 日本武尊, son of Keikō Tennō 景行天皇, the twelfth emperor. As a boy, Yamato Takeru murdered his twin brother by lying in wait for him in the privy, a stratagem repeated in 1578 by the *ninja* 忍者 who assassinated Uesugi Kenshin 上杉謙信; and later, having disguised himself as a beautiful maiden, the young prince killed the two chieftains of the Kumaso 熊襲 clan. After this, perhaps the first reliable references to *ninja* are in the Shōmonki 将門記, a chronicle compiled soon after 940 AD, apparently by a monk from the Hitachi-Shimōsa region. Military chronicles throw a little more light on their activities during the next five hundred years: in the *Taiheiki* 太平記 (fourteenth century), for example, there are many references to *shinobi*.

By this period, certain monasteries, particularly Tendai and Shingon foundations, had become known as places where one might go for guidance in secret military arts, whether of strategy or of combat: Miidera, the Sambōin of Daigoji, and Kuramadera 鞍馬寺 (near Kyōto) being most well-known in this respect. We have already alluded to the institution of the *sōhei*, 'soldier-monks', the idea for which is credited in two quite early sources to Ryōgen 良源 (912–85), head of Hieizan from 966.[96] The oldest surviving school of *ninjutsu*, Togakure-ryū 戸隠流, claims as its founder in the twelfth century one Togakure Daisuke 戸隠大助, who moved from Nagano 長野 to the region of Iga 伊賀, after fighting against the Taira. He is actually preceded in the genealogy by still other names, going back to the beginning of the twelfth century. The details of this lineage may be impossible to verify: but, taken together, evidence from various sources suggests that some organised bands of *ninja* (not necessarily known yet by this name) were operating by the late Heian period (twelfth century), especially in remote and mountainous regions. After the fifteenth century, such recognised *ryūgi* as Katori Shintō-ryū began to include *ninjutsu* in their repertoire; and Sasama Yukihiko has suggested that a further element was contributed to *ninjutsu* at this time by organised bands of *nobushi* 野伏, soldiers of fortune; and by those who undertook more conventional kinds of espionage and intelligence-gathering.[97]

Ninjutsu, like *shugendō*, has incorporated elements of *mikkyō* practice. It

---

96 The truth of the matter is hard to determine: armed monks probably existed still earlier in Japan; and Ryōgen's own role seems ambivalent. See G. Renondeau, 'Histoire des moines guerriers du Japon', in *Mélanges publiés par l'Institut des Hautes Études Chinoises*, tome premier (Bibliothèque de l'Institut des Hautes Études Chinoises, vol. XI; Paris: Presses Universitaires de France, 1957), pp. 159–346, for a detailed discussion.
97 *Cf.* Sasama, (*Zusetsu*) *Nihon budō jiten*, pp. 543–4.

is hard to determine when a particular technique or ritual, such as the *kuji*, entered its extensive repertoire: but its use of strikes to the body (*atemiwaza* 當身技) and its medical lore (used to heal as well as to cause harm) relate to and probably preserve some ancient knowledge and techniques which came to Japan from Korea and China, where they were part of Taoist folklore and Taoist-influenced martial arts. The transmission of *ninjutsu*, and probably also its content, were modified under the settled conditions of Tokugawa rule from the seventeenth century onwards; but it would be wrong to conclude that such unarmed *taijutsu* 體術, '[combat] arts of the body', have no earlier history.[98]

I have not been able to determine when the *kuji* entered *ninjutsu*. It may have occurred first in the sixteenth century, under influence from Katori Shintō-ryū and from *shugendō*, and was probably reinforced during the Edo period, in the eighteenth and earlier nineteenth centuries. At the present time, *ninjutsu* is best represented through the teaching of Hatsumi Masaaki 初見良昭 (b.1931) and his followers, notably the American Stephen K. Hayes (b.1949), who has written or co-authored many semi-popular books about it in English. Hayes seeks to relate his practice to Tendai *mikkyō* doctrine; the guild of instructors owing allegiance to him is known as the Marishi-kai; and, following the example of Dr Hatsumi, and of Hatsumi's own teacher Takamatsu Toshitsugu 高松壽嗣, he also teaches a version of the *kuji*.

Hayes relates that while he was training in Japan he frequently asked Dr Hatsumi for guidance concerning the *kuji*. In the end he returned to the United States with his curiosity unsatisfied; but in 1982, when Dr Hatsumi was visiting him for a *ninja* gathering in Ohio, the question came up again in discussion. Hayes has recently recalled what happened:

> Once and for all to satisfy my need for knowledge, in front of everybody Hatsumi Sensei suddenly turned to me and ordered me to punch him in the back of the head from behind whenever I was ready. Perhaps he noticed the look of horror on my face. He laughed and said he would take all responsibility for whatever happened.

98 There are specific texts on *ninjutsu* that originated in the late sixteenth century, though they were edited in their present form during the Tokugawa period. *Ninjutsu* shares techniques of self-defence (throws, chokes, locks to the joints) with the various schools of *jūjutsu* 柔術, 'arts of pliancy', which also developed above all during the Tokugawa period and are the direct ancestors of modern *jūdō* 柔道 and *aikidō* 合気道. Hatsumi Masaaki, the greatest living master of *ninjutsu* (and related arts), refers to his composite system as *ninpō taijutsu* 忍法体術: see Hatsumi Masaaki 初見良昭, *Togakure-ryū ninpō taijutsu* 戸隠流忍法体術 (Shin Jimbutsu Ōraisha, 1983); also Masaaki Hatsumi, *Ninjutsu: history and tradition* (Burbank, Cal.: Unique Publications, 1981).

35

Again he stated his order to punch him without warning. With that, he turned his back to me and casually waited for my strike, continuing to talk to the crowd. I punched at the back of his head. Without any preparation or set-up whatsoever, he slipped to the side as my fist sailed through the air to where his head had been a fraction of a second before. There is no way he could have seen or heard the punch coming. Sensei then scanned the shocked crowd with his gaze and announced flatly, 'That is *kuji*'.[99]

Here then we have a third level of interpretation: the *kuji* are not just a kind of ritual magic, not just psychological anchors, but a means of developing extra-sensory perception and other psychic powers. Hayes himself has elaborated on this idea, making the point that such ability 'takes time to cultivate, and requires an experienced teacher for guidance', one who will at the same time explain secrets of bodily and mental preparation for the ritual.[100] Dr Hatsumi too has expressed the view that a true understanding and mastery of *kuji* require that one undergo hardship and long training:

Therefore, I say that the *ku* in *kurō* (hardship, heartache) will lead to *kuji*. The *ku* character of *kurō* means suffering. That suffering will produce the strength that empowers your *kuji*. By forging on through hardship, you come to know the overwhelming quality of willpower that enables your intentions to become reality. Of course you realize that what we are talking about here is different from ordinary *kuji*. After you have endured all the hardships, you will transcend this *kuji* and go on to the elevated realization of *jūji*...

One further comment by Dr Hatsumi deserves quotation:

The hand postures and grid cutting are in actuality only one third of the whole *kuji* concept. They represent the role of the physical body in action, which must be joined by the intellect in action and the will in action in order to produce results. The three elements of thought,

---

99 Stephen K. Hayes, 'Golden moments', *Musubi* (Germantown, Ohio: Nine Gates Institute), 17.6 (1993), p. 2. I am obliged to Stephen Hayes for sending me copies of his very interesting newsletter, and for graciously allowing me to quote from it here. I am indebted to him and to J. Courtland Elliott (Toronto) for their generous responses to my questions about the practice of *ninpō taijutsu* today.
100 Stephen K. Hayes, *The ancient art of Ninja warfare: combat, espionage, and traditions* (Chicago and New York: Contemporary Books, 1988) p. 24; *cf.* Stephen K. Hayes, *Ninja, vol. 3: warrior path of Togakure* (Santa Clarita, Cal.: Ohara Publications, 1983), pp. 129–37.

word, and deed coordinated and attuned with each other make up the *ninja*'s *kuji* power principle. The system is in reality a method for learning to remove the gap that separates intention from successful action. Once the *kuji* technique is mastered, the *ninja* then has the power to create physical reality by means of his intention alone. Focused intention becomes completed action itself; cause blends with effect until the distinction fades.[101]

The reference here to the Shingon doctrine of the sanmitsu 三密, 'three mysteries', is noteworthy. It is unnecessary in the present essay to pursue this interpretation further, except to note that for Dr Hatsumi the *jūji* signify love, and create the basis for safety, prosperity and welfare for future generations. (Other contemporary Japanese teachers of martial arts have expressed their ultimate aims in similar terms.) However, 'There is a saying, "Even if you are granted the powers of *kuji*, you are not necessarily granted those of *jūji*".'[102]

CONCLUSION

In the foregoing pages, we have seen how an old Chinese Taoist spell was taken into Chinese Buddhist folklore at an early date, and probably became known in Japan first via Pure Land Buddhism. It may have entered esoteric Japanese practice either through early *shugendō*, or, more likely, through the encouragement of the Shingon monk Kakuban in the twelfth century.

An examination of the various symbolic associations of the *kuji* syllables, and of the sources for them, suggests that in *shugendō*, at least, the ritual

---

101 Foregoing two quotations from Hatsumi, in Masaaki Hatsumi and Stephen K. Hayes, *Ninja secrets from the grandmaster* (Chicago and New York: Contemporary Books, 1987), p. 91, and Hatsumi, *Ninjutsu: history and tradition*, p. 236.

102 Hatsumi, in Hatsumi and Hayes, *Ninja secrets from the grandmaster*, p. 92. In *ninjutsu* the tenth syllable, inscribed on the *kuji* grid, is usually *ki* 鬼, 'demon'. Takamatsu-sensei apparently also taught a separate set of *kuji* syllables, specific to Togakure-ryū, though we are not told what it is: Hatsumi and Hayes, *Ninja secrets from the grandmaster*, pp. 94–5; *cf.* Hayes, *Ninja, vol. 3: warrior path of Togakure*, p. 136). In *ninjutsu*, as in *shugendō*, each syllable has particular associations, whether symbolic or psychological. Possibly the secret syllables are *On-A-nichi-Ma-ri-shi-ei-sowa-ka*, standing for Oṃ Āditya Mārīcī svāhā. This *mantra* is dedicated both to Āditya, the sun-god Sūrya (hence Dainichi Nyorai), and to Mārīcī; and is cited by Sasama, (*Zusetsu*) *Nihon budō jiten*, p. 256, for use in conjunction with the *kuji*. The usual *mantra* for Marishi-ten, also used in kuji rituals, is simply *On-Ma-ri-shi-ei-sowa-ka* (e.g. in *Fuju shū*, No. 202).

crystallised only in the late fourteenth and the fifteenth centuries, though some elements of the practice may be older, and still others may be later. The association of *kuji* ritual with Marishi-ten and with martial arts cannot be traced earlier than the late fourteenth century. The story of Japanese religion during the Ashikaga period has generally been told from the standpoint of Zen; but much was happening at that time in what we may term mainstream Buddhism; and much too was happening at a more popular level, even if it is less well documented. It must be admitted that the suggested chronology, pieced together in this essay from several distinct historical strands, does go slightly beyond the available evidence; but it is consistent with it, and the essay as a whole should provide a new basis for discussion.

In the Tokugawa period, *kuji* rituals were adapted for use not only in many martial arts but also in Nichiren-shū. With the decline of both *shugendō* and the traditional martial arts after the Meiji Restoration, many of these practices were lost; but the *kuji* have lived on into the late twentieth century, both in folk ascetic practice and in certain of the so-called *kobujutsu* 古武術, 'old martial arts', most notably *ninjutsu*. Perhaps unexpectedly, they can also be related to some modern ideas about the workings of the human mind.

2

The worship of Confucius in ancient Japan

I. J. McMullen

INTRODUCTION

Confucius has been the object of religious veneration and sacrifice in Japan for nearly thirteen centuries. Worship has taken a special form, known as the *sekiten* (also read *shakuten*; Chinese: *shidian*) 釈奠 or *sekisai* (Chinese: *shicai*) 釈菜, an originally Chinese ritual, whose distinguishing features are that it has usually been observed on academic premises or associated with institutions of education, and that it has tended to depend for its observance on the sponsorship of those in power. During its long history in Japan, the *sekiten* rite has served as an index and symbol of the commitment of political authority to Chinese Confucian learning as an officially sponsored basis of schooling or system of ideas. Its history is associated with the history of the educational institutions that usually formed its setting. Yet it is also distinct, for, more concisely and more visibly than those institutions, it reveals the nature of official attitudes to the Confucian tradition and its values. Its observance has not been continuous; rather, like the tradition of which it is the religious expression, it has tended to flourish under conditions of political centralisation and stability.

This essay is concerned with the *sekiten* rite in ancient Japan and particularly in the eighth and ninth centuries.[1] Its purpose is to compare the

1 The essay is based on a comparison between the extant ritual directives for the Tang *shidian* and the ancient Japanese *sekiten* ceremonies. In approaching this subject, I have benefited greatly from the thorough and learned article by Iyanaga Teizō 弥永 貞三, 'Kodai no sekiten ni tsuite' 古代の釈奠について, in Sakamoto Tarō hakushi koki kinenkai 坂本太郎博士古稀記念会, comp., *Zoku Nihon kodai shi ronshū* 続日 本古代史論集, 3 vols. (Yoshikawa Kōbunkan, 1972), vol. 3, pp. 355–467. Though my essay adopts a different perspective and occasionally expresses dissent from Professor Iyanaga's views, its debt to his work remains fundamental. On the Tang side, I have benefited greatly also from the knowledge of the cult of Confucius of my brother, David McMullen, without whose help the comparative perspective central to this article could not have been developed. I am grateful also to Glen Dudbridge, Jeffrey Mass and Ivo Smits for helpful criticisms of earlier drafts of this essay. In addition to the Cambridge Workshop on Japanese Religion, earlier versions of this paper were read to seminars at the School of Oriental and African Studies, University of London, and the Nissan Institute of Modern Japanese Studies, University of Oxford,

Japanese versions of the rite with the Chinese ceremony on which they were based, to trace developments in the ritual in Japan and to analyse the significance of departures from the Chinese model. The ancient Japanese *sekiten* offers a highly visible and well-documented example from a field still understudied outside Japan: the adoption, observance and subsequent re-interpretation of Chinese institutions in the ancient period. Like other Chinese institutions adopted by the ancient Japanese state, the *sekiten* embodied values that were, ultimately, to prove to be at variance with those of its adoptive society. Its history in Japan, it can be argued, reflects little less than the history of the attitude of high political authority to the Confucian educational institutions and values on which the Chinese-style centralised imperial bureaucratic state was based. Successive modifications of the observance, many of them subtle, expose particularly a weakening of the symbolic relationship between imperial authority and the bureaucracy on which, in its grandest version, the original Chinese rite was premised. This weakening was, in turn, both a cause and a symbol, both 'model of' and 'model for',[2] the wider failure of Chinese-style institutions in ancient Japan.

ORIGINS OF THE CEREMONY

The state-sponsored sacrifice to Confucius was a relatively late development in the Confucian tradition, and is, in some respects, alien to the original teaching. Indeed, it has been suggested by a modern historian of the rite in China that Confucius himself would have been 'horrified and displeased'[3] by the religious cult of himself of which the rite is the chief expression. That cult reflects a phase in the tradition extending from the Han 漢 (202 BC– AD 220) to the Tang 唐 (618–907) dynasties, sometimes referred to as 'state Confucianism', in which institutions, particularly the performance by the state of objective rituals, received special emphasis.

The earliest references to sacrifices in China on academic premises are found in those canonical ritual texts such as the *Li ji* 礼記 (Book of rites) and *Zhou li* 周礼 (Rites of Zhou) that are held to reflect idealised versions of Han dynasty ritual practices. The references, however, tend to be vague and inconsistent with regard to both the nature and the occasion of the offerings

and I am grateful for some constructive comments from participants. All defects and errors are my own responsibility.

2 Clifford Geertz, *The interpretation of cultures* (New York: Basic Books, 1973), p. 93.

3 John K. Shryock, *The origin and development of the state cult of Confucius: an introductory study* (New York: Paragon Reprint Corporation, 1966; reprint of 1932 edition), p. 176.

that they prescribe.[4] None specifies Confucius as the recipient of offerings. A more detailed picture of the ritual begins to emerge over the Six Dynasties (229–589), the period of three and a half centuries of disunion that followed the Han dynasty. Here again, however, practice among the relatively short-lived dynasties of this period varied considerably. For the most part, observances appear to have been irregular.[5] A rather well-documented observance is recorded for the year AD 443. Here, something of the structure of the ceremony can be reconstructed from verses composed during an ensuing banquet by the poet Yan Yannian 顔延年. Yan's poem is one of a group of 23 extant verses on the *shidian* from the period of disunion.[6] These poems, known as *shidian shi* 釈奠詩 (Jap. *sekiten shi*) seem similarly to have originated during court banquets associated with the rite. Though the practice of banqueting and with it the composition of verses were to die out in Tang China, they were to remain very important aspects of the ritual in its Japanese version.

Yan's poem *Huang tai zi shidian hui zuo* 皇太子釈奠会作 (Composed at the gathering of the crown prince's *shidian*) describes in oblique and high-flown language a ceremony with the following main stages:[7] (i) a lecture in the state academy before a coloured image of the sage; (ii) discussion of ritual texts in the presence and with the participation of the crown prince with imperial readers and interlocutors; (iii) a religious ceremony in the main hall of the academy, consisting of offerings, inspection, dancing and music; (iv) return to the palace and a feast in the presence of the emperor at which Yan's verses were composed.

4 See e.g. *Li chi: Book of rites*, trans. James Legge, ed. Ch'u Chai and Winberg Chai, 2 vols. (New York: University Books, 1967; reprint of 1885 edition), vol. 1, pp. 261, 347, 348–9; *Le Tcheou-li ou rites des Tcheou*, tr. Édouard Biot, 3 vols. (Paris: Imprimerie Nationale, 1851), vol. 2, p. 46.

5 According to the Tang ritual compendium, the *Tong tian* 通典, the rite was observed in the Wei 魏 Dynasty (220–65) on the occasion of state lectures; in the Western Jin 西晋 (265–316) in the state academy in 271 and 293 by the emperors and, on the occasion of the end of a series of lectures, by the crown prince; in the Eastern Jin 東晋 (317–420) by both emperor and crown prince, becoming established on a seasonal basis; in the Liu Song 劉宋 (420–79) by the crown prince in 445; in the Southern Qi 南斉 (479–502) following the Liu Song pattern; in the Liang 梁 (502–57) by the crown prince in 509 and 541; and in the Northern Qi 北斉 (570–6) on the occasion of the crown prince mastering a classic or the foundation of a school. See Tu You 杜佑, *Tong tian*, 2 vols. (Taibei, Da Hua Shuju, 1978; reproduction of Canton edition of 1538), vol. 1, pp. 496–97.

6 For these poems, see Fukuda Toshiaki 福田俊昭, 'Heian chō no sekiten shi' 平安朝の釈奠詩, *Nihon bungaku kenkyū* 日本文学研究 24 (1985): 118–19.

7 For annotations on this poem and a helpful Japanese paraphrase, see *Monzen* 文選, 3 vols., in *Kokuyaku kanbun taisei* 国訳漢文大成 (Kokumin Bunko Kankōkai, 1922), vol. 2, pp. 77–81; see also Iyanaga, pp. 376–9.

It was, however, the Tang dynasty version of the rite that was destined to exert most influence on Japanese practice. Under the Tang, the *shidian* became an element in a state ritual programme that is celebrated, with justice, for its grandeur and sophistication. Confucian-sanctioned imperial ritual became 'one of the principal ... function[s] of the T'ang dynastic state'.[8] The great ritual projects of the dynasty, its accession rites, suburban sacrifices, the imperial cult of ancestors, the climactic Feng 封 and Shan 禪 rites and the construction of the Ming tang 明堂 (Hall of light) symbolically legitimated the dynasty, for they acted out the emperor's claims to mediate between heaven and society. Tang state ritual was, moreover, in an important sense public. More, it has recently been argued, than in previous dynasties, the emperor acted not for himself or his ancestors, but on behalf of the whole empire of 50,000,000 subjects. Tang state ritual practice was characterised by a 'trend ... toward more openness, greater inclusivity of participants, and the seeking of ends that are more public and political than personal and private.'[9] This trend reached a climax in the first half of the eighth century under the great emperor Xuanzong 玄宗 (r.712–56). Concomitantly, the ritual activities of the dynasty were a matter of concern for the whole bureaucracy; they were 'integrated into the bureaucracy as a whole'.[10] Ritual matters were in the forefront of bureaucratic concern, and 'the ritual tradition was accessible to the entire offical body',[11] rather than the preserve of a specialist religious group or caste. This sense of ritual as a public project and of the imperial role in it also as public is an important theme, to which it will be necessary to return. It was an aspect of one of the great achievements of the dynasty, the creation of an ethos of public service focused on the state.

The *shidian* rite was an important element in this grand scheme, and was informed by the same public values. From the beginning of the dynasty, it attracted strong imperial interest and support. Nor is this surprising: together with the cult of Confucius, of which it was the most conspicuous element, the *shidian* was, of course, politically important. From the outset of the dynasty, Tang sovereigns felt obliged to win the support of the Confucian scholarly community in ruling China. This they did precisely through the vigorous promotion of the cult of Confucius. Their measures included imperial

---

8 David McMullen, 'Bureaucrats and cosmology: the ritual code of T'ang China,' in David Cannadine and Simon Price, eds, *Rituals of royalty: power and ceremonial in traditional societies* (Cambridge: Cambridge University Press, 1987), p. 187.

9 Howard J. Wechsler, *Offerings of jade and silk: ritual and symbol in the legitimation of the T'ang dynasty* (New Haven, Yale University Press, 1985), p. 194; see also David McMullen, *State and scholars in T'ang China* (Cambridge: Cambridge University Press, 1988), pp. 10–11.

10 David McMullen, 'Bureaucrats and cosmology', p. 187.

11 *Ibid.*

visits and sacrifice at Confucius' tomb and ennoblement of his descendants. Their most sustained patronage, however, took the form of attending or officiating in person at the metropolitan *shidian* rite at the shrine to Confucius constructed in the official institute of learning, the *guozi jian* 国子監 (state academy directorate). Gaozu 高祖 (r.618–26) did this in 623, 624 and 625; his successor, Taizong 太宗 (r.626–50), in 626, 631, 638 and 640.[12] The ceremony was promoted also outside the capital and, by the end of the seventh century, a system of nation-wide observance was in place at prefectural and county schools. Directives for the service were almost certainly included in seventh-century offical ritual codes, the *Zhenguan li* 貞観礼 (637) and *Xianqing li* 顕慶礼 (658), neither of which is extant. It was, however, a ritual code of the following century, the *Da Tang Kaiyuan li* 大唐開元礼 (Rituals of the Kaiyuan period [713–41]), completed in 732 and regarded by posterity as the supreme codification of Tang ritual practice, that was destined most to influence the mature form of the rite in ancient Japan.

THE *SHIDIAN* IN THE *DA TANG KAIYUAN LI*

The *Da Tang Kaiyuan li* supplies sets of directives for versions of the *shidian* ceremony in descending order of importance.[13] The grandest version prescribed the crown prince as chief celebrant. It was in this version that the mutual dependence of the imperial dynastic house and the bearers of the Confucian scholarly tradition was most subtly and elaborately articulated. Apart from the participation of the crown prince, its most salient difference from lesser versions was that it was followed by a lecture in the hall of the university. This, however, was not a regular form of the *shidian*; it seems to have been performed when the crown prince was of school age.[14] A lesser version of the ceremony, for the 'sons of state' (*guozi* 国子), prescribed the rector of the university as chief celebrant. This was the version that was performed at the twice yearly regular observance at the metropolitan university. Essentially, this was a somewhat scaled-down version of the crown prince's ceremony, with reduced music and no lecture. Prefectural and county versions, further scaled down and with no music or offerings of 'fur and blood,' were also prescribed. Here, prefectural and county officials and academic officers acted as celebrants.

12 David McMullen, *State and scholars*, p. 32.
13 For the text, see *Dai-Tō Kaigen rei*, ed. Ikeda On 池田温 (Koten Kenkyūkai, 1972; photolithographic reprint of edition of 1886; hereafter, *DTKYL*), *juan* 53–4, pp. 292A–302B.
14 Iyanaga, p. 389.

Of these various versions, the crown prince's is most instructive for the purposes of comparison with the Japanese version of the ceremony.[15] The chief recipient of the sacrifice here was Confucius under the title of Kong Xuanfu 孔宣父 (Universal Father Kong). Chinese religious practice, however, commonly prescribed subordinate recipients of sacrifice or 'correlates'. Also included, therefore, were Confucius' leading disciple, Yan Hui 顏回, together with 50 disciples and 21 worthies of the tradition. The rite, like the regular metropolitan spring and autumn observances, took place within the precincts of the state academy directorate at Changan 長安, to the south of the main palace complex. It was conducted on two sites. The religious service proper was held in the *Kongzi miao* 孔子廟 (shrine to Confucius), while the exposition of the classics that followed moved to the *xuetang* 学堂 (lecture hall). The former seems to have housed images of the Sage himself and other major figures in the tradition, whose positions, other sources show, were moved during the course of the dynasty; there were also paintings of worthies of the tradition on its walls. Both buildings were laid out on a north–south axis. They seem each to have formed an open court, bounded on the north side by a hall elevated on a terrace. This raised hall, which was presumably open to the south, formed the space in which the main ritual proceedings were conducted. Access to the terrace was by flights of steps from the court below.

In this, its grandest form, the *shidian* involved a large cast of participants drawn from different parts of the polity, all with precisely prescribed roles both in the preparations and in the ceremony itself. From the imperial side came the crown prince himself as chief celebrant; his tutors; officers and members of his household; and guards. From the academic community came the rector and vice-rector of the university as second and third celebrants; the bearer of the canon; readers; lecturers and honorary lecturers; academic officials; and the student body. In addition, the directives specify grand invocationers; directors of the rites; invocationers; gentlemen ritualists; heralds; ushers; marshals; censors; abstainers; and mace-bearers. Harmonisers, musicians, dancers and cooks were also involved, as were officials from other parts of the bureaucracy: the directors of the offices of music, imperial banquets, fermented drinks and suburban sacrifices. The directives also provide for spectators. Most of these participants in the crown prince's *shidian*, furthermore, would have roles also in the regular twice-annual observances. Also required for the ceremony were a large number of ritual vessels and trays; a total of seventy-three spirit thrones; two sets of the *tailao* 太牢 sacrifice of an ox, a sheep and a pig; wine libations; silk offerings; and specially inscribed tablets. The proceedings were also extended in time, for a preparatory abstinence was required that stretched the ritual over a total of

15 *DTKYL*, pp. 292A–8B.

six days for the major participants. Here was a major ritual effort that required careful co-ordination and planning. Even in its lesser, non-imperial, versions, it could not be other than an important event in the ritual calendar.

The structure of the crown prince's *shidian* resembles that of other rites in which imperial participation was involved. The ritual proceedings were initiated for the crown prince with a three-day period of 'relaxed abstinence', during which he abstained from mourning, contact with the sick, music and official business. This was followed by two days of 'intense abstinence' for which the crown prince, fully accoutred, was installed under guard in a screened precinct within the palace. Other officials participating in the ceremony also observed abstinence, during which they rehearsed the rite. Three days before the ceremony, formal preparation of the sites began, with markers set in place for the main participants. Here, the principle of directionality was of great importance, with the south constituting the most important orientation. Thus, in the exposition phase of the rite, the marker for the crown prince was under the east wall, facing west. The lecture chair, however, was placed under the north wall, facing south, the direction symbolising a pre-eminent authority that, according to Chinese thinking, clearly transcended that of the crown prince in this ritual context.

Preparation of the offerings began in the late afternoon of the eve of the ceremony proper. The director of the bureau of suburban sacrifices supervised the positioning of the ritual vessels; the rector and vice-rector of the state academy inspected the cleansing of the victims in the kitchens; the censors inspected the ritual vessels. Some six hours before dawn, the director of state banquets ordered the cooks to slice the victims; the invocationers took the 'fur and blood' to a sacristy. The victims were then cooked, sliced up and placed on trays for offering. Two and a half hours before dawn, the director of the office of suburban sacrifices brought in the spirit thrones of Confucius, Yan Hui and seventy-one other followers of the tradition. Confucius' spirit throne was placed between the western pillars of the hall, facing east;[16] those

---

16 At first sight, such an arrangement seems odd in a ritual tradition in which directionality was so important, for Confucius would be expected to occupy the ritually pre-eminent south-facing position. Iyanaga suggests (p. 451) that the positioning was determined by the need to accommodate the 72 correlates along the longest, northern wall of the shrine. A more likely explanation, however, seems to be the historical one given in the *Xin Tangshu* 新唐書, recording an imperial edict of 739 (Ouyang Xiu 歐陽修, *Xin Tangshu*, 20 vols. [Peking: Zhonghua Shuju, 1975], vol. 2, pp. 375). Earlier in the dynasty, in the Zhenguan 貞觀 period (627–49), Confucius had occupied a secondary position in the tradition to the Duke of Zhou 周公, who had faced south in the shrine, while Confucius had faced east. Though the Duke of Zhou was no longer sacrificed to in this rite, Confucius' position had not, as late as 739, yet

of Yan Hui and the other worthies of the tradition were apparently accommodated along the northern wall of the shrine, facing south, with provision for an overflow.

The ceremony of sacrifice itself was composed of a series of actions characteristic of Chinese sacrifice to ancestors or other spirits, many of which are clearly derived from the canonical ritual texts. Throughout the ceremony, as in the positioning of the markers, directionality, the orientation of the participants in the symbolically significant four cardinal directions, was again an important principle according to which status relationships among the participants were articulated. Ritual cleansing of the premises by sweeping immediately preceded the main ceremony. The religious offering phase of the rite consisted of a series of offerings: first, by the crown prince himself, of silk banners at the spirit thrones of Confucius and Yan Hui; next, by a grand invocationer, of the 'vessel of fur and blood'; then of a libation by the crown prince at both the main altars, accompanied by a reading of a dedicatory prayer. This prayer was followed by distribution, initiated by the crown prince himself, of the portions of the sacrificial victims. This, in turn, was followed by libations by the second and third celebrants. When these were complete, the banners were buried in a specially prepared pit in the precincts, and the religious phase of the rite was over.

In these proceedings, repetition was involved, both by the same celebrant to different recipients, and by successive celebrants. No doubt this element of repetition helped confer rhythm and coherence on the proceedings. Prostration and bowing, usually in the form of the 'double obeisance' (zaibai 再拜) exchanged among the participants, formed an important part of the ritual, and must have encouraged a sense of involvement, even among those, such as the students, whose role was mainly that of passive onlookers. Offerings were made from a kneeling position. According to a note on the regular, metropolitan version of the ceremony, 'in placing objects, it is done kneeling; when the action is completed, the head is bowed and [the performer] then stands up.'[17] The crown prince was not excepted from this, for 'whenever he receives an object [to make an offering], he inserts his mace in his belt; after he has made the offering, he takes out the mace, prostrates himself, and then rises'.[18] The leading participants were guided by verbal instructions, relayed, probably in a piercing diction and with the vowels protracted, by heralds and marshals. The crown prince's actions were guided chiefly by the general of his bodyguard and members of his household, who also passed the offerings to him. Thus

been moved. In placing Confucius' spirit throne facing east under the western wall, the *Da Tang Kaiyuan li* directives may well have reflected this anomalous situation.
17 *DTKYL*, p. 300C.
18 *Ibid.*, p. 295C.

the imperial and academic roles in the ceremony are to some extent demarcated. The most important actions were accompanied by music, each musical sequence being introduced by the wooden percussive *zhi* 柷 at the signal of the raising of the harmoniser's pennant. Again, the crown prince's role was distinctive, for whenever the directives required him to move, the orchestra played 'the music of everlasting harmony (*yonghe zhi yue* 永和之楽)'. Dancing was employed to mark three points in the ceremony, and singing once. These aesthetic elements must have combined with the dignity of the surroundings, the probably archaic-looking ritual paraphernalia and the carefully guided movements of the main celebrants, to create a rich and solemn atmosphere. The mutual deference ritually displayed between all the participants must also have created a sense of unity transcending hierarchy as the ritual unfolded through its successive stages.

Following the religious ceremony proper, the action moved to a second site, the lecture hall of the state academy directorate, and the ritual entered the more secular phase of the 'exposition of learning'. The crown prince was conveyed to the hall by palanquin and adopted his seat, facing west with an entourage of guards and tutors. All made the double obeisance, with the important, specifically noted exception of the bearer of the classic. His association with the canonical source of the tradition conferred a symbolic ritual precedence on him throughout this phase of the ceremony, even over the crown prince, the representative of supreme political power. When all had adopted their seats in the hall, the reader read from the classic and made his exegesis. A lecturer, facing north, the direction of subordination, asked about points on which he had doubts. The bearer of the classic, sitting in a chair and facing south, clarified them, whereupon other lecturers took their turn to raise questions. When this process was completed, the crown prince made his departure. The whole academic community from the rector down to the students lined the route outside the university (*xuewai* 学外) to see him off.

Such, in brief summary, was the version of the crown prince's *shidian* prescribed in the *Da Tang Kaiyuan li*. The ritual, it is not fanciful to suggest, exhibits features that reflect, in sacralised and idealised form, the values normative in the society which created it. It was, first, a ritual performance that integrated in a subtly articulated ceremony the historically distinct elements of the Chinese imperial bureaucratic state. Representatives of the two main constituents, autocratic imperial power (the crown prince) and the meritocratically selected civil bureaucracy (the rector of the university, academic officials, the students), are brought together in a harmonious and unified performance. Here, the ritual must have derived something of its undoubted dignity and excitement from the fact that, although the university did not provide the only entry to the bureaucracy, registration there greatly enhanced a candidate's chances of success in the competition for office.

The relationship of the various participants throughout the rite is characterised by mutual deference, expressed by the exchange of obeisances. Yet the participants are also assigned precise roles which articulate their relative hierarchical statuses. Thus the crown prince is first celebrant, and the ceremony waits on him for its beginning and end. He is, moreover, protected by a military bodyguard, a symbol, perhaps of the coercive power available to the imperial house and its role in maintaining civil order. It is he who symbolically distributes the food offerings, again, perhaps, as a symbol of the dynasty's stewardship over the productivity of nature. Yet at the same time, the crown prince ritually acknowledges a certain dependence on and subordination to the members of the academic community. He is guided to the site of the ceremony by his tutor. Despite his exalted status, he remains, of course, *in statu pupillari*, and obliged to receive instruction. In the 'exposition of learning', he yields ritual superiority to the bearer of the classic, who does not bow to him and who occupies the ritually pre-eminent south-facing position in the lecture hall during that phase of the ritual.

The academic participants, on their part, provide the precinct to which the crown prince journeys for the rite in what might be interpreted as a symbolic pilgrimage of homage and a public aknowledgement of the authority of Confucian values. In the person of his tutors, Confucian scholars accompany and, where appropriate, guide the crown prince. It is the bearer of the classic who, from a ritually pre-eminent position, explicates the Confucian tradition to all the participants. Above all, however, both imperial and academic participants in the rite unite in an act of homage to the founder of the tradition of learning on which the bureaucracy itself depends for its training, identification of merit, selection and the very moral and political ideals that, in the ideal order of things, inform the whole polity. Thus the crown prince's version of the *shidian* in the *Da Tang Kaiyuan li*, can, with little hyperbole, be interpreted to symbolise the normative structure of the Chinese imperial bureaucratic state and the partnership between the Confucian tradition and imperial power.

In the more abstract terms useful in particular for cross-cultural comparison, the *shidian* can also be interpreted with reference to the values implicit in it. The ceremony centred, of course, on an act of homage to Confucius, and was thus an implicit acknowledgement of the authority of his teachings, with their emphasis on humanity, basic equality and the ideal identity of the moral and political hierarchies. But the *shidian* may also be analysed in terms of the paired contrasts of achievement and ascription and universality and particularism. Here, even though Tang offialdom is conceded to have been still largely recruited from an ascriptive, hereditary aristocratic elite, it was also characterised, as Patricia Ebrey has pointed out, by a 'bureaucratic emphasis on universalistic standards of achievement'.[19] Participation in the *shidian* was arguably to a considerable extent achievement-based and universalistic in the sense that it was, in theory and increasingly also in practice, ultimately enjoyed on the basis of merit. Within the university community, progress and ultimately graduation were regulated by competitive examinations. Even in the case of the crown prince, who participated on the basis of birth, particularism and ascription, lip-service would be paid to the ideology that his position was ultimately contingent upon a universalistic mandate of heaven. In terms of these polarities, therefore, the crown prince's *shidian* may be claimed to incline to achievement and universality, even though in practice these values were still to some extent also constrained by their opposites, ascription and particularism. It was this ritual, latent with these values, that was to be transmitted to Japan in the early eighth century.

The *Da Tang Kaiyuan li* was regarded as the definitive codification of ritual for the Tang dynasty. It did not, however, rigidly determine the details of actual practice.[20] Already, under a decade after the completion of the code, in 739 and 740, the emperor issued edicts intended to enhance further the dignity of Confucius and his tradition and, in particular, the *shidian* rite itself.[21] These edicts came to the attention of Japanese students in China, and are therefore worth noting briefly at this point. The first edict raised Confucius in rank and conferred on him the new title of *Wen Xuan wang* 文宣王 (Cultured universal prince). His position in the Confucian shrine was moved from the west wall, the site specified for his spirit throne in the *Da Tang Kaiyuan li*, to the ritually supreme south-facing position. From this time on, it became a generally accepted principle that 'from the son of heaven to commoners, all face north and acknowledge [Confucius] as their teacher'.[22] By Song 宋 (960–1279) times, indeed, the suggestion that the south-facing position in the shrine belonged to the imperial house rather than Confucius was regarded as sycophantic.[23]

The history of the *shidian* ceremony under the Tang was not, however, one of uniform prosperity. The cult of Confucius suffered some decline in

19 Patricia Ebrey, *The aristocratic families of early imperial China: a case study of the Po-ling Ts'ui family* (Cambridge: Cambridge University Press, 1978), p. 102.
20 David McMullen, 'Bureaucrats and cosmology,' p. 231.
21 Su Mian 蘇冕, Cui Xuan 崔鉉 and Wang Bo 王溥, comp., *Tang hui yao* 唐会要 , *juan* 35 (*Cungshu jicheng* edn, 16 vols.), vol. 6, pp. 637–38.
22 The opinion of Du Mu 杜牧 (803–52), quoted in David McMullen, *State and scholars*, p. 60.
23 *Ibid.*

the aftermath of the An Lushan 安禄山 rebellion (755–62), and there is even evidence to suggest that prefectural and county level observances of the *shidian* were banned for a while.[24] Under Dezong 徳宗 (r.780–804), the cult revived somewhat. However, during the remainder of the dynasty, it seems not to have recovered its former vigour. It may have suffered from two trends in the cultural life of the Tang after the An Lushan rebellion: the increasing prestige of *belles lettres* at the expense of narrower Confucian studies, and the decline of the role of the public state and its institutions in intellectual life. The first of these trends, at least, was to exert an influence in Heian Japan, and it is, in general, important to bear the relative decline of the rite in the later Tang in mind when considering its development in Japan.

THE *SEKITEN* IN JAPAN: THE EIGHTH CENTURY

The first record of the observance of the *sekiten* in Japan is found in the *Shoku Nihongi* 続日本紀, with a notice on 701/2/14:

> *Sekiten*: [note] the *sekiten* hereupon makes its first appearance in Japan.[25]

This notice seems intended to mark a way station in the long process of sinicisation of the Japanese polity that had already begun as early as the late sixth century. The process reached a peak of intensity in the last decades of the seventh and in the early eighth centuries. In 701, the Taihō 大宝 Code, the third and the then most advanced and comprehensive in a series of Chinese-inspired codes of administrative and penal law had been completed. This code made detailed provision for a metropolitan university (*daigakuryō* 大学寮) and for provincial schools (*kokugaku* 国学) on the Chinese pattern. A major function of these offical institutions of learning was identified as the twice-annual observance of the *sekiten* rite to Confucius. The *gakuryō* 学令 (administrative ordinances for schools) ordained that the rite should be performed at government expense at the metropolitan university and provincial schools on the first *hinoto* 丁 day of the second and eighth lunar months.[26]

It is significant that the ordinance for the religious rite to Confucius was

---

24 *Ibid.*, p. 59.

25 *Shoku Nihongi*, in Kuroita Katsumi 黒板勝身, ed., *Shintei zōho kokushi taikei* 新訂増補国史大系, 62 vols. (Yoshikawa Kōbunkan, 1962–7; hereafter *KT*), vol. 2, p. 9.

26 *Ritsuryō* 律令, ed. Inoue Mitsusada 井上光貞 et al., in *Nihon shisō taikei* 日本思想大系, 67 vols. (Iwanami Shoten, 1970–in press), vol. 3, pp. 262.

included in the section of the code dealing with academic institutions, rather than in the ritual programme of the Japanese *Jingikan* 神祇館 (office of deities), the special religious arm of the ancient Japanese state established at this time. The *Jingikan*, however, handled indigenous cults, including the 'Shintō' court rituals most closely associated with the imperial family. It is considered to have played an important role in perpetuating the legitimacy of the traditional, *uji* 氏-based, aristocratic and particularistic pre-reform fabric of Japanese society.[27] The exclusion of the *sekiten* from the main programme of religious ritual of the state was, however, probably not a deliberate attempt to isolate the new, imported cult, for the Tang code itself, which the Japanese legislators followed closely in many matters of organisation and detail, similarly placed the ordinances for the cult under those for the educational institutions.[28] However, in a society which, in contrast to contemporary China, had no tradition of what has been called 'endemic Confucianism',[29] this arrangement must have had consequences that it did not have in China, where the ritual programme of the state as a whole had a Confucian colouring. It may have contributed to institutionalising Confucianism as an alien and elitist tradition, of academic rather than political relevance. At the same time, the isolation of the *sekiten* from the main ritual programme of the Japanese state probably made it easier, as was to happen in due course, to subordinate it to other court rituals.

No details of the 701 observance of the *sekiten* survive. It seems likely to have had a makeshift, tentative character, and was possibly an isolated event, conducted, moreover, in the still temporary capital at Fujiwara kyō 藤原京. At any rate, no further documentation of the rite survives until 705, four years later. In that year, the *sekiten* was performed again as part of an effort by Fujiwara no Muchimaro 藤原武智麻呂 (680–737), to rescue the university from the decline into which it had apparently fallen.[30] Muchimaro had been appointed vice-rector of the university in the third month of 704. Whatever the long-term ambitions of his lineage, his professed motives in reviving the university demonstrate a clear perception, characteristic of 'state

27 Richard J. Miller, *Ancient Japanese nobility: the* kabane *ranking system* (Berkeley: University of California Press, 1974), p. 11.
28 Niida Noboru 仁井田陞, *Tōrei shūi* 唐令拾遺 (Tōkyō Daigaku Shuppankai, 1964; reprint of 1933 edition), pp. 265–71.
29 Arthur F. Wright, 'The formation of Sui ideology, 581–604,' in John K. Fairbank, ed., *Chinese thought and institutions* (Chicago: University of Chicago Press, 1957), p. 88.
30 This and the following details concerning Muchimaro are taken from his biography by the monk Enkei 延慶. See *Kaden (ge)* 家伝下 in Hanawa Hokiichi 塙保己一, comp., *Gunsho ruijū* 群書類従, 29 vols. (Keizai Zasshisha, 1898–1902), vol. 4, pp. 352–4.

Confucianism', of the connection between Confucian learning, imperial power and political and moral order. He knew, according to his biography, that 'schools ... are the source of the influence of kings'. At this early stage, evidently, the sinicisation of the Japanese polity was not perceived to conflict with the interests of an ambitious aristocratic lineage.

It was to be a while, however, before the rite became securely established in the metropolis. It must be assumed that, with the move to the new Nara capital of Heijō kyō 平城京 in 710, a permanent site for the university and its shrine to Confucius was soon created. An edict of 720/2/11 recorded in the *Shoku Nihongi*[31] ordered the two offices of the inspectorate (*kenkō shi* 検校司) and the manufactory of utensils (*zōki shi* 造器司) to make *sekiten* utensils for the office of the palace table (*daizenshiki* 大膳職) and the office of the palace kitchen (*ōiryō* 大炊寮). A decade later, following the spring observance of the *sekiten* on 730/2/11, the middle controller of the left, Nakatomi no Hiromi 中臣広見, was ordered to the university to express imperial appreciation for the efforts of the doctors and students, and to distribute rewards according to status.[32] High authority appeared satisfied. There is no evidence, however, that the rulers of the first half of the eighth century were especially interested in the rite, for, particularly in the case of Shōmu 聖武 (r.724–49), they appear to have been more committed to Buddhism than to Confucianism. But it is not unlikely that by now the rite was an established part of the metropolitan ritual calendar. It is still not clear, however, what form the ceremony assumed.

The history of the Japanese *sekiten* in the mid-Nara period is dominated by the figure of Kibi no Makibi 吉備真備 (693–775), together with Sugawara no Michizane 菅原道真 (845–903), one of two individuals to feature prominently in the surviving documentation of the rite in ancient Japan. Though their roles in the history of the rite were to be different, both men came originally from the lower ranks of the metropolitan rank-bearing bureaucracy. Both, moreover, as is well known, rose to high ministerial rank as the result of direct imperial patronage. In effect, the career pattern of these two men fulfilled the Chinese Confucian meritocratic ideal more closely than usual in ancient Japan. Their achievements were based on their distinction in Chinese learning and their success as scholars in the university. Their association in the documentary record with the rite to Confucius is, therefore, no accident. Kibi's career, particularly, provides insight into the complex political background against which the *sekiten* rite developed in eighth-century Japan.[33]

31 *KT*, vol. 2, p. 79.
32 *Ibid.*, p. 121.
33 Biographical information concerning Kibi is taken from Miyata Toshihiko 宮田

Kibi was the son of 'a lower-ranking military officer'.[34] In 717, at the age of 23, he joined the seventh Japanese official mission to Tang China, where he was to stay as a student until 735. Kibi's extended stay in China thus fell within the Kaiyuan period (713–41) and the long reign of the great Xuanzong. This was a period of dynastic prosperity and confidence, in which the operations of the Tang state, including its patronage of the cult to Confucius, reached their greatest magnificence. It is clear that Confucianism was a concern of Kibi during his stay in China. An interest in the tradition is already suggested by the fact that on 717/10/19, a mere nine days after its arrival in the Tang capital, the Japanese party was granted official permission to visit the shrine to Confucius.[35]

On his return to Japan in 735, Kibi began a career at the Confucian university, being appointed vice-rector. In 741 he was made teacher of the classics to the heir apparent and in 743 head of the heir apparent's household, a post that he held until 747. In 748, a reform of the *sekiten* in respect of its 'vestments, utensils and ceremonial procedures' was carried out that can confidently be attributed to Kibi.[36] His career, however, was adversely affected by a resurgence of Fujiwara political influence under Fujiwara no Nakamaro 藤原中麻呂 (706–64), and he was exiled to Kyūshū in 750. In 751, now aged 57, he was appointed one of two deputy ambassadors in his second embassy to China. It is considered circumstantially very probable that his embassy procured the *Da Tang Kaiyuan li*, the ritual text that was to provide the model for the *sekiten* in Japan, together with news of more recent modifications to the ceremony in China, including those implemented by Xuanzong's edicts of 739 and 740.[37]

In 766, Kibi was appointed minister of the right under the Shōtoku 称徳 empress (r.749–58; 764–70), 'in recompense for teaching us since we were heir apparent'.[38] It must have been the combination of Kibi's academic distinction, his pedagogical role to the empress and his continued proximity to her that secured an imperial progress to the *sekiten* observance in the university on 767/2/7, the sole recorded occasion of a reigning Japanese sovereign attending the ceremony in ancient Japan.[39] The following year,

俊彦, *Kibi no Makibi*, Jinbutsu sōsho 80 (Yoshikawa Kōbunkan, 1961).

34 *Ibid.*, p. 4.

35 *Ce fu yuan gui* 冊府元亀, *juan* 974, quoted in Miyata, p. 22.

36 *Shoku Nihongi*, *KT*, vol. 2, p. 196; see also Kibi's commemorative biography on 775/10/2, *ibid.*, pp. 423–34.

37 Iyanaga, pp. 400; 403.

38 *KT*, vol. 2, p. 336; Miyata, p. 200.

39 *KT*, II: 340. The *Shoku Nihongi* records the rewards to the leading participants on this occasion. The director, imperial lecturer Asada no Makiyo 麻田真浄; the doctor of phonology, Yuan Jinjing 袁晋卿, an expatriate Chinese, who had accompanied

Confucius' title was changed to Bun sen ō (Cultured universal prince), in conformity with Xuanzong's edict of 739.[40]

In the decades following Kibi's death in 775, that witnessed the long reign of Kanmu 桓武[41] (r.781–806) and the successive moves of the capital to Nagaoka kyō 長岡京 and Heian kyō 平安京, the *sekiten* recedes for a while in the extant documentation. Indeed, it was later to be claimed in the intensely sinophile atmosphere of the Jōwa 承和 period (834–48) that it had been 'for more than eighty years neglected and unperformed'.[42] It is difficult to account satisfactorily for this apparent neglect of the rite during these decades. Kanmu himself had started life as a commoner of low court rank. In 766, he had served briefly as rector of the university with the rank of junior fifth rank, upper.[43] This academic experience might have been expected to incline Kanmu to be sympathetic to the university and its claim to foster administrative merit. Indeed, during his reign on 794/11/7, the *kangakuden* 勧学田 (scholarship paddy) for the support of students was increased more than threefold, on the unexceptionable Confucian grounds that 'the ancient kings placed teaching and learning first'.[44] As an ambitious, vigorous and competent ruler himself, Kanmu might have been expected to perceive, as his Chinese and Korean counterparts did, that the position of the emperor could potentially be enhanced by an alliance, over the heads of the hereditary aristocracy, with a meritocratically appointed professional bureaucracy. Indeed, Kanmu is said to have 'attempted to revive the *ritsuryō* system and promoted able men from less influential court families'.[45] Kanmu, furthermore, was certainly alert to the potential value of Chinese Confucian ritual in legitimating the position and actions of the emperor. On two occasions, on 785/11/10 and 787/11/5, he had ordered the performance at Katano 交野, to the south of his new capital at Nagaoka, of the suburban round altar sacrifice

Kibi back to Japan on his return from his first embassy in 735 and was subsequently rector of the university; and the interlocutor, junior secretary of the university Nogi no Mizumichi 濃宜水通, were all promoted. So also, by one rank, were heralds, doctors and students, to the number of 17.

40 *Ibid.*, p. 357.

41 Biographical information on Kammu is taken from Murao Jirō 村尾次郎, *Kanmu tennō*, Jinbutsu sōsho 112 (Yoshikawa Kōbunkan, 1963).

42 *Tsunesada shinnō den* 恒貞親王伝, in Hanawa Hokiichi, comp., *Zoku gunsho ruijū* 続群書類従, 19 vols. (Keizai Zasshisha, 1902–12), vol. 8, p. 47; Iyanaga, p. 415.

43 Murao, p. 25.

44 *Nihon kiryaku zenpen* 日本紀略前篇, *KT*, vol. 10, p. 268; Hisaki Yukio 久木幸夫, *Daigaku ryō to kodai jukyō* 大学寮と古代儒教 (Saimaru Shuppankai, 1968), p. 64.

45 Robert Borgen, *Sugawara no Michizane and the early Heian court* (Cambridge, Mass.:Harvard University Press, 1986), p. 8.

to High Heaven (Kōten 昊天), with his father, the Kōnin 光仁 Emperor (r.770–81), as correlate.[46] These ceremonies, of which there is no previous recorded occurrence in Japan, are considered to have had political significance. Kanmu and his father were descended from the Tenji 天智 (r.668–71), rather than the Tenmu 天武 (r.673–86), line of the imperial family that had reigned hitherto, and their accession represented an important shift of lineage within the ruling dynasty. The suburban sacrifice, an impressive ritual to an unfamiliar, tran-scendent, deity, seems to have been intended to legitimate their position.[47]

Several possible reasons for the apparent lapse of imperial interest in the *sekiten* at this crucial point in its history in Japan may be suggested. Despite his academic experience, Kanmu seems by temperament to have been more drawn to the world of miltary affairs than to scholarship.[48] Though his own rule was relatively free of direct manipulation by Fujiwara oligarchs, Kanmu certainly owed his elevation to crown prince and emperor to Fujiwara support,[49] and he may have felt disinclined to disturb the established hierarchies among the senior nobility.[50] Perhaps an item of ritual policy relating to institutions of learning was perceived as of little account in the context of Kanmu's larger policy objectives, the pacification of the north and the overhaul of the system of provincial administration. He seems to have been aware of the incipient decline of the public ethos of the Japanese state, but the measures that he took to attempt to achieve a sense of identification with the institution of emperor stressed military, rather than civil, lines of authority.[51] Perhaps, also, he was influenced by the relative decline of the ceremony in post-An Lu-shan China itself. He may, again, though suspicious of the institutional power of the Nara temples, have favoured Buddhism, rather than Confucianism, as the source of ritual dignification of his rule. It was during his reign that the seven-day, thirteen-cycle reading of the *Saishōōkyō* 最勝王経 (Suvarṇa-prabhāsottamarāja sūtra), 'the largest-scale annual observance in the Heian

46 For these observances, see Hayashi Rikurō 林陸郎, 'Nagaoka Heian kyō to kōshi enkyū' 長岡平安京と郊祀円丘, *Kodai bunka* 古代文化, 26.3 (March 1974), pp. 11–22.

47 It is interesting also that Kammu is said to have intended, in another Confucian gesture, to wear the Confucian three years' mourning for his father. However, he was, significantly, forced to abandon this for fear of a curse from the Ise shrine because of resulting neglect of worship there (Murao, pp. 182–5).

48 Murao, p. 13.

49 Kammu was particularly close to the Shikike 式家 branch of the Fujiwara; see *ibid.*, pp. 41–2.

50 For an example of Kammu's climbing down in the face of opposition to a hereditarily unqualified promotion, see *ibid.*, p. 88.

51 *Ibid.*, pp. 67–77.

ritual calendar',[52] became established. Perhaps the reason may have to do with the world of geomancy. Kanmu was evidently a superstitious man.[53] He had been born in the year of the ox, and is said to have been 'particularly afraid of the killing and dying of oxen'.[54] The prohibition in 791 and 801 of a popular cult of a 'Chinese deity' involving the sacrifice of oxen in the provinces of Ise 伊勢, Owari 尾張, Ōmi 近江, Mino 美濃, Echizen 越前 and Kii 紀伊 has been related to this imperial obsession.[55] Kanmu can hardly have been unaware that, at least in its original Chinese form, the metropolitan *sekiten* also involved the *tailao* sacrifice of an ox, a sheep and a pig. Later Japanese practice, known from the *Engishiki* 延喜式 (Procedures for ceremonies of the Engi period [901–23]) of 927, was to substitute a large and a small deer for the first two members of this set,[56] but it is not clear exactly when this substitution was made. There remains, circumstantially, at least the possibility that, in the intensely superstitious atmosphere of the time, Kanmu's fearfulness, linked with the association of the *sekiten* with oxen, may lie behind both the substitution and possibly also the decline in imperial patronage of the rite in the final decades of the eighth century and the early years of the ninth. Whatever the reason behind it, the decline of the rite in these decades demonstrates the truth that, at least under a relatively strong emperor, the *sekiten*, and with it also the whole world of values that it symbolised, were vulnerable to the chances of imperial whim.

None the less, it is clear that, although it may not have benefited from direct imperial patronage, the *sekiten* continued to be observed during Kanmu's reign. A kyaku 格 (penal procedure) of 793/5/11 identified a recurring difficulty over the freshness of the sacrificial victims forwarded from the provinces, which in recent years had been sliced before delivery, with the risk of going bad before the ceremony. However, 'with regard to the ritual of sacrifice,

---

52 Kurozaki Teruhito 黒崎輝人, 'Nihon kodai no shinji to butsuji: daijōe to misae o chūshin ni' 日本古代の神事と仏事 ― 大嘗会と御斎会を中心に, in Minamoto Ryōen 源了円 and Tamagake Hiroyuki 玉懸博之, eds., *Kokka to shūkyō* 国家と宗教 (Kyōto: Shibunkaku Shuppan, 1992), p. 65.

53 His two moves of capital may have been, at least in respect of timing, determined by this kind of belief: the first, from Nara to Nagaoka, by the fact that 784 was a revolutionary year (*kōshi* 甲子) in the sexagenary cycle (Hayashi Rikurō, p. 18); the second, to Heian-kyō, by fear of the vengeful spirit of his dead younger brother, the deposed crown prince Sawara 早良 (*Kokushi daijiten* 国史大辞典 [Yoshikawa Kōbunkan, 1979–94], vol. 3, p. 935). On the move of capital from Nara generally, see also Ronald P. Toby, 'Why leave Nara?', *Monumenta Nipponica*, 40 (1985), pp. 331–47.

54 *Kokushi daijiten*, vol. 3, pp. 935–36.

55 Ibid.; for the cult itself, see *Shoku Nihongi, KT*, vol. 2, p. 556; *Nihon kiryaku zenpen, KT*, vol.10, p. 276.

56 *Engishiki*, in *KT*, vol. 26, p. 516.

cleanliness and purity are basic; but to carve up the carcases of the victims is also clearly a part of the laws of ritual'.[57] Accordingly, victims were required to be sent whole to the court of sacrifice. It would seem, therefore, that the rite continued to be observed quietly within the academic institutions, at least at the metropolitan level.

THE *SEKITEN* IN THE NINTH CENTURY

A change came with the reigns of the Saga 嵯峨 (r.809–23), Junna 淳和 (r.823–33) and Nimmyō 仁明 (r.833–50) emperors. These men were ardent sinophiles and promoters of Chinese culture. By around mid-century, the court's interest in things Chinese had reached a fresh peak of intensity. This enthusiasm resulted in a renewal of imperial patronage of the *sekiten* itself. Thus Prince Tsunesada 恒貞親王 (825–84), crown prince under Nimmyō until 842, according to an early biography revived the ceremony after its 'more than eighty year' neglect, and on imperial orders, led 'the one hundred officers to perform the *sekiten*'.[58] Moreover, the ceremony was followed by versifying, from which the prince compiled an anthology. This imperial observance is not specifically mentioned in the narrative section of the standard histories, but has been dated to the early Jōwa period (834–47).[59] There seems no doubt that, whether or not due to this kind of imperial support, in the ninth century the university ceremony, now known to be based on the *Da Tang Kaiyuan li*, was a routine function in the metropolitan ritual calendar. In the provinces, too, the ritual became standardised according to the *Da Tang Kaiyuan li* during the course of the century.[60]

There were, inevitably, occasional difficulties and irregularities, many involving the complex world of taboos and pollutions. In 877, for instance, a bitch littered in the university, and the ceremony, already postponed once, was abandoned.[61] In 879, the autumn ceremony was cancelled because an official had died suddenly on university premises two days earlier.[62] In 884,

---

57 Quoted in *Nihon sandai jitsuroku* 日本三代実録, *KT*, vol. 4, p. 598; see also Miyagi Eishō 宮城栄昌, *Engishiki no kenkyū* 延喜式の研究, 2 vols. (Taishūkan, 1955–7), Shiryō hen 資料篇, p. 430.
58 *Tsunesada shinnō den*, p. 47.
59 Iyanaga, p. 436; cf. p. 415.
60 *Nihon sandai jitsuroku*, *KT*, vol. 4, p. 62, where a memorial of Jōgan 貞観 2 [860] refers to the university procedures following those of the *Da Tang Kaiyuan li* (*daxue guoji* 大学国子 version), and requests that the provincial ceremonies be standardised according to the same authority.
61 *Ibid.*, p. 410.
62 *Ibid.*, p. 456.

the autumn performance was postponed because a mare had suffered a miscarriage in the water office, and, when eventually performed, was further disrupted by a clap of thunder.[63] And in 887, the autumn ceremony was cancelled because an official had shortly before died of fright at an earthquake while inspecting repairs to a government building.[64] The problem of the freshness of the victims recurred. On 885/10/10, an imperial edict referred back to the 793 ruling and, because 'the guards' victims nowadays are extremely putrid and smelly and [have to be] discarded as unusable', ordered once again that fresh victims be submitted.[65]

These irregularities, no doubt, were the exceptions that prove the rule. Their inclusion in the record suggests that, in the second century of its observance in Japan, the ceremony had indeed become routine. Yet behind the facade of apparent regularity, subtle but important developments were taking place during the ninth century in the spirit and structure of the metropolitan ceremony and in its relation with the imperial palace. Cumulatively, they were to take the Japanese *sekiten* far from the public, integrated celebration of the relationship between imperial authority and the bureaucracy and its values of its high Tang model. The causes of these developments were complex. They may have been influenced in part by trends in contemporary Chinese culture; but, in part, they were also caused by indigenous cultural and political factors.

THE PALACE EXPOSITIONS

One of the earliest departures from Tang practice documented for the ninth century is also one of the most striking: the institution of the 'palace exposition' (*uchi rongi* 内論義) in the imperial presence on the day following the formal autumn *sekiten* ceremony itself.[66] The concept of a palace exposition was probably not a radically new one, for rather similar functions in the imperial presence, often in the form of 'debates' (*jianglun* 講論) between proponents of different faiths or 'readings' (*du* 読), had a long history in China.[67] The

---

63 *Ibid.*, p. 570.
64 *Ibid.*, p. 637.
65 *Ibid.*, p. 598.
66 For this ceremony, see Kurabayashi Shōji 倉林正次, 'Sekiten uchirongi no seiritsu' 釈奠内論義の成立, in *Kokugakuin zasshi* 国学院雑誌 86.11 (1985): 328–38.
67 See e.g. David McMullen, *State and scholars*, p. 33, for a debate held in 624, significantly in the state academy directorate, rather than in the imperial palace; and p. 87 for palace readings from the *Yue ling* 月令 book of the *Li ji*. A particularly famous debate was held in 826, with Bo Juyi 白居易 as chairman. See Arthur Waley, *The life and times of Po Chü-i* (London: George Allen and Unwin Ltd., 1949), pp.

staging of a palace exposition in the imperial presence in connection with the *sekiten*, however, may well have been a Japanese innovation. The practice may have followed a recent Buddhist precedent, for the *Nihon kōki* 日本後 紀 records a similar, but Buddhist, *uchi rongi*, on 813/1/14, following the completion of the seven-day reading cycle of the *Saishōōkyō*.[68] The first record of a palace exposition in association with the *sekiten* is found just over two years later, on 815/2/6 with a notice that the Saga Emperor summoned scholars to the palace for *ritsugi* 立義 (establishing meanings).[69] Thereafter, on 825/8/8, following the autumn ceremony, a summons was made to 'doctors and students'.[70] A similar entry for the following year adds that this has become 'an established usage'.[71] This ceremony was clearly intended to satisfy the scholarly enthusiasms of ninth-century emperors and to demonstrate the high place of Confucian learning in the priorities of the state. Indeed, it suggests a level of imperial seriousness and commitment that might compare favourably with that of many Chinese emperors.

Such an established ritual required formal procedures. Though no set of directives for the *uchi rongi* appears to survive from the ninth century,[72] later Heian ritual texts may be taken as some guide to the order of the ceremony, for Heian ritual was inherently conservative.[73] For the *uchi rongi*, the emperor was elaborately installed on a seat within blinds of state in the *shishinden* 紫宸殿 (ceremonial hall) of the palace, with two chamberlains bearing the imperial regalia, four ladies-in-waiting and four imperial secretaries in attendance. Princes and nobles joined the imperial presence. The scholars, five doctors, four graduate students (*tokugyō sei* 得業生) and two interlocutors, were now summoned and assumed positions on the outer south veranda. The duty noble (*shōkei* 上卿)[74] next summoned a doctor by name. The latter announced his own name, bowed twice, advanced two or three paces on his

169–71.

68 *KT*, vol. 3, p. 121; Kurozaki, p. 65.

69 *Ibid.*, p. 131; the term *ritsugi* is usefully glossed in Kurabayashi, pp. 529–30.

70 *Nihon kiryaku zenpen, KT*, vol. 10, p. 321.

71 *Ibid.*, p. 323.

72 But see Miyagi, *Shiryō hen*, p. 435, for a *shiki* 式 (ceremonial procedure) of pre-Engi date specifying the duties of the chamberlains (*kurōdo* 蔵人) at this ceremony.

73 This account is based on Ōe no Masafusa 大江匡房, *Gōke shidai* 江家次第 [*c*.1099–1111], in *Shintei zōho Kojitsu sōsho* 新訂増補故実叢書, 39 vols. (Meiji Tosho Kabushiki Kaisha, 1952–7; hereafter *SZKS*), vol. 2, pp. 260–62.

74 A member of the senior nobility appointed by rota to take charge of court rituals and other ceremonies. See Tsuchida Jikichin 土田直鎮, 'Shōkei ni tsuite' 上卿につ ひて, in Sakamoto Tarō hakushi kanreki kinenkai 坂本太郎博士還暦記念会 comp., *Nihon kodai shi ronshū* 日本古代史論集, 2 vols. (Yoshikawa Kōbunkan, 1962), vol. 2, pp. 565–78.

knees, took up a mace and assumed the seat of the respondent, a red chair placed centrally outside the emperor's blinds of state under the eaves on the south side of the hall. An interlocutor (a lecturer or a graduate student) was summoned and proceeded, also after a double obeisance and on his knees, to a white chair set for him on the outer veranda, again to the south. The doctor, as respondent, read the name of the classic, and the interlocutor raised doubtful points on its content. When the reply was finished, the next interlocutor questioned the respondent on another classic. After the completion of the process, the scholars retired and waited in the eastern court of the palace for their rewards of bolts of cloth according to status. They performed a *haibu* 拝舞 (dance of gratitude) and departed.

The *uchi rongi* following the *sekiten* seems likely to have been conceived as a transposition to the imperial palace of the exposition of learning phase of the *shidian* itself. Direct comparison is, however, complicated by the difference in sites and by the fact that, where in the Tang *shidian* the crown prince is involved, in the Japanese *uchi rongi* it is the reigning emperor himself. The Japanese ceremony may, in fact, be more tellingly compared with another ritual included in the *Da Tang Kaiyuan li*, the *huangdi huang taizu shixue* 皇帝皇太子視学 (viewing of the academy by the emperor and crown prince).[75] This ritual, like the *shidian*, has canonical origins.[76] It also shares with the exposition phase of the *shidian* the feature of an exposition in the lecture hall of the state academy directorate, but is distinguished by the presence there of the emperor himself, as well as the crown prince. The *Da Tang Kaiyuan li* directives for this ceremony prescribe that the emperor's seat be set 'under the northern wall of the hall, in the centre, facing south'. The 'lecture chair' was to be placed 'to the west of the imperial seat, [also] facing south'.[77] The emperor and the leading bearer of the Confucian tradition thus share the pre-eminent south-facing orientation, the emperor superior only in occupying the central position. No doubt, in giving a Confucian scholar a position of gross ritual comparability with the emperor, the drafters of the Tang directives had in mind a passage in the *Xueji* 学記 book of the *Li ji*, which specifically excepted the master of the 'Great College' both from the status of subject and from the north-facing orientation when communicating with the emperor.[78]

As a ceremony of exegesis of the Confucian canon in the imperial presence, the Tang viewing rite is thus structurally the closest Chinese counterpart to

---

75 Text in *DTKYL*, pp. 290C–1C.
76 *Li chi*, vol. 1, pp. 359–61.
77 *DTKYL*, p. 290C.
78 *Li chi*, vol. 2, p. 88: '[T]here are two among his subjects whom the ruler does not treat as subjects . . . According to the rules of the Great College, the master, though communicating anything to the son of heaven, did not stand with his face to the north. This was the way in which honour was done to him.'

the Japanese *uchi rongi*. Comparison, however, suggests important differences. Internally to the ceremony, the ritual deference accorded the Japanese emperor in the *uchi rongi* significantly exceeds that accorded the Chinese emperor in the viewing rite. In the *uchi rongi*, the positions of the emperor and respondent, respectively south- and north-facing, are those ritually symbolic of ruler and subject. The presence of chamberlains bearing the imperial regalia, a feature of the later Heian version of the ceremony even if not already so in the ninth century, seems intended symbolically to reinforce the transcendence of the Japanese emperor over his Confucian scholars. By contrast, in the Chinese viewing rite the south-facing position is shared by the emperor himself and the equivalent of the respondent, the bearer of the canon, symbolically representing the authority of the Confucian teaching and its partnership with imperial power.

Perhaps the most instructive contrast between these two ceremonies is, however, between their sites. The Chinese emperor's presence in the state academy directorate suggests an active engagement with the secular world outside his palace. In locating the ritual within the palace itself, the ritual centre of the realm, on the other hand, the Japanese drew attention to the sacerdotal and symbolic role of their sovereign. This contrast is heightened by the mobility of the Chinese emperor and the immobility of his Japanese counterpart. The Chinese emperor's journey to the state academy directorate for the viewing rite can, like the crown prince's for the *shidian*, be interpreted as a symbolic journey of acknowledgement and homage to the locus of Confucian learning. In the Japanese *uchi rongi*, the movement is reversed: the scholars journey to the palace, rather than the emperor to the university. The emperor's ritual immobility is apt. The *uchi rongi* suggests that the ninth-century Japanese emperors were retreating into notions of sovereignty that, far more than the Chinese, were transcendent, sacerdotal and ascriptive. They were, probably literally as well as metaphorically, screened in their palace from active engagement with the realities of the world outside. Not least, again literally as well as metaphorically, they were distanced from the achievement-based, meritocratic values symbolised by the Confucian university and its most important ritual. At the same time, they were passive, sacred symbols of the genealogical permanence of the Japanese imperial house and the aristocratic, ascriptive social order that supported it and that it legitimated. What the emperors gained in symbolic potency, however, they tended to lose in political power.

At all events, an important consequence of the palace expositions was, in effect, a fragmentation of the unity that had characterised the *Da Tang Kaiyuan li* ceremony. In place of a single, essentially public rite unified by common participation, there are now two. Where the *Da Tang Kaiyuan li* version had brought together representatives of the various elements in the polity in a single, integrated and public ritual, the institution of the *uchi rongi* created a separate, imperial ceremony, divorced from the university, and, given the small number of participants, in effect, private.

FEASTING AND VERSIFYING

The palace expositions were not the only development that threatened to fragment the unity and subvert the original public, Confucian character of the *sekiten* ritual in its adoptive environment. There was also a tendency from the early ninth century to make the *sekiten* the occasion of social and aesthetic diversion, and particularly of versifying in Chinese and the banqueting that provided its social setting. Though these activities had characterised the rite in the Six Dynasties period, neither was an aspect of high Tang practice, and they tended to restrict participation in the rite, to shift its focus and to alter its character.

Some element of feasting and verse composition seems likely to have featured in the Japanese version of the rite from the early days of its observance in Japan.[79] However, if that is so, the tendency to use the rite as the occasion for aesthetic and social pleasure was strengthened in the ninth century. The four decades covered by the reigns from Saga to Nimmyō were, as already suggested, a period of 'rapidly mounting admiration for Chinese culture'.[80] Much of the sinophile energy of these years was directed towards literary production in Chinese, an activity conceived to be conducive to effective imperial government. For this was the period in which the belief that, to borrow the oft-quoted words of emperor Wen of the Wei 魏文帝, 'literature is the great task of regulating the state' was adopted as a slogan for the activities of the Japanese court.[81] This fashion for composing verse in Chinese

---

79 So much is suggested by the survival of a *sekiten* poem from the first decades of the eighth century, for, as already noted, these poems were produced at banquets following the religious ceremony proper. See poem by Fujiwara no Maro 藤原万里, No. 97 in *Kaifūsō* 懐風藻, ed. Kojima Noriyuki 小島憲之, in *Nihon koten bungaku taikei* 日本古典文学大系, 102 vols. (Iwanami Shoten, 1957–68), vol. 69, p. 160. This poem is dated to 717–21 by Fukuda (p. 20).

80 Jin'ichi Konishi, *A history of Japanese literature: volume two: the early middle ages*, tr. Aileen Gatten, ed. Earl Miner (Princeton: Princeton University Press, 1986), p. 68.

81 Quoted in Ōtsuka Hideko 大塚英子, '*Bunshō keikoku*' no hikakubungakuteki ichikōsatsu' 「文章経国」の比較文学的一考察, *Kokubungaku kaishaku to kanshō* 国文学解釈と鑑賞, 55.10 (October 1990), p. 103. I am grateful to Dr Gaye Rowley, Cardiff University, for drawing my attention to this article.

found an outlet in the *sekiten* ceremony itself. Indeed, the revival of the ceremony after its decline following the death of Kibi no Makibi seems to have been due, in part at least, to literary enthusiasm. In the passage from the biography of Prince Tsunesada referred to above, it is the composition of verse and the prince's compilation of an anthology that are the main focus of interest, and seem, at least in the mind of the author, to loom larger than the religious aspect of the rite itself. The prince seems to have inaugurated a fashion. In the ceremony itself, this appears to have resulted in an additional ceremony of feasting and verse composition following the exposition that has no counterpart in the *Da Tang Kaiyuan li* versions of the rite.

Both feasting and the composition of verse are specified following the exposition in the presence of the crown prince, in directives contained in a section entitled *sekiten kōron no gi* 釈奠講論ノ儀 (the *sekiten* exposition ceremony) in the *Jōgan gishiki* 貞観儀式 (Procedures for ceremonies of the Jōgan period [859–76]).[82] Prescribed here is a three stage addition to the formal exposition phase of the ceremony, marked off from the exposition proper by the withdrawal of all participants outside the immediate ceremonial precincts and their re-entry, in hierarchical order, into the court of the lecture hall. This sequence consists of: (i) a banquet for all participants, later to be referred to as the *momodo no za* 百度の座 (refreshments),[83] for which those of high rank are seated in the hall itself, those of lower rank, presumably physically separated from their betters, in adjoining east and west halls. The banquet itself is preceded by a *shaza shashu* 謝座謝酒 (thanks for seating and thanks for wine) in the court, a regular ritual gesture prescribed before an official feast.[84] This banquet consisted of toasts and the distribution of food in wooden boxes, prepared by the bureau of the palace kitchen. This was followed by: (ii) a banquet for those of fifth rank and above, put on by the university itself; (iii) the composition of verse by literati, usually relatively low-ranking officials of the university, in the presence of the court party, simultaneously with expositions staged by students in other disciplines.

Though there is some dispute among historians as to whether the directives of the *Jōgan gishiki* represent original ninth-century formulations or were revised in the tenth century to reflect contemporary practice,[85] external

---

82 Also known as *Gishiki* 儀式; text in *SZKS*, vol. 4, p. 182–85.

83 Iyanaga, p. 454; for the *momodo no za*, see Kurabayashi Shōji, 'Sekiten no momodo no za' 釈奠の百度座, *Kokugakuin zasshi* 86.2 (1985): 1–14. The traditional explanation for the term, which means literally 'hundredfold feast', is given by Ōe no Masafusa (p. 142): 'Chikasuke 允亮 says: "Of old an empress said: 'Those who have devoted themselves to public [service] should be rewarded [with refreshments], even a hundred times a day.'"'

84 See *Engishiki*, 'Kōen' 公宴, in *KT*, vol. 26, p. 993.

85 For Iyanaga's dating of the text to the Jōgan period, see pp. 458–9; for a

evidence shows conclusively that some such social and aesthetic ceremony as outlined above must have been observed. Thus a *Nihon sandai jitsuroku* notice of the omission of the 'refreshments' (the *momodo no za*) in the observance of 872/2/7 confirms that their distribution was the normal practice of the time.[86] External evidence also confirms the composition of verse during the *sekiten* ceremony. From the Jōgan period, records of the themes of *sekiten* verses survive, albeit not for every year. The texts of 29 of these poems are extant, beginning from 867.[87]

The *sekiten*, therefore, became, at least in the eyes of the court, an important social and literary occasion. There is, indeed, evidence that the court's interest in the *sekiten* was confined exclusively to the exposition of learning phase of the ceremony and its sequel. First, a memorial of 860 refers to the metropolitan *sekiten* ceremony as following the *guozi* version from the *Da Tang Kaiyuan li*.[88] This version, used for the regular, twice annual ceremony in Changan, was internal to the university. Its chief celebrant was the rector. It made no provision for the participation of the crown prince or senior nobility, nor for any exposition following the religious rite. The ninth-century Japanese *sekiten* was thus a hybrid, composed of two historically different elements. The exposition in the presence of the crown prince was added, incongruously in terms of the *Da Tang Kaiyuan li* model for the ceremony, to a purely internal university ceremony.

Other evidence also suggests that the court did not participate in the religious rite in the university. In the *Jōgan gishiki* directives for the exposition of learning, the crown prince is assigned the following instruction:

summary of and bibliography on the problems of this text, see entry in *Kokushi daijiten*, vol. 7, pp. 470–1.

86 *KT*, vol. 4, p. 303.

87 Fukuda (pp. 26–7) supplies a list. These verses are generally Confucian in sentiment and contain allusions to the classic that was the subject of the immediately preceding exposition. They cannot be said always to be well-sustained or of the highest literary quality.

> Mid-spring *sekiten*. Heard a lecture on the *Analects* and composed on 'Zhongni 仲尼 [Confucius] is the sun and moon' (vol. 19, p. 24; Legge, tr., p. 348) from the same:
>
> When men possessed the Way, Zhongni was born.
>
> When the heavens above are cloudless, the sun and moon traverse.
>
> Truly, for humankind, the heavens are the same.
>
> We shrink [in awe], cast down our eyes, and venerate the high and bright.

Denshi kashū 田氏家集, in *Gunsho ruijū*, vol. 6, p. 811, poem of Shimada no Tadaomi 島田忠臣 (828–92), dated by Iyanaga (p. 435) to 865 or 869.

88 *Nihon sandai jitsuroku*, *KT*, vol. 4, p. 62, memorial of Wanibe no Ietsugu 和迩部宅継.

The crown prince dismounts from his carriage outside the eastern gate [of the university], and thereupon enters the gate of the shrine [to Confucius]. He ascends to the hall and bows to the Former Sage and the Former Teacher. When this is done, he enters the Todōin 都堂院 [the lecture hall of the university] through the eastern side gate. Ascending the north eastern steps, he enters the door of the hall and assumes his seat.[89]

This directive strongly suggests that the crown prince was not to participate in the religious ceremony itself, but to proceed, after a cursory bow at the image of Confucius and Yan Hui, directly to the exposition. This procedure probably bears little relation to actual practice, for no evidence survives that the crown prince attended even the exposition phase of the ceremony after the mid-ninth century. It does, however, confirm a lack of interest in the religious ceremony proper on the part of the imperial house. A similar inference is to be drawn with respect to the high officers of state from a notice in the *Nihon sandai jitsuroku* for 886/8/1, which refers to the grand minister entering the shrine to Confucius 'after the ritual of sacrifice was over'.[90]

It might be tempting to identify this penetration of the *sekiten* by the social and aesthetic activity of verse composition as a symptom of the growing detachment from political realities and practical administration that is, of course, one theme of the history of the court and high aristocracy during the Heian period. Certainly, there is an air of self-absorption and dilletantism about court culture at this time. However, literature was, of course, conceived to have a political purpose. It is one of several ambiguities in the history of the *sekiten*, that in so emphasising these activities, the Japanese court may have been responding, as earlier it did in a different direction, to contemporary Tang practice. The court of Dezong, in particular, witnessed a renewed emphasis on literature and commitment to 'ceremonies and banqueting,' possibly at the expense of the support of Confucian learning. It has recently been suggested that this development was known to the Japanese through the reports of the sixteenth official embassy that returned in 804 and through other channels, and that it inspired the rather similar developments in the Japanese court.[91] If this argument is correct, the tendency to use the *sekiten* ritual as the occasion for social and aesthetic recreation may have been partly inspired by Tang, as well as by indigenous developments.

At all events, the institution of an exposition with its social and aesthetic sequel patronised by the senior nobility further compromised the original

89 *Jōgan gishiki, SZKS*, vol. 31, p. 183.
90 *KT*, vol. 4, p. 615.
91 Tsukada, p. 104.

unity of the *Da Tang Kaiyuan li* version of the ceremony. The *sekiten* ceremony itself has been divided into two separate, essentially discontinuous, parts. There seem to have been, in effect, two ceremonies: a religious ceremony in the shrine to Confucius, about which the ninth-century sources are uninformative beyond suggesting that it was performed; and an academic, social and aesthetic ceremony in the university's lecture hall. Only the second of these ceremonies received the patronage of high authority and is therefore well documented. And even here, given evidence of the formalisation of the exposition to be presented below, it is not unreasonable to assume that it was its social and aesthetic aspects, the versifying and feasting, that were most attractive to its exalted patrons. When the palace expositions are added to the picture, the *sekiten* will be seen to have divided into three separate parts, each reflecting a different stratum within the Japanese polity: the sacrifice to Confucius that involved, in so far as it followed the *guozi* version of the *Da Tang Kaiyuan li*, only the academic officers and students of the university; the exposition and ensuing feasts and versifying, patronised by the senior nobility; and the palace expositions, put on for the benefit of the emperor. In social and political terms, this fragmentation of the rite reflects the increasing stratification of rank-bearing Japanese society according to the principle of inherited status. In terms of the values identified in the *Da Tang Kaiyuan li* version of the ritual, it destroys the sacralised, architectonic unity that the ritual symbolised. With that loss goes also a loss of the universalism and belief in achievement implicit in the state's unified, collective act of religious homage to Confucius.

OTHER ASPECTS OF THE *SEKITEN* IN THE NINTH CENTURY

The *uchi rongi* must have raised the profile of Chinese learning and letters in Japanese elite society, as it was no doubt intended to do. But by making the palace the centre of scholarly prestige, it must also, ironically, have deflected respect away from the public state institutions of learning and their programme. The failure of the court to involve itself in the religious ceremony in the university must have detracted from the prestige of that institution and its Confucian programme of studies. In subtle ways, also, the fashion for literary composition probably drew prestige away from more narrowly defined Confucian learning and may thus also have contributed to a weakening of the ethos of public service. Other important factors contributed to a decline in the vitality of the cult of Confucius during the ninth century. The cult seems to have declined in vigor in China itself, as already noted. Though the Japanese were to update their academic usages in accordance with Tang practice as late as the mid-ninth century, for instance adopting Xuanzong's edition of the *Xiao jing* 孝経 (Classic of filial piety) for the university curriculum on 860/10/16,[92] it was not the cult of Confucius itself that they felt compelled to strengthen. As the Tang dynasty weakened, moreover, diplomatic relations became less intensive, and the Japanese became less emulous of the Chinese model of the state and its supporting institutions. The second half of the ninth century is seen as a period of waning Chinese influence and the reassertion of Japanese values. At the same time, the Fujiwara consolidated their political ascendancy and monopoly of high office, both weakening the institution of the emperor and rendering the meritocratic principles on which the university was notionally based increasingly irrelevant to the prospects of most men. Within the university, private halls, chief among them the Kangaku-in 勧学 院 of the Fujiwara, must have distorted the public function of the institution. The Kangaku-in was eventually even to assume religious functions on behalf of the Fujiwara and their clan Buddhist temples and Shintō shrines,[93] a role that must have co-existed oddly with the officially ordained public Confucian role of the university. Against this background, it is no great surprise to find further evidence both of a tendency to subordinate various aspects of the *sekiten* to native institutions and values and of a decline of vitality in its observance.

There was, first, a tendency within the exposition phase of the *sekiten* ceremony itself to exalt the ritual status of the crown prince relative to that of the bearers of the Confucian tradition. The evidence for this comes, once more, from the *Jōgan gishiki*.[94] This text contains directives for the setting out of the seats in the university lecture hall for the exposition phase of the rite. The 'high seat' of the bearer of the canon, in accordance with the *Da Tang Kaiyuan li* usage, is 'at the middle portal of the hall, facing south'; the reader faces him; and the interlocutors are between them, a little distance to the west and facing east. The crown prince's seat, however, is to be set not, as in the *Da Tang Kaiyuan li*, against the east wall and facing west, but east of the bearer of the canon and facing south, that is on the same east–west axis and facing in the same direction. In this way, the ritual primacy of the bearer of the canon, if not lost (he is still seated centrally and, apparently, on a higher seat than the crown prince), is at least compromised. The explicit gesture to the transcendence of the Confucian tradition of the *Da Tang Kaiyuan li* is avoided. More strikingly still, in the *Da Tang Kaiyuan li* version of the exposition, the bearer of the canon had, on entry into the court of the lecture

92 *KT*, vol. 4, p. 55–6; Kano Naoki 狩野直喜, *Dokusho san'yo* 読書纂餘 (Misuzu Shobō, 1980), p. 135.
93 Hisaki, p. 147.
94 *SZKS*, vol. 31, p. 182; cf. Iyanaga, p. 452.

hall, been explicitly excluded from bowing to the crown prince. In the *Jōgan gishiki*, however, he and the reader make a double obeisance together, both on entry into the court and on conclusion of the exposition.[95] Even though there is no evidence that the crown prince actually attended the *sekiten* from Jōgan times, it is clear that the drafters of these directives felt constrained to avoid any suggestion that, even notionally, the representative of the imperial lineage might be ritually inferior to the bearers of the Confucian tradition. This feature of the ninth-century *sekiten*, therefore, parallels the ritual exaltation of the emperor in the *uchi rongi*, and reflects the same tendency to downgrade the status of the Confucian tradition relative to that of the imperial lineage.

There was, furthermore, a tendency to subordinate the *sekiten* to less obviously foreign ceremonies in the order of precedence implicit in the court's ritual programme, in effect to marginalise it. As a ritual implicitly of the 'middle' status in the Tang classification, it was, even in the country of its origin, in principle liable to be displaced by 'major' ceremonies.[96] In China, this may have mattered little, since the whole ritual programme had a Confucian colouring. In Japan, however, it implied the subordination of Confucian to 'Shintō' ceremonies. In 820, the ceremony was postponed to the second *hinoto* day of the month because it coincided with the *Ki'nensai* 祈年祭 (also known as the *toshigoi no matsuri*), the rite to pray for a good harvest; it was believed that 'the three victims should be abstained from'[97] during this important ritual. This principle was affirmed, and at the same time an eclipse of the sun made grounds for postponement, in the *Jōgan daigaku shiki* (Procedures for the university of the Jōgan period).[98] Further, an imperial edict of 885/11/10 reaffirmed a previously stated principle that if the day of the sacrifice fell 'before [one of] the various festivals or on the day itself', the use of the three victims and of the pickled hare was to be abandoned and fish to be substituted.[99] The 'festivals' involved here were almost certainly those mentioned explicitly in this context in the *Engishiki* of the early tenth century: the Kasuga 春日, Ōharano 大原野, Sono-Karakami 園韓神 festivals,[100] 'Shintō' observances which had been accorded state-sponsored status as *kansai* 官祭 (official festivals) relatively recently and as a result of the resurgence of Japanese religious and cultural practices in the ninth century.[101] These ceremonies, indeed, can be interpreted to represent a

---

95 *SZKS*, vol. 31, p. 184.
96 Ordinance of the Zhenguan (627–49) period, in Niida, p. 265.
97 *Nihon kiryaku zenpen, KT*, vol. 10, p. 310; Miyagi, *Shiryō hen*, p. 432;
98 *Ibid.*
99 *Nihon sandai jitsuroku, KT*, vol. 4, p. 598.
100 *Engishiki, KT*, vol. 26, p. 516.
101 Okada Shōji, 'The development of state ritual in ancient Japan', *Acta Asiatica* 51 (1987): 27. In Japan it was also the practice from at least the mid-ninth century

reassertion of *uji*-based particularism at the expense of the ethos of the public Chinese-style state. The Kasuga and Ōharano festivals were precisely to honour the Fujiwara house. There is a kind of symbolic appropriateness, therefore, in the fact that these ceremonies were accorded priority over the *sekiten*, which, of course, had, in its original Tang form at least, celebrated a very different, universalistic, set of values.

Moreover, from before the middle of the ninth century, the exposition phase of the *sekiten* itself began to show signs of loss of vitality and of formalisation. In Tang China, the classics chosen for the exposition are thought to have been flexible and 'appropriate to the occasion'.[102] In ninth-century Japan, however, they became fixed in a rigidly prescribed, unvarying order, referred to as *Shichikei rinten kō* 七経輪轉講 (Exposition of the seven classics by rote).[103] This practice was traced historically by the historian of Chinese learning in the Heian period, Kawaguchi Hisao 川口尚夫, for the period 860–900.[104] Iyanaga, however, was able not only to confirm Kawaguchi's findings, but also to demonstrate that the cycle extended back as far as 838.[105] This suggests that in the same decade that the imperial patronage of Confucian exegesis in the palace had reached its peak, the academic aspect of the university ceremony lapsed into formalisation.

Something of the character that the Japanese *sekiten* had acquired by the end of the ninth century is reflected in the career of the scholar-bureaucrat Sugawara no Michizane and his relationship to the rite. Michizane, as already mentioned, was, together with Kibi no Makibi, one of two individuals particularly associated with the rite in ancient Japanese sources. Indeed, he was the author of 12 of the 29 *sekiten shi* (together with one preface) to survive from the Heian period. At first sight, his career suggests a close parallel with that of Kibi, for like him he was of relatively low hereditary court rank, enjoyed a successful academic career and was, during an interlude in Fujiwara ascendancy, spectacularly promoted to the position of minister of the right. However, whereas Kibi contributed to the establishment of the ceremony in Japan, Michizane's relation to the *sekiten* is ambiguous. Just as Michizane's career suggests a man reluctant to challenge the ascriptive values

---

(Iyanaga, p. 410) to cancel the *sekiten* if it fell within the period of an emperor's mourning for an ascendant (*ryōan* 諒闇). Comparative data with the Tang are required to assess the significance of this.
102 Iyanaga, p. 437.
103 Minamoto no Takaakira 源高明, *Seikyūki* 西宮記 [*c.* 955–64], *SZKS*, vol. 6, p. 160.
104 Kawaguchi Hisao, *Heian chō Nihon kambungaku shi no kenkyū: zōtei ban* 平安朝日本漢文学史の研究、贈訂版 (Meiji Shoin, 1964), pp. 130–4.
105 Iyanaga, pp. 416–39.

of the society of his time,[106] so his attitude to the *sekiten* appears much what might be expected of a ninth-century offical of his status. The dating of his *sekiten* verses seems to illustrate the association of the ceremony with relatively low-ranking academic posts, an important function of which was to service the cultural needs of the senior nobility. Of Michizane's 12 *sekiten* verses, all but four were composed between 868 and 886 while he enjoyed the academic career traditional to his family.[107] During these decades, he held rank no higher than junior fifth, upper, and he would have participated in the ceremony in a subordinate capacity, as a professional scholar, charged with the composition of Chinese verse for diversion of the senior nobility. It was not until 891 that his career began to involve him in positions of greater political prominence. Nor, in fact, is there any reason to suppose any particular enthusiasm for the ceremony; Michizane's relatively large number of *sekiten shi* among the extant corpus is a reflection of his prolific talent and the fact that more of his verse survives than of any other *kanshi* 漢詩 poet of ancient Japan. Despite the copious documentation linking Michizane to the ceremony, the evidence does not suggest that he was in any serious sense its revivalist.

The history of the *sekiten* from the end of the ninth century to the close of the Heian period in 1185 must be seen against the general decline of *ritsuryō* institutions, including the state education system, during these centuries. The *sekiten* continued to be observed, but shows a similar pattern of decline and more particularly an intensification of tendencies towards formalisation, subordination to indigenous rituals, the inclusion of more feasting, and abbreviation in performance. However, though lack of space precludes a detailed account here, the rite continued to be observed throughout the ancient period.

SUMMARY AND CONCLUSION

Surveying the nearly half-millennium long history of the *sekiten* rite in ancient Japan, no one could fail to be struck by the seriousness and continuity of the effort involved. There was, clearly, at one level an impressive stability about the ritual life of the ancient Japanese state, particularly in its metropolis. No

---

106 Borgen, p. 273.
107 See *Kanke bunsō Kanke kōshū* 菅家文藻菅家後集, ed. Kawaguchi Hisao, in *Nihon koten bungaku taikei*, LXXII, poem Nos. 14, 23, 28, 41, 55, 81, 88, 139. Of the remaining four, one (No. 220) was composed in 887 in Sanuki 讃岐 where Michizane celebrated the *sekiten* as provincial governor; two (Nos. 396 and 398) in 893, during which he held a variety of posts, including assistant director of the ministry of rites; and one (No. 382) in 895.

Chinese dynasty was to bequeath such a record of continuity. The Chinese pattern, rather, albeit against the background of the secular development of Chinese society, inevitably followed that of the Chinese dynastic cycle. It tended to be one of intense initial imperial commitment followed by an irregular decline and eventual renewal. Indeed, by just past mid-point in the history of the rite in ancient Japan, the cycle of the Tang dynasty had run its course. In 960, when the Japanese *sekiten* was still being conscientiously observed, albeit fragmented and with some loss of vitality, the founding Song emperor revived an evidently lapsed Confucian cult with grand imperial gestures to the Confucian shrine.[108] In 1280, the dynastic cycle was to be renewed yet again. Under the Yuan (1280–1368), the observance of the rite was to achieve new heights of magnificence.[109]

But it is important to distinguish longevity from other aspects of the observance of the rite in Japan. It will have become clear from the foregoing account that, behind its continuity, the history of the *sekiten* in ancient Japan was not static. Rather, the ceremony underwent considerable but often subtle transformation, under the influence of continental developments, the dynamics of domestic historical change and the process of adaptation to indigenous preferences. Three main phases are described above: adoption in the eighth century; adaptation in the ninth; and decline in the tenth to twelfth. There is much, however, that still remains obscure. Thus lack of evidence in the eighth century makes it uncertain how closely the rite ever approximated to its Tang model in this period, when direct contacts between the two countries were at their most intense. That model was expressed in the *Da Tang Kaiyuan li*, and particularly in the grandest version contained in that work, the *shidian* for the crown prince. This version, it was suggested, was characterised by an overall structural unity that mirrored, in a symbolic fashion, the structure of the Chinese polity. Latent in the ritual, also, were both the values of the tradition to which it paid homage and those of the political society that staged it. It matters rather little here that empirically the crown prince's *shidian* was an irregular and possibly not very frequently observed form of the rite. What is important, rather, is that the *Da Tang Kaiyuan li* possessed great prestige and was widely regarded as expressing an ideal ritual order, and that, furthermore, there is ample evidence that in Tang China the more successful emperors were, historically, actively interested in the cult of Confucius.

It is possible that men such as Kibi no Makibi, who had direct experience of the ritual life of the Tang metropolis and its bureaucratic and physical setting, may have attempted in the eighth century to confer on the Japanese

108 Shryock, p. 153.
109 *Ibid.*, pp. 168–80.

rite something of the structural and symbolic unity and the prestige that it had possessed in contemporary Tang China under Xuan zong. The Shōtoku empress' attendance at the metropolitan *sekiten* in 767 does suggest the possibility of an attempt to create the kind of bond between the imperial institution and the cult of Confucius and its bearers that characterised Tang China under its most vigorous and successful rulers. This bond was the essential basis of the imperial public bureaucratic state, but there must ultimately remain a question as to whether it was ever actually comprehended or realised, even briefly, in ancient Japan. All that can be said for certain is that the history of the rite in the mid-eighth century demonstrates conscientious attempts to keep the form of the Japanese ceremony up-to-date with formal developments in Tang practice.

If Kibi was indeed inspired by a serious desire to adopt the informing ethos as well as the outward form of the rite in Japan, his efforts yielded no permanent result. During the closing decades of the eighth century, imperial patronage of the *sekiten* declined precisely at the point at which it might have been most effective. The reasons cannot now be recovered with certainty, but may include the influence of the lower profile of the rite in post-An Lushan China, Kanmu's preference for military, rather than civil, lines of control, his respect for aristocratic privilege, and his superstitious character. At any rate, Kanmu failed to confer imperial benediction on an implicitly meritocratic institution that might, symbolically, have challenged the aristocratic *status quo*. Kanmu was an autocratic ruler and was, moreover, apparently interested in bringing new blood into high office. He might have been expected to use Confucianism to achieve this goal and to overcome the power of Japan's traditional aristocratic particularism. This was apparently the course adopted in neighbouring Silla Korea, where, 'under [an] authoritarian political structure, Confucianism stood in opposition to traditional true-bone privilege and, indeed, developed in partnership with the power of the throne'.[110] Kanmu, however, does not seem to have perceived this same potential in Confucianism, or to have patronised the *sekiten* with the same resourcefulness that he used in staging the suburban sacrifice. Nor does he seem to have considered the university as a potential instrument for enhancement of his own power in this way. The university appears to have followed its own path as a place mainly

110 Carter J. Eckhert, et al., *Korea old and new: a history* (Cambridge, Mass.: Ilchokak Publishers, 1990), p. 52. For an instructive analysis of the relationship between monarchical power, bureaucracy and aristocracy in the Korean context, see James B. Palais, 'Confucianism and the aristocratic/bureaucratic balance in Korea', *Harvard Journal of Asiatic Studies* 44 (1984): 427–68. Palais sees the beginnings of the weakening of Korean aristocratic power under Confucian influence in the Silla period; for him, however, the process was never completed, and Korea remained characterised by a 'balance' between a bureaucratic and an aristocratic political order.

of training for middle to lower ranking bureaucrats, rather than becoming the path to the highest office. Like his autocratic seventh-century predecessors, the Tenji and Temmu emperors, Kanmu does not seem to have conceived it as his mission to use his power radically to alter the fabric of Japan's traditional social order. Nor is this altogether surprising, for Tang China, his model, in many respects, too, remained to a considerable extent an aristocratic society during this period.

Kanmu's early ninth-century successors lacked nothing in enthusiasm for things Chinese and endeavoured to further the process of sinicisation begun more than two centuries before. They seem to have wished to enhance the position of the Confucian university in national life. But they attempted to do so not by broadening access to it socially so much as by attempting to force the higher aristocracy to adopt Chinese learning. For a while, efforts were made and inducements offered to promote attendance at the university even by the sons of senior nobles, whose hereditary privileges were such that it had hitherto conferred no advantages on them. These policies attained a certain success, and the ancient university attained some prosperity during the ninth century. It is important to stress, therefore, that it still did not become a genuinely meritocratic institution itself or the recruiting ground for a universalistic, meritocratic bureaucracy. For one thing, efforts were made to restrict access to the prestigious literature course to the sons of senior nobility. For another, through the operation of the *on 'i* 蔭位 (shadow rank) system, less socially privileged students continued to suffer penalties when, after graduation, it came to the award of rank and office. Furthermore, as the century wore on, private halls became established, and even academic office itself began to be awarded ascriptively, on a hereditary basis.

None the less, over this period imperial patronage of the *sekiten* seems to have been revived for a while, even if largely as an expression of a rather superficial sinophilia and literary enthusiasm. The rite becomes better documented, but the picture that is now revealed is different from the high Tang model. There are already signs of the privatisation of the rite, its penetration by social and aesthetic values and its assimilation to indigenous particularism. The public, unified expression of imperial and bureaucratic homage to Confucius of the *Da Tang Kaiyuan li* has given way to a compartmentalised observance. The institution of the palace expositions and the summoning of scholars to the palace the day following the autumn religious rite in the university symbolically reversed the direction of homage: it is the bearers of Confucianism who acknowledge the transcendence of the imperial lineage. As expressed in the directives for the Japanese *sekiten*, the relationship of Confucianism to the throne is one of subordination, rather than partnership. During the ninth century, these trends intensified. The ceremony effectively split into three parts: a religious rite in the shrine to Confucius in the university for the academic community; a social and aesthetic ceremony for the senior nobility in the lecture hall; and a palace exposition in the privacy of the imperial palace the day following the formal autumn observance in the university. This fragmentation of the rite can be interpreted as a reflection of the structure of Japanese society as it had developed by this time. The university served mainly as an institution to train middle and lower ranking bureaucrats and literati; above them, higher office was monopolised by a few aristocratic lineages, most conspicuously the Hokke 北家 (Northern house) of the Fujiwara; and yet higher stood the emperor, who had by the second half of the ninth century retreated into a predominantly passive sacerdotal role, ritually potent, but politically stifled by oligarchic power. At all levels of this structure, particularism and ascription were the dominant values. None of the parties identified here, in all probability, was hostile to the *sekiten*. Indeed, some, like the sinophile ninth-century emperors, seem to have been actively in favour of it as an ornament to the state's ritual programme and a symbol of its sinicisation. But they were interested only in surfaces.

The history of the rite from the beginning of the tenth century to the end of the ancient period is one of steady atrophy, formalisation and decline. This is not surprising, for the *sekiten* no longer celebrated values relevant to Japanese society. It had become an empty formality.

Why, then, did the *sekiten* rite become fragmented in Japan and eventually atrophy in this way? Or, to put the question differently, why did the ancient Japanese state not sustain its apparent initial commitment to Confucianism? To answer this question would, of course, be to account for a major failure of the Chinese-style polity in Japan and is beyond the scope of this essay. It is, however, possible to conclude with some speculative observations. Various theories are currently advanced to explain the long-term failure of the Chinese style state in ancient Japan. Much attention has focused on the provisions for land distribution as the root cause for the wider failure. Economic reasons have been adduced: that the Japanese society of the time was too small, sparsely populated and technologically backward to make the system work, or, alternatively, that the increasing prosperity of society led the elite to look outside *ritsuryō* institutions to augment its wealth.[111] These economic explanations do not seem immediately persuasive with regard to the history of the *sekiten* rite in Japan. There is little evidence, for instance, that the metropolitan ceremony faltered for lack of funds. It is, however, possible that scale was a factor, and that the aristocratic society of ancient Japan was indeed too small, too stable and mutually well acquainted, perhaps, to stimulate

111 William Wayne Farris, *Population, disease, and land in early Japan, 645–900* (Cambridge, Mass.: Harvard University Press, 1985), pp. 141–4.

the kind of impersonal competition that became increasingly established in Tang China. The relationship of elite society to the traditionally subordinate occupational service groups, many immigrant-descended, may also have inhibited the development of meritocratic competition. Perhaps the broad notion of 'backwardness', if applied to the cultural sphere, is more helpful. It explains, for instance, the slow start in the establishment of the rite. Unlike Tang China, ancient Japan had no established or diffused tradition of Confucian learning. The rite and the Confucian tradition of which it was the salient expression, as has been shown, were largely confined to academic institutions; they were not in any sense popular. They offered no obvious sublunary benefits.

A third, more general explanation is the 'inapplicability theory', which holds that the institutions of the 'Chinese-style centralized state [were] inherently unworkable on Japanese soil'.[112] This theory, in its turn, however, is analytically weak and unpersuasive, leading too easily either to circularity or to a hypostatised notion of Japanese exceptionalism. It seems, however, to lie behind, for instance, Iyanaga's observation that the religious offerings phase of the *Da Tang Kaiyuan li* version of the ceremony was 'remote from Japan', and atrophied there for that reason.[113] But un-Japanese also were numerous other ceremonies and practices in ancient Japan, including, of course, those of Buddhism. So also was the sacrifice of oxen, apparently spontaneously adopted by the people of eastern central Japan at the end of the eighth century and prohibited by the superstitious Kanmu.

More helpful is the well-established view of institutional and cultural historians that the particular institutional structure of the Japanese *ritsuryō* state prevented the development of a close alliance between an autocratic emperor and his bureaucrats. In the Japanese adaptation of the Chinese polity, the *daijōkan* 太政館 and its consultative apparatus, staffed in effect by the oligarchic senior nobility, dominated decision-making. The Japanese emperor, as a consequence, had much less power than his Tang counterpart. This feature of the Japanese *ritsuryō* state opened the way, as no doubt it was designed to do, to the political ascendancy of oligarchic noble lineages. These lineages, notably the Northern house of the Fujiwara, increasingly dominated the court and obstructed the growth of a truly meritocratic and universalistic bureaucracy. They manipulated the institutions of the formally public state to their private advantage, and eventually subverted them. In this way, the Tang concept of the public good, of public service, and of an emperor and bureaucracy acting impartially on behalf of the whole realm, one of the great achievements of the dynasty, did not take deep root, if it can be said ever to have taken root

112 *Ibid.*, p. 141.
113 Iyanaga, p. 462.

at all, in ancient Japan. In terms of value, bureaucratic universalism was replaced by aristocratic particularism.

This explanation is persuasive when related to the history of the *sekiten* in ancient Japan. The phenomena described above deeply influenced the character of the Confucian university and the operation of the examination system in Japan, which, as argued above, never became an accepted avenue to highest office. With the exception of the ninth century, when the literature course became popular among aristocrats, the university functioned, as is well known, as a technical training school for middle and lower bureaucrats. Indeed, of the 641 *kugyō* 公卿 (senior nobility) of the period 701–1200, only 57 or 8.9% were graduates of the university, and only two (three if Kibi is included) university graduates rose to ministerial rank.[114] By contrast, in Tang China 'the examination-recruited elite *did* gradually establish itself as the major factor within the bureaucracy, indeed as the predominant intellectual group within the bureaucracy'.[115] It was surely the sense in Tang China of the academic institutions as a springboard for 'mounting to the blue sky'[116] in the public service of the emperor on the basis of academic success that conferred vitality both on the academic institutions themselves and on the *shidian* in that country. It is thus easy to see the compartmentalisation and privatisation of the rite in Japan precisely as a rejection by an oligarchic, ascriptive society of the Tang version of the ceremony as a celebration of bureaucratic universalism.

In respect of its aristocratic, ascriptive ethos, there is much about Nara and Heian Japan that, despite a formal indebtedness to the Tang, resembles the earlier, shorter-lived polities of the period of disunion in China. Though their power structures may not have been as oligarchic nor their emperors as passive and sacerdotal as in ancient Japan, these polities were also aristocratic and ascriptive, and their courts were often dominated by a small number of aristocratic lineages. Suggestively, some of them were socially or culturally heterogeneous in ways that call to mind early ancient Japan, with its relatively recent influx of peninsula refugees. They, too, however much they acknowledged the meritocratic ideals of Confucianism, recruited officials on the basis of hereditary qualifications through the 'nine rank arbiter system' (*jiupin zhongzheng fa* 九品中正法).[117] The similarities extend also to cultural phenomena. Both in Nara and Heian Japan and in Six Dynasties China, cultural accomplishments were supremely important, and culture generally

---

114 Hisaki, p. 221.
115 Denis Twitchett, *The birth of the Chinese meritocracy: bureaucrats and examinations in T'ang China* (London: China Society, 1975), p. 28 (italics in original).
116 David McMullen, *State and scholars*, p. 12.
117 Ebrey, pp. 17–19.

may be said to have been self-absorbed and inward looking. Thus the poetry of the ancient period in Japan, to which the Japanese devoted such prodigious attention, did not share the public, social concerns characteristic of much Tang verse. Rather, '[p]oets tended to concentrate on the dexterity with which they grasped a subject rather than the subject itself',[118] a style that has been related to the Six Dynasties manner, rather than to the Tang.[119] In this light, it is not surprising that the Japanese *sekiten*, too, should have retained features from the Six Dynasties version of the rite, such as feasting and versifying.

118 Konishi, p. 14.
119 *Ibid.*, p. 21.

3

An early anthropologist? Ōe no Masafusa's
A record of fox spirits

Ivo Smits

If Heian Japan ever knew a child prodigy it was surely the eleventh-century poet and scholar Ōe no Masafusa 大江匡房 (1041–1111). According to his own account, he learned to read at the age of three, studied the *Shiji* 史記, *Hanshu* 漢書, and *Hou hanshu* 後漢書 at the age of seven, and composed his first Chinese poem when he was ten.[1] He set off on a dazzling bureaucratic career, culminating in his appointment as acting Middle Counsellor (*gon chūnagon* 権中納言) in 1094, and he was a trusted adviser of emperor Go-Sanjō 後三条 (1034–73). At the same time, he managed to keep up the family tradition of Chinese scholarship. The Ōe family represented one of the two most important traditions of expertise in Chinese studies in Heian Japan. Masafusa's great-grandfather, Masahira 匡衡 (952–1012), for instance, had been the tutor to emperor Ichijō 一条 (r.986–1011), and Masafusa himself was on three separate occasions tutor to the crown prince. Scholarship meant not only the study but also the practice of poetry and other forms of literature, and Masafusa was a constantly active member of a group of authors in Chinese.

Masafusa was a scholar with a great interest in all aspects of society, even if they were not always fashionable. He wrote several treatises or 'records' (*ki* 記), all of them in Chinese, on social groups such as playgirls (*asobi* or *yūjo* 遊女) and itinerant entertainers (*kairaishi* 傀儡子), and in general showed an urge to describe the world of men in which he lived. In this respect one might call him an anthropologist *avant la lettre*.[2]

His fascination lay not only with the human, but also with the supernatural. He wrote several treatises on fairly orthodox religious subjects, such as the *Honchō shinsenden* 本朝神仙伝 (Lives of Japanese immortals), the *Zoku*

1 *Bōnen ki* 暮年記: *Gunsho ruijū* 群書類従 (hereafter *GR*) vol. 6 (Keizai Zasshisha, 1904), p. 972. Cf Kawaguchi Hisao 川口久雄, *Ōe no Masafusa* (Yoshikawa Kōbunkan, 1968), pp. 20–21.

2 His *Yūjo ki* 遊女記 and *Kairaishi ki* 傀儡記. See also Kawaguchi, *Ōe no Masafusa*, pp. 197-201. *Kairaishi* (literally 'puppeteers') were a people whose way of life and social status in Heian Japan rather resembled those of gypsies in Europe. They wandered about the country, and made a living by performing little shows, singing, and prostitution.

honchō ōjōden 続本朝往生伝 (Lives of Japanese saints, continued), and the *Kōbō Daishi den* 弘法大師伝 (The life of Kūkai). One of the eerier subjects he turned to is the well-known magic animal, the fox. Masafusa wrote a short treatise concerning this animal, and called it *A record of fox spirits*, or the *Kobi ki* 狐媚記. It is rather short, and written in Chinese, the scholar's language. In it he lists a number of cases of apparent fox apparition in Kyōto in the year 1101.[3] These cases are fascinating material, and it is somewhat surprising that very few modern scholars have devoted their attention to the treatise. The first was M. W. de Visser, at time of his death Professor of Japanese Studies at Leiden University, who published a series of articles about Japanese and Chinese folklore: in 1908 it was the turn of the foxes. De Visser's merit lies mainly in the thoroughness with which he collected his data. Within two and a half pages he gives a partial translation and a summary of Masafusa's study of fox witchcraft.[4] Two well-known Japanese scholars have devoted a page each to the *Kobi ki*: one of the grand old men of Heian *kanbungaku* 漢文学 studies, Kawaguchi Hisao, and Konishi Jin'ichi. Their views on the matter will be discussed below. To my knowledge, the only scholar who has devoted a full-length article to this work is Komine Kazuaki, who published an extensive review in 1985.[5] In English there is an earlier translation of *Kobi ki* by Marian Ury, which appeared in 1988.[6]

Masafusa was one of the first writers in Japan to pay such attention to the fox. It is not clear when the Japanese came to regard the fox as an animal gifted with special powers. In the eighth century, foxes were already regarded as creatures whose appearance had mantic significance for good or ill. Perhaps it is in this connection that the *Zokutōritsu* 賊盗律 (Laws concerning robbery, 702) forbade the harassment of foxes.[7] Ritual fox worship had found its way into Japan from China in the tenth or eleventh century at the latest.[8]

---

3 Masafusa was Acting Governor (*gon no sochi* 権帥) of Dazaifu 大宰府, Kyūshū, from 1097 to 1102, and was not in the capital in 1101.

4 M. W. de Visser, *The fox and the badger in Japanese folklore,* extract from *The Transactions of the Asiatic Society of Japan* 36.3 (Yokohama: Fukuin, 1909); for the *Kobi no ki*, see pp. 32–4.

5 Komine Kazuaki 小峰和明, 'Ōe no Masafusa no *Kobi ki*: kanbungaku to kōsetsu no hazama de' 大江匡房の狐媚記―漢文学と巷説のはざまで, *Chūsei bungaku kenkyū* 中世文学研究 11(1985):127–44.

6 Marian Ury, 'A Heian note on the supernatural', *Journal of the Association of Teachers of Japanese* 22 (1988): 189–94. I learned of the existence of this prior translation only while correcting the proofs of this article.

7 De Visser, pp. 12–19.

7 Ylva Monschein, *Der Zauber der Fuchsfee: Entstehung und Wandel eines 'Femme-fatale'- Motivs in der chinesisischen Literatur* (Frankfurt am Main: Haag und Herchen, 1988), p. 24.

Nevertheless, stories about foxes and their efforts to play pranks on people, either by bewitching them or assuming human form, are rather few until the *Konjaku monogatarishū* 今昔物語集 (late eleventh century).[9] Yet none of these stories is as systematic an inventory of fox witchcraft as is Masafusa's *Kobi ki*.

The best-known literary role of the fox is probably that of the *femme fatale*: it will change itself into a beautiful woman and seduce men. Usually this is just a prank, but at times it may well be a serious love affair. This particular feature of the fox originates in China, where fox transformation stories arose in the Six Dynasties period (*c.* fourth to sixth centuries). One may speak of a positive boom in stories about seductive fox spirits (*humei* 狐媚) during the Tang dynasty (618–907), when the scene shifts from the world of the peasant to the milieu of the literati. These developments are brilliantly discussed by Ylva Monschein in her dissertation about the *femme fatale* motif in Chinese fox stories.[10] The fox as beautiful woman already figures in eighth-century Japan.[11] In the *Genji monogatari* 源氏物語, as well, there is the scene in the Tenarai 手習 chapter in which Ukifune 浮舟 is mistaken for a fox.[12] Perhaps the most fascinating example in Japan is that of Tamamo no mae 玉藻前: in the fourteenth century she was believed to have been the beautiful and learned concubine of either emperor Konoe 近衛 (r.1141–55) or Toba 鳥羽 (r.1107–23), and to have caused the emperor's illness and other disasters.[13] Masafusa's word for fox spirit is *kobi*: the same word that was used in China to indicate seductive fox beauties, but Masafusa apparently does not use it in the same meaning as the Chinese *humei*. I will discuss his concept of 'fox spirits' below.

Another type of fox is the bewitching or illusionist fox. The *Konjaku monogatarishū* gives us a rich variety of this species, and it is this fox that figures prominently in the *Kobi ki*. It plays pranks on man, not so much by

9 De Visser, pp. 19–32; Jolanta Tubielewicz, *Superstitions, magic and mantic practices in the Heian Period* (Warsawa: Wydawnictwa Uniwersytetu Warszawskiego, 1980), pp. 74–8.

10 See note 7.

11 The eighth-century *Nihon ryōiki* 日本霊異記, for instance, contains a story about a man who marries a beautiful woman who turns out to be a fox. Even after he has discovered the woman's true nature, he cannot forget her, and at his wish she comes every night and sleeps with him, and she is therefore called Kitsune ('come always', as well as 'fox'): *Nihon koten bungaku taikei* (hereafter *NKBT*) 日本古典文学体系 70, (Iwanami Shoten,1967), pp. 66–9.

12 *Genji monogatari* 源氏物語, *NKBT* 18, pp. 341–8.

13 De Visser, pp. 8, 51-54: cited from *Kagakushū* 下学集 (1444) and *Nikkenroku* 日件録 (1453).

transforming itself but rather by make-believe: it can transform objects and situations.

Let us now turn to Masafusa's account of witcheries that troubled Kyōto in the year 1101:

> In the third year of Kōwa 康和 (1101) the capital witnessed many strange cases of fox spirits. These miracles occurred in various forms and at various places. At first the foxes held banquets before Suzaku Gate 朱雀門, with horse dung for rice and cow bones for vegetables. They then spread out their delicacies behind the Ministry of Ceremonies, and before the gates of princes, court nobles, and warriors. People called these incidents 'the Great Fox Parties'.

The palace complex has always seemed particularly prone to harassment by foxes. Suzaku Gate was the main entrance to the palace complex. The Ministry of Ceremonies (Shikibushō 式部省) was the first building to the right after entering the Suzaku Gate. In 888 the empress fell ill, and the abbot Sōō 想応 chanted sūtras for three days. On the fourth day the empress had convulsions, and suddenly a supernatural fox (*reiko* 霊狐) appeared which vanished when the abbot said a *mantra*. As soon as the fox was gone, the empress recovered. Bad omens were seen in the early tenth century: foxes howling, copulating, climbing roofs, urinating in the emperor's quarters, and so on.[14] Fujiwara no Yorinaga 藤原頼長 (1120–56) recorded in his diary in 1144 how a boy of fifteen years was seduced by a young woman in the Imperial Storehouse and caught a severe venereal disease with a nasty ulcer. Since the boy had been stared at a few days earlier by a fox that had come out from under the eaves, it was assumed that the girl and the fox were one and the same. 'I never heard of such strange things before', commented Yorinaga.[15] Since much of Heian literary life focused on the palace complex, it is perhaps only natural that it should have become the setting of many accounts of magical incidents.

The next case in Masafusa's record is one of joy-riding. At night two or three young courtiers, accompanied by some women, force their way into an ox carriage which is parked outside the Kamo Shrine, and force the ox boy to drive them along the river. They are met on their way by a Captain of the Right Military Guard, who is astonished to see their red robes glowing in the dark. The courtiers then disappear, after giving the ox boy a red fan. The next day, the boy discovers the prints of fox paws on the carriage, and he sees that

---

14 De Visser, p. 35: cited from *Fusō ryakki* 扶桑略記 (twelfth century).

15 *Taiki* 台記 1144/5/13: *Shiryō taisei* 史料大成 23 (Kyōto: Rinsen Shoten, 1982), p. 123. The Imperial Storehouse, or *osamedono* 納殿, was situated in the Giyōden 宜陽殿.

the fan has changed overnight into a bone. Not only that, he also falls seriously ill, and dies a few days later. The owner of the carriage is so terrified that he wants to burn the vehicle, but he has a dream: a deity asks him not to, and says he will reward him for the ride. The next year, the owner is promoted to Assistant Librarian. Red is a colour associated with foxes, probably because of their fur.[16] The connection of the dream and the fox motif also is one to which Monschein draws attention: foxes will revisit people in dreams, assuming a human form, in order to thank or punish them.[17]

The tendency to assume that anything out of the ordinary must be a fox is illustrated by the incident in which emperor Horikawa 堀河 (r.1086–1107) is followed by a mysterious horseman who gallops out of sight through Suzaku Gate as soon as he is asked who he is. This, too, is considered by Masafusa to be a case of fox spirits.[18]

The victim of the fourth story is a bishop (risshi 律師).[19] He is visited by an old woman who asks him to come to her house, as she would like him to hold a service for her. When the priest arrives at the beautifully ornate private chapel, things already seem a bit strange: the owners of the place are nowhere to be seen, for instance, nor is there anyone to attend on him. He sets to work, but as soon as he jingles his prayer bell the lamp lights turn green and the offerings change into dung. 'Everything was an offence against the regulations.' The poor bishop makes his escape, and when he returns the next day to look for the house it is gone. This tale is a classic example of fox pranks: the foxes assume a human form (the old woman) in order to lure someone into their trap; they change the appearance of things (the stylish hall and the offerings); they try to have the priest eat dung (the offerings). The

16 See also Monschein, p. 30. De Visser thinks that the glow is due to the fox-fires (*kitsunebi* 狐火), which foxes supposedly emit by stroking their tail, but the red robes as a substitute for the reddish fur seems a more likely explanation: De Visser, p. 33, n. 3.

17 Monschein, p. 83.

18 The fox's supposed habit of misleading man came, by extension, to explain anything abnormal. In the Heian period, the fox already was mainly seen as an evil force: it was even said that 'the fox belongs to the household of Enma, the King of Hell'. This explains the practice of 'fox hunting' (*kitsunegari* 狐狩), which still exists in the west of Japan as an annual ceremony on 14 and 15 January. Anne-Marie Bouchy, 'Le renard, élément de la conception du monde dans la tradition japonaise', *Études mongoles ... et sibériennes* 15 (1984): Le renard: tours, détours & retours, pp. 33–4; Komine, pp. 136–7. Komine's quotation is from the *Chūgaishō* 中外抄 (1137–1154, told by Fujiwara no Tadazane 藤原忠実, recorded by Nakahara no Moromoto 中原師元; entry for 1139/5).

19 This tale is mentioned in the *Fukuro zōshi* 袋草紙 (*ca.*1160) as well. Sasaki Nobutsuna 佐々木信綱, ed., *Nihon kagaku taikei* 日本歌学体系 (Kazama Shobō, 1956), 2, p. 47.

complete disappearance of the house is also a classic feature of such stories.

Foxes have a preference for cemeteries. They often live inside the graves, which are obvious places to find skulls required in order to assume human form. The fox must balance a human skull on its head to change itself into a woman or a man.[20] This may be the reason that the fox who buys a house in the fifth tale moves it to the cemetery in Toribeno 鳥部野, Higashiyama 東山 (where, again, the money paid for the house changes overnight into worthless rubbish). A more prosaic explanation for foxes' preference for graves is probably that they hope to find some food there. This may very well explain the 'Great Fox Parties' at Suzaku Gate as well: foxes are known to eat dung and bones, just like dogs.

Masafusa ends his record by citing cases of fox witchery in China. He mentions two famous seductive fox beauties. The first is Daji 妲己, the concubine of king Zhou 紂 of the Shang 商 (c.1550–c.1100 BC). She was captured by him in a campaign against the Yousu 有蘇, and afterwards she prompted him to such cruelties and crimes that these caused the downfall of the dynasty. Yet Daji was so captivatingly beautiful, that even king Wu, the founder of the subsequent Zhou dynasty, could not kill her and left this job to his old chancellor.[21] The second reference is to a classic of Chinese *chuanqi* 伝奇 (wonder stories) literature: Shen Jiji's 沈既済 *Renshi zhuan* 任氏伝 (Story of Lady Ren).[22] Ren was a fox that turned itself into a beautiful woman, and went to live with a man named Zheng 鄭. She led a happy life until she and her partner moved house: on their way they met a pack of hounds, the fox's old enemy, and she was killed by them. This happened in Mawei 馬鬼: Shen intended it as an allusion to the story of Yang Guifei 楊貴妃, the concubine of the Tang emperor Xuanzong 玄宗 (r.712–48), who was executed at the same spot. Masafusa then comments:

> I had not yet believed all these Chinese stories, but now such apparitions have truly been seen in our country [i.e. Japan] as well. Even though we have arrived at the Latter Days of the Law, the supernatural appearances are as of old. Is it not extraordinary?

Masafusa's concept of a fox spirit is not clearly defined. The word he uses is *kobi*, the same word which the Chinese usually use to refer to foxes who changed themselves into beautiful women (*humei*). The cases Masafusa cites from Chinese sources are indeed classic examples of the seductive

---

20 Monschein, pp. 78-81. The fox may also do it by putting grass on its head, like hair.
21 Monschein, p. 155.
22 See note 39.

beauty of foxes. Yet, as we have seen, the instances Masafusa gives of fox witchery in Japan cannot be called seductive fox spirits. Rather, they are illusionist foxes, cases of *koyō* 狐妖 (Ch. *huyao*, 'fox wonders'). The question is, of course, whether it is useful to apply such strict definitions to these terms. Masafusa himself may have felt no need to categorise, or perhaps he decided that the word *kobi* had a literary appeal.

Masafusa's little treatise is far from complete: he makes no mention, for example, of fox possession, or *kitsunetsuki* 狐付. Nowadays this is probably the best-known type of fox witchery.[23] Fox possession seems to have become widespread from the fifteenth century onward, although it was known in Heian Japan as well. In Fujiwara no Sanesuke's 藤原実資 (957–1046) diary, for instance, we read that the high priestess of Ise 伊勢, the Saigū 斉宮, was possessed by a fox, giving strange oracles.[24]

> The Saigū's voice was wild and loud, not to be compared with anything, and her oracle said that the acting Head of the Saigū Bureau Fujiwara no Sukemichi 藤原相通 was no good and his wife mad and disturbed. She wanted small treasure houses built, and called them the Inner and the Outer Shrine. She also summoned all kinds of people, and for days and nights on end had them perform *kagura* 神楽 and crazy dances. In the capital mediums began to worship foxes, madly declaring them to be the Great Deity of Ise. These things are not as they ought to be: the strange worship of deities, the neglect of offerings, it all is not as in former days, and it surely means no respect for the divine. It is a grave lapse of these Latter Days of the Law.

What prompted a scholar like Masafusa to devote a treatise to a witch animal like the fox? The answer may very well lie in the social and political situation of the period. In the early twelfth century the period when the court was the centre of political power was coming to an end. Power was shifting. In part it was shifting to the provinces, to men who neither had nor wanted to have a part in the traditional structures of politics and economics. This had an effect on the position of those who had always relied on those very same structures for their survival, but now found themselves side-tracked in the

---

23 Carmen Blacker, *The catalpa bow: a study of shamanistic practices in Japan* (London: Allen & Unwin, 1975), especially pp. 51–68; Bouchy, 'Le renard', pp. 17–70.
24 *Shōyūki* 小右記 1031/8/4: *Dai Nihon kokiroku* 大日本古記録 (Iwanami Shoten, 1964), *Shōyūki kan* 9, p. 16; *Konjaku monogatarishū* 今昔物語集 vol. 26, No. 17, relates another case of a fox which enters a body.

struggle for power: scholars, professional poets, and petty officials. The term that has been coined to convey their feelings is *mappō ninshiki* 末法認識: the realisation that their world was coming to an end, and that they did not see a way out. As the historian Tsuda Sōkichi (1873–1961) wrote in the early Taishō period, and as generations of Japanese scholars have repeated ever since:

> One came to feel that intellectual ability, which before had always been cherished as the ruling principle both of individual life and of society (even though physical power was approved of up to a certain point), could no longer sustain the influence and culture of the then nobility; and since the world was gradually coming to an end and one was rendered powerless, one came to doubt the value of that intellectual ability, and even, as a last resort, turned to powers beyond man.[25]

Some think that Masafusa's treatise is to be seen in this light. To a scholar like Kawaguchi Hisao, the *Kobi ki* is a symbolic tale: it is a story of social crisis and spiritual desperation.[26] Komine Kazuaki claims it is a moralistic tale: it is a mirror for a sick society, reflecting the other side of the lustre of *insei* 院政 culture and politics; and the man who holds up this mirror hopes that he can guide his country to the right track.[27] Konishi Jin'ichi takes a less pessimistic view: Masafusa is a classic example of the Late Heian intellectual who, following a trend from the Chinese mainland, turns to popular motifs for his writings. Fox transformation tales came from China, where, by the middle of the Tang dynasty, the literati had taken over the elaboration of this part of folklore. Konishi casually reverses Yanagita Kunio's theory of the 'lowborn, upward-moving model' (meaning that motifs originating among the common people are taken up by intellectuals), and proposes the 'highborn, downward-moving model': his view is that the elaborate fox tales from China were picked up by Japanese intellectuals, and afterwards became a popular motif in Japan.[28] The point of positing such a

---

25 Tsuda Sōkichi 津田左右吉, *Bungaku ni arawaretaru waga kokumin shisō no kenkyū* 文学に現はれたる我が国民思想の研究, vol. 2 Kizoku bungaku no jidai 貴族文学の時代, in *Tsuda Sōkichi zenshū* 津田左右吉全集 *bekkan* 別巻 2 (Iwanami Shoten, 1966), p. 439.

26 Kawaguchi, *Ōe no Masafusa*, pp. 294–5; and *Heianchō no kanbungaku* 平安朝の漢文学 (Yoshikawa Kōbunkan, 1981), pp. 197–8.

27 Komine, pp. 142–3.

28 Konishi, Jin'ichi 小西甚一, *Nihon bungeishi* 日本文芸史, vol. 3 (Kōdansha, 1986), pp. 30–3. See also his *A History of Japanese Literature*, vol. 1, 'The Archaic

reversal seems unclear, since all the material we have comes from the intellectual milieu (we have no written material from the common people in those days), and therefore it is difficult to trace the course of fox folklore in early Japan until Masafusa's day. Practically all *setsuwa* 説話 collections, for instance, date only from the eleventh century onwards.

Yet one supposes that Konishi is quite right in pointing to China. One should keep in mind that Masafusa wrote his 'record' in Chinese, and not overlook the implications of this choice. He chose the scholar's language, and thereby gave his subject a character that went beyond the anecdotal. He structured his essay by limiting himself in both time and space – Kyōto in the year 1101 – and by putting the Japanese cases in a larger context. Masafusa derived his anthropologist's stance from his Chinese counterparts. He knew very well, as is clear from his quotations, that it was considered respectable by the Chinese literati to write about people in the lower regions of society and about folklore. In Heian Japan, however, where this was not an obvious thing to do, Masafusa belonged to an avant-garde. This is not to say that we should deny Masafusa his share of *mappō ninshiki*. One might even say that his scholar's eye saw the decline of his times more clearly, and that the *Kobi ki* is an attempt to structure and overcome the hidden anxieties of Late Heian intellectuals.

A RECORD OF FOX SPIRITS, BY ŌE NO MASAFUSA[29]

In the third year of Kōwa (1101) the capital witnessed many strange cases of fox spirits. These miracles occurred in various forms and at various places. At first the foxes held banquets before Suzaku Gate, with horse dung for rice and cow bones for vegetables. They then spread out their delicacies behind the Ministry of Ceremonies,[30] and before the gates of princes, court nobles, and warriors. People called these incidents 'the Great Fox Parties'.

Assistant Librarian Minamoto no Takayasu 源隆康[31] went to pay

and Ancient Ages', translated by Aileen Gatten and Nicholas Teele (Princeton: Princeton University Press, 1984), pp. 419–20.

29 *Kobi ki, GR* 6, 968–9; and *Honchō zoku monzui* 本朝続文粋, in *Nihon bungaku taikei* 日本文学体系 (hereafter *NBT*) vol. 24 (Kokumin Toshosha, 1957), pp. 748-750. The latter version seems more accurate; it is the text reprinted in *Nihon shisō taikei* 日本思想体系 (hereafter *NST*) vol.8 (Iwanami Shoten, 1970), pp. 165–67. I should like to thank Dr B. J. Mansvelt Beck of the Sinological Department, Leiden University, for his help in the early stages of my translation.

30 *Shikibushō* 式部抄. It was the first building to the right on entering Suzaku Gate.

31 As the story will show, he was not yet Assistant Librarian at the time of this

reverence to the Saiin 斉院 of the Kamo 賀茂 Shrine.[32] His carriage stood outside the gate. When night fell, two or three young courtiers, accompanied by some women, forced their way into his carriage and drove away in the moonlight. They crossed Kamo River and arrived at the river bank at Seventh Avenue, where they were met on their way by the Secretary of the Right Military Guards Nakawara no Iesue 中原家季. In the carriage their red robes seemed to glow: one could see their colour, even though it was night. The Secretary silently thought it strange that the boy driving the ox could not bear the hardship and fell flat on the road begging for mercy. The courtiers gave him a red fan, and suddenly went away. On the crossbar of the carriage which the courtiers had leaned upon there were prints of fox paws. The ox boy went home. The next day he discovered the paw-prints and found that the fan was a calf's horn.[33] He then fell ill, and died a few days later. His master was terrified and wanted to burn the carriage, but he had a dream in which a deity appeared and said: 'Please do not burn it. I will reward you for the use of it.' The next year, a letter of appointment made him Assistant Librarian.

The emperor[34] was having his temple[35] built, and as forty-five nights had not yet passed he returned in such a way as to avoid an unpropitious direction.[36] Suddenly he was escorted by a horseman who had raised both left and right sleeves, covering his face. Behind them followed several servants of the Chamberlain's Office with their trailing cap bands,[37] among them

incident. Takayasu's father, Morotaka 師隆, was Secretary of the Saiin Bureau (*Saiin no suke* 斉院次官): there may be a link there.

32 The Saiin was a virgin imperial princess, serving as the priestess of the Kamo 賀茂 Shrine, and had the same rank as the Saigū 斉宮 of the Ise Shrine.

33 *Kenritsu no hone* 繭栗骨 ('cocoon-chestnut horns'): the com-parison of a calf's first horns to silkworm cocoons or chestnuts dates back to the *Li ji* 礼記.

34 Emperor Horikawa (r. 1086–1107).

35 *Goganji* 御願寺, or *chokuganji* 勅願寺, were temples build at imperial request; they were under the protection of the state and were meant to ensure the emperor's well-being.

36 *Kataimi* 方忌, or directional taboos, played an important role in Heian life. At times, certain deities were supposed to stop at certain points of the compass, and then that direction was considered temporarily unlucky or closed. This is probably a case of the 'Great general directional taboo' (*daishōgunhō* 大将軍方), which could last for three years. In the case of long-lasting directional taboos the taboo was observed only once every forty-five nights or only for a full forty-five days. See Bernard Frank, *Kata-imi et kata-tagae: Étude sur les interdits de direction à l'époque Heian*, Bulletin de la maison franco-japonaise, nouvelle série 5, 2-4 (Isseidō Shoten,1958), pp. 154–64.

37 Both *kotoneri* 小舎人 and *kurōdo* 蔵人 were officials from the *kurōdodokoro* 蔵人所, the Chamberlain's Office. The trailing bands of their caps (*suiei* 垂纓) indicated that they were civil servants (*bunkan* 文官), as opposed to military servants (*bukan*

Assistant Professor Fujiwara no Shigetaka 藤原重隆 (1075–1118) who, thinking it strange, addressed the horseman. Without offering any information in reply, the man galloped through Suzaku Gate and in the twinkling of an eye he was out of sight.

The bishop Zōchin 増珍 (1036–1109) was famous for his teachings of the Buddha's Law. Once an old woman came to see him and said: 'I would like to have a mass said. Do come and visit me.' The bishop promised to come. Towards the evening, the old woman came again, and the bishop complied with her wish. They arrived at a hall in a private house on the corner of Sixth Avenue and Suzaku Avenue. The hall was as majestically adorned as it ought to be; but even though they had arranged for a ceremony of offerings for the priest, there was no one to wait on him. Behind a screen someone clapped his hands, and suddenly a cup of wine was brought in. The bishop thought it strange, and did not dare touch any of the food before he sat down to chant sūtras. At the first tone of his prayer bell the lamp light suddenly turned green, and the food offerings turned out to be dung and filth and such like. Everything was an offence against the regulations. He was quite upset, and half-dead with fright he fled. The next day he tried to find the house, but it had disappeared without a trace.[38]

A certain man bought a house on Kyōgoku 京極 Seventh Avenue. Somewhat later he tore the house down and went to Toribeno,[39] where he used the remains of the house for burial materials. What he had given as payment for the house had originally seemed gold, silver, and silk, but the next day it all turned out to be a fraud: worn sandals, old shoes, rooftiles, pebbles, bones, and horns.

Ah! Many such fox miracles are cited in historical records. Daji, the concubine of the last Yin emperor, was in fact a nine-tailed fox.[40] Lady Ren became someone's wife, but when they arrived in Mawei she was chased to death by a pack of hounds.[41] Either these foxes bring about the downfall of student Zheng,[42] or they teach the classics in old graves.[43] I had not believed all

武官), who wore them curled up.

38 This story also appears in *Fukuro zōshi*: see note 18.

39 Toribeno was a cremation field and graveyard in Higashi-yama, Kyōto.

40 Daji seduced king Zhou of the Yin 殷 (or Shang) dynasty, and incited him to commit crimes which brought about the downfall of the dynasty in ca. 1100 BC.

41 This is the *Renshi zhuan* by Shen Jiji (*ca.* 740–*ca.* 800). Ren was a fox that turned itself into a beautiful woman. Mawei, about 50 km west of Changan 長安, was the place where Yang Guifei was killed; the tragic end of Shen's story is a reference to the fate of Yang Guifei.

42 Zheng was the man who fell in love with Lady Ren.

43 This is a reference to a story from book 18 of the *Soushen ji* 捜神記 by Gan Bao

these Chinese stories, but now such apparitions have truly been seen in our country as well. Even though we have arrived at the Latter Days of the Law, the supernatural appearances are as of old. Is it not extraordinary?

干宝 (first half of the fourth century ad) about Professor Hu 胡 ('Turk') who suddenly disappears and then turns out to be an old fox who lives in a grave where he teaches a class of foxes. The next sentence in the text, 或為紫衣公到県許其女屍事在個儻, is completely unintelligible and is left out in the translation.

4

Religion in the life of Minamoto Yoritomo and the early Kamakura bakufu

Martin Collcutt

This essay examines the religious interests of Minamoto no Yoritomo 源頼朝 (1147–99) and the role of religion within his warrior regime, the bakufu, in Kamakura during his lifetime. Its inspiration is threefold: to understand better the role of religion in the life of Yoritomo and medieval warrior society, to see more clearly how the various existing strands of religion – Buddhist, Shintō, and syncretic, and 'old' as well as 'new' – were integrated into people's lives, and to explore the interaction of religion with politics in the early Kamakura bakufu.

Few of the English language studies of the Kamakura bakufu have much to say about Yoritomo's religious concerns.[1] There has been little attempt to define his religious interests or to hint that religion may have been important to him in assuaging some of the guilt of killing; that it may have been invoked in his devotion to deceased ancestors; that it was useful in rallying spiritual sanctions and the support of shrines and temples in his struggle against the Taira 平; and that it may have been important in defining the character of the early Kamakura bakufu and strengthening vassal loyalties. In Japanese, where there have been excellent studies of religion and the medieval 'state' (*kokka* 国家), it is only very recently that attention has begun to be focused on the role of religion in the daily lives and political activities of Minamoto Yoritomo, his wife Masako 政子 and her family, and the warrior society of eastern Japan.[2]

---

1 Minoru Shinoda, *The founding of the Kamakura shogunate* (New York: Columbia University Press, 1960) does discuss 'The legal and moral basis of Yoritomo's government' on pp. 100–13. His translation of the first part of *Azuma kagami* 吾妻鏡 (hereafter *AK*) included in the same book also provides examples of Yoritomo's religious interests. I have retranslated many of these passages in order to bring out their precise religious content more clearly. Miyazaki Fumiko's recent article on 'Religious life of the Kamakura bushi: Kumagai Naozane and his descendants', *Monumenta Nipponica* 47 (1992): 435–67, does not deal with Yoritomo or the bakufu directly but it has much to say about the religious interests of Kumagai and other warrior vassals, *gokenin* 御家人, in early Kamakura society.
2 Satō Hirō 佐藤弘夫, *Nihon chūsei no kokka to bukkyō* 日本中世の国家と仏教 (Yoshikawa Kōbunkan, 1987), and Sasaki Kaoru 佐々木馨, *Chūsei kokka no shūkyō*

90

This essay, then, explores the following questions. Was Minamoto Yoritomo simply a shrewd, politically adept warrior chieftain indifferent to spiritual or religious concerns? If not, what did he believe in or find important in his spiritual life? How, if at all, did these interests carry over into his daily life and leadership of the Kamakura bakufu and eastern warriors? What religious institutions were created in Kamakura and what was their role in the life of the bakufu? What impact did Hōnen's re-interpretation of Pure Land Buddhism or the Ch'an (Zen) practices brought back from China by Eisai 栄 西 and other monks have on Kamakura, and when and how did those influences begin to be felt?

RELIGION IN THE LIFE OF MINAMOTO YORITOMO AS DESCRIBED IN THE *AZUMA KAGAMI*[3]

In his own day, and afterwards, Yoritomo enjoyed a reputation as a fair and just administrator. He was very conscious of his moral reputation and its contribution to the the righteousness and legality of his cause.[4] There were instances in which he made judgements in favour of complainants against his own vassals.[5] He also, on occasion, showed magnanimity in sparing the

kōzō 中世国家の宗教構造 (Yoshikawa Kōbunkan, 1988), both examine the religious interests and policies of the Kamakura warrior regime. They do not, however, go deeply into the role of religion in the personal lives of Yoritomo and those around him. Older, but still useful, studies of religion and medieval politics or the medieval 'state' include Kuroda Toshio 黒田俊雄, *Nihon chūsei no kokka to shūkyō* 日本中世 の国家と宗教 (Iwanami Shoten, 1975), Kawai Masaharu 河合正治, *Chūsei buke shakai no kenkyū* 中世武家社会の研究 (Yoshikawa Kōbunkan, 1985), and Toyoda Takeshi 豊田武, *Shūkyō seido-shi* 宗教制度史, *Toyoda Takeshi chosakushū* 5 (Yoshikawa Kōbunkan, 1982).

3 The standard modern edition of the *Azuma kagami* is that by Kuroita Katsumi 黒 板勝美, in volumes 32 and 33 of *Shintei zōho kokushi taikei* 新訂増補国史体系 (Yoshikawa Kōbunkan, 1965). There is a helpful modern rendering by Nagahara Keiji 長原慶二 and Kishi Shozō 貴志正造, eds., *Zen'yaku Azuma kagami* 全訳吾妻 鏡 (Shin-Jinbutsu Ōraisha, 1976). Shinoda translates most, though not all, of the entries for the period 1180–85. His focus is on politics rather than religion, so I have thought it best to retranslate the passages I cite in order to clarify and highlight the descriptions of religious ceremonies, buildings, statues, and ideas. Footnotes are cited in such a way that readers can easily refer to any edition of the *AK*. It should be noted that dates have not been converted from the Japanese *nengō* and lunar calendar: 1180/8/19, for example, is only an approximation of Jishō 4/8/19. The converted date would be several weeks later.

4 Minoru Shinoda, *The founding of the Kamakura shogunate*, pp. 100–13.

5 For instance the complaint by the monks of Sōtō-zan 走湯山 temple that his warriors were despoiling its lands. *AK*, Jishō 治承 4 (1180)/8/19.

lives of former enemies or in accepting their offers of future loyalty. After the battle of Ishibashi-yama 石橋山, in which he came close to destruction, he not only accepted the support of Edo Shigenaga 江戸重長 and Hatakeyama Shigetada 畠山重忠, both of whom had opposed him, but promoted them over men who had been loyal for much longer.[6] After successful battles he frequently pardoned the majority of those who had fought against him. On several other occasions he spared the life of a captive, or grieved at his death, when he learned that the man, like Yoritomo, was devoted to the *Lotus sūtra*.[7] In these moments he showed himself capable of genuine compassion, anguish, and guilt.[8]

But Yoritomo was not a paragon of virtue. Although we tend to think of him, remote from battle, in his roles as institution builder, administrator, strategist, and shogun, we should not forget that he not only organised the struggle against the Taira, but also fought against Taira supporters on the battlefield. If he did not kill with his own sword, he ordered the deaths of many warriors, some his own supporters, whom he regarded as threatening or treacherous. Yoritomo had blood on his hands. And he was aware of it. This awareness must have accounted for many of his acts of compassion, magnaminity, and religious devotion. The awareness of his sinfulness was brought home to him starkly at the ceremonies marking the restoration of Tōdaiji 東大寺. He was impressed by the venerable Sung Chinese monk Chen Hejing 陳和卿 and asked, through the Japanese monk Chōgen 重源, for an audience. When he was refused repeatedly on the grounds that he had taken many lives, Yoritomo is said to have shed tears in recognition of his guilt.[9] Like most warriors he could be cruel and violent in killing, or cool and calculating, or legally minded or, occasionally, quite arbitrary, as in his decision to have the young Shimizu Yoshitaka 志水義高, a boy betrothed to his eldest daughter, killed for no other reason than that he was the son of Minamoto Yoshinaka 源義仲 (1154–84), whom Yoritomo had distrusted. In an age in which there was a powerful belief in *onryō* 怨霊, the restless spirits of those who had died violently or unhappily, Yoritomo was, for most of his life, haunted by *onryō*, many of whom he had created. During the years of struggle against the Taira there were frequent reminders of the imminence of dead spirits, not only in times of battle, but at executions, the viewings of the heads of fallen friends and enemies, and the grisly exposure of fallen enemy

---

6 *AK*, Jishō 4 (1180)/10/6.

7 *AK*, Yōwa 養和 1 (1181)/7/5. See also Jishō 4 (1180)/7/5; Bunji 文治 2 (1186)/7/25; and Bunji 5 (1190)/9/15.

8 Kawai Masaharu, *Chūsei buke shakai no kenkyū*, p. 98.

9 *AK*, Kenkyū 建久 6 (1196)/3/13. Kawai Masaharu, *Chūsei buke shakai no kenkyū*, p. 98.

heads to public display in Kyōto and Kamakura.

It would have been a cold and nerveless person who felt no need for spiritual solace in the face of battle and single combat, or who saw no merit in assuaging the restless spirits of fallen family members, vassals, and enemies. Yoritomo had spent his childhood in Kyōto. He was cultured and had a taste for the arts. As his treatment of captives and his encounter with the Sung monk indicates, he was not an unfeeling monster. It should not surprise us, then, that Yoritomo had a rich and complex personal religious life.

According to the *Azuma kagami*,[10] religious concerns and actions surface at the most critical period of Yoritomo's life: his decision to respond to the appeal (*reishi* 令旨) from Prince Mochihito 以仁王, issued on the ninth day of the fourth month of Jishō 4 (1180) to rally the Minamoto and other warriors, temples, and shrines to overthrow the Taira. The proclamation itself was couched in religious as well as political terms. Mochihito proclaimed war against Kiyomori and the Taira, 'who would usurp the throne and destroy the Buddhist Law'. He claimed the anti-Taira war was a moral cause that would be vindicated by its spiritual as well as military success. He placed his trust not only in the support of the Minamoto and other warriors but in the gods and Buddhas:

> We rely not only on man's efforts but on the help of providence as well. If the political authorities, the Three Treasures of Buddhism, and the native gods, *kami*, aid us, people throughout the country will also support our cause.[11]

The proclamation, carried to Kamakura by Minamoto Yoshimori 義盛 (Yukiie 行家), was delivered to Yoritomo at the Hōjō 北条 residence in Izu on the

---

10 The *AK* presents some problems as a source. It was compiled late in the thirteenth century, long after the death of Yoritomo, and is regarded as a very pro-Yoritomo, pro-Hōjō work. Having said this, it is also important to point out that it was compiled from earlier materials and, while there may be some slanting of political events, there was probably less of an impulse to distort, or add to, the entries relating to religion. It is used here because it is the best available source on this subject. It may well be an authentic record. But readers should bear in mind that this is the *AK* account, that it is less than comprehensive, and that it may embellish the record in places. The accounts of religious ceremonies generally ring true for the late twelfth century and could, or would, hardly have been invented at a later period. For a recent discussion of the validity of the *AK* as an historical source see Gomi Fumihiko 五味文彦, *Azuma kagami no hōhō* 吾妻鏡の方法 (Yoshikawa Kōbunkan, 1990).

11 Jishō 4 (1180)/4/ 9. The document cited in *AK* is of disputed authenticity. It is probably only a reconstruction of Mochihito's call to arms. However, it is likely that Mochihito, who badly needed the support of temples and shrines, would have invoked religious as well as political and military sanctions against the Taira.

twenty-seventh day of the fourth month. He was probably well aware of the nature of the appeal before he actually opened it.[12] His first act, according to the *Azuma kagami*, was to call on Hachiman 八幡, patron *kami* of the Minamoto, for divine support in whatever might follow. Wearing ceremonial robes, Yoritomo received the appeal and immediately bowed respectfully towards distant Otokoyama, a hill outside Kyōto that is the site of the Iwashimizu 石清水 Hachiman shrine.[13]

Before Yoritomo or any other Minamoto chieftain could do much to help Mochihito, the Taira discovered the plot. The prince fled to Onjōji 園城寺 (Miidera 三井寺) and thence via Uji 宇治 towards Nara. He and his companions were caught by the Taira at Uji[14] and either cut down or forced to take their own lives. It is worth noting that the temples of Onjōji and the Kōfukuji 興福寺 and Tōdaiji 東大寺 in Nara which responded to the prince's appeal thereby earned the enmity of the Taira but, to their ultimate advantage, developed good relations with the Minamoto in the Kantō.

During the summer months Yoritomo continued to try to raise forces in the east to topple the Taira. He also called upon the efficacy of the *Lotus sūtra*.[15] According to the *Azuma kagami* entry for the fifth day of the seventh month (1180), Yoritomo had set himself the task of reciting one thousand passages from the sūtra but was having trouble completing the invocations. The Buddhist priest Kakuen 覚淵 of Sōtō-zan 走湯山, clearly an expert in numerology and the magical powers of the number eight, was able to justify Yoritomo's reduction of the number of recitations to eight hundred:

> The sky is clear and wind light. Yesterday summoned Mon'yōbō Kakuen, the chief monk of Sōtōzan, by letter. He arrived today at the Hōjō residence. The Military Protector (*buei* 武衛) [Yoritomo] addressed the venerable priest: 'I have long had a heartfelt wish to gain the merit of reciting a thousand passages of the *Lotus sūtra*. As an earnest of my sincerity I have invoked the sūtra for several days, but now things have flared up and it will be difficult to fulfil my vow in the coming days. I wish instead to turn over (*tendoku* 転読) eight hundred sections of the sūtra for the Buddha.[16] What do you think?' Kakuen answered: 'Although you are not completing one

---

12 The monk Mongaku 文覚 is said to have been acting as liaison between Yoritomo and the anti-Taira faction in Kyōto.
13 *AK*, Jishō 4 (1180)/4/27.
14 *AK*, Jishō 4 (1180)/5/26.
15 On the role of the *Lotus sūtra* in Japanese culture see George and Willa Tanabe, eds., *The Lotus sutra in Japanese culture* (University of Hawaii Press, 1989).
16 *Tendoku* is rapid 'reading' of a sūtra done by fanning its pages.

thousand recitations, it shows respect for the Buddha to offer eight hundred.' Then, making an offering of incense and flowers before an image of the Buddha, Kakuen explained: 'Your lordship is a member of the clan of the Great Bodhisattva Hachiman. Your lordship upholds the eight chapters of the *Lotus sūtra*. Your Lordship, as the recipient of the will of Hachiman Tarō 八幡太郎 (Minamoto Yoshiie 源義家), is the leader of the brave warriors of the eight provinces of the east. It is within the palm of your hand to subjugate the eight major crimes of the rebel clan of [Kiyomori] the lay priest of the eighth avenue (Hachijō). This your Lordship can do by reciting eight hundred passages of this sūtra.' The Military Protector (Yoritomo) was impressed [by Kakuen] and, upon the conclusion of the meeting, presented him with gifts, which Kunimichi, the secretary, took for him. At nightfall the priest left. He was barely outside the gate when he was recalled. [Yoritomo] said to him: 'When the world is returned to peace and order I will give you at Hirugashima those donations (*fuse* 布施) I should have given you today.' Kakuen, in great joy, took his departure.[17]

In addition to the intervention of Hachiman and the Buddhas and Boddhisattvas active in the *Lotus sūtra*, Yoritomo also hoped for the support of the *kami*. He was doubly pleased, then, to recruit two men who could both fight and conduct Shintō rituals:

There is a person [warrior] called Saeki Masasuke 佐伯昌助. He is priest of the Sumiyoshi Shrine of Chikuzen Province. Last year on the third day of the fifth month he was banished to Izu Province ... Now Masanaga 住吉昌長 of Sumiyoshi, the younger brother of this Masasuke, has come to pay respects to Yoritomo for the first time. Nagae Yorikane 永江頼隆 also came to pay respects. He is a descendant of a priest of the Great Shrine of Ise and, in recent years, a retainer of Hatano Yoshitsune 波多野義常. He has now turned against his lord to serve Yoritomo. As these two have secretly indicated their desire to serve the Minamoto cause, and as they are deeply versed in matters of Shintō ritual, it is reported that they have been permitted to join his followers so they can conduct prayer ceremonies (*kitō* 祈祷).[18]

By the eighth month, Yoritomo felt he had sufficient support from eastern *bushi* 武士 openly to challenge the Taira. On the sixth day of the eighth

17 *AK*, Jishō 4 (1180)/7/5.
18 *AK*, Jishō 4 (1180)/7/23.

month he set the day of attack for the seventeenth of that month. Naturally a propitious day had to be chosen. This was done through divination conducted by his new Shintō ritualists:

> 6th day. Calling [Abe] Kunimichi 阿倍国道 and Sumiyoshi Masanaga before him, [Yoritomo] had them conduct a divination ritual [to determine the best day and hour for the attack]. It has been set for the coming seventeenth between three and and five in the morning.[19]

On the sixteenth day of the eighth month Yoritomo was forced to postpone the hour of launching the attack. In doing so, however, he was anxious that the postponement not impinge on one of the most important religious and symbolic ceremonies in Kamakura warrior society, a *hōjō-e* 放生会, or release of living creatures from captivity, to be held on the eighteenth:

> 16th day. Raining ceaselessly since yesterday. Prayers were offered for victory in the battle tomorrow. Sumiyoshi Masanaga conducted the ritual (*kitō*) to exorcise the spirits of heavenly and earthly disaster. The Military Protector [Yoritomo] participated and himself handed over the mirror to Masanaga. The secretary Nagae Yorikane performed one thousand purifications (*oharae* 御払え). The Sasaki brothers should have arrived today. At dusk they still have not arrived. Tomorrow at dawn Kanetaka should be killed. Lacking the warriors to attack Kanetaka, who should have died at at dawn tomorrow, there is some leeway and [Yoritomo was compelled to postpone the attack]. The eighteenth is the day for the Buddhist ceremony of the liberation of living things from confinement (*hōjōe*) which His Lordship has observed before an image of the Goddess of Mercy, Shō-Kannon 聖観音, for many years since his boyhood. It is hard to break this.[20]

On the seventeenth, the morning he had hoped to launch the attack, Yoritomo was still awaiting the arrival of the four Sasaki brothers. They did not arrive until the early afternoon. In the meantime he had prayers said at the nearby Mishima Shrine, one of a number of shrines and temples in the Izu area for which the Hōjō clan and Yoritomo had particular veneration:

19 *AK*, Jishō 4 (1180)/8/6.
20 *AK*, Jishō 4 (1180)/8/16.

17th day. Clear. This being a day for worship (*jinji* 神事) of the *kami*, at Mishima Shrine, his lordship sent Adachi Morinaga 安達守長 to worship on his behalf and make an offering at the shrine.[21]

Once the Sasaki brothers arrived, Yoritomo decided to attack the compounds of Taira Kanetaka 平兼隆 and the vice-governor Tsutsumi Nobutō 堤信遠 near Mishima by moonlight that night. This marked the opening thrust in Yoritomo's struggle to overthrow the Taira. By dawn on the eighteenth his warriors had slain Kanetaka and his followers, and Yoritomo was able to inspect the severed heads.[22]

Fearing that military campaigning would prevent him from purifying himself by doing his daily recitations from the Buddhist sūtras, on the eighteenth Yoritomo asked the nun Hōon 法音, teacher of his wife Masako, to pray and make purification on his behalf:

> 18th day. Over the years the Military Protector (*butei* 武衛), has been accustomed to performing religious rites (*ongongyō* 御勤行) every day without fail, whether or not there was need for purification. He is disturbed that he will have to neglect these daily prayers because of the wars. There is a nun called Hōon of Izu-san 伊豆山. She instructs Her Ladyship (*midaidokoro* 御台所) [Masako] in the sūtras. She has lived a chaste and blameless life. He asked Her Ladyship to request this nun to perform the daily prayers on his behalf. A list of the prayers has been sent to her. The nun has indicated her acceptance.[23]

As Yoritomo began to assume a more prominent political and military role in Izu and throughout the Kantō, local shrines and temples appealed to him for redress of grievances. In order to gain their support in his military campaigns he listened to their complaints and promised help in the future, if he was successful against the Taira. One Izu temple with which he had especially close ties was Sōtō-zan, whose abbot Kakuen had sanctioned Yoritomo's reduction of the *Lotus sūtra* incantations from one thousand to eight hundred. Sōtō-zan was a center of devotion to the syncretic Buddho-Shinto deity Izu Gongen 伊豆権現, revered by the Hōjō family and by Yoritomo and other Izu warriors. On the nineteenth day of the eighth month the monks of Sōtō-zan complained that warriors, many of them Yoritomo's followers, had been violating its lands:

21 *AK*, Jishō 4 (1180)/8/17.
22 *AK*, Jishō 4 (1180)/8/17.
23 *AK*, Jishō 4 (1180)/8/18.

Recently warriors coming and going between Doi and Hōjō have been using the lands belonging to Sōtō-zan as a short cut. As a result there have been many conflicts. The monks of Sōtō-zan have complained [to Yoritomo] that the warriors have been committing outrages on their lands. Today the Military Protector sent them a letter. In it he consoled them. He declared that, when peace and order are restored to the world, he will donate estate holdings (*shōen* 荘園) to the temple, one in Izu and another in Sagami. This will surely enhance the glory of the Izu Gongen[24] in the Kantō. In this way the anger of the monks was quickly appeased.[25]

Yoritomo cemented this relationship with Sōtō-zan by having Masako stay there for safety during his campaigns:

At night Her Ladyship went to Sōtō-zan and called on Mon'yō-bō Kakuen. She was accompanied by Kunimichi and Masanaga. Her Ladyship will lodge here quietly while the world remains disturbed.[26]

The following day, the twentieth, Yoritomo and his followers moved from Izu into Sagami. They established a position at Ishibashi-yama and raised their standard in the first full-scale encounter with Taira forces:

20th day ... The Military Protector leading at first only the vassals (*gokenin*) of the two provinces of Izu and Sagami, left Izu province and set out for Doi village in Sagami.[27]

23rd day. Heavy rain fell at night. This morning at 3:00 a.m., the Military Protector, accompanied by Hōjō and his sons, [Adachi] Morinaga, [Etō] Shigemori, and Doi Sanehira 土肥実平, led three thousand horsemen to Mount Ishibashi in Sagami where they established a camp. Carrying the standard to the top of which was attached Prince Mochihito's pronouncement was [Nakahara] Naka Shirō Koreshige 中四郎惟重. [Nagae] Yoritaka, holding a pole to which were tied sacred white paper emblems (*hakuhei* 白幣), attended his master.[28]

---

24 *Gongen* is the term used for a Shintō deity who appears as the earthly manifestation of a Buddha and is worshipped at both shrines and temples. The amalgamation of Buddhist and Shintō beliefs and cults was a characteristic feature of the religion of this period in samurai society as elsewhere.
25 *AK*, Jishō 4 (1180)/8/19.
26 *Ibid.*
27 *AK*, Jishō 4 (1180)/8/20.
28 *AK*, Jishō 4 (1180)/8/23.

The gods did not smile on Yoritomo at Ishibashi-yama. He was defeated and forced to flee for his life and go into hiding. Perhaps one good omen for the future was the recovery of a rosary which Yoritomo had lost on the battlefield:

> 24th day ... Later [Sakata] Ieyoshi 家義 sought out Yoritomo. He brought with him a rosary (gonenju 御念珠). The Military Protector had dropped it earlier in the day during the course of the battle. It was a rosary familiar to many of his men from Sagami who had hunted with his lordship in the past. Yoritomo had missed it earlier and been greatly upset. Thus he was overjoyed to retrieve it and thanked Ieyoshi repeatedly.[29]

A rosary was not the only religious icon Yoritomo was accustomed to carry with him. He also carried in his top-knot a tiny silver statue of Kannon. This statuette, with its religious ties to the Bodhisattva of compassion, was clearly of the the deepest personal meaning to him. Yoritomo was born and spent his childhood in Kyōto. It is said that at the age of three he was taken by his wet nurse to the Kiyomizu temple in Kyōto where the principal image was a statue of an eleven-headed Kannon, Jūichimen Kannon 十一面観音. According to the *Azuma kagami* the nurse prayed for Yoritomo's future well-being and for fourteen nights had dreams in which the image appeared. She later gave an image of Kannon to Yoritomo who treasured it as a talisman and object of worship. To have it with him at all times and to express his veneration, he kept it in his topknot. He was, however, afraid he might be captured with it still on him and ridiculed:

> 24th day. ... In the meantime Yoritomo removed from his topknot a statuette of the Goddess of Mercy (Shō Kannon) and installed it in a cave. When he was asked of the meaning of this by [Doi] Sanehira, Yoritomo replied, 'If my head is taken by Kagechika and his men, and they see this image in my hair, I would be ridiculed as commander-in-chief of the Genji.' The Military Protector explained that when he was an infant of three his wet nurse had shut herself in Kiyomizu temple to offer prayers for his future welfare, and after twenty-seven days of prayer she received a divine revelation in a dream. Thereupon she obtained this two-inch image of the Goddess of Mercy and presented it to him.[30]

29 *AK*, Jishō 4 (1180)/8/24.
30 *AK*, Jishō 4 (1180)/8/24.

The statuette obviously meant a lot to him. Later in the year, after his fortunes had begun to turn and he had established a stronger base at Kamakura he retrieved the statuette from the cave.[31]

In the succeeding month Yoritomo was trying to make a stand in the east and raise troops. He frequently called on the gods to help him. In the ninth month, for instance, he worshipped at the Sunosaki Myōjin 洲崎明神 shrine in Awa province. He vowed that if his prayers for the arrival of all the warriors he had summoned were answered, he would present to the shrine a benefice of merit rice lands to promote the glory of its deity.[32]

The preceding examples should be sufficient to give us an idea of the range of Yoritomo's personal religious interests during one of the most critical periods in his life. As depicted in the pages of the *Azuma kagami*, Yoritomo displayed a complex and genuine interest in religion. He was obviously eager to win the support of temples and shrines in the Izu, Hakone, and Awa provinces in his struggle to raise forces to take on the Taira. But he wanted more than the financial and military support of shrines and temples, he wanted their intercession with the deities of Shintō and Buddhism including Hachiman, Gongen, and Myōjin. To secure this divine support Yoritomo frequently worshipped and purged himself of pollution.

At a deeper personal level Yoritomo, if we can trust the *Azuma kagami*, also felt strong and enduring devotion to Kannon and to the *Lotus sūtra*. We may detect some diminution of devotion in his excuses to cut the recitation of the *Lotus sūtra* from 1,000 to 800 and to have a nun offer daily prayers on his behalf. The other side of the coin is that the *Azuma kagami* makes it clear that he did perform 800 incantations and that he took the pains to have the nun replace him when war prevented him from offering daily prayers. He also recited the *Lotus sūtra* daily for the repose of his father, Yoshitomo, who had been killed in Kyōto and whose remains Yoritomo would later reinter in the mortuary temple of the Shōchōjuin in Kamakura.[33] A later incident mentioned in the *Azuma kagami* underlines both the possibility of acts of compassion towards enemies and Yoritomo's devotion to the *Lotus sūtra*. He pardoned an enemy warrior when he learned of that warrior's own devotion to the *Lotus sūtra*:

---

31 *AK*, Jishō 4 (1180)/12/25.
32 *AK*, Jishō 4 (1180)/9/5. *Myōjin*, like Gongen, refers to a Buddha manifest in the form of the Shintō deity. On Jisho 4/9/12 Yoritomo granted a rice field to this shrine. On the previous day he visited an estate (*mikuri* 御厨) belonging to the Ise shrine and vowed to make further grants of *mikuri*, sacred lands, as offerings to the gods. (*AK*, Jishō 4/9/11)
33 *AK*, Bunji 文治 1(1185)/8/30. See below.

Yōwa 1 (1181). Seventh Month. Fifth Day. Nagao Shinroku Sadakage 長尾新六定景 has been pardoned [by Yoritomo]. At the battle of Ishibashi last year, when he killed Sanada Yoichi Yoshitada 佐那田餘一義忠, the Military Protector had punished him for his insolence and placed him in the custody of Okazaki Shirō Yoshizane 岡崎四郎義実, the father of the man whom he had killed. Yoshizane is by nature a compassionate man. He did not ask for Nagakage's head but merely had him pass the days as a prisoner and gave him a copy of the *Lotus sūtra*, which he has been reading unfailingly every day. Last night Yoshizane received a message in a dream which he related to the Military Protector. 'As Sadakage is my son's enemy, it is hard for me to rest until we kill him. However, as a believer in the teachings of the *Lotus*, hearing him intoning the sūtra my resentment (*onnen* 怨念), has at last subsided. If we kill him would it not adversely affect the spirit of Yoshitada [my dead son]?' The Military Protector, wanting to ease his feelings, said : 'To relieve your feelings I will issue a pardon. I too am a devotee of the *Lotus sūtra*. Your request will be fulfilled immediately.' Thus Sadakage was pardoned.[34]

In these respects Yoritomo's devotional life was probably not very different from that of other eastern warriors: a blend of devotion to Shintō and Buddhism, with considerable trust in divination as a guide in critical moments. Where Yoritomo seems to have differed from many other warriors was in the strength of his personal devotion to Kannon and the *Lotus sūtra* and in his consciousness of Hachiman as the protective deity of his ancestors and the Minamoto warrior clan. In the next section we will look at Yoritomo's religious concerns as they are expressed in the building of his new warrior capital in Kamakura and the shrines and temples built to satisfy his, and his family's, spiritual needs and provide a spiritual buttress for his regime.

RELIGIOUS LIFE IN KAMAKURA: THE TSURUGAOKA HACHIMAN SHRINE AND RELATED TEMPLES

Historians tend to discuss Yoritomo's garrison town of Kamakura as an exclusively political creation. They hasten to describe the institutions and councils of the bakufu or the novelty of appointments of *jitō* 地頭 and *shugo* 守護. Most say little, if anything, about religious and ritual activities there. Political institution-building was, of course, a major concern of Yoritomo.

34 *AK*, Yōwa 1 (1181)/7/5.

He was creating his bakufu to regulate a growing military regime while at the same time waging a war against the Taira. But just as religious concerns shaped his personal life, so too religious and ritual interests were never far from his thoughts in his political affairs. For him the religious and ritual dimensions of rule were at least as important as the political and institutional. He did not conceive of Kamakura solely in political terms. The building of religious sites there went hand-in-hand with the building of political institutions during and after the military struggle with the Taira. For Yoritomo, victory over the Taira called for the harnessing of spiritual, as well as political and military energies. And even when it became clear that the Taira could be defeated, the intervention of gods and buddhas was needed to protect his family, satisfy personal spiritual needs, sustain the bakufu, and provide a focus for vassal loyalties and unity. In fact religious and political aspects were so interwined that it is hard to separate them.[35]

We see this interaction of religion and politics – the ancient Japanese term *matsurigoto* 政, implying ritual as well as government, seems appropriate to describe it – from the moment Yoritomo set foot in Kamakura in the tenth month of 1180. Even as he was drumming up support against the Taira and planning institutions of warrior rule in the east, he moved immediately to provide a religious heart for his new garrison town by first moving, then enlarging, the Minamoto tutelary shrine to Hachiman. And very shortly after that he ordered the building of several other Buddhist temples including the Shōchōjuin 勝長寿院, Yōfukuji 永福寺, and Jibutsudō 持仏堂. This section will briefly examine the role of these shrines and temples in the life of Yoritomo and his family, and in Kamakura warrior society.[36]

The Tsurugaoka Hachiman Shrine (Tsurugaoka Hachimangū 鶴岡八幡宮), or Tsurugaoka shrine-temple (Tsurugaoka Hachimangū-ji) as it was also known, was the shrine dedicated to the Minamoto clan *ujigami* 氏神. At first a family shrine, it later became the principal site for the conduct of bakufu prayer services. With the Usa 宇佐 Hachiman in Ōita 大分 and the Iwashimizu Hachiman in Kyōto, it became one of the great national shrines to Hachiman. The Great God Hachiman (Hachiman Ōkami 大神, Buddhist Hachiman

---

35 Yoritomo, of course, was not unusual in his concern for the religious aspects of rule. All medieval warrior families worshipped family deities, and sponsored priests and nuns, shrines and family temples (*bodaiji* 菩提寺). They called on their spiritual and economic support in time of war.

36 There were other early Kamakura period Buddhist temples such as the Daijiji 大慈寺 built by Minamoto Sanetomo 源実朝 or the Jufukuji 寿福寺, of which Eisai (1141–1215) 永西 was the founder. These, however, were built after Yoritomo's death, and fall outside the scope of this chapter.

Daibosatsu 大菩薩) was revered as a protector of the nation.[37] The fact that Yoritomo provided such an elaborate setting for worship of Hachiman in Kamakura indicates both Yoritomo's personal devotion and his determination to make Hachiman a unifying force for the Kamakura *bushi* class. The shrine eventually became a center for devotion by ordinary people as well.

Even before his entry, Kamakura had a spiritual character, one that he was at pains to foster as he enlarged the town and made it the site of his bakufu.[38] One reason for Yoritomo's choice of Kamakura as a garrison was its strong spiritual connection with his Minamoto ancestors.

The origin of the Tsurugaoka Hachimangū is said to date from the eighth month of 1063 (Kōhei 康平 6) when Minamoto no Yoriyoshi, in gratitude for his victories in the Former Nine Years' War, welcomed the *kami* of the Kyōto Iwashimizu Shrine to the Yuhi district on the coast of Kamakura. The shrine later fell into disuse but was rebuilt by Yoritomo's ancestor, Yoshiie. It became a centre of devotion for Kantō *bushi*, especially for the Minamoto clan. According to the *Azuma kagami*:

> This shrine was established in the eighth month of Kōhei 6 (1063) during the reign of the ex-emperor Go-Reizei. Minamoto no Ason Yoriyoshi, the governor of Iyo, secretly welcomed the spirits of the Iwashimizu Shrine so that he might offer prayers to the ancestral gods for his subjugation, in response to imperial decree, of Abe Sadatō. Originally built in the Yuhi district of this province, the shrine, now known as the lower sub shrine (*wakamiya* 若宮), was repaired during the second month of Eihō 永保 1 (1081) by Minamoto no Ason Yoshiie, governor of Mutsu.[39]

37 On the history of the Hachiman cult, see Nakano Hatayoshi 中野幡能, *Hachiman shinkō shi no kenkyū* 八幡信仰史の研究, 2 vols. (Yoshikawa Kōbunkan, 1976).

38 In addition to a small Hachiman shrine, there had been several other temples in the area prior to Yoritomo's entry. These included the Sugimoto-dera 杉本寺 and a cave temple. Recent archaeological research suggests that there may have been other temples in the area of Imakōji 今小路, although there are no written records of their existence. Fragments of temple roof tiles from one temple that is thought to date from the Nara period have been found in substantial quantities. There is evidence, too, of a temple site that may have been a provincial temple, *kokubunji* 国分寺, in the Nara period. With the exception of Sugimoto-dera, however, these temples do not seem to have been active in 1180. On this see *Kamakura shishi – shajihen* (Yoshikawa Kōbunkan, 1959) 鎌倉市史、社寺編, p. 157.

39 *AK*, Jishō 4 (1180)/10/12. Note: a *wakamiya* 若宮, literally 'young shrine', is a sub-shrine or small shrine, usually built within the precincts of a principal shrine. The term also meaning 'young prince' was sometimes applied to shrines built especially for imperial princes.

Yoritomo entered Kamakura on the sixth day of the tenth month of 1180. After spending the night in a peasant's house, his first acts on the following day were to visit the Wakamiya Hachiman shrine and view the remains of his father's, Yoshitomo's, former residence:

> Yoritomo first visited the Tsurugaoka Hachimangū to worship. Then he viewed the remains of the residence of deceased Councillor of the Left [Yoshitomo] at Kamegayatsu. Yoritomo had planned, after inspecting the site, to build his own residence there but the terrain was not wide enough. Moreover, Okazaki Taira Shirō Yoshizane had built a temple there to perform memorial services [for Yoshitomo]. He therefore said he would abandon the plan.[40]

A few days later, 10/11, Masako and the Buddhist priest Senkōbō Ryōzen 専光房良暹 of Sōtō-zan arrived.[41] By the following day Yoritomo had decided to move the existing Hachiman Wakamiya shrine. Although it is not clear from the records, it is quite likely, that Yoritomo discussed this decision with Masako and Senkōbō.[42] On the occasion, Yoritomo purified himself and acted as his own priest, having selected the site in consultation with the gods by drawing a lot:

> 12th day. Weather clear. At 3:00 a.m. in order to venerate his ancestors, he [Yoritomo] went to Kitayama in the Kobayashi district where he designated a place for the construction of a shrine and ordered the Tsurugaoka Shrine to be transferred to this site. Senkō-bō has been named temporary Intendant (*bettō-shiki* 別当式), while [Ōba] Kageyoshi 大庭景義 has been appointed to administer the affairs of the Shrine-temple (*gūji*). Meanwhile, in order to purify himself, the Military Protector has been observing abstinence from animal food. With regard to the location of the shrine, since there was still some question as to the wisdom of abandoning the old for the new site, the matter was put to divine decision. The Military Protector himself, drawing a lot before the altar, decided on the location. Although the building has not yet been decorated, the roof has been thatched.[43]

---

40 *AK*, Jishō 4 (1180)/10/7.
41 *AK*, Jishō 4 (1180)/10/11.
42 On the Hachiman-gū's place in Kamakura and the bakufu see Matsuo Kenji 松尾剛次, 'Buke no "shuto" Kamakura no seiritsu' 武家の首都鎌倉の成立, in Ishii Susumu 石井進, ed., *Miyako to hina no chūsei shi* 都と鄙の中世史 (Yoshikawa Kōbunkan, 1992).
43 *AK*, Jishō 4 (1180)/10/12.

This is the origin of what came to be known as the 'Wakamiya' (young shrine). It is from the Wakamiya that the better known Tsurugaoka Hachimangū developed. At first the shrine was quite simple. The first building was only a temporary structure, and it was rebuilt the following year.[44] The pillars were of pine with a reed-thatched roof. In addition to the sanctuary for the *kami* (*shinden* 神殿), there were cloister corridors and a five-storey pagoda. A lake was built at the approach to the shrine.[45] In Yōwa 2 (1182), at the time of Masako's pregnancy with Yoriie, Yoritomo ordered that the road to the shrine be straightened:

> For the convenience of worshippers the winding road between Tsurugaoka shrine and Yui bay has been straightened. Yoritomo had long planned to do this, but had done nothing so far. However, his concern that Her Ladyship, now with child, might make pilgrimages to the shrine has prompted him to initiate the project.[46]

Devotion to Hachiman was the most important religious activity at Tsurugaoka shrine.[47] The Minamoto house developed strong devotion to Hachiman from the time of Yorinobu (968–1048), his son Yoriyoshi (998–1075), and his grandson Yoshiie (1041–1106). They founded branch shrines of the Iwashimizu Hachimangū in the Kantō and Tōhoku regions in step with their conquests there. They probably became attached to the Iwashimizu Hachiman through their guard duties and other service in the imperial court. Members of the Seiwa Genji 清和源氏 were sent as messengers by the imperial court to Iwashimizu. Moreover, they believed that Hachiman was a defender of the nation and an expert in military affairs.[48] From that time on the Hachiman cult spread quickly in *bushi* society, where it was

---

44 See *AK* entries for Jishō 5(1181)/5/13; Jishō 5/6/27; Jishō 5/7/8. This last entry states, 'The carpenters from Asakusa have arrived and they have begun work on the sub-shrine,Wakamiya. First the sacred body (*shintai* 神体) was removed to a temporary hall. The Military Protector paid his respects ... On the fifteenth of the coming month it is planned to return the sacred objects to the main hall Construction of the shrine should be completed by then'.

45 *AK*, Yōwa 2 (1182)/3/24.

46 *AK*, Yōwa 2 (1182)/3/15.

47 On the cult of Hachiman in Kamakura bushi society see Miyazaki, 'Religious life of the Kamakura bushi', pp. 453–6.

48 Toyoda Takeshi, *Shūkyō seido-shi*, p. 518; Hagiwara Tatsuo 萩原龍夫, *Chūsei saishi soshiki no kenkyū* 中世際祝組織の研究 (Yoshikawa Kōbunkan, 1962), p. 99; Ebe Yōko 江部陽子, 'Tsurugaoka Hachimangū hatten no sankaitei to Minamoto Yoritomo no shinkō' 鶴岡八幡宮発展の三楷梯と源頼朝の信仰, *Shintōgaku* 神道学 63 (October 1969), p. 18.

linked to the Seiwa-Genji's military tradition in the eastern provinces.

Yoritomo respected and maintained the relationship with the Iwashimizu Hachimangū but he also wanted the Kamakura Hachimangū to be more than an eastern satellite of Iwashimizu which had very strong connections with the court and the Buddhist temples of the capital. By moving and refurbishing the old Yui Shrine, Yoritomo tightened the relationship between Hachiman and his house, the main lineage of the Seiwa-Genji, by making the deity his *ujigami*.[49] He exercised direct authority over the foundation and regarded it as his house's family shrine (*ujiyashiro* 氏社). Through this arrangement Yoritomo asserted his position as successor of Yoriyoshi and Yoshiie, and warrior entitled to lead the Seiwa Genji and to perform the rituals to the protective *kami*.[50]

Yoritomo quickly brought the Wakamiya shrine into spiritual action in his campaign against the Taira. Four days after the relocation, on the sixteenth of the month, Yoritomo ordered that religious services be held 'for the protection of the nation' (*chingo kokka* 鎮護国家). He also began to provide for the economic support of the new shrine:

> At the Lord Protector's request religious services (*gongyō* 勤行) lasting throughout the day were begun at the Tsurugaoka Wakamiya. The three venerable Buddhist sūtras dedicated to the protection of the nation, namely the *Hokke-kyō*, *Nin'ō-kyō* 仁王経, and *Saishō-ō-kyō* 最勝王経 were chanted, together with the *Dai-Hannya-kyō* 大般若経, *Kanzeon-kyō* 観世音経, *Yakushi-kyō* 薬師経, *Jumyō-kyō* 寿命経, etc. They were offered by shrine monks (*gusō* 供僧). [Yoritomo] granted Kuwabara village as shrine domain land.[51]

It is difficult to know exactly how often Yoritomo visited the Wakamiya for worship but he certainly made frequent use of it when he was in Kamakura and set the first day of each month as a special day for worship there.[52] The ritual seems to have been a combination of Shintō and Buddhist elements – the offering of a sacred horse to the gods followed by prayers and offerings for deceased spirits combined with chanting of Buddhist sūtras – conducted

49 Hagiwara, pp. 99–100, 112–13.
50 Ebe, pp.19–20.
51 *AK*, Jishō 4 (1180)/10/16.
52 The *AK* does not provide entries for the first day of every month. Where entries are made for the first day, some record visits to the shrine by Yoritomo; others do not. We can assume he made the visits attributed to him (if the *AK* is reliable). He may also have gone on first days for which there are no entries or the entries deal with other subjects. All we can say is that, judging by *AK*, he went on a number of first days.

under the supervision of a Buddhist priest. Religious rituals were followed by entertainments and contests, sometimes in the grounds of the shrine, and by banquets:

> Jishō 5 (1181).[53] First Month. First Day. At 5 a.m. The Military Protector went to Tsurugaoka Wakamiya to worship. Suspending all the usual activities for the day, he has ordered that the morning of the first day of each lunar month be a day of worship at this shrine[54] ... He set out on horseback. He arrived at the worship hall. Senkōbō Ryōzen was waiting here to attend His Lordship. First a sacred horse was led to the altar. Usami Sukeshige 宇佐美祐茂 and Nitta Tadatsune 新田忠常 presented it. Then he listened to a reading of the *Lotus sūtra* as offerings of food (*kuyō*) were made to the spirits of the dead. After the service Chiba Tsunetane 千葉常胤 gave a feast [in His Lordship's honour] at his residence. A three-foot carp and an abundance of fruits and wine were served.[55]

Several more first-of-the-month visits are recorded, so it seems fair to say that when Yoritomo was in Kamakura, and free of urgent business, he did observe the monthly visits. But he also visited the shrine on other occasions. In Jishō 5 (1181), intercalary second month, for instance, Yoritomo vowed to visit the shrine for seven days in succession to pray for victory and peace:

> From today, and for the next seven days, [Yoritomo] has vowed that he will worship at the Tsurugaoka Wakamiya for the return of peace and tranquility. This is for the pacification of the outbreak of insurrections in the east and the west. He visited the shrine before dawn [today]. A sacred dance was performed.[56]

In the beginning the Wakamiya was a small, private, family shrine (*ujiyashiro*). In step with the institutional development of the bakufu from the mid-1180s to the 1190s, the Tsurugaoka Hachimangū came to be recognised

---

53 The era name was changed from Jishō 5 to Yōwa 1 on the fourteenth day of the seventh month.
54 'As the day for offering *hei* (*nusa*) to the shrine'. *Nusa*, originally cloth offerings, were symbols of divinity made of cloth or paper and hung on a pole.
55 *AK*, Jishō 5 (1181)/1/1.
56 *AK*, Jishō 5 (1181) intercalary 2/21. The record for the 27th day of the month states that 'Yoritomo worshipped at the Wakamiya for the seventh day, thus fulfilling his vow' (Jishō 5, intercalary 2/27).

107

not only as the *ujiyashiro* of Yoritomo's house but also as the shrine of the bakufu guardian deity – in other words, an official government institution.

The above accounts suggest that in the early days, although some individual *gokenin* were called upon to accompany Yoritomo to the shrine, they seldom participated in either Tsurugaoka Hachimangū's management or ceremonials. In time, however, *gokenin* took a more active part in religious ceremonies organised by Yoritomo or the bakufu. Several factors were probably at work here. Kantō *bushi* families had their own family divinities. However, they were increasingly drawn to worship Hachiman too. As Yoritomo's power increased, *bushi* naturally wanted to associate their fortunes, and their houses, with his. One obvious way to do this was to share in the ritual activities devoted to Hachiman. From Yoritomo's point of view, persuading, or allowing, other *bushi* to worship his family divinity was one way of extending his power over them and attaching them to his house and his goals. It is noticeable that as his influence grew from 1181 he made *gokenin* contribute to the support and maintenance of the Tsurugaoka Shrine as well as join in its ceremonies. Yoritomo ordered Kumagai Naozane to participate in the Hōjō-e at Tsurugaoka Hachimangū. Naozane's son, Naoie, frequently attended shrine ceremonies, and many other eastern *gokenin* took part in these rites.[57] Even high-ranking vassals were expected to provide materials and labour for reconstruction projects and even to perform personally such menial jobs as carrying stones and leading carpenter's horses. In this way Yoritomo obliged the *gokenin* to acknowledge that they belonged to his house and were subject to his authority.[58] As Miyazaki states: 'This development of the shrine provided Yoritomo with a firmer theoretical basis for making the *gokenin* render service to its deity, and many of them increasingly came to take part in religious ceremonies in Hachimangū. They also performed various other tasks necessary for maintaining the shrine, such as repairing buildings, cleaning the sacred enclosure, guarding the precincts and providing lamp oil'.[59]

Hachiman was indeed a very fitting patron for the bakufu as well as the Minamoto house. He ranked among the most powerful divinities in the indigenous pantheon and enjoyed as much respect as even the deity of Ise,

57 Miyazaki, 'Religious life of the Kamakura bushi', pp. 453–6. According to Itō Seirō 伊藤清郎, the members of fifty-three *gokenin* houses from the eastern provinces, including all the major ones, participated in religious ceremonies at Tsurugaoka Hachimangū from 1185 to 1198: 'Kamakura bakufu no gokenin tōsei to Tsurugaoka Hachimangū' 鎌倉幕府の御家人統制と鶴岡八幡宮, *Kokushi danwakai zasshi* 国史談話会雑誌 (Feb. 1973), pp. 20–1.

58 *AK*, Jishō 5 (1181)/7/20 and Yōwa 2 (1182)/3/15.

59 Miyazaki, 'Religious life of the Kamakura bushi', p. 455. She cites Ebe Yōkō, 'Minamoto Yoritomo to Tsurugaoka Hachimangū: shūkyō seisaku no ichirei toshite' 源頼朝と鶴岡八幡宮－宗教政策の一例として, *Shintōgaku* 54 (1967): 56–7.

the ancestral deity of the imperial house and major guardian of the imperial court. Hachiman had a powerful military aspect and at Usa and Iwashimizu had been revered for centuries as a protector of the state.

But the Tsurugaoka Shrine did not only have religious and ritual functions. It increasingly took on quasi-official functions. As Miyazaki points out, Yoritomo also stressed the shrine's significance as a symbol of unity among the eastern *bushi* rallying around the bakufu vis-à-vis outsiders, particularly the imperial court. Clerical officials coming from Kyōto to serve in Kamakura were required to pledge their loyalty to the bakufu at the shrine. Official messengers from the court and documents issued by the emperor were formally received at the Shrine. When he made Shizuka, the captured lover of his estranged half-brother Yoshitsune, dance at the shrine, Yoritomo told her that those who dedicated any arts to its deity must pray for blessings on the eastern provinces and, above all, on the bakufu.[60]

In Kenkyū 2 (1191)/3/4 the shrine was badly damaged by fire. In the 11th month of that year Yoritomo welcomed the *kami* of the Iwashimizu Hachiman to a new site higher in the hills above the Wakamiya. This was the origin of the main shrine, Hongū, and laid the basic pattern of the Hachimangū as a combination of Wakamiya and Hongū. This layout persists today. It should be remembered, however, that the medieval Tsurugaoka Hachimangū was very different from the Shintō shrine that millions of tourists now visit on their rounds of the Kamakura sights each year. The present shrine is a product of the government-enforced separation of Buddhism and Shintō (*shinbutsu bunri* 神仏分離) movement in early Meiji. Until Meiji, Tsurugaoka Hachimangū had Buddhist was well as Shintō buildings, images, and clergy. In the separation all the Buddhist buildings in the Hachimangū were destroyed, Buddhist images, ritual implements, and texts scattered, Buddhist monks excluded, and most traces of Buddhism removed from the Shrine. Visiting the Hachimangū today it is easy to overlook its Buddhist past but it is clear from the records that from early in its history a variety of Buddhist buildings existed within its precincts and that Buddhist as well as Shintō priests lived and performed rituals within the precincts. The chief priest of the Hachimangū was a Buddhist monk. Its character was that of a shrine-temple complex (*jingū-ji* 神宮寺) dedicated to Hachiman, and in many early documents it was actually referred to as Hachimangūji, the Hachiman shrine-temple.

There is no Kamakura period map of the shrine. The closest we can get to a vizualisation of the early medieval Tsurugaoka Hachimangū is a plan of the shrine drawn in the late sixteenth century, Tenshō 19 (1591), when Hideyoshi ordered Tokugawa Ieyasu to rebuild the shrine. This is a ground

---

60 Itō Seirō, 'Kamakura bakufu no gokenin tōsei', pp. 24–5; *AK* Genryaku 元曆 1 (1184)/4/15; Kenkyū 3 (1192)/7/26; and Bunji 2 (1186)/4/8.

plan showing the walls and buildings in the interior of the shrine precincts. By comparing this plan with older written records it is possible to establish an impression of the medieval character of Tsurugaoka. The sixteenth-century map shows the Wakamiya shrine below and to the south-east of the main shrine (Hongū 本宮), with the two shrines joined by pathways and steps.[61]

The Hongū was located in the hills to the north, the highest point in the complex. This was opened in Kenkyū 2 (1191)/11/21 when the sacred body (*shintai*) of Hachiman from Iwashimizu was invited to enter.[62] The main buildings of the Hongū were a Prayer Hall (*haiden* 拝殿) and the Sanctuary (*shinden*). These were surrounded by a cloister with a two-storey gate to the south. The Hongū, as the centre for devotion to Hachiman, became the focal point of the whole complex. Here, after 1221, lectures on the *Saishō-ō sūtra* (*Saishō-ō-kyō*) and *Lotus sūtra* were held. Especially lavish were the great *Ninnō-e* 仁王会, the most important official ceremonies of the bakufu held at Hachimangū, in which one hundred invited monks prayed for peace in the Kantō and the realm at large. We can gauge the importance of this ceremony by the fact that it was first held to pray for bakufu victory on the day following the departure of warriors from Kamakura to fight in what is known as the Jōkyū war.[63]

The Wakamiya, on a lower level than the Hongū, looms as large on the plan as the Hongū, suggesting that it was equally important in the medieval period. Wakamiya had its own Sanctuary and five sub-halls. These sub-halls were built after Yoritomo's death, between 1206 and 1217. Eleven monks were attached to them and offered daily prayers for bakufu intentions. The residence for monks was to the north-west of the shrine precinct.[64] As at many other temples and shrines throughout Japan, Buddhist monks offered prayers and offerings to Shintō *kami* in an easy blending of Shintō and Buddhist ritual.

The Wakamiya, too, was surrounded by a roofed cloister. It was, in fact, like the cloister of a Buddhist temple. The cloister was used for the ritual of 'turning the pages' (*tendoku*) of the *Saishō-ō sūtra*. Dances and musical

61 See *Kamakura shishi shajihen*, pp. 66–7. For amended plans of the Hachimangū in Kyōhō 享保 17 (1732) and 1591 see Matsuo, 'Buke no "Shuto" Kamakura no seiritsu', pp. 112–13. Matsuo analyses the two ground plans and provides a helpful description of the shrine in the late medieval period.
62 An elaborate ceremony was held with gifts of horses to the new shrine. *AK*, Kenkyū 2 (1191)/11/21.
63 Since it was not introduced into Kamakura until well after Yoritomo's death, the Ninnō-e 仁王会 falls outside the scope of this paper. See Matsuo, 'Buke no "Shuto" Kamakura no seiritsu', pp. 124–9.
64 The residence of the shrine monks was called the Nijūgobō 二十五坊. It lay behind the Hachimangū in Kita-no-tani 北の谷.

performances were also offered here in honour of Hachiman and as prayers for peace in the Kantō. During *hōjō-e* young women danced here. It was in this cloister in 1186 that Shizuka Gozen 静御前, the lover of Yoshitsune, danced in lament for Yoshitsune before Yoritomo and Masako. Yoritomo admonished her that dances in the cloister were in honour of Hachiman and to pray for the intentions and success of the bakufu.[65] Sumō wrestling offerings were also made here. The cloister also served to mark off the shrine precincts, the area sacred to the *kami*, from the Buddhist buildings elsewhere in the compound.

Just to the south of the Southern Great Gate of the Wakamiya, but still within the lower precincts of the shrine, was an open area used for mounted archery (*yabusame* 流鏑馬) and other festive activities performed before the gods and buddhas. It was in this sector, approached across a 'red bridge' and through a Shintō gate (*torii* 鳥居) that the festivals for the release of living creatures (*hōjō-e*) were conducted.

CEREMONIES AT THE HACHIMANGŪ

In addition to the religious ceremonies and the regular expressions of devotion to Hachiman and the *kami* mentioned above, the two great annual events held at the Hachimangū were the *hōjō-e* and, after 1221, the *Great Ninnō-e* 大仁王会.

According to the *Azuma kagami* entry for Jishō 4 (1180)/7/16, Yoritomo was concerned lest battle plans interfere with a *hōjō-e* to be held on the eighteenth of the month. Apparently Yoritomo had observed this ceremony before an image of Kannon since his childhood.[66] In Bunji 3 (1187) he instituted the *hōjō-e* as a large-scale ceremony to be held at the Hachimangū annually on the fifteenth day of the eighth month. As part of the festivities a mounted archery contest was also held at the shrine.

The *hōjō-e* became the biggest festival in Kamakura, for commoners as well as *bushi*. It was a combination of Buddhist memorial service and martial festival. At first it was held on one day, the fifteenth of the month. From Kenkyū 1 (1190) it was carried over onto the sixteenth as well. On the fifteenth the shrine was first blessed by the sacred palanquin bearing the divinity. The shōgun descended from his horse at the southern entrance, walked across the red bridge into the compound, and visited Wakamiya and Hongū shrines. Gifts of horses were presented to the gods, and the ceremony of releasing birds and fish into the pond, accompanied by the chanting of the

65 *AK*, Bunji 2 (1186)/4/8.
66 See above.

Lotus sūtra, was held. The Buddhist part of the ceremony was probably borrowed from the Iwashimizu Hachimangū. But whereas at Iwashimizu the *Saishō-ō-kyō,* advocating the efficacy of saving life, was chanted, in Kamakura the *Lotus sūtra,* favoured by Yoritomo, was used.[67] There was also a performance of dance in the cloister of the Wakamiya.

The following day saw the equestrian events, including the riding of horses given to the shrine by the shōgun, mounted archery, and horse racing. The highlight was the mounted archery. At first, five mounted bowmen shot at the targets. Later as many as sixteen competed. Temporary seats were set up for the spectators. Because horsemen and spectators vied in lavish dress for the occasion the bakufu in 1261 had to issue a prohibition against ostentation (Kōchō 1 (1261)/2/20 *Kamakura bakufu tsuika hō* 追加法).

Yoritomo's motives in emphasising and formalising the *hōjō-e* can only be guessed at. From childhood he had had some interest in the Buddhist practice of releasing living creatures from captivity. It is also possible that he thought of it as a fitting memorial service for warriors, Taira as well as Minamoto, who had died in the wars. In this sense it provided some relief from the sense of guilt he undoubtedly carried. He may also have seen it as a means of strengthening vassal loyalties and asserting order and hierarchy in Kamakura warrior society. Participation in the *hōjō-e,* the procession, and the equestrian events was both an obligation (*gokenin-yaku* 御家人役) and an honour for *gokenin* who lived in the eastern provinces. And those who lived in more distant regions were required to participate in ceremonies at their principal provincial shrines.[68] Warriors vied in the quality of gifts they presented and were especially proud to show off their riding and archery skills in the *yabusame* included in the *hōjō-e.*[69] The bakufu was thus able to use access to the *hōjō-e* as one means of demonstrating favour and strengthening loyalty and hierarchy among its vassals. Wounded pride and status consciousness no doubt sparked the quarrel between Yoritomo and his leading vassal, Kumagai Naozane, who objected to being asked to set up archery targets when his fellow *gokenin* were allowed to ride on horseback in the 1187 ceremonies.[70]

Yoritomo and the Minamoto family did not have a monopoly of devotion to Hachiman. Hachiman was a powerful and well-regarded *kami,* venerated for centuries at the Usa, Iwashimizu, and other shrines. Many warriors,

---

67 Matsuo Kenji, 'Chūsei toshi Kamakura' 中世都市鎌倉, in Gomi Fumihiko, ed., *Toshi no chūsei* 都市の中世 (Yoshikawa Kōbunkan, 1992).

68 See Ishii Susumu, 'Chūsei seiritsuki gunsei kenkyū no ichi shiten' 中世成立期軍制の一視点, in *Shigaku zasshi* 史学雑誌 78.12 (1969): 16–17.

69 Ebe, 'Tsurugaoka Hachimangū hatten' p. 29.

70 Miyazaki Fumiko, 'Religious life of the Kamakura bushi', pp. 435–67.

however, were probably first encouraged to worship the deity through their participation in bakufu-sponsored *hōjō-e*.[71] Yoritomo restricted them from freely holding ceremonies at Tsurugaoka Hachimangū and praying for their own benefit there but this did not prevent them from taking Hachiman as their *ujigami* and establishing shrines in their own domains.[72] The spreading Hachiman cult, with its focus in the lavish ceremonies of the Tsurugaoka *hōjō-e*, thus served as a means of enhancing vassal loyalty and unity.

OTHER RELIGIOUS SITES: SHŌCHŌJUIN, YŌFUKUJI, AND JIBUTSUDŌ

The Hachimangū remained the central official religious site of the Kamakura bakufu. But several other religious sites were built by Yoritomo to cater to his ritual and religious requirements. These included the Shōchōjuin, Yōfukuji, and the Jibutsudō. They were built to satisfy strongly felt needs. The Shōchōjuin 勝長寿院 (South Hall) was an expression of Yoritomo's strong filial and ancestral devotion to his father, Yoshitomo. The Yōfukuji was built as a memorial for Yoshitsune and the many warriors on both sides who had died in the Genpei wars. Once the temples were built, they were integrated into the pattern of warrior life and government in Kamakura.

The Shōchōjuin was the family mortuary temple (*bodaiji*) for Yoritomo's father, Yoshitomo, and the Minamoto clan. Yoritomo had long wanted to build a mortuary temple for his father. He selected a site and held the ground-breaking ceremony for what was then called the 'South Chapel' late in 1184.[73] Yoritomo commissioned the Buddhist sculptor Seichō 成朝 from Nara to make the images. Seichō arrived in the following year and began to fashion a sixteen foot (*jōroku* 丈六) statue of Amida for the new building.[74] Yoritomo's father had been killed in Kyōto by the Taira. Yoritomo was naturally eager to have the remains brought to Kamakura and re-buried in the mortuary temple. With the destruction of the Taira, he was able to achieve this in the autumn of 1185:

> Eighth month. Thirtieth day. The Second Rank [Yoritomo] has always made filial devotion to his ancestors his main concern, but he has not yet been fully able to achieve his aim. Since the cruel and premature death of his father [in the Heiji Disturbance], Yoritomo has read the *Lotus sūtra* daily and prayed for the salvation of the

71 Ebe, 'Tsurugaoka Hachimangū hatten', p. 30.
72 Toyoda, *Shūkyō seido-shi*, pp. 522–5.
73 *AK*, Genryaku 1 (1184)/11/26.
74 *AK*, Genryaku 2 (1185)/5/21.

departed spirit. To demonstrate his respect and reverence for his father, Yoritomo has planned to build a temple in his honour. Desiring to place his father's remains at rest there, he has secretly sought the ex-sovereign's sanction to have his father's remains transferred to this temple. On the twelfth of this month the ex-sovereign, in recognition of [Yoritomo's] great services, ordered an official to exhume Yoshitomo's head from its burial place near the east prison in Kyōto and instructed that, together with the head of [Kamada Jirō] Masakiyo 鎌田二郎正清, it be delivered to Kamakura. Ōe Kintomo 大江公朝 was appointed to bear the heads. He arrived from the capital today. The Second Rank went out to the banks of the Katase river to meet him. The remains were carried by disciples of Mongaku in containers hung from their necks. The Second Rank received them personally and carried them back to Kamakura. On this occasion, instead of his usual ceremonial robe of coloured silk he wore a plain white robe.[75]

Three days later, with appropriate ceremony, the remains of Yoshitomo and Kamada Masakiyo were re-interred in the grounds of the South Chapel (10/3).[76] The monk Kōgen of Onjōji, officiating priest for the dedication ceremonies, arrived in Kamakura on the twentieth.[77] Seichō's gilt statue of Amida was installed on the following day when a copy of the prayer to be read at the chapel dedication was also received in Kamakura.[78] The dedication, a lavish affair, attended by *gokenin* and their wives as well as Yoritomo and Masako, was held on the twenty-fourth day of the tenth month. The temple was renamed Shōchōjuin.[79] Later, as the Shōchōjuin was extended, Lotus Halls (Hokkedō 法華堂) for Masako and Sanetomo were added. It remained a center of ancestral worship of Yoshitomo and devotion to Amida and the *Lotus sūtra* throughout the Kamakura period. The importance of Shōchōjuin in the Kamakura religious world is shown by the fact that it – not the Hachimangū – was chosen as the site for the forty-ninth day memorial service for former emperor Go-Shirakawa 後白河 in 1192.[80] Up until 1225 it was not uncommon to have memorial services involving one hundred monks at Shōchōjuin. The Hachimangū did not monopolise public religious functions

75 *AK*, Bunji 1 (1185)/8/30.
76 *AK*, Bunji 1 (1185)/9/3.
77 *AK*, Bunji 1 (1185)/10/20.
78 *AK*, Bunji 1 (1185)/10/21.
79 See *AK*, Bunji 1 (1185)/10/24 for a detailed account.
80 *AK*, Kenkyū 3 (1192)/5/8. This was a so-called 100-monk memorial service (*kuyō* 供養). *AK* provides details of numbers of monks and gifts to them.

in the early period. However, after 1225, all such large-scale public functions tended to be held at the Hachimangū. This shift in the religious world probably paralleled a shift in the location of the bakufu in 1225 from Ōkura to a site nearer Tsurugaoka. The Shōchōjuin was allowed to go to ruin in the Muromachi period.[81]

Yoritomo built the Yōfukuji in 1189 immediately after his conquest of the northern Fujiwara to offer prayers for the spirits of Yoshitsune, Fujiwara Yasuhira 藤原泰衡, and the many other warriors who had died in the Genpei wars or in the north-eastern campaign. In Bunji 5 (1189) Yoritomo had gone to Hiraizumi in his northern campaign to capture Yoshitsune and punish the Fujiwara there for shielding him. Yoshitsune eluded him by taking his own life. He did, however, destroy the northern Fujiwara family before returning to Kamakura. He was reportedly astonished by the splendour of the great two-storey hall of Chūsonji 中尊寺 in Hiraizumi, known as the Daichōjuin and determined to build a similar one in Kamakura. It was also known as the 'Two Storey Hall' (Nikaidō 二階堂) and the Temple of the Three Halls (Amida and Yakushi Halls were later built to the right and left of Nikaidō), and must have been a large and imposing temple complex.

Construction work began late in 1189.[82] However, because of a fire in Kamakura, work was delayed until the autumn of 1192, when they began digging the pond.[83] The paintings on the doors and the wall behind the Buddha image were completed late in the tenth month.[84] They are thought to have been based on those in the Golden Hall of Mōtsuji 毛越寺 in Hiraizumi. The memorial service dedicating the new building was held on the twenty-fifth of the eleventh month, with Kōken, the monk from Miidera who had given the kuyō for Shōchōjuin, officiating.[85] Later on, other buildings were added. These included a Yakushi Hall for veneration of the Buddha of Healing, an Amida Hall, and a three storey Pagoda. In the following year a great memorial service was held in the Amida Hall. The intention was to recreate the ninefold Pure Land (kubon jōdo 九本浄土) of Amida in this present world. This form of Amida devotion was similar to that practised by the Heian nobility hoping for rebirth in the Pure Land. It did not necessarily presage the ready acceptance of Hōnen's simplified version of Pure Land Buddhism by Yoritomo or the senior members of the Kamakura bakufu. The Yōfukuji maintained its character

---

81 The site has not been excavated, so the scale and layout of the original Shōchōjuin are not known.

82 *AK*, Bunji 5 (1189)/12/9 .

83 *AK*, Kenkyū 3 (1192)/8/24. On the 27th of the same month a disciple of the Ajari Jōkū 阿闍梨静空, the monk Shōgen 静玄, was called in and asked about garden design for the pond before the main hall.

84 *AK*, Kenkyū 3 (1192)/10/29.

85 *AK*, Kenkyū 3 (1192)/11/25.

as a centre of traditional Pure Land belief throughout the Kamakura period, but it seems to have burned down in the early fifteenth century and not been rebuilt.

The Jibutsudō, or Hall Containing Buddhas, was also built not far from the Hachimangū. This building later served as a Lotus Hall, Hokkedō, and became both a centre for devotion to the *Lotus sūtra* and the mortuary temple for Yoritomo. In the late summer of 1194, for instance, Masako returned from Izu in time to perform the seven days of autumn equinox ceremonies in the Jibutsudō. This involved chanting of the *Lotus sūtra* before statues of Śakyamuni Buddha, Amida, Miroku, Kannon, Monju, and Fudō.[86] A few days later, she held a large-scale memorial service for Kiso Yoshitaka, the betrothed husband of her eldest daughter who had been killed in childhood on Yoritomo's orders. After Yoritomo's death it was designated his mausoleum and naturally it became the centre of veneration of his spirit. On the anniversary of Yoritomo's death (1200/1/13) Masako, who had taken the tonsure, held the first year memorial service for him at the Jibutsudō. Hōjō Tokimasa and a large number of warriors attended. The Zen monk Eisai officiated. Masako presented a Sakyamuni triad and a mandala made from her own hair in the form of the Sanskrit letter 'A'.[87]

The above provides a sketch of the main religious buildings constructed in Kamakura during Yoritomo's lifetime. Through the religious, ritual, and festive activities conducted in them we can get some idea of the range of religious interests of Yoritomo and his close family and warrior advisers. It is clear that great importance was attached to religious activities on a personal level and as part of the operation of the bakufu and warrior society. Many of these activities, perhaps the majority, were prayer services, known as *kitō*, for some kind of intention or another. The clergy who dominated the new religious establishment in Kamakura until well into the thirteenth century were monks whose function was to lead such prayer services.

The Hachimangū eventually became the most important centre and combined private and public, Shintō and Buddhist, and ritual and festive functions. The Shōchōjuin was built as a mortuary temple for Yoritomo's father and combined a strong Buddhist character with aspects of ancester devotion. The Yōfukuji, with its Pure Land emphasis, commemorated the spirits of warriors who had fallen in battle, and may be thought of as a site for the pacification of restless spirits. The Jibutsudō reflected the very powerful current of devotion to the *Lotus sūtra* running through the religious life of the age as well as the personal devotions of Yoritomo and Masako. It also served as a site for veneration of Shaka, Kannon, Fudō, Miroku, and Monju, all of

---

86 *AK*, Kenkyū 5 (1194)/ Urū 8/2
87 *AK*, Shōji 正治 2 (1200)/ 1/13.

whom were important devotional figures in warrior society.

These shrines and temples were headed by monks of the older schools of Buddhism, especially monks from Nara and Onjōji who served as chief priest or Intendant (*bettō*). In the lifetime of Yoritomo the Shintō-Buddhist establishment in Kamakura was dominated by Buddhist monks of the older schools who had undergone ordination at either the Tōdaiji Kaidan'in 東大 寺戒壇院 or the Enryakuji 延暦寺 platform. These were official monks (*kansō* 官僧), whose function was to pray for the intentions of the shōgun, bakufu, and nation just as in Kyōto or Nara they would have offered similar prayer services for the imperial family, the court, and the nation. It is important to remember that until the mid-Kamakura period it was the monks of the Tsurugaoka Hachimangū, Shōchūjuin, and Yōfukuji who played the leading role in Kamakura religious life as the officiating monks for the bakufu. It was not until the mid-thirteenth century that Zen and Ritsu monks came to play leading roles in the bakufu structure of ceremonial prayers for worldly blessings.

Even the Hachimangū, which had Shintō priests, was under the supervision of a Buddhist cleric. The Hachimangū comprised both shrines and temples. From the layout of the buildings it might seem that the shrines had primacy. The office of Shintō priest (*kannushi* 神主) at the shrine was entrusted hereditarily to the Ōtomo family in 1191. But the Buddhist monk who supervised the administration quickly assumed considerable influence. Yoritomo appointed Buddhist monks whom he respected as Intendants for the Hachimangū. Senkōbō Ryōzen of Sōtō-zan was first given temporary appointment. A more permanent Intendant was installed in 1182 when the venerable abbot Engyō 園暁 came from Miidera (Onjōji) to Kamakura.[88] These religious institutions were very much under the direction of Yoritomo and the bakufu and it is clear from the records that they shared information and were subjected to the same rules of conduct. The *bettō* and monks of the three temples consulted each other and were in close touch with the bakufu on matters affecting any of their institutions. Edicts affecting one temple were also addressed to the others.[89]

WARRIOR INTEREST IN THE PURE LAND AND ZEN

It is important, finally, to add a word or two about the acceptance of Pure Land and Zen in Kamakura society. What progress had been made by the

---

88 *AK*, Juei 1 (1182)/9/23
89 Matsuo, 'Buke no "Shuto" Kamakura no seiritsu', pp. 118–19, cites a law issued in 1242 to the *bettō* 別当 of the three temples forbidding priests' attendants to wear swords. This sprang from violence in the monks' quarters at Shōchōjuin.

time of Yoritomo's death in 1199?

In the case of Pure Land Buddhism, there is no doubt that Yoritomo and Masako had a strong devotion to the traditional Pure Land teaching of the kind prevalent in late Heian period Tendai monasteries and widely accepted by the court nobility and the northern Fujiwara. Buildings, statues, texts, and practices all demonstrated an interest in Amida and the Pure Land. This interest was shared by Yoritomo's in-laws, the Hōjō, and by other Kamakura *bushi*. The fact that Yoritomo built temples symbolising the realisation of the Pure Land in Kamakura seems to have had an impact on *bushi* around him. His father-in-law, Hōjō Tokimasa, for instance, built the Ganjōjuin 願成就院 in Izu in 1189 in honour of Yoritomo's conquest of the Fujiwara in the north. He installed Amida Nyorai as the principal image (*honzon* 本尊) giving birth to the Pure Land in this world. He also installed statues of Fudō and Bishamonten made several years earlier by Unkei 運慶 in Nara. Wada Yoshimori 和田義盛, another leading warrior chieftain serving Yoritomo, also commissioned an Amida triad from Unkei as well as images of Fudō and Bishamon for his Jōrakuji at Ashina (Yokosuka).[90] This Pure Land devotion was traditional, aristocratic, Pure Land Buddhism derived from the court and capital, or from Nara or the northern Fujiwara. Moreover it was not exclusive. In Kamakura warrior society it was mixed with strains of devotion to the tantric deities Fudō Myōō and Bishamonten as well as the *Lotus sūtra*, Yakushi, Kannon, Jizō, and many other deities.

During Yoritomo's lifetime, Hōnen 法然 (1133–1212) in Kyōto was forging a more radical Pure Land teaching. He started advocating the exclusive practice of the *nenbutsu* 念仏 in 1175 and wrote the *Senchaku hongan nenbutsu shū* 撰択本願念仏集 for Kujō Kanezane in 1198, a few months before Yoritomo's death. There is no record of Yoritomo being in touch with, or influenced by, Hōnen, though it is quite likely that he had heard of him and of his emphasis on the *nenbutsu*. The first fully-fledged Pure Land preacher to spread Hōnen's teaching in Kamakura seems to have been Ryūkan 隆寛 (1148–1227) who arrived in 1227. Well before this, however, Hōnen's advocacy of the *nenbutsu* as the easy path to the Pure Land in an age of decline had found ready acceptance among *bushi* in Kyōto and Kamakura. A number of Kantō *bushi* accepted Hōnen as a teacher and took Pure Land names. These included the bakufu houseman Utsunomiya Yoritsuna (Renshō) and his younger brother Akinari (Shinjō), as well as Kumagai Naozane and

---

90 Miura Katsuo 三浦勝男, 'Chūsei bushi-tachi no inori' 中世武士達の祈り, in Miyama Susumu 三山進, ed., *Zusetsu Kamakura bukkyō* 図説鎌倉仏教 (Shinchōsha, 1988), pp. 244–5 (see photo on p. 244).

his son.[91] Yoritomo's leading vassal Hatakeyama Shigetada is said to have asked Hōnen about the Pure Land *nenbutsu* and the preparations for becoming a monk. These examples and other references found in such sources as the *Hōnen shōnin gyōjō ezu* 法然上人行状絵図 show that many Kamakura *bushi* were interested in the single-practice Pure Land teaching being advocated by Hōnen during the lifetime of Yoritomo. Several of them associated with Hōnen and his disciples while on guard duty in Kyōto and brought news of the new religious movements in the capital back to Kamakura.

However, the Pure Land teaching that Hōnen taught in Yoritomo's lifetime still had a very strong Tendai and aristocratic flavour. Hōnen was still viewed as a Tendai monk with strong Pure Land interests rather than the founder of a new Pure Land school. As the example of Kumagai Naozane shows, even those *bushi* who were most attracted to Hōnen's teaching did not abandon their involvement in bakufu-sponsored religious activities in Kamakura. Nor did they abandon their traditional family *kami*, the *ujigami*. There is no record of an officially sanctioned exclusive *nenbutsu* practice in Kamakura during Yoritomo's lifetime, or for some years thereafter.

A similar situation prevailed in the case of Zen. Although Eisai brought Ch'an practices back from his second journey to China well before Yoritomo's death, he was at first mainly active in Kyūshū and Kyōto, and even there seems to have advocated not exclusive meditation but a mixed practice involving scholastic (Tendai) and Tantric (Shingon) elements as well as *zazen* 座禅. Eisai did not go to Kamakura until after Yoritomo's death. He served as the officiating monk at the first memorial service for Yoritomo and won the patronage of Masako, Yoriie, and Sanetomo. Masako granted him land for the building of Jufukuji which later became a Zen temple. The *Azuma kagami* records more than a dozen meetings between Masako and Eisai. It is clear that that she respected and trusted him and that he gave her spiritual solace at a very difficult time in her life – she had just lost her second daughter as well as Yoritomo. It is quite likely that he talked to her of Zen. He may even have introduced her to *zazen*. But there is no record of this. All the *Azuma kagami* entries present him as traditional Tendai monk leading prayer services for bakufu intentions. Nor is there any indication in the *Azuma kagami* that Masako or Kamakura *bushi* associated with Eisai as a Zen priest or were at all interested in Zen practice. The acceptance of Zen in Kamakura, like that of Hōnen's Pure Land teaching, comes well after Yoritomo's death and requires separate treatment.

91 Miyazaki, 'Religious life of the Kamakura bushi', provides an excellent description of Naozane's Pure Land belief in the context of his other religious interests.

119

5

Rethinking Japanese folk religion: a study of Kumano Shugen

Miyake Hitoshi

SHUGENDŌ AND THE HISTORY OF JAPANESE FOLK RELIGION

I understand 'folk religion' to refer to religion that arises from within daily life and reflects aspects of production and consumption in the daily lives of ordinary people, in contrast to world religions such as Christianity, Islam, and Buddhism, in which a founder has advocated teachings and doctrines based on his or her religious experience and upon which a religious organisation is established. Folk religion consists of annual observances (*nenchū gyōji* 年中行事), rites of passage, rituals for avoidance of misfortune, and various myths and traditions. Religion in Japan developed with these folk religious elements as its fundamental background. Thus I will first give an outline of folk religion in Japan, and then place the topic of this paper, Kumano Shugen, within this framework.

Japanese folk religion is centred around belief in, and rituals focused on, the *kami* カミ of places such as mountains and the sea – thought to be an 'other world' – as well as the myths and traditions concerning these figures. The religion known as 'Shintō' came into being through the process of welcoming, enshrining, and celebrating the *kami* of sacred places (*reichi* 霊地) and accepting them as guardian deities of the family (*ie* 家) or village (*mura* 村). The influence of religions introduced from abroad was also an important factor, and as a result of this influence some people entered the holy spiritual regions of the mountains and performed ascetic practice under the guidance of 'mountain men'. These people were able to draw on the power of the *kami* and became religious figures who performed magico-religious activities. The ascetics (*keza* 験者) of the esoteric Buddhist Shingon and Tendai traditions are representative of these figures. During the Heian Period (794–1185), people who had cultivated such practices and attained magical powers were called *shugenja* 修験者. This marks the beginning of Shugendō 修験道 as a distinct religious tradition.

It is necessary here to make some attempt to place Shugendō within the history of the development of folk religion in Japan. Folk religion in Japan is based on animism, and involves nature worship. The notion of the divine, or of spirits/gods, is a two-layered structure: the indigenous local spirits (*kami*

カミ) and those that were introduced from the outside (*kami* 神) and conferred power on the indigenous *kami*. In earlier times people enshrined and celebrated the indigenous *kami*, and sought to control and protect their lives through magically manipulating these spirits. Then even more powerful figures in the forms of 'Buddhas' were introduced from abroad. At the same time many techniques for manipulating and controlling these forces were also introduced in the forms of shamanism, Taoism, and esoteric Buddhism. Around the ninth and tenth centuries, *shugenja*, people who had cultivated these techniques and experienced ascetic practices in the mountains, began to appear in large numbers, and eventually formed the religion called Shugendō.

Around the twelfth and thirteenth centuries, the way of thinking called *hongaku shisō* 本覚思想 (the idea that all things are inherently enlightened) became very popular among the members of the Tendai school on Mt Hiei 比叡. It was assumed that all things have the nature of the Buddha, that even the plants and earth possess buddhahood. It is not an exaggeration to say that this way of thinking is animism in Buddhist garb. Tamura Yoshirō 田村芳朗 has proposed that all of the so-called new Buddhist movements of the Kamakura period (1185–1333) were based in some way upon this Tendai idea of *hongaku shisō*: Zen and Shugendō sought to realise Buddhahood within this life through various practices; the Pure Land schools of Buddhism sought to attain Buddhahood in the next life by chanting the Buddha's name (*nenbutsu* 念仏); the Nichiren 日蓮 school sought to establish a Buddha-land on this earth.[1]

Ancestral veneration took root later, in the sixteenth and seventeenth centuries, with the establishment of the social structures of the family (*ie*) and village (*mura*), and funerary practices and rites for the ancestors assumed an important social role. Eventually, the Buddhist establishment came to be responsible for such matters, and in the Edo Period (1600–1868) the lives of people in local societies were structured around a number of religious 'authorities': clan or local guardian spirits for regional security (Shintō); the family or clan temple for funerals and ancestral rites (Buddhism); and Shugen or esoteric Buddhist establishments for the healing of disease or avoidance of misfortune. One can identify these religious figures who performed magico-religious prayers (*kaji-kitō* 加持祈祷) as *yamabushi* 山伏 (*shugenja*), Buddhist priests (*sōryo* 僧侶), or Shintō priests (*shinshoku* 神職), but in fact the three types were all combined. However, after 1868 the Meiji government ordered a separation of 'Buddhist' and 'Shintō' elements, and outlawed Shugendō. It sought to establish a State Shintō with Ise Shrine as its centre and all the local clan deities with their own place within this overriding structure. One

---

1 Tamura Yoshirō, *Kamakura shinbukkyō shisō no kenkyū* 鎌倉新仏教思想の研究 (Kyōto: Heirakuji Shoten, 1965).

result of the outlawing of Shugendō was that many new religions sprang up to take its place and respond to the human need for fulfilling worldly aspirations. After the Second World War, Shugendō regained its independent status and once again began an active role in the religious life of the Japanese people.

The study of folk religion in Japan has so far taken one of two major standpoints. The first is to seek an indigenous Japanese folk belief that remains even today among the Japanese people; this approach is best represented by the work of Yanagita Kunio 柳田国男 (1875–1962). The attempt to seek an ancient prototype for Japanese culture in the practices and texts of ancient Japan is best represented by the work of Origuchi Shinobu 折口信夫 (1887–1953). The recent work of Takatori Masao 高取正男, which emphasises the distinction between Buddhist and Shintō customs, can also be classified under this approach.[2] As we can see from the fact the Yanagita himself referred to his studies as *shin-kokugaku* 新国学 (new national studies), this approach is an extension of the *kokugaku* (national studies) of Motoori Norinaga 本居宣長 (1730–1801) and Hirata Atsutane 平田篤胤 (1776–1843).

The second approach is to focus on the beliefs of ordinary people who do not limit their religious affiliation to any one religious tradition, and thereby attempt to grasp the function of these religious practices. Studies based on this approach include the archaeological examination of artifacts and relics and the study of poetry and literature in works such as the *Man'yōshū* 万葉集 and traditional diaries and tales; these can all be taken as material for the study of folk religion. In such an approach, the content and function of folk religion become the focus of attention, and there is no attempt to find a kind of 'indigenous' element.

In light of this analysis, I believe we can say that the Japanese, in response to their perceived needs, have absorbed various religious traditions from abroad and blended them to create their own particular kind of syncretistic folk religion. From this perspective, it is necessary to examine the process and the ways in which the Japanese have absorbed various foreign religions, blended them with indigenous elements, and created a particular kind of folk religion. For this purpose it is necessary to study this 'blending/syncretism of *kami* and buddha' (*shinbutsu shūgō* 神仏習合) and the religious traditions that are most representative of this kind of syncretistic religion, that is, Shugendō and the new religions.

My concern is the study of Shugendō, and I seek to examine the formation of Japanese folk religion within the thought patterns, rituals, and organisation of these syncretistic religions. The rest of my paper will be devoted to a

---

2 *Shintō no seiritsu* 神道の成立 (Heibonsha, 1979).

study of Shugendō in the Kumano region as a specific example of the kind of research I have outlined above.[3]

SHUGENDŌ AND THE ORIGIN OF THE 'THREE MOUNTAINS OF KUMANO'

Shugendō is a religious tradition that took the form of an organised religion around the ninth and tenth centuries when ancient Japanese religious beliefs and practices in the mountains were influenced by religions such as Taoism and esoteric Buddhism imported from abroad. The practitioners gained supernatural powers through ascetic practice in the mountains, and utilised these powers mainly through performing magico-religious activities. Shugendō was found at sacred mountains throughout Japan, but the form that was most influential throughout the country was the Shugen that first developed in the Kumano 熊野 region of the present Wakayama 和歌山 prefecture and around the mountain Kinbu-sen 金峰山 in the Yoshino 吉野 region of the present Nara 奈良 prefecture.

Kumano consists of the three areas of Hongū 本宮, Shingū 新宮, and Nachi 那智, and thus is referred to as the 'three mountains of Kumano' (Kumano Sanzan 熊野三山). Kumano Shugen was at first connected with the Tendai temple of Onjōji 園城寺 (also called Miidera 三井寺), but from the fourteenth century came under the control of the Kyoto temple Shōgo-in 聖護院. This branch of Shugendō eventually came to be known as the Honzan-ha 本山派.

Kinbu-sen was also known as Kane-no-mitake 金の御岳 ('hills of gold'), and is well known as the focus of a pilgrimage made by the Heian period aristocrat and politician Fujiwara no Michinaga 藤原道長 (966–1027). The central object of worship in the Shugen of Kinbu-sen is Kongō Zaō Gongen 金剛蔵王権現, a figure venerated by En no Ozuno 役小角, the Nara period thaumaturge and supposed founder of Shugendō. This Mitake faith spread throughout the country, and at the present time Yoshino is the headquarters of the Kinbu-sen Shugen Honshū 金峯山修験本宗 organisation. Around the fifteenth century, shugenja of 36 temples in the Kinki 近畿 area founded an association of 36 leaders (sendatsu 先達), the Tōzan Sanjūroku Shōdai-sendatsu Shū 当山三十六正大先達衆, with its headquarters at Ozasa 小篠

---

3 Miyake Hitoshi 三家準, *Shugendō shisō no kenkyū* 修験道思想の研究 (Shun-jūsha, 1985), *Shugendō girei no kenkyū* 修験道儀礼の研究 — 増補版 (Shunjūsha, 1970), *Shugendō jiten* 修験道辞典 (Tōkyōdō Shuppan, 1986), and *Kumano shugen* 熊野修験 (Yoshikawa Kōbunkan, 1992).

deep in the mountains of Kinbu-sen. By the sixteenth century, these leaders and their *yamabushi* followers had shifted their headquarters to Sanbō-in 三宝院, a sub-temple of Daigoji 醍醐寺 in Kyōto, and were known as the Tōzan-ha 当山派 branch of Shugendō. This and the Honzan-ha discussed above formed the major branches of Shugendō.

There are many more famous sacred mountains connected to Shugendō, including Mt Katsuragi 葛城 in Nara Prefecture (where En no Ozuno is said to have practised), Mt Haguro 羽黒 in the Tōhoku 東北 region in northern Japan, Mt Hiko 彦山 in Kyūshū, and Mt Ishizuchi 石鎚 in Shikoku. Today there are many independent Shugendō organisations: Honzan Shugen-shū 本山修験宗 (formerly the Honzan-ha), Shingon-shū Daigo-ha 真言宗醍醐派 (formerly the Tōzan-ha), Kinbu-sen Shugen Honshū, Haguro-san Shugen Honshū, Ishizuchi Honshū, Goryū 五流 Shugendō, and so forth. As we can see from this brief history of Shugendō, Kumano Shugen and its offspring – the Honzan-ha – has been the main stream running throughout its history. That is the reason I have chosen to focus on Kumano Shugen.

Kumano is mentioned in the *Kojiki* 古事記 as the burial place for Izanami-no-mikoto, one of the *kami* who, in Japanese mythology, gave birth to the land of Japan. As we can see from this myth, Kumano has from ancient times been considered an 'other' world. There are three major shrines in Kumano: Hongū Taisha 本宮大社, Hayatama Taisha 速玉大社 in Shingū, and Nachi Taisha. The central *kami* of Hongū shrine is Ketsu-mi-miko no kami 家津美御子神, known as a tree deity. The corresponding Buddhist figure was believed to be Amida Nyorai 阿弥陀如来. The central *kami* of Shingū's Hayatama shrine is Kumano Hayatama no kami 熊野速玉神, believed to have come from the other side of the sea. The corresponding Buddhist figure was believed to be Yakushi Nyorai 薬師如来. The central *kami* of Nachi is Kumano Fusumi no kami 熊野夫須美神, with the corresponding Buddhist figure believed to be the Bodhisattva Senju ('thousand-armed') Kannon 千手観音菩薩. In later times, however, each of the shrines enshrined the *kami* of the other shrines, and they are as a group referred to as the Kumano Sansha Gongen 熊野三社権現 (avatars of the three Kumano shrines).

Nachi is also the location of the temple Seigantoji 青岸渡寺, which enshrines another form of Kannon: Nyoirin 如意輪 ('wish-fulfilling jewel'), and the temple Myōhō-zan Amidaji 妙法山阿弥陀寺. Also, in medieval times there were many people who departed on boats from the beach of Nachi out to sea to the west in hopes of reaching Fudaraku 補陀落, the Pure Land or paradise of Kannon.

According to the *Kumano gongen gosuijaku engi* 熊野権現御垂迹縁起, which is the oldest extant written record on Kumano and was included in the *Chōkan kanmon* 長寛勘文 of 1163, the *kami* of Kumano was originally Shin

晋, the 'divine prince' of the land deities of Mt Tian-tai 天台 in China.[4]
These *kami* are said to have flown to Japan, stopping first on Mt Hiko in
Kyūshū, Mt Ishizuchi in Shikoku, Mt Yuzuruha 諭鶴羽 in Awaji 淡路, and
so forth until finally arriving at places in the Shingū area such as Kannokura
神倉 and Asuga 阿須賀 and the Hongū area. Here they were discovered by a
hunter named Chiyosada 千与定 and were first enshrined as the avatars of
Kumano.

A large number of *shugenja* gathered in the Kumano area throughout
history. From around the eighth century they would practise at Kumano and
heal diseases through the use of magical powers. Some of the most famous
include the figure of Eikō 永興, who was considered a bodhisattva; Jōzō 浄
蔵, who first conducted ascetic retreats at Nachi Falls in the tenth century;
Ōshō 応照, who sacrificially burnt his body at Nachi; Zendō 禅洞 of Hongū,
whom tradition credits with being the first to practise asceticism on Mt
Ōmine; and Ragyō 裸行, who practised at Kannokura and is said to have
discovered Nachi Falls with the guidance of Kannon.

SHUGENDŌ AND THE DEVELOPMENT OF THE 'THREE MOUNTAINS OF KUMANO'

Pilgrimage to the Kumano area (Kumano *mōde*) by members of the Imperial
and aristocratic families became very popular during the period of Insei 院政
retired emperors (1086–1198). The retired emperor Uda 宇多 participated in
a Kumano pilgrimage in 907, and was followed by emperor Kazan's 花山
visit to Nachi in 987. When retired emperor Shirakawa 白河 went on a
pilgrimage to Kumano in 1090 he visited all of the areas of the Kumano
Sanzan under the guidance of the monk Zōyo 増誉 of Onjōji. Shirakawa
later granted the temple Shōgo in to Zōyo. Also at that time the steward
(Bettō 別当) of the Kumano Sanzan was appointed to the official government
rank of *hōkyō* 法橋. As a result the Kumano Sanzan area became bound up
with the central authorities in Kyōto. According to the *Kumano bettō keizu*
熊野別当系図 (lineage of the Kumano stewards), this lineage of Kumano
stewards continued until the time of Shōtan 正湛 in 1284.

Pilgrimage to Kumano became very popular during and after the time of
retired emperor Shirakawa. Shirakawa himself made the pilgrimage nine
times, retired emperor Toba 鳥羽 21 times, retired emperor Go-Shirakawa 後
白河 34 times, and retired emperor Go-Toba 後鳥羽 28 times. Go-Shirakawa
was an especially devout pilgrim, and in 1160 he enshrined the Kumano

---

4 *Chōkan kanmon* in *Gunsho ruiju*, Zatsu no bu 18,463巻, 26輯: *Shinkō gunsho ruiju* 新校群書類従 20 (Naigai Shoseki, 1940).

Gongen at the Hōjūjiden 法住寺殿 sanctuary on the imperial palace grounds in Kyōto. He renamed the sanctuary Shin-Kumano-sha (new Kumano shrine), and appointed Kakusan 覚讃, the head priest (kengyō 検校) of the Kumano Sanzan, as kengyō for this shrine. During this year Go-Shirakawa also had the temple Zenrinji 禅林寺 of Higashiyama in Kyōto enshrine the Nachi avatar (gongen 権現), and also renamed this temple 'Shin-Kumano-sha'. Later it was known as Nyakuōji-sha 若王子社.

There were Shugen practitioners throughout the Kumano Sanzan. Those centred at Hongū were organised around the elders of five temples known as the Nagatoko-shukurō-goryū 長床宿老五流. The long and narrow shrine buildings used for ascetic practices were known as nagatoko. The yamabushi who used these building were called nagatoko-shū 長床衆. The nagatoko-shū of Hongū practised all along the long path from Kumano, past Ōmine, and into Yoshino, but they centred their activities at the spots known as Jinzen 深仙 and Zenki 前鬼. The Shugen centred at Shingū included unmarried Buddhist priests (shūto 衆徒), Shintō priests (shinkan 神官), and 'Buddhist' priests who served at 'Shintō' shrines (shasō 社僧); there were also ascetics among the shasō who were called nagatoko-shū.

The Kannokura hijiri practised on the mountain overlooking Shingū known as Kannokura. The Shugen at Nachi included those who practiced retreats at one or more of the 48 waterfalls of Nachi. They were called Nachi takigomori-shū 瀧籠衆 ('those who practise retreat at a waterfall').

THE RITUALS AND THOUGHT PATTERNS OF KUMANO SHUGEN

As the pilgrimage to Kumano became more and more popular, the kami enshrined at Kumano also increased in number. By the middle of the twelfth century the kami had increased to 12, and were called Kumano jūnisho gongen 熊野十二所権現 (the 12 avatars of Kumano). These 12 avatars were the three mentioned above, plus the five Ōji 王子 ('princes'): Wakamiya-ōji 若宮王子 (originally Amaterasu-ōmikami; the corresponding Buddhist figure was Jūichimen Kannon 十一面観音), Zenji no miya 禅師宮 (the corresponding Buddhist figure was Jizō 地蔵), Hijiri no miya 聖宮 (the corresponding Buddhist figure was Ryūju 龍樹 [Nāgārjuna]), Chigo no miya 児宮 (Nyoirin Kannon), and Komori no miya 子守宮 (Sho Kannon). The rest consisted of the four guardian deities of Ichiman Jūman 一万・十万 (Fugen 普賢 and Seishi 勢至), Kanjō jūgosho 勧請十五所 (Shaka 釈迦), Higyō Yasha 飛行夜叉 (Fudō 不動), and Meji Kongō 米持金剛 (Bishamonten 毘沙門天). Ketsu-mi-miko, whose corresponding Buddhist figure was believed to be Amida Nyorai, was also known as Shōjōden 証誠殿.

In addition to these 12 avatars, the *nagatoko-shū* of Hongū venerated Shūkongōjin 執金剛神 as their guardian deity. In Shingū, the Asuga 阿須賀 Shrine on the banks of the Kumano River enshrined the Yatagarasu 八咫烏 ('eight-legged crow'), whose corresponding Buddhist figure was Daiitoku Myōō 大威徳明王; Takakuraji no mikoto 高倉下命 (Aizen Myōō 愛染明王) was enshrined at Kannokura. Both of these shrines were closely related to Shugen activities. At Nachi, Hirō 飛瀧 Gongen was enshrined next to the 12 Kumano avatars in the shrine at the waterfalls. Together these figures were known as the 13 avatars of Kumano. There is also a Nyoirin-dō at Nachi that enshrined Nyoirin Kannon. This later became Seigantoji 青岸渡寺, the first spot on the 33 centres of the Saigoku Kannon pilgrimage.

According to the Shugen shinan-shō 修験指南鈔, compiled in the fourteenth century during the heyday of Kumano Shugen, the original form of Shōjōden, the central deity of the 12 Kumano avatars, was Jihi Daiken-Ō 慈悲大頭王 ('king of compassion and great insight'), ruler of the Indian kingdom of Magadha and a descendant of Śākyamuni.[5] This ruler had as his family retainers two elders named Gaken 雅顕 and his brother Chōkan 長寛, who were descendants of Śākyamuni's disciple Kāśyapa. Jihi Daiken-Ō married Gaken's daughter and had two sons. The descendants of these families came to Japan to save the Japanese people. The king became Shōjōden, the two princes became Musubi 結 and Hayatama 速玉, and Gaken became Kanjōjūgosho. Gaken's younger brother Chōkan became the deity of Fushimi Inari 伏見稲荷 in Kyōto and vowed to protect those who went to Kumano on pilgrimage. The *Ryōbu mondō hishō* 両峰間答秘鈔, compiled a little later than the previous text, claimed that Gaken came to Japan and became En no Ozuno.[6] Unlike the story in the *Kumano gongen gosuijaku engi*, these texts claim that the Kumano avatars originally were the descendants of Śākyamuni and served as retainers for a ruling family in India.

The rituals of the Kumano pilgrimage at this time were recorded in 1427 by the monk Jitsui 実意 of Jūshin-in 住心院 in his diary *Kumano-mōde nikki* 熊野詣日記, after he served as *sendatsu* 先達 (guide) for Ashikaga Yoshimitsu's 足利義光 consort Kitano-dono 北野殿. Kitano-dono entered a room for purification (*shōjin-ya* 精進屋) on the 16th day of the ninth month, and maintained a pure lifestyle until setting out on the pilgrimage. They departed on the 20th day of the month, leaving Toba by ship and travelling down the Yodo River. Upon reaching Osaka they visited Tennō-ji and paid their respects to the Buddha-relics enshrined there. Rituals such as *hōhei* 奉幣 (an offering

---

5 See the text of *Shugen shinan-shō* in *Shintō taikei* 神道大系 75 (Shintō Taikei Hensankai, 1988).
6 See the text of *Ryōbu mondō hishō* in *Shugendō shōso* 修験道章疏 2 (Nihon Daizōkyō Hensankai, 1919).

of a wand with hemp and paper streamers), *kagura* 神楽 dances, and oracles (*takusen* 託宣) were performed at the major shrines along the way such as Fujishiro 藤白, Kirime, Inabane 稲葉根, Takijiri 瀧尻, and Hosshin-mon 発心門. At the sea near Tanabe they performed *shiogori* 塩垢離 (purification with sea water) and crossed the rapids at San-no-se near Takijiri on foot. Upon reaching Hongū they performed *hōhei, gongyō* 勤行 recitations, *kagura* dances, and oracles. Next they travelled by boat down the Kumano River to Shingū, and then by sea to Nachi, where the same sorts of rituals were performed. At Nachi, in addition to the above rituals, sūtras were ritually buried (*maikyō* 埋経). After finishing the pilgrimage to all three mountain centres, the same road was followed back. Before going home, a final service was performed on the tenth day of the tenth month at Fushimi Inari in thanks to the deities for protection and a safe trip. Note that during this pilgrimage to Kumano, oracles were performed repeatedly at many stages along the way.

Kumano Shugen is slightly different at each of the three areas. There is no site for ascetic practice close to Hongū, so the Shugen of this area involved entering the mountains and travelling as far as Ōmine and Yoshino. Two of the characteristic practices of Hongū Shugen are the practice of spending a retreat in the mountains over the New Year by the Misoka 晦 *yamabushi*, and the Jinzen initiation (*kanjō* 灌頂) performed at Jinzen. At Shingū there was the practice of the Kannokura *hijiri*, who fasted and kept watch over the 'eternal flame' in preparation for the fire festival. At Nachi there was the practice of retreat near a waterfall for practising austerities by sitting under the waterfall.

THE REGIONAL DISPERSION OF KUMANO SHUGEN

As the practice of the Kumano pilgrimage spread among the retired emperors, aristocratic families, and members of the *bushi* 武士 class, an increasing number of manors (*shōen* 庄園) were donated to Kumano organisations. During the period of the retired emperors, many manors in the Kii 紀伊 area were donated by members of the imperial or aristocratic families. During the period of the Northern and Southern dynasties (1336–92) both the Northern and Southern factions sought the military support of those in the Shingū area, thus leading to the donation of a number of manors. Such donations gradually dwindled after that time. Areas in which there were more than three manors belonging to Kumano authorities were as follows: Kii, 22; Tōtōmi, eight; Bizen, six; Ise, Suruga, and Mimasaka, four each; Mikawa, Tajima, and Awa, three each. Manors belonging to the Shin-Kumano and Nyaku-ōji shrines in Kyōto included 8 in Bichū, 5 in Yamashiro, 4 each in Settsu and Harima, and 3 in Awaji. It should be noted that the manors belonging to Kumano and Shin-Kumano were mostly places conveniently located by the sea – Awa and locations along the Seto inland sea, Ise, Mikawa, Tōtōmi, and Suruga. This indicates that Kumano authorities favoured manors that were conveniently located for the transport of goods by sea. The Kumano Gongen were enshrined at these manors and became centres for the activity of Kumano *sendatsu*. During the Sengoku period (1467–1568), however, members of the warrior (*bushi*) class attacked the manors, and eventually they became economically unprofitable to maintain.

At this point the Kumano organisations found it better to depend on 'tourism' rather than the manors for economic subsistence, that is, on patrons (*danna* 旦那) who visited Kumano on pilgrimage from around the country. These patrons were led to Kumano by *sendatsu*, and their specific religious needs, such as the performance of prayers and arrangements for lodging, were taken care of by escorts known as *oshi* 御師. The first *oshi* make their appearance during the pilgrimage of Fujiwara no Munetada 藤原宗忠 in 1109, as recorded in the *Chūyūki* 中右記.[7] The retired emperors and aristocrats who made pilgrimages to Kumano during the period between 1090 and 1221 had their needs taken care of by certain *bettō* (steward) families, but from around the end of the thirteenth century, as pilgrimage became popular also among the warriors and ordinary people, priests from Kumano began to fulfil the role of *oshi*. There were *oshi* affiliated with each of the three Kumano regions, but the *oshi* from the Nachi area, affiliated with temples such as Rōno-bō 廊之坊 and Jippō-in 実報院, were particularly active during the fourteenth and fifteenth centuries.

Sendatsu would lead their patrons to certain *oshi* of the Kumano area, and then would be responsible for taking care of various needs, such as ritual purification before departing and rituals to be performed at sacred sites such as Ōji 王子, for acting as guides along the way, and so forth. During the period of retired emperors, these duties were performed during the pilgrimage of a retired emperor or member of the aristocracy by a high-ranking priest of a famous temple. From around the end of the twelfth century, however, more and more pilgrimages to Kumano were undertaken by warriors, their servants, and ordinary people, and a variety of types of *sendatsu* developed in response to these new needs. When a *sendatsu* brought his patron to an *oshi*, he would present a petition (*ganmon* 願文) listing his own, and the patron's, name and address. Thus the *sendatsu* acted as a go-between for his patron and an *oshi*,

---

7 Entry for Tennin 天仁 2.10.26: *Shiryō taisei* 史料大成, vol. 10 (Naigai Shoseki, 1934), p. 448.

and henceforth a relationship was established whereby this patron's family would always depend on this *oshi* for services such as lodgings and religious rituals. The *oshi* would then receive financial support from the *sendatsu* and patron on the occasion of each pilgrimage. Such *sendatsu* and patrons thus became the source of economic support for those in the Kumano area. Eventually, among the *oshi* the rights to patrons became the object of the transfer and sale of rights, and collateral for loans. In such cases the *ganmon*, containing the name of the *sendatsu* and patrons, would be used as a legal document. An *oshi* also kept records and a register of the names of the *sendatsu* and patrons affiliated with him. Such historical records, such as deeds of transfer or sale, collateral for loans, petitions, and registers, are called *oshi monjo* 御師文書. About 1,500 such records are preserved at the Kumano Nachi Taisha, and about 250 at Hongū Taisha.

A look at these *oshi monjo* shows that the number of patrons steadily increased between the fourteenth and sixteenth centuries. Once the Sengoku period began at the end of the fifteenth century, however, rights to serve patrons were frequently sold. At this time Rōno-bo and Jippō-in at Nachi bought up many of the rights to the *oshi* patrons and increased their influence in the area. Areas of Japan in which the largest number of such patrons and *sendatsu* were from are as follows: 92 patrons and 78 *sendatsu* from Ōmi; 90 and 55 respectively from Mutsu; 75 and 42 from Musashi; 69 and 76 from Iyo; 67 and 28 from Ise; 53 and 22 from Echigo; 50 and 36 from Awa; 46 and 18 from Kōzuke; 44 and 7 from Suruga; 40 and 22 from Yamato; 36 and 22 from Sanuki; and 36 and 21 from Settsu. Note that these areas are in the north-western part of Japan (Mutsu, Kōzuke, Musashi, Echigo); areas that can be reached conveniently by sea (Ise, Suruga, Settsu, Shikoku); and geographically close areas such as Yamato and Ōmi.

Historically, the earliest centres for such activity were among the *sendatsu* of the Kinki and Chūbu areas, later spreading to the Chūgoku and Kantō areas, and finally to Echigo, Tōhoku, Shikoku, and Kyūshū. The activities of the *sendatsu* in the Kantō and Tōhoku areas continued well into the Sengoku period in the early sixteenth century.

Next, based on the *oshi monjo*, let us look at the different types of *sendatsu* and patrons. First there were *sendatsu* directly affiliated with *oshi* from the very start, such as the 'Jippō-in *sendatsu*'. These were only a minority, however. The second type were *sendatsu* who came to Kumano from another area and then travelled around the country inviting and soliciting patrons to go to Kumano on pilgrimage. These are called *yugyō* 遊行 (wandering) *sendatsu*. These people were called 'Ise ajari', 'Wakasa ajari', and so forth depending on their place of origin. The third type were called *zaichi* 在地 (regional representative) *sendatsu* because they stayed in a certain

130

local area, such as a sacred mountain like Nikkō, a certain large shrine or temple, or a Kumano manor, and served there as Kumano *sendatsu* and representatives of Kumano Shugen. The fourth type were Honzan-ha *sendatsu* affiliated with places like Shin-Kumano or Shōgo-in in Kyōto, or members of the 36 Tōzan-ha *sendatsu*. These were called Shugen *sendatsu*. The fifth type were religious figures other than Shugen *sendatsu*. These include the Nenbutsu-hijiri 念仏聖 of the Jishū 時宗, Yin-Yang masters 陰陽師, and lay people who served in the role of *sendatsu*.

Next, patrons included priests and nuns of regional shrines and temples, family members of warrior families or their servants, and common people such as farmers and merchants. In general, at first wandering *sendatsu* would lead religious members of a regional temple or shrine on a Kumano pilgrimage. Then the religious members of a regional temple or shrine would become a 'representative' *sendatsu*. This pattern can be found in many areas. Also, in the Kantō and Tōhoku areas most of the patrons were from warrior families or their servants, whereas in the Kansai area many of the patrons were merchants or artisans.

Finally, let us take a look at developments in the organisation of *sendatsu*. First, as we can see in the *Ise ajari montei-hiki* 伊勢阿闍梨門弟引 (Guide for Ise ajari disciples), there were various special types of *sendatsu* and their disciples, and it appears that it was the disciples who actually accompanied the pilgrims to Kumano. These *sendatsu* and their disciples are referred to, respectively, as the *hon-sendatsu* 本先達 and *toki-no-sendatsu* 時の先達; the person who actually accompanied the pilgrims to Kumano was sometimes called *michi-sendatsu* 道先達. Second, as this kind of sharing of responsibilities developed, titles such as *dai-sendatsu* 大先達 and *shō-sendatsu* 小先達, that distinguished superior and inferior ranks, began to be used. Third, there appeared hereditary *sendatsu* families, wherein the role of *sendatsu* was handed down from generation to generation. These families would often place a member of their family in various regions, and these would act as *sendatsu* for patrons in those regions. For these *sendatsu* families, the original, first-generation *sendatsu* was called *konpon sendatsu* 根本先達. The Mochi-watatsu 持渡津 *sendatsu*, who were active in the northern part of Japan (Ōshū) from the end of the thirteenth century and into the fourteenth century, are representative of these families. Fourth, the temple families (*inge* 院家) of Shōgo-in were appointed the regional representatives as *sendatsu*. These formed the base of the later Honzan-ha organisation.

In addition to these types of organisation, there were also groups of ascetics who gathered around Kumano *sendatsu* in areas such as the northern part of Ōmi, the Shirakawa area of Mutsu, and in Sagami. The Tōzan Sanjūroku Shō-dai-sendatsu, an organisation of *sendatsu* in the Kinki area, is thought to be an outgrowth of such a group. Also, in places such as Ōmi, Kyōto, Ōsaka and Sakai, groups of lay people gathered around *sendatsu* to organise pilgrimages to Kumano.

Branch shrines of the Kumano Gongen, like those of Hachiman, Ise, and Inari, sprang up across the country. A map of their distribution shows that these shrines developed along the sea coast following the Kuroshio current: to the north-east from Mie and Aichi to Shizuoka, Kanagawa, Chiba, and Fukushima; and to the south-east to Kōchi, Kagoshima, and as far as Okinawa. There are also many Kumano shrines along the Seto inland sea coast. This reveals that the dissemination of the Kumano Gongen was closely related to sea travel. Also, during the period of retired emperors, the Kumano Gongen were enshrined as the guardian deities of the manors that belonged to Kumano. There are records of enshrining the Kumano Gongen among the warriors in the period of the Northern and Southern courts, and such enshrining was conducted by Kumano *yamabushi* and Kumano *bikuni* 比丘尼 (nuns) from the Sengoku period up to the Edo period. In any case it is clear that the Kumano Gongen enshrined across the country were the focus of activity by Kumano *sendatsu*.

THE DEVELOPMENT OF KUMANO SHUGEN

The *bettō* system began to lose its authority in Kumano from around the end of the Kamakura period. In its stead the Kumano Sanzan *kengyō* officials gained political power owing to support from the manors, and eventually came to dominate the Kumano Sanzan area. The post of Kumano Sanzan *kengyō* had been held by the head (*chōri* 長吏) of Onjōji since the time of Zōyo. In the latter half of the fourteenth century, however, Ryōyu 良瑜 of Shōgo-in (the Onjōji branch temple) was appointed *kengyō*. Ryōyu was very active: he began the practice of the Jinzen *kanchō* initiation in Ōmine, and 16 times filled the central role of *chūdan* 中壇 in *godanhō* 五壇法 ceremonies sponsored by Ashikaga Yoshimitsu. Eventually his successors at Shōgo-in were appointed to the post of Kumano Sanzan *kengyō*. Also, the temple Jōjō-in 乗々院 of the Shin-Kumano Nyakuōji *bettō* in Higashiyama was appointed as Kumano Sanzan *bugyō* 奉行 by Ashikaga Takauji 足利尊氏, and assisted the *kengyō*, and eventually came to be responsible for control over the Kumano Sanzan and the Kumano *sendatsu*. From around the end of the fourteenth century, Nyakuōji guaranteed the position of *sendatsu* to Kumano *sendatsu*, and in exchange received part of the fees that the *sendatsu* were paid by their patrons.

Dōkō 道興 (1465–1501) of Shōgo-in, seeking to organise all of the

Kumano *sendatsu*, especially those in the Mutsu and Kantō areas, left Kyōto in 1486 and travelled around through the Hokuriku and then the Kantō and Tōhoku areas over the next year. During these travels Dōkō visited a large number of Kumano *sendatsu*, staying at the lodgings of the major *sendatsu*. He also practiced mountain austerities at the major sacred mountains such as Hakusan, Tateyama, Mt Fuji, and Nikkō, made pilgrimages to shrines and temples throughout the country, and enjoyed the hospitality of the local governor of these places. It should be added that Dōkō was the elder brother of Konoe Masaie 近衛政家, the current *kanpaku*, and was retained by the shōgun Ashikaga Yoshimasa 足利義政. Thus the Kumano *sendatsu* in the local areas expected his protection, and joined his bandwagon.

From around the middle of the sixteenth century (1532–55), the head monk of Shōgo-in began to grant the status of *nen-gyōji* 年行事 to important local Kumano *sendatsu*. In turn the *nen-gyōji* were given responsibility for organising the local *yamabushi* of a certain area and the *sendatsu* who would guide patrons to Kumano and other sacred sites. They were also responsible for the distribution of charms, and other religious activities. Shōgo-in received a portion of the income from this activity. The area controlled by one of these *nen-gyōji* was called *kasumi* 霞 (territory for religious activity). Moreover, the local governor permitted Shōgo-in to appoint the *nen-gyōji*, and guaranteed the activity of the *nen-gyōji* in the part of his *kasumi* that belonged to the domain.

This method of governing by Shōgo-in is a different style from that of the Kumano *oshi*. The Kumano *oshi* stayed in Kumano and received offerings directly from their patrons who visited Kumano. Shōgo-in, on the other hand, appointed Kumano *sendatsu* as *nen-gyōji* and guaranteed their control over the *yamabushi* and their right to conduct prayers and purification rites, and to guide their followers in their *kasumi* to sacred places. In turn Shōgo-in received a part of the income that the *nen-gyōji* and *yamabushi* earned through these activities.

In sum, the organisation of Kumano Sanzan consisted of the relationship between the *oshi* and *sendatsu*/patrons. In contrast, the Shōgo-in organisation emphasised direct control of the *sendatsu* by the headquarters (Shōgo-in), and did not include the patrons.

In the Edo period, the head of Shōgo-in (the Kumano Sanzan *kengyō*) left the general management of the Kumano organisation to the Nyakuōji (Kumano Sanzan *bugyō*) and the temple families directly related to Shōgo-in. They controlled the 27 *sendatsu* (i.e. the religious rulers of the *kuni*), the *nen-gyōji* of *gun* (districts), the assistant *nen-gyōji* (*jun-nen-gyōji*), and the subordinate *yamabushi* under the authority of Shōgo-in. In this way the organisation of Kumano Shugen that used to be based on a relationship

133

between *oshi* and patrons, eventually developed into the Honzan-ha, the centralised organisation of *yamabushi*.

Finally I would like to say a few words about the influence of Kumano Shugen on Japanese folk religion. Worthy of note so far as ideas are concerned are the stories about the origin of the Kumano deities as avatars of divine personalities from China and India. In Japan, there were traditionally 12 figures identified as the *kami* of mountains (*yama no kami* 山の神), and these stories gave character and content to the *twelve* deities and provided them with authority. With regard to organisation, what is important is that the Honzan-ha that developed out of Kumano Shugen put down deep roots in local areas around Japan during the pre-modern era. It responded to the needs of the local villagers by providing religious festivals, prayers, and rituals, and leaders for pilgrimage to sacred sites. In its organisation of pilgrimages and ascents of sacred mountains it took as its model the organisation of *oshi*, *sendatsu*, and patrons that originated in Kumano. In addition, *shugenja* have had a great influence on Japanese folk religion through their participation in village rituals, folk arts, annual observances, rites of passage, and prayers and incantations.

English translation by Paul L. Swanson

6

Keeping the faith: *bakuhan* policy towards religions in seventeenth-century Japan

Peter Nosco

INTRODUCTION

Two questions that continue to provoke lively debate in studies of early-modern Japan are, first, how ambitious the *bakuhan* 幕藩 enterprise was, and, second, how successful this state was in achieving its ambitions. Most scholars accept the premise that the domainal (*han*) and central (*bakufu*) governments of Tokugawa (1600–1867) Japan cumulatively exercised unprecedented social and political control, but the totalitarian or 'absolutist' properties of *bakuhan* government remain arguable.[1] The issues are complex and often confusing, since the Tokugawa state's control over individuals appears at times, especially during its first half-century, and in principle, to have been near total, and at other times, as well as in practice, to have been relatively relaxed.

Analyses of *bakuhan* power have often included some reference to policies concerning religious institutions, but these studies have been in various ways limited. They have tended to focus on either the experiences of the Buddhists or those of the Christians, and have not drawn insights from the comparative analysis of both. In general, they have accepted state policy toward religion uncritically, equating the declaration of policy with its effective enforcement, and they have been written either by political and institutional historians who underestimated the utility of *bakuhan* religious policy as a barometer of its power, or by students of culture whose understanding of the political dimensions of their subject has been at best naive.

Further, most of these studies have emphasised, if not overemphasised, the *bakuhan* state's power vis-à-vis religions and religionists by extrapolating from the state's early successes in this arena. In brief and in its most commonly

1 Mary Elizabeth Berry succinctly summarises the orthodox understanding that the 'shogun and the daimyo of the Tokugawa period collectively monopolized a previously dispersed authority over land and its resources, military force, law and judicature, cities and commerce': 'Public peace and private attachment: the goals and conduct of power in early modern Japan', *Journal of Japanese Studies* 12 (1986): 237. James W. White has written that 'the major reason for stating that Tokugawa Japan approached absolutism is not because it was so very absolute, but because the absolute states of Europe were not so very absolute themselves': 'State growth and popular protest in Tokugawa Japan', *Journal of Japanese Studies* 14 (1988): 6.

stated form, this view regards Oda Nobunaga's 織田信長 (1534–82) destruction of the Enryakuji 延暦寺 and Ishiyama Honganji 石山本願寺 fortresses in 1571 and 1580 respectively, and the crushing of the Shimabara 島原 rebellion in 1638 as bracketing a period of intensified state control of religion that set the tone for the remaining two centuries of Tokugawa rule. This is not to say that these events were not of a watershed nature: the military power of the temples was broken by Oda Nobunaga's campaigns; these temples were eventually brought under the authority of the *bakuhan* state; and the Shimabara rebellion was the last major, and in many ways the most dramatic, instance of resistance to the state in the seventeenth century. Nonetheless, the question of state religious policy in seventeenth-century Japan was altogether more complex than the standard accounts suggest.

In this essay, I compare the state's policies toward Christianity and Buddhism, examine continuities and discontinuities in religious policy from the late sixteenth century to the seventeenth, and attempt to evaluate critically evidence of both the state's enforcement of, and the populace's compliance with, its stated religious policies during the seventeenth century. I also argue three points. First, while the succession of elites responsible for the unprecedented consolidation of power in Japan that occurred from roughly 1570 to 1651 sought to bring religions and religious institutions under their absolute control, the limits of such a totalising strategy were already apparent to bakufu and domainal leaders by the mid-seventeenth century. Second, as a response to this apprehension of its own limitations in this area, the *bakuhan* state began, and for two centuries and more continued, tacitly to accept its inability to control what individuals believed, even as it sought in other ways to expand its administrative authority over religious institutions. And third, the state thereby allowed what Warren and Laslett have termed 'private-life secrecy' in the sphere of religion.[2]

EARLY RELIGIOUS POLICY UNDER NOBUNAGA AND HIDEYOSHI: THE EFFORT TO ACHIEVE MILITARY CONTROL, 1571–98

The most conspicuous manifestations of the religious policies of the Oda and Toyotomi 豊臣 regimes are those that most obviously concerned power and resulted in death. These include the military defeat of the warrior monks of the Tendai 天台 sect's spiritual centre at Enryakuji on Mt Hiei 比叡 in 1571,

2 Barbara Warren and Barbara Laslett, 'Privacy and secrecy: a conceptual comparison', in Stanton Tefft, ed., *Secrecy: a cross-cultural perspective* (New York: Human Sciences Press, 1980), pp. 25–34.

the surrender of the Pure Land sect's Ishiyama Honganji fortress in 1580, and the execution by crucifixion of 26 Christians in Nagasaki in 1597. The reason for this level of violence, at least against the Buddhists, was that the major Buddhist institutions had collectively amassed levels of control over land and individuals that exceeded that of all but the most powerful daimyō. Commanding armies that included both legions of the faithful and professional security forces, the largest of these institutions, like the Tendai headquarters on Mt Hiei and the Ishiyama Honganji fortress, were fundamental obstacles to anyone aspiring to absolute control over the main island of Honshū. Oda Nobunaga's campaigns against these foes took the better part of a decade and resulted in the deaths of tens of thousands of people.

His preoccupation with military control notwithstanding, Oda Nobunaga was clearly aware of the civil-administrative dimension of policy toward religious bodies and established a number of precedents in this area which were later adopted by the Tokugawa bakufu. As early as 1575, in the midst of his military campaigns against the militant Pure Land Buddhist faithful (*monto*, 門徒), he established the equivalent office of what in the Tokugawa period was known as the office of *Jisha bugyō* 寺社奉行, or Commissioner of Temples and Shrines.[3] Further, in 1579 he utilised the format of a 'debate' at his Azuchi 安土 castle between monks of the Pure Land and Nichiren 日蓮 sects in order to resolve a dispute between the two. This proved to be the first of a succession of such performances during the next century in which Japan's central government was drawn into internecine religious conflicts in the role of reluctant arbiter.

Perhaps because the Buddhists were no longer a meaningful political or military threat after Nobunaga's death in 1582, and perhaps also because, unlike Nobunaga, his ambitions included subjugation of the Christian stronghold of Kyūshū, Toyotomi Hideyoshi 豊臣秀吉 was more concerned with Christianity and less with Buddhism than Nobunaga had been. At times Hideyoshi reversed religous decisions made by Nobunaga, as when he ordered the Pure Land 'victors' in the Azuchi debate of 1579 to return to the Nichiren representatives the document admitting defeat that the latter had submitted to the former. More often than not, however, Hideyoshi's religious policies continued trends or tendencies begun by Nobunaga, as in his appointment of Maeda Gen'i 前田玄以 (1539–1602) a cleric formerly trusted by Nobunaga, to administer religious matters as his commissioner of shrines and temples, or again in his destruction of the Shingon 真言 faithful at Negoro 根来, which differed from Nobunaga's bloody campaigns against Mt Hiei and

---

3 Neil McMullin, *Buddhism and the state in sixteenth-century Japan* (Princeton: Princeton University Press, 1984), pp. 225–6.

Ishiyama Honganji only by being smaller in scale.[4]

Hideyoshi's political, military, and religious goals inevitably overlapped, as in his 'sword hunt' which proved as helpful in the confiscation of weaponry from the major Buddhist fortresses as from his enemies among the daimyō. At times lessons learned in one arena proved transferable to another, as when Hideyoshi threatened with crucifixion those peasants who concealed their fields from his cadastral surveyors.[5] Throughout his career, Hideyoshi remained flexible and was prepared to change his religious policy whenever necessary to meet those circumstances that would suit his political or military ends.

To summarise the key features of the religious policies of Oda Nobunaga and Toyotomi Hideyoshi, one observes that both were more concerned with what the leaders and members of religious communities controlled, did, or threatened to do, than with what they believed or averred. Whenever representatives of religious communities sought their intervention to address issues of doctrine or belief, both Nobunaga and Hideyoshi resisted being drawn into such discussions unless, as in the 1579 Azuchi debate, other ends might be served. The Hideyoshi years represent a transition in religious policy from the Nobunaga era, when the principal intention was to neutralise the Buddhist institutions militarily, to the Tokugawa Ieyasu 徳川家康 years when, as we shall see, the effort was redirected almost exclusively toward political and economic control. The key administrative differences between Hideyoshi and Nobunaga in the area of religious policy concerned not the general goals of control over land and persons, but such specifics as attitudes toward individual denominations or creeds, as seen in the execution of the Nagasaki Catholics which was ultimately more significant for what it heralded than for what it accomplished.

THE IEYASU YEARS, 1597–1616: THE EFFORT TO ACHIEVE POLITICAL AND ECONOMIC CONTROL

Tokugawa Ieyasu (1542–1616) was the first of the unifiers to use religious policy as an instrument of purely political and economic, as opposed to military, control. Nevertheless, like Nobunaga and Hideyoshi before him, his

4 Maeda Gen'i was also one of Hideyoshi's original Five Commissioners (Gobugyō 五奉行) of the capital, Kyōto.

5 Wakita Osamu, 'The social and economic consequences of unification', in *The Cambridge history of Japan* (Cambridge: Cambridge University Press, 1991–), vol. 4, p.109.

initial exposure to it concerned a military issue and came in the form of the need to respond to an insurrection of Pure Land Ikkō 一向 faithful in Mikawa 三河 in 1563–4. Since many of Ieyasu's retainers were of this Ikkō faction, quelling the insurrection provided the young Ieyasu with valuable experience in the 'diplomacy' of religious policy.[6] Further, those religious traditions to which the most state attention was devoted during the regimes of Nobunaga and Hideyoshi, the Christians, the True Pure Land and *fuju fuse* 不受不施 Nichiren Buddhists, were precisely those that for the most part prospered during the years of Ieyasu's rule from the death of Hideyoshi in 1598 until his own death in 1616.[7]

Of all Buddhist denominations, it was the Nichiren *fuju fuse* extremists who received most of Ieyasu's reluctant attention. The issue that provoked the crisis was not new and had already proved difficult for Hideyoshi. The Nichiren sect had generally viewed Toyotomi Hideyoshi with favour by comparison with Nobunaga, principally because Hideyoshi had ordered the Pure Land monks to return to them the document admitting defeat in the Azuchi debate. In 1582, however, the office of Maeda Gen'i, who had been charged with the oversight of temple and shrine affairs, ordered each of the so-called 'ten sects' of Buddhism to send one hundred monks to participate in a monthly memorial service for Hideyoshi's ancestors at the newly-built Myōhōin 妙法院 Hall of the Great Buddha (Daibutsuden 大仏殿) in Kyōto. This became an issue in the Nichiren sect, since to comply with it meant compromising the centuries-old *fuju fuse* principle, which held it to be impermissible for the faithful either to accept offerings from, or to offer alms to, those outside the sect.

At a meeting of the Nichiren leadership held at the Honkokuji 本国寺 in Rokujō 六条, Kyōto, the majority supported an accommodationist position of endorsing participation on a 'one time only' basis; but a fundamentalist, extremist faction, led by Nichiō 日奥 (1565–1630), opposed even this limited participation and withdrew from the meeting. Hideyoshi reacted to this slight, as he perceived it, from Nichiō's faction by granting a request from the Pure Land sect to be ranked higher than the Nichiren sect, which was as a result demoted to the sixth rank among the ten participating denominations. The accommodationists petitioned Hideyoshi in 1598 to intervene and punish Nichiō for refusing to comply with his demand, but Hideyoshi seems never to have responded to the petition and died later that year. Perhaps because they were seeking to impress Hideyoshi's successor with their obedience, the

---

6 Tamamuro Fumio 圭室文雄, *Nihon bukkyōshi: kinsei* 日本仏教史―近世 (Yoshikawa Kōbunkan, 1987), p. 6.

7 As opposed to the relatively brief period from 1603 to 1605 during which he actually held the position of shōgun.

Kyōto accommodationist temples in 1599 pressed their cause anew with Tokugawa Ieyasu. Anxious to avoid being drawn into what he perceived to be a matter internal to the Nichiren sect, Ieyasu offered generous terms of compromise, which Nichiō nonetheless rejected. Interpreting Nichiō's response as a challenge, Ieyasu then ordered the Nichiren sect's disputants to debate their differences before him at Ōsaka Castle, and as a result of his 'defeat', Nichiō was exiled to Tsushima 対島 from 1600 until 1612, when he was pardoned by Itakura Katsushige 板倉勝重, successor to Maeda Gen'i as Ieyasu's Superintendent of Temples and Shrines (*jisha bugyō*). The *fuju fuse* minority and the accommodationist majority achieved a reconciliation in 1616 even though some members continued their quarrel in the form of treatises and rebuttals.[8]

From 1601 to 1615 there was a flurry of legislation directed against the other major Buddhist sects and intended to begin the incorporation of their temples politically and economically within the nascent structure of the *bakuhan* state. Between 1601 and 1615 no fewer than 44 regulatory directives were directed at specific temples or sects.[9] Interestingly, the Nichiren sect was untouched by this legislation, for the state's persecution in earnest of the *fuju fuse* extremists did not begin until late 1616, after Ieyasu's death.

Despite the impressive volume, this legislation was in all likelihood not particularly onerous for the temples and sects concerned, since it was written by Ieyasu's trusted advisor on spiritual matters, the Zen monk Konchiin Sūden 金地院崇伝 (1569–1633), and was based largely on drafts, and

8 In order of composition, these include Nichiō's *Hokkeshū shomonryū kindan hōse jōjō* 法華宗諸門流禁断謗施条々 (1615), Nichiken's 日乾 *Ha ō ki* 破奥記 (1615), Nichiō's *Shūgi seihōron* 宗義制法論 (1616), Nichiken's *Hōse juyōron* 謗施受用論 (1622[?]), and Nichiō's *Kindan hōseron* 禁断謗施論 (1624). The *Shūgi seihōron* summarised the reasons for non-participation in the memorial service as follows: (i) it is forbidden to worship in front of the Buddha of another sect; (ii) it is wrong that the Nichiren sect has been assigned a lower place than the Pure Land; (iii) Hideyoshi was never a believer in the Lotus sūtra; and (iv) the Kyōto Shoshidai 所司代 (deputy) had upheld the right of the Nichiren sect to practise their faith in the manner of their choosing. See Tamamuro, 'Kakure daimoku' かくれ題目, in Kataoka Yakichi 片岡弥吉 et al., *Kinsei no chika shinkō* 近世の地下信仰 (Hyōronsha, 1974), p. 140.

9 Tamamuro, *Edo bakufu no shūkyō tōsei* 江戸幕府の宗教統制 (Hyōronsha, 1971), pp. 13–17. The 1601 legislation concerned the conduct of monks on Mt Kōya 高野 and sought to distinguish administratively the *gyōnin* 行人, 'lay brothers', on Mt Kōya from the *gakuryō* 学侶, or traditional clergy. Of the remaining 43 directives, 33 were directed at Tendai and Shingon temples, while the remainder went largely to Pure Land and Zen 禅 temples of the Sōtō 曹洞 and Rinzai 臨済 sects, with one going to the Hossō 法相 sect, and in addition there was the *Shie hatto* 紫衣法度 of 1613.

responses to those drafts, submitted by the institutions themselves. In this respect, the significance of the regulations lies less in their restrictive character than in their attempt to establish through precedent the principle of the bakufu's right to intervene in the administration of temples and shrines. The legislation thus effectively brought to an end the tradition of immunity that temples had enjoyed during the medieval period, when various forms of secular authority were regarded as not valid within temple precincts. It also defined the essence of the priestly vocation to be the study of doctrine and the maintenance of discipline, requiring priests to affiliate with temple organisations, thereby limiting the possibility of 'free-lance' proselytism.[10]

Tokugawa Ieyasu's religious policies even touched the imperial court. One important source of income for the court had been the right to confer *shie* 紫衣, or 'purple robes', upon prelates. In 1613 the bakufu issued regulations, again drafted by Sūden, that required the prior approval of the bakufu for any imperial decisions to confer *shie*. Though both Nobunaga and Hideyoshi had sought to enforce their authority over the imperial court in religious matters, Ieyasu's initiative concerning the 'purple robes' represented interference with one source of imperial revenue and heralded the more stringent regulations of the *Kinchū narabi ni kuge shohatto* 禁中並公家諸法度 ordinances of 1615 governing the conduct of the imperial household and the courtiers.

Another expansion of religious policy during Ieyasu's rule was the attempt to organise all temples by sect into a system of main temples and branch temples, giving substantial doctrinal, administrative and policing authority to the designated main temples.[11] This system was well advanced in the Kantō 関東, or Eastern Provinces, prior to Ieyasu's death, but only later reached the same stage of development in the Kansai 関西, or Western Provinces.[12] Though it applied only to the Buddhists and was initially less than national in its application, this was yet another important step in the effort to construct a comprehensive organisational system for all religious institutions, and thereby eventually to incorporate them within the *bakuhan* structure.

It is against this backdrop that one can contextualise Ieyasu's policies toward the Christians. Again, matters of personal faith were not his principal concern whether in his dealings with the Christians or in his responses to the

---

10 Tamamuro, *Edo bakufu no shūkyō tōsei*, pp. 20–2, and *Nihon bukkyōshi: kinsei*, pp. 5, 25–6.

11 Takano Toshihiko 高埜利彦, *Kinsei Nihon no kokka kenryoku to shūkyō* 近世日本の国家権力と宗教 (Tōkyō Daigaku Shuppankai, 1989), p. 86.

12 Tamamuro, *Edo bakufu no shūkyō tōsei*, pp. 33, 45. Shingon temples were an exception: they appear to have been brought under equal measures of control throughout Japan prior to Ieyasu's death in 1616.

Buddhists, and his response to the Christians and their creed followed much the same pattern as his response to the *fuju fuse* controversy. After initial reluctance to be drawn into the controversy at all, he preferred to search for a compromise, and once convinced that further negotiation was unlikely to bear fruit, he responded decisively.

Ieyasu was for most of his life anything but the anti-Christian autocrat that many studies suggest. The number of Christians in Japan approximately doubled from about 150,000 to 300,000 during the years between Hideyoshi's death and the last years of Ieyasu's life. Further, this interval also roughly coincides with the only period (1598–1614) when a Roman Catholic bishop was allowed to remain in continual residence in Japan. In fact, until just two years before his death, Christianity flourished in Japan as never before. It was not until Ieyasu's suspicions regarding the political loyalty of the Christian daimyō and his distrust of the foreign clergy outweighed his inclination toward religious tolerance that the bakufu forbade Christianity throughout Japan, in the eighth month of 1612. The systematic persecution of Christians began with the expulsion of the clergy (the decree is untitled) in 1614.[13] Even though not a single Christian was executed because of his or her faith during the years of Ieyasu's rule, Christianity in Japan began to decline in response to the persecution initiated during the last years of his life.

RELIGIOUS POLICY FROM 1616 TO 1639: CONSOLIDATION OF CONTROL

The principal developments after 1616 in state policy toward religion include the formal proscription of the *fuju fuse* faction, the intensified persecution of Christians, and a new emphasis on encouraging apostasy. This was also a crucial period of transition in religious policy in Japan, as the limits of the *bakuhan* state's capacity to control thought and belief first became apparent. It was during these years, between the death of Ieyasu in 1616 and the final *sakoku* 鎖国 edict in 1639, that the greatest number of executions of Christians occurred. In just 23 years the number of Christians in Japan was reduced almost by half to 150,000, roughly the number at the time of Hideyoshi's death. In other ways, however, the Christians emerged with surprising signs of strength. For example, the Jesuits alone claimed more than 17,000 adult

13 The effect of these measures was immediately apparent; for example, in 1612 the Inaba 稲葉 family, daimyō of Usuki in Hyūga, reversed their hitherto sympathetic attitude toward Christianity and began their own persecutions. See Murai Sanae 村井早苗, *Bakuhansei seiritsu to kirishitan kinsei* 幕藩制成立とキリシタン禁制 (Bunken Shuppan, 1987), p. 68.

baptisms during the years from 1614 to 1626, and since Jesuit clergy were smuggled into the country after the 1614 expulsion order, the number of Jesuit clergy in the country actually increased to 36 by the year 1621.[14]

Since existing policies were increasingly perceived by the bakufu to be less than wholly effective, Tokugawa Iemitsu 徳川家光, who succeeded his father Hidetada 秀忠 (1579–1631) as shōgun in 1623, at first attempted simply to intensify enforcement of the policies without altering their substance. Some 50 Christians were burnt at the stake in 1623, one year after 55 Christians had been executed in Nagasaki. These executions went some way towards achieving the goal of suppressing Christianity, but the success was by no means complete. For example, the fact that some 150,000 Christians renounced their faith during these years is partial evidence of the success of the bakufu's anti-Christian policy, but at least as remarkable is the fact that some 150,000, for the most part poorly trained, commoner Christians dared to sustain their faith in blatant violation of bakufu law and at considerable risk to their lives.[15] From the perspective of the various Roman Catholic missions to Japan, it was fortunate that by this point their leadership had for over a decade been preparing the faithful for the anticipated oppression and the possible future absence of clergy and need to move 'underground'.[16]

There was also a new emphasis on apostasy, which is illustrated by the story of the Japanese Jesuit priest Antonio Ishida. His treatment is interesting because it suggests that the *bakuhan* state was prepared to tolerate limited compliance with its religious directives. Ishida became the personal project of Takenaka Uneme 竹中采女, Nagasaki Commissioner (*bugyō*) from 1626 to 1633, yet despite imprisonment and probable torture he refused to apostasise and even rejected an offer made by Takenaka in 1631 allowing him to believe whatever he pleased so long as he publicly submitted to the shōgun's policies.[17]

---

14 Jurgis Elisonas, 'Christianity and the daimyō', in *The Cambridge history of Japan*, vol. 4, pp. 301–72.

15 Christians who renounced their faith and converted to Buddhism do not seem to have gravitated toward any one particular sect. Of some 121 Christians in Hirado 平戸 who renounced their faith, 31 registered at Nichiren temples, 25 at Pure Land temples, 25 at True Pure Land temples, 37 at Zen temples, and 3 at Shingon temples. See Murai, *Bakuhansei seiritsu to kirishitan kinsei*, p. 171.

16 The efforts made on behalf of the Santa Maria sodality are illustrative. In 1617 Geronimo Rodrigues wrote the *Gojōten no Santa Mariya no mikumi*, with a section outlining the responsibilities of the group's leadership, and in 1621 Anotonio Janone wrote a a set of organisational principles for the sodality entitled *Santa Mariya no mikumi no okite* さんたまりやの御組の掟 which he felt 'everyone in the membership should know'. See Kataoka Yakichi, 'Kakure kirishitan', in Kataoka et al., *Kinsei no chika shinkō*, p. 32, and Peter Nosco, 'Some problematic issues in the study of the "underground" Christians', *Japanese Journal of Religious Studies* 20.1(1993): 10.

17 George Elison, *Deus destroyed: the image of Christianity in early modern Japan*

One discerns here a new distinction acceptable to the state between what might be termed style and substance, a distinction that was to be further sharpened later and to which we shall return.

The bakufu's policy toward the *fuju fuse* extremists again in various ways parallels that toward the Christians, just as does the *fuju fuse* faction's response anticipate that of the Christians. Nichiō's exile seems not to have impressed the Kyōto *fuju fuse* temples any more than did the persecution of Christianity impress the Christians. At the time of Nichiō's pardon in 1612, fully one-half of the Nichiren temples in Kyōto supported his position, and the *fuju fuse* principle was officially recognised by the bakufu in 1620.[18]

It was the death of shōgun Hidetada's wife in 1626 that precipitated a crisis. Just as had been the case three decades earlier with the memorial services for Hideyoshi's ancestors, the issue again revolved around an order to attend a funeral service, this time for Hidetada's wife. The accommodationist faction attended the services, but the extremists, now led by Nichiju 日樹 (1574–1631), refused to do so. In 1629 the accommodationists pressed their suit against the extremists anew with the Commissioner for Shrines and Temples. In response to their suit yet another 'debate' was held between the factions in 1630, as a result of which the *fuju fuse* faction and its practices were officially proscribed. In a gesture emblematic of the often perfunctory nature of religious policies at this time, in the fourth month of 1630 Nichiō was again exiled, despite the fact that he had died in the previous month, along with Nichiju and the other leaders.

As Tamamuro Fumio has observed, what began essentially as a doctrinal issue, represented by various priests identified with specific temples, developed into a feud between temples and finally into a contest between the bakufu and the Nichiren sect over the issues of the separation of church and state and state control of religion.[19] The fact that the Ikegami Honmonji 池上本門寺 temple, the new spiritual headquarters of the extremists, was in Edo surely contributed to the bakufu's perception of it, if not as a threat, then at least as a defiant element, and for this reason the interests of the bakufu and the Nichiren accommodationists converged in the suppression of the extremists. Like the Christians, the *fuju fuse* extremists went 'underground', though their sanctuary

---

(Cambridge, Mass.: Council on East Asian Studies, Harvard University, 1973), pp. 188–9, and Herbert Cieslik, *Kirishitan jinbutsu no kenkyū* キリシタン人物の研究 (Yoshikawa Kōbunkan, 1963), pp. 98–107.

18 The principal official in this case was again Itakura Katsushige of the Samuraidokoro 侍所. See Jeffrey Robert Hunter, 'The *fuju fuse* controversy in Nichiren Buddhism: the debate between Busshōin Nichio and Jakushōin Nichiken', unpublished PhD dissertation (University of Wisconsin at Madison, 1989), pp. 200–9.

19 Tamamuro, 'Kakure daimoku', pp. 165–6.

lay not within the relatively sequestered community of the village, but rather within the labyrinthine network of Nichiren temples which, it will be recalled, had been essentially exempted from the flurry of temple-directed decrees of the preceding Ieyasu years. Because their underground movement was veiled in this manner, it proved impossible for the government to eliminate the *fuju fuse* faction.

In 1631 the bakufu issued a decree to all main Buddhist temples (*honzan* 本山) ordering them to provide exhaustive lists of their branch temples throughout the country, prohibiting the construction of new temples without bakufu permission, and forbidding the naming or renaming of a branch temple without authorisation from the main temple. This represents yet another attempt to regulate at least one aspect of what was otherwise proving to be a difficult situation, but compliance with this decree was at best partial. The Pure Land sect was the first to comply, taking just over one year to submit its list; a number of the other major sects followed suit over the next ten years. However, the resurgent True Pure Land sect submitted no registers; the registers submitted by the Tendai sect were incomplete; and in general the registers tended to be more detailed for the eastern parts of the country than for the western. In fact the registers did not become complete until 1786–95.[20]

Furthermore the registers drawn up in compliance with this decree provide the most compelling evidence of the *fuju fuse* faction's resistance to the state's attempts to proscribe it. Of the 1,075 temples recorded on the Nichiren sect's list of 1633, the Ikegami Honmonji, the principal *fuju fuse* temple, had 165 branch temples. Of course, not all of these temples were necessarily involved in the clandestine pursuit of *fuju fuse* practices, but a list compiled 30 years later for the sect's internal use listed 134 of them (81%) as retaining this extremist character. Similarly, a list compiled in late 1633 of the branch temples of the Myōkakuji 妙覚寺, another spiritual centre for the extremists, listed 84 temples as entirely *fuju fuse* in character and an additional seven temples as partially within the fold.[21] Clearly, despite the bakufu's relative success in incorporating the country's temples within the administrative structure of the *bakuhan* system, it was not proving easy to ensure that both Christians and Buddhists complied in matters of belief and practice.

In its dealings with the imperial court also the bakufu began to sense the limitations of its power even as it continued to enforce, at times heavy-handedly, a measure of compliance. In 1627 Emperor Go-Mizunoo bestowed the coveted *shie* upon prelates of the Daitokuji 大徳寺 and Myōshinji 妙心寺 temples, without obtaining the bakufu's prior approval as the 1613 bakufu restrictions

---

20 Takano, *Kinsei nihon no kokka kenryoku to shūkyō*, p. 86; Tamamuro, *Nihon bukkyōshi: kinsei*, p. 51; and Tamamuro, *Edo bakufu no shūkyō tōsei*, pp. 51–2.
21 Tamamuro, 'Kakure daimoku', pp. 167–70.

required. As a result, in what came to be known as the 'Purple robes incident' (*shie jiken* 紫衣事件), the bakufu in 1627 simply declared the conferred robes to be invalid and arranged for their confiscation. When a number of priests from the Daitokuji and Myōshinji, including Takuan Sōhō 沢庵宗彭, complained about this, the bakufu ordered them into exile. For his part, the hapless but ever defiant Emperor Go-Mizunoo abdicated in 1629 in a final, albeit fruitless, gesture of defiance against the bakufu.[22]

It was not until 1635, after the death of Sūden, that the bakufu formally instituted the office of *Jisha bugyō* as a continuing office. It was typically headed by *fudai* 普代 daimyō (three at first, later as many as five), whose responsibilities included not just oversight of the administration of temples and shrines, but also supervision of such inhabitants of the margins of Tokugawa society as *bikuni* 比丘尼 nuns, actors, and blind court musicians (*kengyō* 検校), as well as teachers of such subjects as linked verse, yin-yang divination, *go* 碁 and *shōgi* 将棋. One indication of the importance that the bakufu attached to this office is the fact that the *Jisha bugyō* were more powerful than other *bugyō* since they could initiate inquiries and even begin a trial without soliciting prior bakufu permission, and had the independent authority to pass sentences up to the severity of exile.[23]

Other legislative developments related to religious policy are hard to date. The temple-registration system (*terauke shūmon* 寺請宗門), for example, which the bakufu may have initiated as early as 1613–14, was not applied nationally until 1635. This, of course was the legislation that required all individuals to register with a parish Buddhist temple. Similarly, the oldest examples of the *Shūmon jinbetsuchō* 宗門人別帳 registers are believed to date from 1634 in the Christian stronghold of Hirado 平戸, 1638 in Mino 美濃, and 1641 in Ōmi 近江, but such registers did not become a nationwide practice until around 1660.[24] In their most common format, these registers included each individual's name, age, relationship (e.g., 'oldest son'), temple name, and denominational affiliation, and listed these details household by household. The *gonin-gumi* 五人組 system of mutual responsibility was initially implemented to provide disincentives for sedition and anti-social behaviour, though this too proved useful for sniffing out proscribed religious activity.[25]

---

22 Murai, *Bakuhansei seiritsu to kirishitan kinsei*, pp. 152ff, and 'Shie jikengo no chōbaku kankei' 紫衣事件後の朝幕関係, *Kinsei bukkyō* 近世仏教, vol. 6, no. 1 (1983).

23 Tamamuro, *Edo bakufu no shūkyō tōsei*, pp. 52–3.

24 *Ibid.*, pp. 80–1.

25 *Ibid.*, pp. 76, 80–2.

RELIGIOUS POLICY 1640–97: THE NEW LIMITS OF THE POSSIBLE

During the decades before 1640, it is clear that for the first time in Japanese history certain religious communities were proscribed and subjected to intense and systematic persecution, and equally clear that members of those communities showed remarkable resilience in resisting the bakufu's measures. The *bakuhan* state's response to its initial apprehension of the limits to its power in the religious arena was on the one hand to enact legislation, like the *sakoku* directives, that is conspicuous for its excessive character, and on the other hand to search for procedures that would enable the state to ensure at least nominal compliance with its directives.

By contrast, the religious policy of the years from 1640 to 1697, the last year for nearly a century in which anyone was executed for violation of the state's religious policy, may best be understood as an attempt to resolve the contradictions betwen the harshness of the state's publicly proclaimed policies and the limited reality of what was understood to be achievable.[26] In this respect, the religious policies of the second half of the seventeenth century generally appear geared to consolidating the gains already made in the ongoing effort to incorporate religious institutions within the *bakuhan* structure, by, for example, adding an anti-Christian article to the 1663 revision of the *Buke shohatto* 武家諸法度 (Regulations governing military households). In matters of personal faith and belief, the state grew ever more dependent on mechanisms to demonstrate nominal compliance with directives that it increasingly understood to be unenforceable.

After the Shimabara Rebellion of 1637–8, Christians, particularly on Kyūshū and its surrounding islands but also in other parts of Japan, were in significant numbers driven 'underground', where they continued to practise what they believed to be the fundamentals of their Christian faith. The fact that the Christians chose to conceal their proscribed religious activities with a veil of various, largely Buddhist, activities and objects made their detection particularly difficult for the *bakuhan* authorities, but this defensive practice also generated a degree of confusion among the 'underground' Christians in matters of belief that did not become fully apparent until they ended their concealed existence some two centuries later.

From the middle of the seventeenth century onward, the *bakuhan* state relied principally upon an annual inquisition in order to root out violators of its prohibitions on Christianity and the *fuju fuse* faction. In 1640 Inoue

---

26 The next instance of an execution for violation of religious policy occurred in 1790: Anesaki Masaharu 姉崎正治, *Kirishitan shūmon no hakugai to senpuku* 切支丹宗門の迫害と潜伏 (Kokusho kankōkai, 1987; reprint), p. 299.

Masashige 井上正重 (1585–1661) was appointed to the new position of *Shūmon aratame no yaku* 宗門改役 (Office of the inquisitor). Despite impressive initial successes, he eventually encountered evidence of the failure of the anti-Christian policies, such as the discovery in 1657 of over 600 Christians in Ōmura 大村 and of hundreds of Christians in Usuki 臼杵 in Hyūga 日向.[27] In a document entitled *Kirishito ki* 契利斯督記, Inoue described in 1658 the new tactics of discovered Christians as follows: 'the suspects, when questioned as to whether they were Christian, at first hid nothing at all and responded that they were. Nowadays, however, they conceal their religion as best they can'.[28] This practice of concealing their faith is important, because the evidence overwhelmingly supports Inoue's assertion that the adherents of proscribed creeds had in earlier decades either recanted or confessed but now made every effort to conceal their beliefs. It is apparent that, at least among pockets of Christians, dissumulation in matters relating to personal faith had by the middle of the century become a recognised defensive practice.

Inoue, who was a celebrated inquisitor, now discerned the limitations of the state's methods of enforcement of its religious policies, and I believe that this recognition underlies the *bakuhan* state's retreat from demanding obedience to insisting on what amounted to no more than nominal compliance. As his record indicates, Inoue understood that performance of the *efumi* 絵踏, a widely used test of faith that required suspected Christians to trample on sacred images, and the provision of information for the religious census of the *Shūmon aratame*, had met initially with self-incriminating candour on the part of suspects but that these same methods later encountered increasingly sophisticated strategies of dissimulation and prevarication. Evidently, obedience in matters of personal faith was proving less amenable to enforcement than obedience in other matters, for a religious census posed challenges that made a national cadastral survey almost simple by comparison, and this in a land with a long history of the oath as a personal covenant.[29]

Even though many Christians survived into the 1660s and early 1670s, they were no longer regarded as much of a threat by local authorities, certainly at least in part because they outwardly lived the lives of exemplary citizens, particularly as cultivators of the soil, and there is evidence that the bakufu by this point began to reverse or at least relax its punishments for violation of religious policy. For example, whereas some two-thirds of the Ōmura Christians refused in 1657 to disavow their faith and were executed, roughly a decade

27 Elison, *Deus destroyed*, p. 192.
28 Anesaki, *Kirishitan shūmon no hakugai to senpuku*, p. 86.
29 Berry, 'Public peace and private attachment', p. 262.

later, when some 30 Christians were discovered in Usuki in 1668 by the Nagasaki Superintendent, not one was executed; they were instead arrested and imprisoned, and several died in prison. When the circumstances of their arrest, sentencing, and imprisonment were reported to the Commissioner of Inquisition (*Shūmon bugyō*) in Edo, an approving reply came in the form of a letter.[30]

Further support for the view that by the second half of the seventeenth century the bakufu had lost interest in executing violators of religious policies, even the ban on Christianity, comes from the writings of Engelbert Kaempfer, a German physician in the employ of the Dutch trading mission on Deshima island in Nagasaki harbour. Kaempfer describes the *shūmon aratame* as an annual inquiry throughout the country into 'what religion, belief or sect each family, or its individual members belong to'. According to Kaempfer, the inquiry usually followed by some days or weeks the *efumi*, 'trampling over the Images of our blessed Saviour, and the Virgin Mary ... as a convincing proof of their abhorrence of the Christian Religion'. Kaempfer further describes the manner in which local Nagasaki officials, having completed a census of their neighbourhood, proceeded 'from street to street, and house to house' until the inquiry was complete:

> After the Inquisitors have seated themselves on a mat, the landlord, his family, and all his domesticks, of both sexes, old and young, and whoever else lodges in the same house, and sometimes also the next neighbors, if their houses be not big enough for the act to be celebrated therein, are called together into the room, where the ... images [of our Blessed Saviour extended on the cross, and that of his holy Mother, or some other saint] are laid upon the bare floor, after which the Jefumi Tsio or Secretary of the Inquisition, takes the list of inhabitants, and reads their names, one by one, compelling them to appear as they are call'd, and to walk over the said Images with their feet. Young children, as Yet not able to walk, are by their mothers taken upon their arms, and held down to touch the Images with their feet ... After they have gone in this manner thro' all the streets and houses of the town, the inquisitors themselves trample over the Images, ... serving as witnesses for each other ...

In 1691 he visited more than 50 imprisoned Christians in Nagasaki. According to his account, as recently as 1688 three suspected Christians had been added

---

30 Murai, *Bakuhansei seiritsu to kirishitan kinsei*, pp. 71–2. Further, after 1674 there were virtually no more arrests of Christians in Usuki: Anesaki, *Kirishitan shūmon no hakugai to senpuku*, p. 270.

to the prisoners' ranks, and he remarks that, 'knowing little more than the name of our Saviour and his blessed Mother, they are so zealously attached to it that they chuse rather to die miserably in gaol, than by renouncing their faith, which they are often compeled to do, to procure their liberty.' He states that they are no longer executed 'as they were formerly, without mercy, and consideration of their great simplicity, and the little necessity there is at this time to shew much severity.' Indeed, this convergence of 'consideration' with the limits of the practicable suggests that by the 1690s the state had reconciled itself to the reality that its religious policies were only nominally enforceable, and that there was no longer anything to be gained from the wholesale execution of violators.[31]

This conclusion is supported by the circumstances of the *fuju fuse* movement which encountered comparable resistance and obstacles. Since the movement survived underground, hidden within the network of Nichiren temples, the 'disguise' was perfect. In the *Fuju fuse chō* register of temples not in compliance with bakufu law, which was compiled in the 1660s, some 134 Nichiren temples were listed. In 1661 and again in early 1663 the Minobu Kuonji 身延久遠寺, headquarters of the Nichiren accommodationist majority, drew the attention of the Commissioner of Temples and Shrines to the suspected non-compliance of the extremists on such occasions as the thirteenth anniversary of the funeral for the late shōgun, Tokugawa Iemitsu. Receiving no satisfaction from these efforts, Minobu in 1663 wrote to the senior councillors (*rōjū* 老中) Sakai Tadakiyo 酒井忠清 and Inaba Masanori 稲葉正則 complaining of three Nichiren temples that were not submitting to its authority, and protesting that the power of the *fuju fuse* faction was growing as a result of what was perceived to be the shōgun Ietsuna's 家綱 lenience toward them. The bakufu's response came in 1665 with the prohibition of the *daimoku* 題目 and *nenbutsu* 念仏 confraternities (*kō* 講) and a pledge to uncover *fuju fuse* extremists; but neither the prohibition nor the pledge appear to have lead to much in the way of results.[32]

The *Fuju fuse jiinchō* 寺院帳 (Register of *fuju fuse* temples), prepared in 1667 by the Minobu Kuonji temple, is a telling piece of evidence in this

31 Engelbert Kaempfer, *The history of Japan*, translated by J. G. Scheuchzer, 2 vols. (New York: The Macmillan Company, 1906; reprint), vol. 1, p. 330, vol. 2, pp. 85–6, 121–2,

32 Tamamuro, 'Kakure daimoku', pp. 168–73. One tactic used by the state is remarkable for its apparent innocence. From late in 1665 the bakufu insisted upon receipts for donations (*jiryo* 寺領) it made to temples suspected of harbouring *fuju fuse* elements; for the issue of such a receipt would, of course, constitute evidence of betrayal of the *fuju fuse* principle, while refusal to issue one would constitute circumstantial evidence of non-compliance with the law.

connection. Accusing some 49 temples of suspected participation in the proscribed tradition and grouping the temples according to their perceived degrees of non-compliance, it demonstrates that the movement remained strongest in the provinces of Musashi 武蔵, Kazusa 上総, and Sagami 相模, in other words in those areas under the very nose of the Edo bakufu.[33] As had occurred in its attempt to eradicate Christianity, the fundamental problem for the *bakuhan* state in all this was the difficulty of proving what was ultimately a matter of belief. As a response, the bakufu in 1669 issued a decree that excluded temples identified with the *fuju fuse* traditions from the *terauke* system, and ordered those who previously had registration certificates from those temples to obtain new certificates from other temples. This sought to use the *terauke* and *gonin-gumi* systems to expose *fuju fuse* extremists in the same manner as these systems were intended to expose Christians, but in all likelihood practitioners of proscribed Buddhist movements had by the late 1660s learnt the same defensive skills in dissimulation and prevarication that Inoue had observed a decade earlier among Christians. One consequence of all this activity was that, after 1669, one might be imprisoned simply for being accused, without corroboration, of being a *fuju fuse* extremist, in much the same manner as someone accused of the crimes of being a Christian, conspiring against the bakufu or being an instigator of a farmers' riot.[34] The diminished incidence of religious trials in the eighteenth century, however, suggests that the state's dependence upon informants and self-incrimination had resulted in a corpus of legislation the enforcement of which ran counter to the economic interests and social practices of local communities.

At the same time as it was retreating from its efforts to control what people believed, the bakufu was nonetheless intensifying its efforts to achieve administrative control of Buddhist institutions throughout Japan, as may be seen from a key piece of legislation issued in 1665, the *Shoshū jiin hatto* 諸宗寺院法度 (Regulations for temples of various sects). The decree contained a total of fourteen articles of which nine were issued under the seal of the shōgun, Ietsuna, and an additional five were issued by the senior councillors. Those issued under the shōgun's seal tended to be more administrative in nature and demanded that the sects devote greater attention to the preservation of correct ceremonial and the qualifications of their clergy; sustain the system of main temples and branch temples and the registration of parishioners; avoid factionalism and report those who violated the law; prohibit the unauthorised sale of temple lands or a temple's treasures; and exercise greater control over covenants between teachers and students. The remaining articles issued by the senior councillors dealt with such sumptuary matters as priests'

---

33 *Ibid.*, pp. 168–73.
34 *Ibid.*, pp. 184–6.

clothing, the prohibition of women residing within temple precincts, and so on.[35]

The pattern one observes, then, during the half-century following the *sakoku* edicts includes two familiar elements: first, an intensification of measures designed to provide evidence of nominal compliance with bakuhan policies in the religious arena, coupled with the state's retreat from its attempt to control what individuals believed; and second, greater consolidation and incorporation of religious institutions within the administrative structure of the *bakuhan* state. Since the state's policies regarding matters of individual belief depended for enforcement upon either the self-incriminating testimony of suspects or the testimony of informants, both of which conflicted with the interests of local communities as well as of individuals, the result of these efforts was to encourage them to develop their skills of concealment and to lead the state toward an acceptance of the limits on its ability to carry out its policies.

PRIVACY, SECRECY, AND RELIGIOUS POLICY

The erosion of the long-hallowed notion of the mutual dependence of Buddhist (*buppō* 仏法) and secular law (*ōbō* 王法) during the century following the Ōnin 応仁 war (1467–77) opened the way for the separation of church and state in Japan in a manner that allowed members of religious institutions like the Ishiyama Honganji to subordinate themselves to the constituted political order while retaining the essentials of their faith.[36] Conversely, it also created a conceptual framework that would be used in the seventeenth century to justify behaviour that violated the state's religious policies.[37]

This separation of church and state, and, more importantly, the attempts by the latter to control and the former to evade control, may also be regarded as responsible for the genesis of what Alida Brill has called 'private-life secrecy' in religious matters in early-modern Japan. As the nascent *bakuhan* state sought to extend its absolutist ambitions to areas of personal faith,

35 Tamamuro, *Edo bakufu no shūkyō tōsei*, p. 93; *Nihon bukkyōshi: kinsei*, pp. 83–92.

36 Galen Amstutz, 'The Honganji institution, 1500–1570: the politics of True Pure Land Buddhism', unpublished PhD dissertation (Princeton University, 1992), p. 272, Oguri Junko 小栗純子, 'Kakure nenbutsu' かくれ念仏, in Kataoka et al., *Kinsei no chika shinkō*, pp. 210–13, 228–9.

37 Hunter has discerned in Nichiō's writings an awareness of 'the manner in which [church and state] may interact as institutions, without religious significance': 'The *fuju fuse* controversy', p. 290.

individuals in Japan became practised in unprecedented forms of religious dissimulation and prevarication as the first line of defence against the state's religious policies. Unwilling to abandon its claims to authority in this area, the state responded by constructing mechanisms to secure no more than nominal compliance, which was tantamount to complicity with the resistance to its demands.

In her study of the concept, Brill has demonstrated that privacy has a number of seemingly 'natural' or instinctive properties even though it is obviously culture-bound in that it arises from 'the desire or the attempt to be protected from invasion, intrusion, exposure'. According to this perspective, personal privacy may appear to represent a victory of sorts on the part of the individual, but such privacy is inevitably 'granted to an individual only when others agree to honor [it], be it by compliance with the law or community custom.'[38] In other words, either the state or the community, or both, are complicit wherever privacy is present. Secrecy, by contrast, is a form of defence. As Warren and Laslett have discerned in their differentiation of privacy and secrecy, secrecy is 'not only a strategy for hiding acts or attributes that others hold in moral disrepute, but it is also a means to escape being stigmatized for them'.[39] Thus one way of regarding this issue is to see religious secrecy, a form of defence, as to some extent being supplanted by religious privacy, which requires complicity, as the *bakuhan* state came tacitly to acknowledge the limited effectiveness of its policies. Alternatively, one may similarly regard the clandestine exercise of proscribed religion that occurred in Japan during the seventeenth century, again in Warren and Laslett's terms, as 'private-life secrecy', the justification of which was less an independent or counter-ideological enterprise 'than a response to ideology: a desire to avert the full wrath of whatever powerful groups are in control of the definition of "undesirable elements"'.[40]

At first, during the 1570s, the 'problem' with religious institutions for would-be unifiers in Japan was their control of major landholdings, large-scale security forces, and leagues of faithful willing to bear arms in support of their creed. The attempt to control Japan's religions began with the attempt to break their military and economic power, and only when that task was complete did the unifiers' attention turn in earnest to political and administrative control over religions and religionists. Throughout much of the world at this time, religion was serious business, as attested to by the fact that 'three of the four largest rebellions in early-modern Europe', as well as the largest rebellion in

---

38 Alida Brill, *Nobody's business: paradoxes of privacy* (Reading, Mass.: Addison-Wesley Publishing Co., 1990), pp. xv, xvii.

39 Warren and Laslett, 'Privacy and secrecy', p. 26.

40 *Ibid.*, p. 29.

early-modern Japan, 'had religious overtones' to them; but it is naive to suggest, as some have done, that the bakufu succeeded through force in totally eliminating selected religions.[41]

Controlling what people believed proved to be far more difficult for the bakufu than controlling what they averred, and controlling what they averred proved more difficult than controlling what they did. One reason for this difficulty is that religions, by their very nature, disclose what purports to be extraordinary while encoding that which is ultimate.[42] This dual character of religions, with one foot, as it were, in the spotlight and the other in the shadows, has been evident in Japan since the earliest recorded times. The difficulties for the state, however, in its attempts to control religions, were evident in the numerous reversals and transmogrifications of religious policy in late sixteenth- and seventeenth-century Japan, which undermined the formation of state-endorsed rationales for compliance. It is in this sense significant that it was not until religious policy stabilised after the 1660s that one finds the effective production and penetration of statist ideology in Tokugawa Japan.[43]

By that point, however, it was too late for the state to control what people believed, for not only had dissimulation become part of the *modus vivendi* of those who dared challenge the state's religious policies, but the *bakuhan* officials charged with enforcement were already aware of this fact and invited the persecuted to dissemble in the form of nominal compliance. This genesis of 'private-life secrecy' in religious practice is made remarkably clear by the experiences of the Jesuit priest Antonio Ishida, imprisoned in 1629 by the Nagasaki Commissioner, Takenaka Uneme, who was responsible for the new emphasis on apostasy and was assisted by his Confucian adviser, Saitō Gonnai 斎藤権内. It was on the occasion of his interrogation in 1631 that Takenaka reminded Ishida that his primary allegiance was to the shōgun and that expression of that allegiance lay in obedience to his sovereign's decrees; and, if he would only acknowledge this obedience, he might 'continue

---

41 White, 'State growth', p. 13; he argues (p. 14) that the bakufu was successful in eliminating Christianity.

42 Kees Bolle, ed., *Secrecy in religions* (Leiden: E. J. Brill, 1987), pp. xii–xiii, 1; see also John Middleton, 'Secrecy among the Lugbara', in *ibid.*, p. 41. This identification of secrecy with religion is at times so strong that some scholars have gone so far as to identify secrecy as 'a form of religious experience': Ian Mackenzie, ed., *Secret societies* (New York: Holt, Rinehart and Winston, 1967), p. 18.

43 Herman Ooms, *Tokugawa ideology: early constructs, 1570–1680* (Princeton: Princeton University Press), argues that ideological closure was first achieved in Japan in the writings of Yamazaki Ansai 山崎闇斎.

to believe what he pleased in his own heart'.[44] Private-life secrecy in the realm of belief was now for the first time present in Japan, and nothing between heaven and earth could eradicate it. In the same manner that the would-be and actual unifiers retreated on other fronts ultimately unnecessary for the maintenance of public order, they likewise retreated in the enforcement of religious policy as it concerned individual belief.

44 Elison, *Deus destroyed*, p. 189. This entire affair is described in greater detail in Cieslik, *Kirishitan jinbutsu no kenkyū*, pp. 98–107.

7

Heavenly affinities and discrepancies: Fr Leturdu's early ethnographic account of Okinawa (1846–1848)

Patrick Beillevaire

Fr Pierre Marie Leturdu (1821–61) set foot on Okinawa on 2 May 1846, aged only twenty-four. He was brought there from Macao aboard the *Sabine*, a French corvette under the command of Captain Nicolas François Guérin. Born in the rural town of Quintin, in northern Brittany, Leturdu had felt a precociously early call to the missions. Unlike most of his colleagues, who had previously exercised diocesan responsibilities before opting for the missions, he had joined the Parisian seminary of the Société des Missions Etrangères before completing his training, on 15 March 1844. His ordination took place in December the same year. On 10 March 1845 he left France, destined never to return.[1]

Leturdu was to spend almost twenty-eight months on Okinawa, finally leaving in August 1848. Upon his arrival there he met another priest, his former teacher Théodore Augustin Forcade (1816–85), who had been living on the island since May 1844, accompanied by a Chinese catechist. They were preparing to leave Okinawa temporarily, on board some other French ships which were expected to reach Okinawa soon. Forcade had been the first Christian missionary to attempt to resume the evangelisation of Japan, which had been interrupted some two hundred years earlier. Until his time, Westerners had visited Okinawa only for short periods. The longest known sojourn had been that of Captains Murray Maxwell and Basil Hall, in 1816, and that lasted no more than six weeks.[2]

The Ryūkyū Islands were at first attached to the Vicariate of Korea established by Rome in 1832. From 1846, they were included in the newly created Diocese of Japan, of which Forcade was appointed the head. The little reliable information available in the early 1840s about the Ryūkyūs, which were, however, renowned for the mild manners of their inhabitants, induced him to think that they should be more promising than any other land in the Far East for missionary activity. Despite the prompt and stern opposition

---

1 A short biography of Leturdu is found in A. Launay, *Mémorial de la Société des Missions-Etrangères* (Paris: Séminaire des Missions-Etrangères, 1916), II, 396–7.
2 See B. Hall, *Account of a voyage of discovery to the west coast of Corea and the Great Loo-Choo island* (London: John Murray, 1818).

shown by the authorities to every aspect of Christian teaching, Forcade continued throughout his two-year residence to nourish the hope that the evangelisation of the islands would be possible. In his opinion, the attitude of the authorities was an impediment that could be removed by the application of external pressures. Yet it became all too clear to his successor, Leturdu, that the situation would never improve without a radical change in the policy of the bakufu in Edo. Consequently, the Ryūkyū Islands gradually came to be seen as a mere threshold to Japan where missionaries could at least profit from the opportunity to acquire the rudiments of Japanese for the purpose of propagating the faith later on.

A total of eight priests, all of them sent by the Société des Missions Etrangères, resided in Okinawa between 1844 and 1862 (the mission was suspended between August 1848 and February 1855). During their lengthy stays, extending for most of them from two to six years, they sent numerous letters to their colleagues and superiors, of which only a few have so far been published. These letters were conveyed to China by the annual tribute-ship despatched from Okinawa or by the occasional Western vessel. Two books also came out of their experiences: Forcade's fragmentary diary, published in the year of his death, and a collection of letters addressed by the talented Louis Théodore Furet (1816–1900) to the founder of French japanology, Léon de Rosny.[3]

Leturdu distinguished himself by being the author not only of occasional letters but also of a report that is exceptional in that it evinces a true curiosity about Ryūkyūan culture hardly found, Furet's letters apart, in the writings of his colleagues. This document, deposited in the archives of the Société des Missions Etrangères, is addressed to the members of the central council of the Oeuvre pour la Propagation de la Foi (Society for the Propagation of Faith), an institution based in Lyon which was founded in 1822 under the inspiration of Pauline Jaricot to serve the purpose of gathering moral and financial support for the missions. The Report is in the form of a manuscript, divided into two parts and comprising in all 101 pages.[4] Leturdu wrote it in

---

3 T. A. Forcade, 'Le premier missionnaire du Japon au XIXe siècle', *Missions Catholiques* (Lyon), 17 (1885): 201 *et seq.*, and *Le premier missionnaire du Japon au XIXe siècle* (Lyon: Missions Catholiques, 1885); L. T. Furet, *Lettres à M. Léon de Rosny sur l'Archipel japonais et la Tartarie orientale* (Paris: Maisonneuve, 1860).

4 In a letter addressed to the superior of the seminary of the Missions Etrangères, dated 24 December 1848 at Hong Kong, Leturdu announced that he had just completed a report on the Ryūkyūs, written at the request of Forcade, and that he was going to send it along with an 'extract' from his diary: Archives of the Société des Missions Etrangères, vol. 568, p. 490. Though the report was intended for presentation to the council of the Oeuvre pour la Propagation de la Foi in Lyon, he thought it best to secure the consent of his superior first. He also suggested that the report be rewritten

1848 when he was back in Hong Kong. It is largely based on a slightly shorter and not so easily legible abridged version of the diary, now lost, that he kept during his residence on Okinawa. In places the Report simply paraphrases what remains of the diary.[5]

The first and less original part of the Report appeared as a letter, with substantial cuts, in volume 21 of the *Annales de la Propagation de la Foi* (1849), a publication edited by the society of the same name. The only author to have examined the document in its entirety, along with the diary, seems to have been the priest F. Marnas when he was writing the chapters on the Ryūkyū Mission for his book on Christian revival in Japan, first printed in 1896. While historically accurate, his work is imbued with apologetic concerns and makes no use whatsoever of Leturdu's ethnographic observations. It is my intention here to focus attention on precisely these forgotten aspects of Leturdu's writings, as well as on the correspondences he sought to establish between the Christian creed, or the Catholic version of it, and local beliefs. Apart from Marnas' book, there is an article on Forcade and Leturdu by Professor T. Hatakenaka, but this deals only marginally with the diary and makes no mention of the unpublished part of his Report.[6]

Neither Forcade nor Leturdu had studied Chinese when they arrived on

by a copyist in Paris before being sent to Lyon. The fine hand in which the Report now kept in the Archives is written, is so different from the casual hand employed by Leturdu in his diary and his letters as to make it clear that it is the work of a copyist. Leturdu's original has, however, not yet been found. Another problem arises concerning the date of the Report. While the first part is dated 27 January 1849 at Hong Kong, the end of the second part is dated 26 February 1848, also at Hong Kong. This is obviously a mistake, for Leturdu was still on Okinawa in February 1848, and, as mentioned in the letter cited above, he set to work on his report only after his arrival in Hong Kong. The date of the second part should therefore be amended to read 1849.

5 The abridged form of the diary and the Report are in volume 568 of the archives of the Société des Missions Etrangères, bearing the following titles: 'Journal de Lioukiou (Oukigna)' (pp. 348–72), 'Rapport sur Liou-Kiou (Rapport à Messieurs les membres du conseil central de Lyon), (pp. 511–75), and 'Suite du Rapport sur Liou-Kiou' (pp. 380–415). Unpublished letters from Forcade and Leturdu are to be found in volumes 568 and 569. Hereafter references to these documents will be made simply in the form of a page number: each volume of the Archives, despite the heterogeneity of their contents, has been paginated throughout.

6 F. Marnas, *La religion de Jésus (Yaso Ja-kyô) ressuscitée au Japon dans la deuxième moitié du XIXe siècle* (Paris: Séminaire des Missions Etrangères, 1931 [reprint of 1896 edition]), vol. 1, pp. 183–204; Hatakenaka Toshirō 畠中敏郎, 'Forukādo to Ruturdu: Okinawa no kirishitan fukkatsu' フォルカードとルテュルデュー 沖縄の切支丹復活, in *Nantō, sono rekishi to bunka* 南島その歴史と文化 (Daiichi Shobō, 1980), vol. 3, pp. 123–50. Leturdu's report is listed in G. H. Kerr, *Okinawa, the history of an island people* (Rutland and Tokyo: Charles E. Tuttle, 1958), p. 505, but apparently Kerr had no access to it.

Okinawa. What they knew of Japan at that moment is difficult to evaluate. No surviving records indicate whether any special preparation for the Far East was added to the ordinary theological courses followed at the seminary of the Missions Etrangères.[7] One may, however, surmise that it could not have amounted to more than reading a few celebrated works and listening to experienced elders. Until their departure the missionaries were usually ignorant of which area, anywhere from India to Korea, they would be dispatched to, and the decision concerning their final assignment rested with local procurators.[8] Only then could they really start learning something precise about the cultural context of their mission. While on Okinawa, Forcade tells us that he read the letters of Francis Xavier and of some other Jesuits who had travelled to China and Japan.[9] One may guess that Leturdu benefited from the same material. In his diary, for instance, he once quotes Luis Frois about the Bon festival (365). Moreover both missionaries had glanced through Charlevoix's *Histoire du Christianisme dans l'empire du Japon* (1715), or through some abridged edition, but they seem not to have known his larger work *Histoire et description générale du Japon* (1736), which reproduces Engelbert Kaempfer's information on the Ryūkyū Islands. Forcade had also taken with him excerpts on Japan from the geographers Malte-Brun and Balbi, and he mentions the story of the Polish Count Benyowsky who claimed to have come across hospitable Christian villagers after a shipwreck near some northern Ryūkyū island.[10] On the whole, it is not an exaggeration to say that, apart from the fate of the early Christians, neither Forcade nor Leturdu displayed any keen interest in Japanese culture and society as such. In particular, they appear only slightly acquainted with religious data collected in sixteenth- and seventeenth-century Japan and found thereafter in various reference books. Furthermore, they remained unaware of the well-informed articles on the Ryūkyūs, based on British and Chinese accounts, which were published in the *Nouvelles annales des voyages, de la géographie et de l'histoire* during the early nineteenth century.

More surprising is the fact that they never mention a memoir on the Ryūkyūs written by Antoine Gaubil, a French Jesuit of the Peking mission.

---

7 The library of the seminary was looted during the Revolution and was only partially restored during the following decades.

8 In Leturdu's case the decision was taken in Macao by Fr Libois.

9 T. A. Forcade, 'Lettre de M. Forcade, missionaire apostolique du Lieou-Khieou, à M. Libois, procureur des Missions Etrangères à Macao, Grande Luchu, Tu-maï, Bonzerie d'Amiku, le 12 août 1845', *Annales de la Propagation de la Foi* (Lyon), 18 (1846): 377.

10 *Ibid.*, 380, 377. In an unpublished letter from Okinawa, Forcade says he is also using a map printed in 1839: letter to Libois, 2 August 1845 (Archives, vol. 568, pp. 29ff).

The main source used by Gaubil was the official report of Xu Baoguang 徐
葆光 (?–1723), a Chinese envoy sent to Okinawa in 1719 for the investiture
of king Shō Kei 尚敬 (1700–51). Among other things, Gaubil's memoir
contains information on beliefs and language which should have been of
immediate interest to the missionaries. First published in 1758, in *Lettres
édifiantes et curieuses*, it had been reprinted several times during the first
decades of the following century and was easily available in the 1840s.[11]
However, there can be no doubt that its contents were known to Forcade and
Leturdu. It is cited, but with no indication of the author, by the explorer
Dumont d'Urville in his *Voyage pittoresque autour du monde* (1834–5),
surely the most widely read documentary fiction of mid-nineteenth-century
France, and a work often used as a guide-book by missionaries and navigators
alike. Forcade mentions that he and his companions brought a copy with
them when they disembarked on Okinawa in 1844 and that local officials
were amazed by the illustrations in the chapters on the Ryūkyū islands,
redrawn from those of British narratives. He clearly read it carefully, for in
his correspondence he disagrees with its version of the 1609 invasion of the
Ryūkyū islands by Satsuma because it concealed the permanent takeover by
Satsuma that ensued.[12] But like Dumont d'Urville, the only source to which
Forcade refers is the account given by a 'Chinese diplomat', Xu Baoguang
(spelled Supao-koang by Dumont d'Urville). Further, the historical information
presented in the first part of Leturdu's Report is obviously a close paraphrase
of Gaubil's memoir itself. However, unlike the latter who relied solely on
Chinese views, Leturdu clearly acknowledges the Japanese domination over
the Ryūkyūs since the begining of the seventeenth century, and he holds
Japan responsible for the 'ruin' of the kingdom (554). His transcriptions of
names are also more appropriate than Gaubil's. His chapter on geography, on
the other hand, scarcely owes anything to Gaubil. It brings forth original
data, some derived from his own observations.

Dumont d'Urville's *Voyage pittoresque* exerted considerable influence
upon the minds of the first French visitors to Okinawa. Based on the narratives
of W. R. Broughton (1804), B. Hall (1818), J. M'Leod (1817), and F. W.
Beechey (1831), it draws a glowing picture of the country and of its inhabitants.
Different from all their neighbours, they were described as cordial, honest,
hospitable, peaceful, and open-minded. To many a visitor Okinawa was simply
reminiscent of the Golden Age of mankind. Forcade's first letters are filled
with an optimism reflecting such a view. Yet, at the time of his arrival, there

11 P. Beillevaire, 'Au seuil du Japon. Le mémoire du P. Gaubil sur les Ryûkyû et
ses lecteurs', *L'Ethnographie*, 108(1990): 15–53.
12 Forcade, *Le premier missionnaire*, p. 15; *idem*, 'Lettre de M. Forcade', pp.
378–9.

were already hints that the friendly reception the British had met with had been simply a safe means by which the alarmed and defenceless Okinawans could try to prevent foreigners from lingering. Relations were bound to deteriorate once the missionaries forced their presence upon them. Though the Ryūkyū kingdom passed officially for a vassal state of China, visitors had not taken long to guess that Japan took an interest in various aspects of its policy. They could sense, in particular, that the strict instructions to keep them at distance emanated from Japan. Japanese junks also – sometimes up to twenty-one, writes Leturdu – could often be seen on station in Naha harbour, clear evidence of important trade links with the northern neighbour (553). In fact the kingdom was directly under Satsuma's thumb, not Edo's, but paradoxically this would remain almost completely unnoticed by the Europeans until the late 1850s.[13] To Forcade and Leturdu, the king thus appeared to be a puppet manipulated by a mysterious and invisible 'Japanese mandarin' based in Naha, whom they took for a representative 'of the imperial court', meaning the bakufu in Edo (pp. 546, 552).

One month after its arrival the *Sabine* was joined as expected by two other warships flying the French flag. Admiral J. B. Cécille, in command of the division, had been commissioned to negotiate a treaty of amity and commerce with the Ryūkyū government. Cécille was himself a fervent Catholic sincerely devoted to the missions, but his 'rude and arrogant' behaviour, as the American historian G. H. Kerr aptly qualified it, was fully supported, if not fostered, by Forcade. The negotiations took place at a remote and inconvenient location more than 50 kilometres north of Shuri chosen by the admiral himself; communications with the palace were thus difficult and hampered by inevitable delays. One reason put forward by the Ryūkyū officials

13 Accounts of the conquest of the Ryūkyū islands by Satsuma had curiously sunk into oblivion. One already finds in the seventeenth-century records of the British East India Company, and later in Kaempfer, a clear indication of the role Satsuma played in the Ryūkyū islands. In 1832, during a brief stay, the Prussian-born missionary and doctor Charles Gutzlaff had also noticed junks from Satsuma in Naha harbour: C. Gutzlaff, *Journal of three voyages along the coast of China* (London: Frederick Westley and A. H. Davis, 1834), p. 362. Though Satsuma's influence on the Ryūkyū kingdom is never mentioned in any of Leturdu's or Forcade's writings, the notes of a French officer who visited Okinawa in 1848 bear witness to Leturdu's awareness that 'a delegate from the Prince of Satsuma, [a] mysterious proconsul' lived in Naha. It is also said that Leturdu vainly tried to meet him: E. Jurien de la Gravière, *Voyage en Chine et dans les mers et archipels de cet empire pendant les années 1847–1848–1849–1850*, 2 vols. (Paris: Charpentier, 1854), vol. 1, pp. 222–3. All through the Edo period, Satsuma turned to its own advantage the official relations between the Ryūkyū kingdom and the Chinese empire by trading secretly with the latter. Sometime in the late 1850s, the Shimazu daimyō would also try to buy weapons from the French through the instrumentality of the Ryūkyū government.

for refusing to sign a treaty with the French was their fear that Japan would immediately break off commercial relations with the kingdom, which would have dire consequences for them.They endeavoured to conceal their close links to Satsuma as well as their general allegiance to Japan, and tried to make the French believe that all trade relations with Japan were mediated by Tokara, a group of tiny islands located in the northern part of the archipelago.[14] Cécille did not neglect to cite the treaty recently concluded by France with China to bend the wills of his interlocutors, but to no avail. After a month of apparently fruitless discussions, tired of the delaying tactics of the local officials, he decided to head northwards and try his luck in Nagasaki. The three ships weighed anchor on 17 July, carrying away Forcade and his Chinese assistant. Leturdu was left alone; the admiral alluded to military reprisals if his safety and his freedom of movement were not guaranteed. Like Forcade two years earlier, he had been introduced to the Ryūkyū officials as a would-be interpreter, officially needed by the French government; for that purpose he was to be given 'books and teachers' so that he could learn the local language (supposedly standard Japanese). At the last moment, Ryūkyū officials orally consented to that request, with obvious reluctance.[15] On his departure Forcade already knew that he had been appointed bishop of the new diocese of Japan, although this was to exist only on paper for many years. It was several months before the consecration could take place; but in any case, despite his proclaimed intentions, he never returned to Okinawa, to Leturdu's utter dismay, nor did he ever visit mainland Japan.

As a general rule at the Missions Etrangères, a missionary, especially when fresh from the seminary, was not to be left alone for very long. In order to alleviate the hardships caused by Forcade's prolonged absence, Leturdu was joined in September 1846 by another colleague, Mathieu Adnet, formerly vicar in Verdun. Already ailing at the time of his arrival, his health steadily deteriorated. He finally died, probably of tuberculosis, on 1 July 1848 (he was born in 1813). The Report contains a moving account of the agony of his death struggle. On his death Leturdu received messages of condolence from a

---

14 Kerr, *Okinawa*, pp. 276–8; Shimajiri Katsuyoshi 島尻克美, 'Bakumatsu-ki ni okeru Ryūkyū ōfu no ikokusen taisaku - Furansu kansen rairyū jiken o chūshin ni' 幕末期における琉球王府の異国船対策 － 仏艦船来琉事件を中心に, in *Ryūkyū － Oki-nawa, sono rekishi to Nihon shizō* 琉球・沖縄 － その歴史と日本史像 (Yūsankaku, 1987), p.136; Forcade, *Le premier missionaire*, pp. 104, 111, 145. Later in life Cécille was given the honorific title of 'count' by Pope Pius IX. French officers were usually not so openly supportive of the missions, though the propagation of the faith was then generally considered to be desirable for the expansion of commerce: see the introduction to Forcade, 'Mer Bleue: Archipel de Liou-Tchou', *Revue de l'Orient*, 10 (1846): 257–8.

15 Forcade, *Le premier missionnaire*, p. 134.

royal minister and from the 'governors' (*kwan* 官, J. *kan*) of Shuri, where the palace was located, and of Naha. Though filled with apparent concern for the fate of the bereaved missionary, the messages were considered by him to be 'a show of civility devoid of any serious commitment' ('des politesses qui n'engagent à rien'; p. 533). Nonetheless three officials and a procession of people wearing white garments escorted the deceased to his last abode near the shore (still visible today in Tomari harbour). A young man carried the cross, another the holy water. All of them attended the mass celebrated by Leturdu and so, he says, were given the opportunity to see 'that if we do not worship the dead, at least we do know how to honour them' (p. 534).

The first part of the Report recalls the harsh conditions under which, as Forcade had before them, he and Adnet had been forced to live. Housed in the Seigenji 聖現寺, a Shingon temple located on Ameku 天久 (spelt Amiku in the Report, in accordance with local pronunciation) hill in Tomari 白村 (Tumai in the local dialect), then a village on the northern fringe of Naha, they were at the beginning kept under the constant surveillance of men posted outside. A simple sneeze could cause their guards to rush into the building. Each time they went for a walk they were closely spied upon too. Whenever they proceeded along a road, refusing to pay attention to warnings that they should proceed no further, people around were forcefully chased away. Although they were eventually granted more freedom, discussions with ordinary people were rare and proselytising was out of the question. But they were never forbidden to say mass daily. Prevented from buying food directly on the market, they also discovered that the official intermediaries imposed upon them were making them pay three, six, or even more times the going rate for goods and were, moreover, supplying them with goods of low quality (pp. 365–6).

It took Leturdu and Adnet some time to obtain from the authorities a partial application of the hard-won oral agreement concerning the study of the language. To comply with their wishes they were given some books, the nature of which remains unclear, and received assistance from several teachers. But the missionaries soon complained that they were deliberately being taught only the written language, in order, as they supposed, to prevent them from talking to the people. Like Forcade, Leturdu still thought that the language spoken on Okinawa was not substantially different from mainland Japanese. In his circumstances of isolation and hardship, he was sustained in his studies of the language by the idea that they would one day be useful for future missions to Japan.[16]

16 It was not until September 1849 that Forcade, on route from Macao to Hong Kong, learnt from a Japanese castaway that the 'Ryūkyū language, for the study of which he had worked so hard without teachers or books, was in short just a bad

Besides historical and geographical information, the first part of the Report contains an interesting comment on Okinawan houses (pp. 550–1). Leturdu starts by denying them any aesthetic value, although acknowledging their tidiness: 'How could you describe as beautiful those wooden houses, only single-storied, with no architecture ... Imagine a cage divided into compartments and you will have an idea of Japanese houses'. Despite this outright condemnation, there follows a description of their general tripartite design: the room on the east, he explains, is reserved for the chief of the household and for visitors, the middle one is for ancestor worship, and the third, on the west, to which the kitchen is often annexed, is the place where women and children ordinarily stay during the daytime; the rear of the building is taken up with smaller rooms. It escaped his notice that the domestic architecture he described not only expressed a prevailing functional pattern but also evoked patterns of space symbolism that could be seen at both village and island level.[17] While the houses of poor peasants had only one room where family members huddled together, and a thatched roof instead of a tiled one, the nobility lived in large and beautiful dwellings in the middle of a yard surrounded by walls set back from the street. 'As is generally the way in Japan', Leturdu writes, 'people of importance hide themselves behind walls; it gives the cities a stern appearance, well in accordance with the kind of government that rules them.' But to his surprise he could find no guard around the Shuri palace where 'the king, his minister and the first three mandarins reside'; it seemed that it had been left to the protection of two 'stone-lions' (*shishi* 獅子): 'Indeed, our European notions are quite inappropriate here!' (p. 547).

The Report is especially noteworthy for its second part, which is devoted to religious subjects. Leturdu managed to collect information by inquiring from his language teachers during classes, or by talking with monks and with ordinary people that he happened to meet while he explored the countryside around Naha.[18] It seems that he became conversant enough with the Naha dialect after a few months. His study of language had been facilitated by the earlier work of Forcade who compiled a Ryūkyū lexicon comprising some six thousand words, which has unfortunately been lost. He soon managed to have the agreement that he thought had been concluded by Admiral Cécille

patois, very difficult to understand for the inhabitants of the larger islands [of Japan]': letter dated 18 September 1849, cited in Marnas, *La religion de Jésus*, pp. 216–17.
17 P. Beillevaire, 'Spatial characteristics of human temporality in the Ryūkyūs', in J. Hendry and J. Webber, eds, *Interpreting Japanese society* (Oxford: JASO, 1986), pp. 76–87.
18 On one occasion also Leturdu set out alone on a trip to the north of the island in search of an old man and a child who had mysteriously visited him before; this trip lasted 13 days (Report, p. 539; Journal, p. 369).

1 Ainu *iyomande* ritual; Kotan nr. Lake Kutcharo (Hokkaido) March, 1954. Preparations for the ritual: women pound rice and millet in a wooden *nisu*, holding heavy *yutani* poles.

2 Yanaka Torizō (left) and Kikuchi Ginosuke, both in their late seventies (1954), were perfectly conversant with all ancient traditions concerning the *iyomande*, and knew by heart the many prayers relating to this important event.

3 Two young and strong men have climbed on the bear's cage and perform a ritual dance, holding in their hands the ropes with which they will presently secure the bear.

4 The bear has been lifted out of his cage and is paraded around the village; a mock hunt is enacted by the men, who shoot blunt harmless arrows at him. This part of the *iyomande* is called *hepere tukan*. The women in a large circle go on dancing, clapping their hands and singing *(upopo)*.

5 Ekashi Kikuchi Ginosuke (age 77) and the bear, with some of its gifts. Ekashi Kikuchi is about to deliver a long prayer in Ainu, chanted with a very deep voice, expressing the hope that the bear, as messenger of human beings to the gods, will carry good news of the honourable treatment received, and will soon 'return again' to the world of men.

6 The bear has been dispatched or 'sent off' (*iyomande* means 'sending off'), by suffocation between two heavy poles. The carcass is reverently displayed on some mats at the feet of the *nusa* altar. Four *ekashi*, (from left to right) Yamaya Haruzō, Yanaka Torizō, Kikuchi Ginosuke and Maeda Sentarō, are preparing to chant prayers and messages for the bear, 'the little god'.

7 Feast indoors. Each of the three *iyomande* days ends with crowded feasts. Libations are offered to *Kamui Fuchi*, godess of the hearth, and to other gods of the Ainu pantheon. On the last evening the bear's meat, stewed, is offered to all participants.

and the local authorities translated into Okinawan ('en oukignain'; pp. 349). In a letter to procurator Libois dated 28 September 1846, he announced that he intended to translate into 'Japanese' the *Dialogues of Gonçalvez*, which had been given to him by Forcade, and a Latin–Chinese dictionary.[19] Neither of these projects came off. For one thing, the teachers were accused of being inefficient. The missionaries also deplored the fact that they were frequently replaced, probably for fear that they would develop some attachment to the foreigners.

Leturdu's comments on local culture are rarely free of explicit value judgements. As often as not, his approach aims at refuting or depreciating the point of view of his informants. Occasionally, he states, he would not hesitate to suggest to them how shallow or inconsistent they seemed to him. For that reason the Report, besides being a valuable eye-witness account, should also be considered to reflect the intellectual baggage of the missionaries, the ways in which they perceived cultural otherness, and the values that they considered to justify their intrusion into a foreign culture with the avowed purpose of transforming it. It shows in a crude way, especially by means of its diction, the weight of the observer's cultural background. Certainly naïve compared with the anthropological perspectives of today, this document nevertheless encourages us to ponder the relationship between claims to universalism – whether religious, legal or moral – and the drive for domination.

At the end of October 1847, Leturdu and Adnet were given the opportunity to witness the preparations for the funeral of king Shō Iku 尚育 (1813–47). Though they were prevented from attending the ceremony proper by 'more than five hundred men', they described the event as the 'apotheosis of a new *kami*', 'reminiscent of the apotheosis of the too famous Taykosama [i. e. Toyotomi Hideyoshi] sworn foe of the word Christian' (pp. 543, 383). The successor, king Shō Tai 尚泰 (1843–1901), was only nine years old, but Leturdu was not expecting any political disturbance, nor any change in his own situation: 'the one who [really] governs did not die, the Japanese mandarin still lives on'; 'the king who passed away was a mummy, another mummy is going to replace him, and that will be the end of it' (p. 543). On the following day, he celebrated All Saints' Day and found comfort in reflecting on the superiority ('la sublime sagesse') of the Christian faith that offered honest and charitable men and women as models, 'simple and pure souls' giving rise, 'not to adoration … but to respect and imitation', whereas Japanese

---

19 This passage (Archives, vol. 569, pp. 36–7) can also be understood to mean that he wanted to have his language teachers translate them for him. He mentions in his diary that the 'interpreter' who translated the agreement for him had been immediately relieved of his position. Some ten years later Furet published an Okinawan version of the Pater Noster: Furet, *Lettres à M. Léon de Rosny*.

religion compelled 'a slave people to worship the dust' of 'oppressive' and 'corrupted' men transformed into gods (p. 384). He made a pretext of Adnet's weakness and of the fact that they had 'no part in the privileges of local people' for refusing to comply with the official interdiction on eating meat, fish, and eggs for fifty days after the king's death (p. 542). As he pointed out, fishermen had not stopped putting to sea and pigs were as usual being taken to the slaughterhouse.

In one passage in the Report Leturdu notes that the religion of the people concerned only *kami* and *hotoke* (locally pronounced *futuki*): their cult consisted 'solely of going six or seven times a year, on certain fixed days, each family separately, to the temples or to some high places, to offer them grains of rice, wine or tea' (p. 387; he designated them indiscriminately either as gods or as deities). In fact he had previously distinguished three sorts of deities worshipped by Okinawans: *kami*, *hotoke*, and ancestors, for which he gave no native word. *Kami*, a word he proposed to translate as 'spirit or genius', 'are beings that cannot be seen, nor touched, nor represented...'; 'they are beyond number and fill the earth, the sea, the air'. 'Their thrones are sacred stones'; 'those stones ... receive [are the witnesses of] oaths, wedding promises, and all important agreements.' (pp. 380–1) For the *hotoke*, temples were erected. As to the ancestors, 'their sanctuaries are the tomb and the tablet ...' But he found it difficult to be more precise on the respective attributes of *kami* and *hotoke*: 'I was never given', he complains, 'a clear idea of the difference they make between *kami* and *hotoke*' (p. 384). He observes that indeed both comprise deified humans, for instance kings for the former and Buddhist legendary figures for the latter, and beings endowed by nature with a divine essence. He discerned in the *kami* the most primitive deities of the country, whereas *hotoke* and ancestor worship had been brought in more recently by monks and Chinese settlers. In so far as Okinawa is concerned, he was also right when he stated that, unlike *hotoke* which were always given the appearance of 'idols of stone, wood or metal', there were no representations of *kami*. His observation that there were 'benevolent *kami*' and 'wicked *kami*', 'some protecting humans, others abusing them', brought him to wonder whether wicked *kami* were wicked 'through their own fault or by nature'. Their origin puzzled him too: did the Okinawans think that they were created beings? A touch of irony comes out when he comments that 'all this is left unsaid in the Okinawan catechism' (pp. 380–1). He placed Jizō bosatsu 地蔵菩薩, devoted to 'childhood [which is] so exposed to dangers', among the *kami*.

It was not without deep astonishment that Leturdu found in the *kami* 'so complete a notion of our angels'. Both, he wrote, share 'the same spiritual essence, the same division in two camps, the same functions towards man' (p. 381). 'It is true', he added, 'that the notion of angel is perhaps the best preserved in all idolatrous countries.' The idea he expresses here of a primeval religious lore, which could in his view only have been thoroughly transmitted to Christian countries, was one that was widely accepted by traditionalists in his time. The sole difference that he identified between *kami* and angels is that the former possess a divine nature and are consequently regarded as 'independent and sovereign beings', whereas the latter are not. Still, he notes, he found among members of the aristocracy the opinion that 'the *kami* are nothing other than intermediary beings between heaven and men', so that they would be even closer to angels: 'Men, they say, being too unworthy to address heaven directly... have their wishes and their prayers received by the *kami* and taken by them to heaven' (p. 382). Leturdu had to acknowledge, however, that the influence of conversations they had had with his predecessor, Forcade, could readily be discerned here. It was obvious to him, whatever they said, that they were confusing heaven with the sky (French, of course, has only the one word, *ciel*, for both concepts). What they were referring to, he explains, 'when their reasoning is put under pressure', is nothing other than the physical realm above, with 'the sun, the moon, and all there is up there'. None the less, nobles and common people would altogether appear somehow dissatisfied with their *kami*, betraying 'a vague idea of some other being that they are unable to account for'. Referring to the 'testimony of Tertullian', Leturdu thought he was justified in taking this for the evidence of 'a naturally Christian soul, having at heart the idea of a unique and supreme god'.

From the standpoint of modern ethnography, Leturdu's observations are undoubtedly biased, but they do contain some reliable information. Ryūkyūan culture does in fact differentiate between two kinds of primordial *kami*. Firstly there are those dwelling in the sky, who are called *tin nu kam* 天の神, and secondly there are those dwelling at the bottom of the sea or somewhere towards the horizon, a place which is generally called *nirai*, a notion cognate with the Japanese *ne no kuni* 根の国 and *tokoyo* 常世 found in the *Kojiki* 古事記 and *Nihon shoki* 日本書紀 myths.[20] Moreover, according to a widespread belief imported from China, the *kami* of the kitchen fire, *fii nu kam* 火の神, are conceived as go-betweens reporting human deeds to the *kami* of the sky at the end of each year.[21]

Leturdu does not seem to be aware that, unlike in Japan, Buddhism had never been deeply rooted in Okinawa. Recalling the 'evil role' played by

20 C. Blacker, *The catalpa bow: a study of shamanistic practices in Japan* (London: George Allen & Unwin, 1975), pp. 73–5, 325.
21 Kubo Noritada 窪徳忠, *Chūgoku bunka to nantō* 中国文化と南島 (Daiichi Shobō, 1981), p. 350; P. Beillevaire, 'Spacial characteristics of human temporality in the Ryūkyūs', p. 78.

Buddhist monks in the repression of Christianity in sixteenth- and seventeenth-century Japan, he understandably had no reason to grieve over the wretchedness and the poor reputation that they now enjoyed: 'Today, these poor priests, reduced to a small number [only 35 we are told below], are held in general contempt; they are called ignorant, lazy, and good-for-nothing; the mildest of their critics say that they are totally degenerate and that they are being maintained simply out of regard for Antiquity which bequeathed them' (p. 385). The reason he puts forward to explain their low numbers is that they 'do not marry, [that] they cannot eat but rice and vegetables; [that] they have to lead a rather secluded life: all this, albeit one knows that in reality the bonzes are living as everybody else, has a look of austerity that frightens and rebuffs' (p. 386). Apparently discouraged, they would spend their meditation time either sleeping or smoking, and many of them had become so addicted to alcohol 'that all of their earnings go on it' (p. 380).

Generally ignorant of Japan's complex cultural history, the Catholic missionaries thought, right up to the 'opening' of Japan in the 1850s, that they would find their foremost enemies in the Buddhist clergy. They were apparently confident that popular religious practices, loosely structured as they were, would not be able to resist Christian teaching, but they were particularly afraid that the Buddhist church might prove to be an obstacle, rivalling their own hierarchical organisation and also enjoying the backing of the government. Leturdu noted, therefore, with satisfaction, that the monks seemed to be deprived of the high esteem and influence they had been able to boast of in the days of Francis Xavier. In his view, their present state was a clear punishment for the evil influence they had exercised against the early Japanese Christians. In his diary he bluntly notes: 'Poor bonzes: funerals apart, nobody calls upon them'. People would even 'insult them by sacrificing to hotokes without their help' (p. 361). Eventually he came to deplore what he called the 'coldness for religious things' of the Okinawans, which he attributed to the monks' neglect of the practice of religious teaching and to the lack of public religious ceremonies (pp. 361, 363). The weakened foes were now being blamed for having failed to maintain their social standing and, as a result, for not having sustained the faith of the people.

What Leturdu had learned about the life of the historical Buddha, Shaka (=Śākyamuni), termed by him 'father of the bonzes', led him to think that the whole story had in fact been made up from particulars relating to the story of Christ (pp. 387–9). This forgery, he thought, would have occurred soon after the introduction of Christianity to India, in the age of the Apostles, the local Buddhist clergy having been at once impressed by the life and doctrines of the founder of Christianity. So for him, it was only supposed borrowings from Christianity that could account for the success met by Buddhism in

Asia. What he could now observe made him feel confident enough to assert: 'nowadays Bonzism is a dead body, no longer living in the mind or in the heart of the people. If it is still occupying the ground, it is just a matter of habit and also because the people have nothing to put in its place. But come the Gospel, they will bury the corpse at once!'

Leturdu usually takes Okinawa to be representative of all Japan. However, in some parts of the Report, he clearly sets the religious situation in Okinawa apart from that in Japan. 'No nunneries are found in the Ryūkyūs', he wrote, 'but they still exist in Japan. Bonzes are also in great number there. Processions and public sacrifices are performed as in St Francis Xavier's time. The Japanese need religious exercises, whereas in the Ryūkyūs they are totally indifferent to that matter' (pp. 380–1).

Leturdu gives earnest consideration to the explanations provided by Okinawans about the fate of souls after death. It is noticeable that for him, although he was no exception among the missionaries, the fear of death was the main incentive for believing in God. So, implicit in his inquiry there is the hope that the Okinawan people could be interested in getting from his teaching a more coherent perspective and eventually be converted. He observes that common people and monks alike 'believe in another life, a happy one for good people, an unhappy one for the wicked' (p. 390). But the fact that the Buddhist monks also believed in reincarnation ('metempsychosis' is the word he uses) quite puzzled him. So he asked them how it was possible for a soul to be at the same time located in an animal, in a tablet, in a tomb, in paradise, or in hell. Though he could never get an answer, he says, he had read somewhere that each person possessed several souls: but then, he wonders, why would those souls 'not partake of the same reward or punishment?' (p. 389). He hastened to add that 'it would be unjustly severe to expect any rationality from pagan creeds'. As for the contradiction he perceived between, on the one hand, the notions of paradise and hell, and, on the other, the belief in reincarnation, his tentative explanation was that the souls condemned to hell could be redeemed by giving money to the monks who intercede with the gods through their prayers (for that reason he calls them, with a touch of irony, 'friends of the gods'; p. 392). Still, those souls afterwards had to dwell in the bodies of some base animals before being given a new opportunity to be reborn as a man. The souls of people who had committed only mild offences, although they would escape being thrown into hell, would have to undergo a purgatorial period of some sort before reaching the 'Elysian Fields' (p. 393).

Although Leturdu had the idea that in theory Buddhist monks ought to be pantheist, he found most of them well aware of the distinction to be made, as he put it, between the 'infinite Being' and 'limited beings' (p. 390). As for

169

the nobles, he regretted that their acquaintance with Chinese books had made them religious nihilists. A discussion with a monk, whom he introduced as a kind old man, gave him occasion to express his own opinions about Confucianism. Though he concedes that one may accept Confucianism as a social philosophy, he goes on to regret that 'it provides no sound rules for conducting one's private life'. Moreover, he regarded its concept of God as much too vague, and deplored that fact that it had nothing to say about the punishments a soul could expect after death (p. 391).

After Shaka, Leturdu assigned four other 'famous' deities to Buddhism. As regards the first, Amida, he confessed that he 'knows nothing, save that it is one of the gods related to Tartarus' (p. 393). The other three happen to be in fact local *kami*, and in the Report he recorded tales circulating about them (p. 393–7). One was Buza, who was supposed to be helpful to shipwrecked people. The second was Futenma Gongen-ganashii 普天間権現, the goddess attached to Futenma Gū 普天間宮, one of the most popular shrines on the island.[22] The third *kami* was represented by a tale about a farmer named Mikaru-ganashii; this is but one version of the widespread tale of Hagoromo, the woman with a feather, or 'winged', gown. Leturdu's overall comment about these tales is that: 'One has to admit that a more than average faith is needed to trust such stories.' He also gives us an idea of his attitude towards his interlocutors: 'When we were told such things, we could not help starting to laugh. They looked offended and used to say that we should not be told anything because we were incredulous, that it has however always been taken for granted that extraordinary things occurred in olden times about which all the ancients agree. But they eventually laughed with us too' (p. 397). The myth of the origins of the kingdom in the first part of the Report, in fact reproduced from Gaubil, also amazed him for being very exotic, 'a tale that one would believe to have been borrowed from the history of the Egyptians or Scythians' (p. 562).

Leturdu took a particular interest in the Bon festival which occurs in Okinawa between the thirteenth and the seventeenth day of the seventh lunar month. His report quotes a popular tale about its origin: a child, ill-treated by his stepmother, longs desperately for his dead mother and thinks of dying himself; an old man, touched by his distress, tells him that he can see his mother once a year, about the middle of the seventh month, by peeping with a bamboo into her tomb; doing so, the child sees his mother and confesses his sorrow to her; she begs him to stay alive and, instead of letting himself die, to visit her again at the same time; as instructed, the child gets into the habit of bringing offerings every year to the tomb where his mother appears

22 *Ganashii* is an honorific term. *Gongen* is transcribed *gounnguinn* in the Report, in accordance with local pronunciation.

in the shape of a butterfly (p. 399–400). Leturdu describes how on the first day of the festival, at sunset, each family welcomes the souls of its departed members and guides them to the house where they are served a meal in front of the ancestral altar: 'then, one keeps silent for half an hour because the souls are eating!' (p. 398). When this is over, 'they all leave the ancestors' room except the old man, who probably stays there to inquire about that other world where he soon will go'. These four days are a time of great rejoicing. On the last evening, torches are lit again and the family walk in procession from the altar to accompany the souls back to the door: 'at that moment begins the strangest of all ceremonies. For fear that one of the souls, too fond of good living, might succumb to its desire to stay, everyone grasps a stick and starts hitting out in every place to chase away any poor soul which might have such a desire.' The author terms these doings 'barbarous' and says 'he teased Okinawans a lot, asking them where that affection for their ancestors of which they were so proud had gone'. 'They answered with laughter: "we have been taught so to believe and to act."' He also points out, as another matter for derision, the incoherence of a ritual forcing souls to walk all their way back home to restore themselves while they are proceeding to paradise. Only in his diary does he mention that he had learnt that explanation from the Jesuit Luis Frois.

A whole chapter of the Report is concerned with 'tombs and funerals'. There are two kinds of tombs, says Leturdu: 'some have the shape of a horseshoe as in China, others are dug like caves in the hills as in Japan' (pp. 401, 358). The coffins, he notes, are square in shape and the deceased stands inside with the legs pressed against the chest. When someone is on the point of dying, moanings fill the house, mixed with the faint sound of a bell intended to ward off evil spirits. After the death, the loud cries of professional wailers are heard all around. 'If the house has a few bowls of rice to give to bonzes, one, two, three of them are called, at will' (p. 402).[23] Once, accompanied by Adnet, he dared to join a funeral procession in spite of the whispers of the participants. Two 'mumbling monks' walked in front of the coffin, 'a kind of kennel painted in red and embellished with gold'. Their heads were swinging so fast that they looked to him 'like weathercocks during a typhoon'. After giving some details concerning funeral attire, 'superstitious banners', and the offerings brought to the tomb, the Report indicates the length of the period of mourning required and the afflictions to be endured by mourners according to the degree of kinship. During the first fifty days following a father's or a mother's death, 'one had better die than live', it notes, and 'one spends days and nights next to the tomb' in 'a small

---

23 This sentence concerning the monks is derogatory in French, with the use of the word *écuelle* for 'bowl'.

straw hut called a mourning house' erected for that purpose (pp. 403–4). Memorial services were subsequently performed on fixed days, until the final ritual of bone-washing, but these were said to be the concern only of women. Probably confusing Okinawa with Japan, Leturdu appears to hold the view that it had earlier been the practise to burn the dead on funeral pyres, not leave them to decay, whereas now, he observes, cremation is only practiced in the case of monks (p. 402). In his diary he remarks that 'ancestor worship is more alive than the cult of *kami* and *hotoke*' and he gives a brief but accurate account of the patrilineal system based on strict primogeniture that is the rule in Okinawa: family-groups are divided into stem and branch households, and, despite having a collective tomb, each branch keeps separate custody of the ancestral tablets of its successive heads (p. 365).[24]

The Report also contains a brief socio-linguistic analysis of honorific forms with a few Okinawan sentences cited as supporting evidence. This is intended to demonstrate the deep concern for social hierarchy that infused, or, as Leturdu thought, marred, the daily life of the people. The introductory remarks betray the long-nurtured resentment of the Catholic Church against the Japanese authorities responsible for its banishment: 'Japan, as one knows, is not exactly a land of freedom. Besides the despotic autocrats who rule with terror and arbitrary decisions, everybody's superior is a despot. Mandarins lord it over nobles, nobles over common people, the master over his slaves, the father over his wife and his children. Language necessarily mirrors so deep a servitude...' (p. 406) The unavoidable pressure of hierarchy, in Okinawa as in Japan, would have found a direct expression in the constant usage of suffixes 'that make verbs have an almost unending length'. The author records other non-linguistic data that seemed to him to carry the same sense of social differentiation: styles of hairdressing, hairpins made of gold, silver, or copper, caps of different colours, and garments.

Okinawan women, he found, suffered from the most servile of conditions, constantly devoted as they were to a husband who is their 'lord and master' (p. 410). 'As in all pagan countries, which take no part in the regeneration of man by the woman [i.e., the Virgin Mary], women live here under the burden of the Curse. They are slaves, victims of Eve's sin' (p. 358) He also denounced the nobles' monopoly on education, which in his view perpetuated the people's bondage (p. 408).

Leturdu's general feeling about the Okinawans, that they are gentle and easy-going but shallow people, spontaneously more inclined to chat and drink than to work, differed little from the views expressed by Engelbert Kaempfer one and a half centuries earlier. 'They work out of necessity',

---

24 Until recently, contrary to the prevailing custom in Japan, Okinawans were reluctant to destroy the mortuary tablet following completion of the memorial services.

Leturdu writes. 'Their social behaviour is polished, corruption seems to be unknown'; furthermore, 'no spectacle [entertainment] can be seen', a fact about which the missionary would hardly complain' (pp. 412–13). However, their politeness appears to him tinged with flattery and obsequiousness, and the fear they had for their masters would impel them to lie. Nevertheless, he remained confident that Okinawans could easily be converted: 'it is impossible to imagine a country with a better disposition and presenting fewer obstacles' (p. 535). The people 'are righteous, they do not believe in idols, they feel no attraction towards any state-sponsored cult, which, anyhow, is not found on Okinawa; they do not crave for luxury or for that consuming activity that results from feverish trade', so they shared all the virtues that supposedly belonged to the rural and anti-republican France of the age, as illustrated in some of Balzac's novels.

Several times Leturdu seems to deplore the fact that neither temple meetings nor processions could be observed in Okinawa. Once, however, as reported in the diary, he and Adnet witnessed an event which they thought bore some resemblance to a procession. It was 'a trip on the waters made by fishermen'. What the author then relates in lively terms is the *haarii* festival, a ritual competition enacted once a year to bring about a good harvest. His description reads as follows:

> ... it takes place on the 4th [day] of the 5th month. During our first year we witnessed the departure ceremony. It was 5:30 a.m. We were saying our prayers when the sound of tom-toms reached our ears. This quite intrigued us, as never before had we heard such a thing. We authorized ourselves to interrupt our meditations and take a look. We went out and got to where the ceremony was taking place. One individual carrying a large oar was leading the way; three banners followed; then, thirty seamen in full dress, each with an oar and a piece of wood. In one place lay the tail and the head of a dragon. A little farther, we set eyes on another, smaller, one. These are the two dragons Gee and Xin, worshipped in China, and the story of them can be found in the *Documenta rationis*.[25] Here, nothing is known about them, even Confucius' story remains unknown. 'We do here as in China', that is their first and last motivation. But let us return to the procession. It reached the bottom of a tree standing at the entrance to Tumai. A woman arrived and

25 The author of the *Documenta [rectae] rationis* was Bishop Jean-Louis Taberd: *Documentatio rectae rationis, seu forma instructionis ad usum alumnorum sinensium, anamitarum* ... (Serampore: Missions Etrangères, 1839). His book was intended to facilitate missionary work in China and Vietnam.

offered a sacrifice. This over, she retired. Thereupon men came to present rice and sake out of which they soon made a libation in their stomachs [i.e., they drank it]. It was curious to watch them presenting in turn the cup to their gods before drinking it themselves. When that first sacrifice was completed, a boat of many colours was brought in. The thirty rowers squatted inside. The tail of the long snake was then fastened to the front of the boat, and its head to the rear with one of the two tom-tom carriers standing next to it. At a signal from the tom-tom player, the oars were raised and then smoothly entered the water, which sprouted each time into the air, as a kind of libation probably, while the banners were rhythmically swung by their carriers before the snake god's head and tail! The boat thus came and went thrice in front of the bystanders. At that moment, as the tom-tom sound accelerated, the oars quickened and it moved away, heading towards Nafa where a similar boat was awaiting Tumai's in order to go alongside it to an old palace, fallen in ruins, where a sacrifice was to be offered to the god that invented boats. The men rowed with prodigious speed. Their leaders were writhing, stretching out their arms, shaking their whole bodies like demons. The reason for such behaviour is that the more intense the efforts and the contortions are, the more pleased the god is. The journey there and back took three hours during which the tom-tom sounded continuously. The rest of the day was spent idly. The victim of the sacrifice is a pig on which, together with sake, they feasted on the spot. Some other people told me that the two snakes or dragons are simply a representation of the dragon controlling the sea. It causes whirlwinds by sucking up the water to quench its thirst. If someone disappears at sea, they offer sacrifices, asking it to bring back the soul to the tablet set up by the children of the deceased (pp. 363–4).

Apart from his rather contemptuous depiction of the consumption of the offerings by the participants themselves, which might betray embarrassment at the similarity to the essence of the Mass, Leturdu unwittingly points out here two important original features of Okinawan culture: the female predominance in rituals and the use of pork for offerings. Had he known that they were not quite in accordance with Buddhist principles prevailing in mainland Japan, his attention might have been more specifically drawn to them. He was somewhat better informed about Chinese customs, and was of course right when he attributed a continental origin to the ritual competition he observed.[26] It is also, incidentally, possible to discern a foreshadowing of

26 It is said that dragon boat race festivals were introduced to Okinawa during the

the diffusionism versus functionalism controversy in the irritation felt by the missionary-ethnographer when he discovered that there was no necessary close connection between the origin of a ritual and its actual meaning for the people who perform it. Like the Jesuits in China he used the word 'sacrifice' to denote any offering or oblation to the gods or to the ancestors, without implying actual or symbolic blood-shedding. Even though there can be no doubt that in his opinion Christ's was the only worthy sacrifice, Leturdu never appears hesitant to use that word in the Okinawan context.

Addressing his superiors, he expressed the hope that the Ryūkyū islands would be the 'cradle of Japan's religious regeneration' (p. 573). The only serious hindrance, that had haunted the missionaries since the seventeenth-century persecutions, would remain the Japanese government itself. Like all of his colleagues, Leturdu was convinced that Japan's conversion to Christianity was only prevented by her despotic rulers. Their 'selfish interest', their 'contempt for the people' would lead them to oppose the diffusion of Christianity and therefore the salvation of their subjects with all means at their disposal. It was because he no longer believed in the possibility of an autonomous future for Okinawa that he was harshly critical of the bakufu, the government in Edo: 'What is adorned with the name of the Kingdom of Okinawa [Oukigna] is nothing but a province or a department of Japan. The reason that it is called a kingdom, a word that should properly refer to an independent state, lies in the vanity of Japanese monarchs who wanted the ancient local kings to retain their original title after they had submitted, in order to have the vainglory of ruling over kings instead of state commissioners. That sounds much better' (pp. 545–6).[27] There are only two possibilities left, he says, for the future: 'a first-order miracle that will show everybody, brighter than the day, that God stands on our side; or, better, the paralysis of Japanese potency thanks to foreign intervention. Unless this happens, there is no hope that this country could be converted' (pp. 535, 354).

By 1848, when he was in Hong Kong, the second of these possibilities was beginning to look probable. He was then in a position to announce to his correspondents that the Americans were preparing an expedition to force the opening of Japan. To this end they would, he said, be ready to occupy a part of the empire. As serious consideration was being given at the same time to the establishment of a shipping-route for steamers by the Ryūkyū islands,

sixteenth century by Chinese settled in Kume village: W. P. Lebra, *Okinawan religion. Belief, ritual and social structure* (Honolulu: University of Hawaii Press, 1966), p.145.

27 More than ten years were to pass before the role of Satsuma was fully appreciated. Captain Jurien de la Gravière blamed only the 'slavish habits' of Ryūkyū officials for preventing them from resisting the 'moral pressure' of Japan: de la Gravière, *Voyage en Chine*, vol. 1, p. 226.

there were good reasons to suppose that Okinawa might be the chosen place. Moreover, he foresaw that the British might swiftly follow the Americans. Since the island had been deprived of all its defences by the Japanese, he was expecting no special difficulties for the Americans: '[The Japanese] could well be duped by their own policy!' (p. 554). Whatever future developments might be, the Report concludes the matter with a fine piece of rhetoric: 'We owe it to the saints who are so fervently praying for the missions' (p. 415).

The tone was not always so optimistic in the diary or in the letters. At times he seems desperate that he might have no conversions to his credit. Near the end of his stay, he complained that his mission was like a 'barren woman' (p. 372). But it is not altogether clear whether his essential motivation was the salvation of other people or his own salvation through suffering. He welcomed the hardships he was enduring, he says, because they 'associate him with Christ's pain and then with his glory'.[28]

Leturdu is probably the only missionary of that period who dared to worry explicitly about the alliance between the cross and the gun, even though he remained thoroughly ambivalent. He admits that he would not mind seeing 'Religion' introduced into Japan with the help of France. He judges this method to be 'fairly human' but feels at the same time that it should not be 'the usual way' (p. 348). He is fully aware that it is precisely because 'Japanese emperors' were once convinced that missionaries were nothing but the 'envoys of Western powers' that they have conceived such a hatred for them. To his diary he confides: 'And as a matter of fact, the first missionaries coming back after two hundred years are carried by men-of-war, settled by men-of-war, and would gain freedom thanks to men-of-war. A fine confirmation of [the] prejudice [of Japanese]!' And, he adds, 'that idea was hurting us'. At other times he appears frankly irritated by the political standpoint of the Okinawan and Japanese authorities: '... we are considered to be governmental emissaries; for what purpose? I do not know. Would our government need to send people to prepare the roads and the minds for a foreign invasion if its intent were to seize this miserable island, an invisible spot on the earth!' Observing that the policy so far followed by Western governments seemed to have no effect whatsoever on the attitude of the Japanese authorities, he concludes that 'it is better to force one's way into Japan than not to enter at all', and feels finally reassured that 'the gun appears to be the only means that Providence is desirous of using for the opening of an Empire to the Gospel.'[29]

The relationship between power and religion was not understood by the missionaries consistently, for their own interests had a considerable hold on

28 Letter to Libois, 22 July 1846: Archives, vol. 569, p. 14.
29 Letter to Thivet, 22 September 1847, Archives, vol. 569, p. 58.

their minds. Forcade especially, and to a lesser extent Leturdu, who was a man of milder manners, were prompt to denounce the hold of Okinawan or Japanese authorities over religion, failing to notice that they themselves did not hesitate to call upon their government when necessary and to threaten their unwilling hosts with its possible intervention. Vague agreements were forced upon the other party, any infringement of which could always be tactically alleged to justify military action, as was indeed the case in 1847 in the bay of Tourane, on the Vietnamese coast, in an incident involving this same Forcade.

The very day before Leturdu's arrival, another missionary, Bernard Jean Bettelheim, had taken up residence on Okinawa with his family. A dedicated but self-assured man, he was a member of the Church of England sent to Okinawa with funds from the Loochoo Naval Mission, a society founded by one of Captain Hall's officers.[30] Though beyond the scope of this paper, the relations between the Roman Catholic priests and the British missionary are themselves of interest. The linguistic skills and the unfailing zeal of the latter obviously irritated the French priests. But Bettelheim was probably no more tolerant than they were of Okinawan customs and beliefs. As he was a heretic in the eyes of the Catholics, his friendly overtures were promptly rejected with minimal politeness. Leturdu considers him to be 'the other enemy ... more dissimulating and no less dangerous' than the local authorities.[31] In writings intended to be read by colleagues and superiors, the French priests could certainly not afford to show the faintest sign of dealings with a 'Protestant'. It is striking that passages dealing with him have been deleted from those of their writings (including Forcade's) which were published. In fact, there are hints in Leturdu's diary that, as time passed, especially when Adnet's health worsened, some fellow-feeling arose based on their shared experience of life in seclusion.[32]

Leturdu left Okinawa on 27 August 1848 aboard the *Bayonnaise*, the first French ship to visit Okinawa since the departure of Admiral Cécille's division. Profoundly grief-stricken by the death of his colleague, and now convinced that Forcade would not come back, he embarked without hesitation. He had no real choice anyway. The commanding officer, Captain Jurien de la Gravière, had received written instructions to take the missionary away or, if

30 Kerr, *Okinawa*, pp. 279ff; Y. Teruya, 'Bernard J. Bettelheim and Okinawa: a study of the first protestant missionary to the island kingdom, 1846–1854' (unpublished PhD dissertation, University of Colorado, 1969).
31 Letter to Thivet, 22 September 1847: Archives, vol. 569, p. 58.
32 See also the testimony of E. Jurien de la Gravière in *Voyage en Chine*, vol. 1, pp. 221–2, 229.

he refused, to tell the Ryūkyū authorities that he was remaining on his own responsibility (p. 372). After some time spent in Hong Kong, Leturdu was assigned to the mission to Guangdong and Guangxi provinces. He was never to return to Okinawa, nor ever to visit any other part of Japan.

8

Accommodating the alien: Ōkuni Takamasa and the religion of the Lord of Heaven

John Breen

INTRODUCTION

Ōkuni Takamasa 大国隆正 (1792–1871), a *kokugakusha* 国学者 of the Tsuwano 津和野 domain, is a key figure, arguably *the* key figure, in the intellectual history of the Meiji Restoration. Hattori Shisō 服部之総 was perhaps the first historian to note this. Nearly half a century ago, he commented on Ōkuni's writings that they provided the frame for the 'picture' of the Charter Oath, that they alone promised to unravel the complexities of Shintō in Restoration Japan.[1] In the longer term, Hattori believed Ōkuni furnished the blueprint for the foreign adventurism and mercantilism that, for him, were part and parcel of Meiji 'absolutism'.[2] It was at about the same time, too, that Maruyama Masao 丸山真男 was depicting Ōkuni as a major player in bakumatsu 幕末 intellectual history, bracketing him alongside Sakuma Shōzan 佐久間象山 and Yoshida Shōin 吉田松陰 as 'the keenest of xenophobes' and yet 'the most vigorous advocate of open country politics'.[3] No doubt because Hattori and Maruyama failed to support their weighty claims for Ōkuni Takamasa, subsequent work on bakumatsu and Restoration intellectual history – and even work specifically on late Tokugawa *kokugaku* – tended to overlook Ōkuni Takamasa and his writings. He remained, for many years, a forgotten intellectual. Recently, however, there has been

This essay draws on several earlier studies I have made of Ōkuni Takamasa's thought. See especially Breen, 'Bakumatsu ishinki no shintō shisō' 幕末維新期の神道思想 in Yasumaru Yoshio 安丸良夫 and Miyachi Masato 宮地正人, eds., *Kindai Nihon shisō taikei* 近代日本思想体系 5, 'Kokka to shūkyō' 国家と宗教 (Furoku geppō 付録月報, 4) (Iwanami Shoten, 1988), and Breen, 'Shintoists in Restoration Japan: towards a reassessment', *Modern Asian studies* 24 (1990): 579–602. A different version is due to appear shortly in *Nihon rekishi*.

1 Hattori Shisō, 'Zettaishugi no tsugiki' 絶対主義の接木 (originally written in 1949), in *Kurofune zengo, Hattori Shisō zuihitsushū* 黒船前後 服部之総随筆集 (Chikuma Shobō, 1966), pp. 109, 114.
2 *Ibid.*, pp. 106–7.
3 Maruyama Masao, *Nihon seiji shisōshi kenkyū* 日本政治思想史研究 (Tōkyō Daigaku shuppankai, 1952), p. 348.

179

something of a 'rediscovery' of the man; and evidence to support the views of Hattori and Maruyama is just now beginning to surface.

Tamagake Hiroyuki's 玉掛博之 seminal study of Ōkuni's views on theology and history has revealed a thinker of a very different sort from Hirata Atsutane 平田篤胤 and his bakumatsu disciples.[4] If it was ever true of the Hirata group that they were 'obsessed with the vision of antiquity', it was most certainly not the case with the politically aware, forward-looking Ōkuni and his followers.[5] Takeda Hideaki 武田秀章 subsequently demonstrated, *inter alia*, the critical role played by Ōkuni and his disciples Fukuba Bisei 福羽美静 and Kamei Koremi 亀井茲監 in the ritual and religious policies of the early Meiji government. Fukuba and Kamei, like Ōkuni himself, were clearly men whose views were at one with the Restoration leadership, and, incidentally, quite at odds with those of the Hirata faction.[6]

The present study draws on the recent work of Tamagake, Takeda and others to explore Ōkuni's thought from a different perspective. In short, it seeks to analyse the changing attitudes towards Christianity evident in Ōkuni's writings from the open-ports period (1853–4), through the high point of the anti-foreign movement (1862–3) and beyond, to the Restoration period (1867–8). Three considerations seem to make this a worthwhile topic to pursue. Firstly, Christianity was, throughout the period under consideration, a constant preoccupation for Ōkuni Takamasa, inseparable from his perception of the Western challenge. Secondly, there is, in Ōkuni's thought, a striking 'flexibility', to use Hattori's term,[7] and, to anticipate the conclusion, this flexibility – this capacity for accommodation – is manifest in Ōkuni's attitude not only to Western 'techniques', but also to the Western 'ethic' of Christianity. In other words, Ōkuni's thought opens up the possibility of an approach to the West in bakumatsu Japan that was neither the rejection of all things foreign, technological and ethical alike, of Ōhashi Totsuan 大橋訥庵, nor the ambivalence of Sakuma Shōzan, Yoshida Shōin and Yokoi Shōnan 横井小楠 that countenanced the accommodation of technology on the one hand,

---

4 Tamagake Hiroyuki, 'Bakumatsu ni okeru "rekishi" to "shukyō" – Ōkuni Takamasa ni okeru shūkyōron to rekishiron to no kanren o megutte' 幕末に置ける『歴史』と『宗教』 — 大国隆正における宗教論と歴史論との関連をめぐって, *Tōhoku Daigaku Bungakubu Nenpō* 東北大学文学部年報 31 (1982).

5 Yasumaru Yoshio, *Kamigami no Meiji Ishin* 神々の明治維新 (Iwanami Shoten, 1979), p. 48.

6 Takeda Hideaki, 'Kindai tennōsaishi keisei katei no ichikōsatsu' 近代天皇際祀形成過程の一考察, in Inoue Nobutaka 井上順孝 and Sakamoto Koremaru 阪本是丸, eds., *Nihongata seikyō kankei no tanjō* 日本型政教関係の誕生 (Daiichi Shobō, 1987).

7 Hattori Shisō, 'Aoyama Hanzo' 青山半蔵, in *Kurofune zengo*, p. 341.

whilst rejecting the ethical on the other. The third justification relates to Takeda's demonstration of the profound influence that Ōkuni's ideas had on the religious policies of the Restoration government. Given that this was so, it is reasonable to suppose that the study offered here of Ōkuni's views on Christianity in the period leading up to the Restoration might provide useful insights into the 'inside' of Restoration policy on religion in general, and on Christianity in particular.[8]

THE 'POSSIBILITIES' OF ŌKUNI SHINTŌ (OPEN-PORTS PERIOD:1853–4)

Ōkuni Takamasa's views on Christianity at this and any other time need to be set briefly in the context of his perception of the world and the West.[9] These are perhaps most lucidly expressed in *Gyojū mondō* 馭戎問答 (Dialogue on coastal defence), a text written and presented to Tokugawa Nariaki 徳川斉昭 in 1854. Its main argument went as follows. Recent years had seen the appearance of ever larger numbers of foreign vessels off Japan's coastline, entirely fitting for an age commemorating the 2,500th anniversary of Emperor Jinmu's 神武 accession. It was but one sign that the world was to be 'renewed'. 'It is a reason to rejoice!' The anger and resentment of many Japanese, their insistence that the foreigners be driven off, were all easy for Ōkuni to understand, but they were, he argued, feelings that arose from an inadequate grasp of the plans that Amaterasu had in store for Japan.[10]

The 2,500th anniversary of Jinmu's accession marked, for Ōkuni, a time more significant still than the 312th, the 625th and the 1,250th anniversaries, each of them epochal in its own way.[11] This new age would witness the spread of Ōkuni's Shintō throughout Japan and the world and, accompanying it, the establishment of a new global order centred on Japan, and Amaterasu's descendant, the emperor. That the unfolding of this new global order depended

8 I have offered a reinterpretation of Restoration religious policy in 'Emperor, state and religion in Restoration Japan: 1868–1877', unpublished PhD dissertation, Cambridge University, 1992.

9 I have benefited here from Tamagake, 'Bakumatsu ni okeru rekishi to shūkyō', and Takeda Hideaki, 'Peri-raikō to Ōkuni Takamasa' ペリー来航と大国隆正, *Shintōgaku* 神道学 140 (1989): 12–39.

10 *Gyojū mondō* in *Ōkuni Takamasa zenshū* (Yūkōsha, 1927; hereafter referred to as *Zenshū*), vol. 1, p. 5.

11 For Ōkuni and history, see, in addition to Tamagake, Arakawa Hisao 荒川久男, 'Ōkuni Takamasa no kakuunron ni tsuite – sono rekishikan no ichikōsatsu' 大国隆正の革運論について ― その歴史観の一考察, *Kōgakkan daigaku ronsō* 皇学館大学論叢, 7.1 (1981).

on the 'accommodation', in some as yet unexplored form, of foreigners, and not their expulsion, goes without saying.

Ōkuni's positive approach to the West's *démarche* was sustained by two things: an obsessive interest in contemporary world developments on the one hand, and unswerving faith in Amaterasu on the other. As early as 1818, Ōkuni had studied Western learning in Nagasaki with Yoshio Gonnosuke 吉夫権之助 and had, thereafter, determined to 'study the world to benefit the Way of this great nation'. Most of his knowledge was gleaned from geographical works by scholars of Western studies, such as Mitsukuri Shōgo's 箕作省吾 *Kon'yo zushiki* 坤興図式 (Descriptive geography of the world) (1845–6).[12] If in 1854 he was not yet an expert on the West, his attitude to the knowledge he was acquiring promised to make him one: 'One should regard Western science', he wrote, 'as a legacy of Sukunahikona 少彦名 [a deity prominent in the first chapter of the *Nihon shoki* supposed to have assisted in the creation of the world]; Japanese scholars should avail themselves of it. [Western knowledge] is a virtue bestowed on us by Sukunahikona ... it is a proper way, by no means contravening the sacred classics'.[13] Western knowledge could also, then, be accommodated in some way or other within Ōkuni's branch of the Shintō tradition of learning. Ōkuni's faith in Amaterasu, the second factor, is apparent enough from the foregoing, but we should pause to note the *possibilities* that this faith – so limiting in theory – contained. For, it was precisely his belief in the gods, in Amaterasu above all, that justified the importation of Western knowledge, and the same belief that made the advent of Westerners a matter for rejoicing. In short, it was Shintō beliefs that gave Ōkuni an enthusiasm that set him apart from intellectual contemporaries of his, like Fujita Tōko 藤田東湖, Sakuma Shōzan and Yokoi Shōnan.[14] What, then, were the implications of this preoccupation with the West, and this Amaterasu faith, for Western religion?

Of three immediately discernible implications, the first is what we might call Christianity's 'theological accommodation'. The example *par excellence* concerns Ōkuni's theories of cosmogony. As Arakawa has demonstrated, Ōkuni's encounter with Western theories of creation in works by Yamamura Saisuke 山村才助 and other *rangakusha* prompted him to make a drastic revision of the *Nihon shoki* 日本書記 (Chronicles of Japan) and the *Kojiki*

---

12 On this, see especially Arakawa Hisao, 'Ōkuni Takamasa no chūkōkigenron ni tsuite – sono rangaku to no kakawariai' 大国隆正の中興紀元論について — その蘭学とのかかわりあい, *Kōgakkan daigaku ronsō*, 3.6 (1984).
13 *Gakuunron* 学運論, *Zenshū* vol. 4, pp. 78–80.
14 On Fujita Tōko, Sakuma Shōzan, Yokoi Shōnan and their respective views of the West, see Uete Michiari 植手通有, *Nihon kindai shisō no keisei* 日本近代思想の形成 (Iwanami Shoten, 1973).

古事紀 (Records of ancient matters) creation stories.[15] Ōkuni rearranged the traditional pre-world into five ages corresponding to the five he discovered in Yamamura's *Seiyō zakki* 西洋雑記 (Miscellaneous notes on the Western world), itself indebted to Gottfried's *History of the West* (1660).[16] Both the Christian original and Ōkuni's revised version begin with creation, but where the former ends with the revolutionary event of Christ's death, Ōkuni's concludes with the revolutionary event of Jinmu's accession. In this revised schema, Adam, Eve and Cain all had their part to play. 'There were many sacred beings who sped through the air from one country to the next [in the Age of the Gods]. It is likely that Adam and Cain were themselves such sacred beings'.[17] 'Adam may well have been a spirit born of Itakeru no kami, who took Eve as his wife and then opened up the Western world'.[18] Ōkuni's view that 'there is no need to doubt either Western or Japanese theories of creation' comes, then, as little surprise.[19] The Christian creator and Christ himself were also accommodated: 'the creator in Christianity is a being that appeared as a consequence of the will of Takamimusubi no kami 高御産巣日神.'[20] Again, 'I hear that the founder of the Christian religion was born of a virgin, and was a teacher from his earliest days. If this is in fact the case, he may perhaps have sprung from Hiruko'.[21] The temptation to dismiss all this as typical nativist nonsense should be resisted. Ōkuni, albeit from a Shintō perspective, is clearly trying to understand; his instinct is not to reject, but to accept and explain.

The second feature of Ōkuni's view of Christianity is an extension of the first, and further evidence of the 'possibilities' inherent in Shintō universalism. That is, it is almost impossible to find him referring to Christianity with terms denoting 'perniciousness' like *jashū* 邪宗, *jakyō* 邪教 and *yōkyō* 妖教. It is true that Ōkuni is nowhere to be found denying Christianity's perniciousness in the early 1850s, but his reluctance to employ terms of the *jashū* ilk is an inevitable result of his belief that Christianity occupied some as yet ill-defined place within Shintō theology. We shall return to this question below, but here it should be noted that the absence from his writings of such emotive terminology offers a striking contrast to the anti-Christian polemic

15 Arakawa, 'Ōkuni Takamasa no chūkōkigenron', pp. 9–14.
16 *Ibid.*, p. 9.
17 *Gyojū mondō*, p. 127.
18 *Ibid.*, p. 128.
19 *Ibid.*, p. 129.
20 *Naobinotama hochū* 直毘霊補注, *Zenshū*, vol. 2, p. 193.
21 *Bunbu kyojitsuron* 文武虚実論, p. 216; *Zenshū*, vol. 1, p. 5.

of Confucianists, of Mito 水戸 scholars and of Buddhists, too, in this open-ports period.[22]

The third dimension to add to Ōkuni's view that Christianity is neither theologically incompatible nor *necessarily* pernicious is his conviction that its practice must, under no circumstances, be permitted in Japan. Justification for this is offered in the *Bunbu kyojitsuron* 文武虚実論 (Literary and military learning: truth and falsehood) of 1853, and the *Gyojū mondō* of 1854.

> The reason for the frequent visits of foreign vessels to our shores is quite simply that they wish to disseminate throughout Japan the Christian way of friendship and love. It is a frightful prospect ... It is not that Confucianism, Buddhism and Christianity have nothing to say about the virtues of loyalty, piety and chastity. It is simply that they dilute them. They are diluted by comparison with the loyalty, piety and chastity here in Japan. The religion of the Lord of Heaven proclaims the way of friendship and love, and people are easily intoxicated by it. They willingly give money to friends; they help the sick, and seek nothing in return. Their nourishing of orphans, for example, may seem to be excellent, but it is, in fact, a very bad way. When Christians form themselves into societies, neither lord nor father can hold sway over them.[23]

Gyojū mondō adds a metaphysical dimension. Ōkuni begins by pointing out that the true religion of the Lord of Heaven is anyway already practised in Japan under the name of *mototsu oshie* 本教. Its central deity is Amenomi-nakanushi no kami 天御中主神, and the presence of the characters for 'heaven' 天 and 'lord' 主 in the name of Amenominakanushi constitute evidence enough of the original truth of the Japanese creed. But the main point Ōkuni makes is that the Japanese religion is distinguished by its insistence on the principle of 'loyalty to the centre (本)', while Western religion teaches 'loyalty to the periphery (末), and not the centre.[24] Some explanation is called for.

---

22 For Confucianists, see Yamamoto Yukinori 山本幸規, 'Bakumatsu gojusha no kirisutokyōkan – Asaka Gonsai *Yōgai kiryaku* ni miru' 幕末御儒者のキリスト教観 一 安積良斎『洋外記略』にみる, *Dōshisha daigaku kirisutokyō shakai mondai kenkyū* 30 (1982); for Fujita and others of the later Mito School, see Uete, *Nihon kindai shisō no keisei*, pp. 24–7; for Buddhists, see especially Gesshō 月性, *Buppō gokokuron* 仏法護国論, in Yasumaru Yoshio 安丸良夫 and Miyachi Masato 宮地正人, eds., *Kindai Nihon shisō taikei* 近代日本思想体系 5, 'Kokka to shūkyō' 国家と宗教, pp. 215–22.
23 *Bunbu kyojitsuron*, p. 400.
24 *Gyojū mondō*, pp. 111–12.

Essentially, Ōkuni grants Christianity a semblance of loyalty, piety and other virtues, but these are 'diluted' and by no means compatible with Japanese loyalty and piety. The 'centre' and 'periphery' are key, metaphysically rooted ethical terms. The 'centre' refers to Amenominakanushi, to the Japan he created, to Japanese Shintō, to the Japanese emperor and above all to his divine ancestress, Amaterasu; 'periphery' refers to the 'opposites' of these: foreign countries, their creator, rulers, people and ethical systems. Loyalty, of the sort preached in Christian lands, is not 'centred' and is, precisely for this reason, dangerous: 'The harm of the religion of the Lord of Heaven is profound. It is vital to prevent its entry into Japan'.[25] It is clear enough then that, despite terminological differences, Ōkuni's objections to the practice of Christianity in Japan were fundamentally similar to those voiced by the vast majority of his contemporaries.

One final point remains to be made. That is, that there is an inherent contradiction here, between his unswerving belief that Amaterasu had guided Western nations to Japan on the one hand, and his conviction, on the other, that Christianity, compatible in some theological form with Shintō, would wreak havoc upon Japan's social order. The next section considers developments in this contradiction at the height of the anti-foreign period, 1862–3.

CHRISTIANITY PERNICIOUS AND TRUE
(ANTI-FOREIGN PERIOD: 1862–3)

The height of the anti-foreign movement in Japan saw Ōkuni at his most prolific. *Sonnō jōi isetsuben* 尊王攘夷異説弁 (Revering the emperor and expelling the barbarians: a divergent view), *Sonnō jōi shinsakuben* 尊王攘夷神作弁 (Revering the emperor and expelling the barbarians: heaven's plan), *Shinri shōgen* 真理小言 (The heavenly principle: some comments) and *Kyūjō ichiran* 球上一覧 (Scanning the globe) are all the products of these turbulent years.[26] Together, these texts point to certain shifts in Ōkuni's view of the

25 *Ibid.*, p. 113.
26 *Sonnō jōi isetsuben* and *Sonnō jōi shinsakuben* are in *Zenshū*, vol. 2; *Shinri shōgen* has been published with a commentary by Takeda Hideaki in 'Shiryō: Ōkuni Takamasa no *Shinri shōgen* ni tsuite – kaisetsu to honkoku' 史料大国隆正の真理小言について 一 解説と翻刻, *Kōgakkan daigaku shintō kenkyūjo kiyō* 皇学館大学神道研究所紀要, 6 (1990); for *Kyūjō ichiran* I have used, Mori Mizue 森瑞枝, 'Ōkuni Takamasa *Kyūjō ichiran* – honkoku to chūshaku' 大国隆正球上一覧 一 翻刻と注釈, *Nihon bunka kenkyujo kiyō* 日本文化研究所紀要, 64–5 (1989–90).

West which must be set out first before developments in his perception of Christianity can be analysed. [27]

The major difference between the 1850s and the 1860s is the greater breadth of knowledge about Western politics and Western society that Ōkuni had now acquired. This new knowledge he derived from geographical works and gazetteers from the hands of China-based missionaries such as Elijah Bridgman's *Hai guo tu zhi* (Kaikoku zushi) 海国図誌 (Illustrated geography of maritime nations) (1843), Daniel Macgowan's *Zhong wai xin bao* (Chūgai shinpō) 中外新報 (Chinese and overseas gazette) (1854), Richard Way's *Ti qiu shuo lüe* (Chikyū setsuryaku) 地球説略 (A brief account of world geography) (1856), and Alexander Wylies' *Liu he cong tan* (Rikugō sōdan) 六合叢談 (Tales from around the world) (1857–8), as well as Commodore Perry's personal account of his expedition to Japan, which was published in Japan in 1859 as *Nihon kikō* 日本紀行.[28] It is likely that the extent of Ōkuni's interest and knowledge at this time was on a par with that of such men as Yokoi Shōnan. Ōkuni's *Kyūjō ichiran*, for example, was a pioneering study in two volumes of the political and social institutions of England, America, France, Russia, Holland, China, Turkey and Prussia.

Ōkuni differed from the majority of his peers not only in the depth of his knowledge, but also in his attitude towards the prevailing view of the West, which found expression in the *jōi* slogan. Ōkuni attacked *jōi* thought for 'labelling foreigners beasts and demanding their expulsion': 'it is natural enough that people should think in this way, perhaps, but if the truth be known, such thoughts do not accord with the wishes of Amaterasu'.[29] Indeed, such anger as Ōkuni vents at this time is turned less on foreigners, than on the 'oblivious *kokugakusha*' and other Japanese who had no feel for the epochal changes in the air.[30] Ōkuni did, indeed, speak of *jōi* as the 'Great Way', but his interpretation of the term was quite different from that in society at large. 'The *jōi* I speak of is not a formal, skin-deep *jōi*; rather it is *jōi* defined by the true and great way; [by which I mean that] it has, as its principal object, a stirring of loyalty for the Japanese emperor in the hearts of

---

27 I have benefited greatly here from Takeda, 'Bunkyū Keiō nenkan no Ōkuni Takamasa' 文久慶応年間の大国隆正, *Nihon bunka kenkyujo kiyō*, 64 (1989): 105–39.
28 *Ti qiu shuo lüe*, *Zhong wai xin bao* and *Liu he cong tan* are referred to in *Sonnō jōi isetsuben*; *Hai guo tu zhi* and Perry's *Nihon kikō* are cited in *Kyūjō ichiran*.
29 *Sonnō jōi isetsuben*, p. 358. A typical example of contemporary *jōi* sentiment is expressed in the assassination note left by the Mito domain participants in the Sakashitamon 坂下門 incident: see Ishii Kanji 石井寛治, *Taikei Nihon no rekishi* 体系日本の歴史 12, 'Kaikoku to Ishin' 海国と維新 (Shōgakkan, 1993), p. 112.
30 *Sonnō jōi isetsuben*, p. 346.

foreigners.'[31] The *jōi* objective was not, then, the expulsion of foreigners but rather their 'edification' – and that of ignorant Japanese – by some means or other, in matters pertaining to Japan and its emperor of divine descent. Clearly, this position is predicated upon the accommodation of foreigners in Japanese society.

Against this background of improved knowledge about the West on the one hand, and Ōkuni's striking re-interpretation of *jōi* on the other, what developments in his view of Christianity can be detected? The first point to make is that this new political and social knowledge was accompanied by a new appreciation of the role played by religion in the development of Western society. Indeed, for Ōkuni, it was the edifying influence of Christianity that explained how, in a matter of very few years, England was able to become 'one of the most powerful nations on earth':

> The people of that country put it down to the fact that they changed their religion. By this they mean that, although originally they had had Catholicism, they later replaced it with the Protestant creed that Luther had established ... There were many outstanding figures in Protestantism who, in concert with the King and his ministers, gave wealth to the nation. [In England and] other countries, they elect religious leaders and pay them respect ... In the present age, so widespread are the edifying effects of the religion that one even hears it said that neither man nor woman can enter society unless they are acquainted with [such Christian arts as] astronomy, geography, literature, Chinese, mathematics and physics.[32]

The 'thriving' of the American nation, too, could be explained in terms of its rejection of Catholicism in favour of Protestantism.[33] Ōkuni's understanding that there were 'two' Christianities – his firmer grasp, that is, of the history of Christianity – is an important development in itself. Catholicism was the original religion, but after Peter's demise there were no great leaders, and so it declined progressively: 'after Protestantism's departure from Catholicism, many were the outstanding leaders that the former produced; many, too, the outstanding followers of the creed '[34] It was, he now understood, a sub-sect of Catholicism that the Portuguese had brought to Japan in the sixteenth century, and that was, indeed, a pernicious creed: 'Even followers of Christianity in modern-day England, America and other countries say that it

31 *Ibid.*, p. 339.
32 *Kyūjō ichiran*, pp. 278–9.
33 *Ibid.*, p. 290.
34 *Ibid.*

was a pernicious creed.'[35] If the Portuguese variant of Christianity – at least that brought to Japan – was, indeed, pernicious, where did that leave Ōkuni's view of the rest of Christendom? This we must now explore in Ōkuni's writings of the early 1860s.

One distinctive feature of Ōkuni's discussions of Christianity in *Shinri shōgen*, *Sonnō jōi isetsuben* and *Sonnō jōi shinsakuben* is that they adopt a 'dialogue' format. Maruyama Masao regards the dialogue as characteristic of Japanese polemical writing. He may well be correct, but he errs in arguing that *kokugaku* 'dialogue' of the Edo period never goes beyond 'the most simplistic sermonising from a single viewpoint'.[36] At least, Ōkuni's dialogues on Christianity do not fit this stereotype. In the texts cited above, for example, Ōkuni allows the questioner a full defence of Christianity as well as some severe criticisms of Shintō. What follows is an extract from the questioner's part in *Shinri shōgen*. It is played by 'a certain student of Western studies':

> A certain student of Western studies had this to say ... The Kirishitan sect is known even in Western society as an evil creed. Protestantism, however, is not a creed that uses magic to cast spells over people. It is a religion based on what people in China call benevolence ... [Western nations, urged on by Protestant-inspired feelings of benevolence and love,] are sometimes moved to take action, in the name of Heaven, against countries like China – and Japan in recent years – on the grounds that their refusal to engage in trade and friendship is in breach of the laws of heaven. However, they never, without reason, wreak violence on other lands; rather, if there were a cruel regime in a country of a different language, such that the people could no longer endure its cruelty, they would then overthrow that regime ... But they would never, without good cause, 'steal' another nation ... If Japan must borrow a foreign way with which to rule the people, then it should cast aside the pathetic creeds of Confucianism and Buddhism, and follow the vastly superior way of Christianity ... How excruciating it is that these narrow-minded scholars of Japan should be so proud as to follow the ancient creeds of Confucianism and Buddhism, and should proclaim Shintō, a creed too worthless to imagine, as the way of this nation![37]

35 *Ibid.*, p. 292.
36 Maruyama Masao, 'Nihon shisōshi ni okeru mondōtai no keifu' 日本思想史における問答体の系譜, in Maruyama Masao, *Chūsei to hangyaku – tenkeiki Nihon no seishinshiteki isō* 忠誠と反逆 ― 転形期日本の精神史的位相 (Chikuma Shobō, 1992), p. 248.
37 *Shinri shōgen*, pp. 121–2.

One is reminded here of Yokoi Shōnan after his conversion to 'open-country' politics upon reading *Hai guo tu zhi* in 1856.[38] Yokoi, it will be recalled, suggested that the Christianity of today and that brought to Japan in the sixteenth century by the Portuguese and Spanish were 'as different as clouds are from mud', and that the former was in essence an 'ethical doctrine in accord with the will of heaven';[39] further, that 'it goes without saying that foreign nations do not work unwarranted violence upon other lands'. Again, it was Yokoi's view that Shintō was 'totally absurd and nonsensical'.[40] It may be that Ōkuni had Yokoi in mind here. Be that as it may, it is of interest that he was ready to lend an ear to this Yokoi Shōnan-type position. The question that concerns us, though, is what differences there were between their respective positions on Christianity.

'Christianity is a most harmful creed', Ōkuni writes; 'its practice must never be permitted in Japan.'[41] But he adds a rider to blur this clearest of statements: 'If it were, in fact, to be permitted, the common people should be told that it is an evil religion whose ways they should not follow'.[42] Clearly, then, Ōkuni is looking ahead to a time when Christianity would be permitted in Japan under some arrangement or other, even if he could not give it his approval. It is of more than incidental interest, too, that Ōkuni offers no counter to the Western studies student's points. For example, he passes by without challenge the proposal that the government cast aside Confucianism and Buddhism and replace it with the superior religion of Christianity. He does not offer in his defence either earlier claims that Christian ethics are inferior and incompatible with those of Shintō. He does not, it is true, retract them, but the only justification he articulates for his continued and unqualified rejection of Christianity has nothing to do with Shintō ideology at all. It is that 'the headquarters of the Christian religion are sited overseas; this could mean that national wealth is transported out of Japan, and the nation could suffer impoverishment as a result'.[43]

Ōkuni's riposte to the student's defamation of Shintō is marginally more spirited. 'It is true that Shintō until now has been very much the pathetic

---

38 On Yokoi's 'conversion', see Uete, *Nihon kindai shisō no keisei*, p. 85.

39 Yokoi Shōnan to Murata Shijū (Ansei 3.12.21) in *Nihon shisō taikei* 日本思想体系 55 (Iwanami Shoten, 1971), p. 479. It needs to be pointed out that despite Yokoi's 'progressive' views of Christianity he never advocated its 'accommodation' within Japan. His approach to the West remained of the 'Western techniques, Eastern ethics' variety throughout his life, and this despite the assertions of his assassins in 1869 that he was plotting to disseminate Christianity throughout Japan.

40 *Ibid.*, pp. 480, 476.

41 *Shinri shōgen*, p. 122.

42 *Ibid.*

43 *Ibid.*, p. 123.

creed', but Ōkuni's own Shintō was of a different order: 'it takes [the pursuit of] truth as its core aim; it strives to teach the ethical way; its richness is manifest in astronomy, geography and all of creation.'[44] In short, then, with the important exception of their understanding of Shintō, Ōkuni's views of the West and its religion are, if not identical to, at least not poles apart from those of his Western studies student.[45]

This same period sees, in addition to the above shifts in Ōkuni's perception of Christianity, new developments in his Shintō thought. They are an extension of the 'theological accommodation' analysed in the previous section. A few brief comments here will suffice. For example, *Shinri shōgen* introduces concepts of heaven and of 'mutual help'. These concepts, new to Ōkuni Shintō, are almost certainly introduced now in order that Shintō may be seen to be capable of accommodating the defining Christian concepts of heaven and friendship and love: 'Takamagahara 高天原 in the ancient texts is what Confucianists really refer to when they talk of Jōten 上天; it is what Buddhists mean when they talk of Tendō 天堂 and what in the West is known as Heaven'; 'the Shintō truth of mutual help (*aitasukuru makoto*) is what the Confucianists mean when they talk of benevolence; what the Buddhists mean when they speak of charity; and what Christianity means by friendship and love'.[46] What makes Japan special, however, is that it alone has the doctrine of 'loyalty to the centre'. For Ōkuni, evidence that Japan alone has that doctrine, and that it is superior to all others, exists in the unending line of emperors.[47]

This expansion of Shintō's parameters would seem to be a sign of Ōkuni preparing himself and his creed for some day in the future when Shintō and Christianity would meet on Japanese soil. In sum, it is anyway clear that the contradiction inherent in Ōkuni's approach to Christianity – that although it is not an evil creed, and can be accommodated within Shintō theologically, its practice should not be permitted in Japan – has yet to be resolved. In defiance of the extreme anti-foreign environment in which he wrote, he makes no change to his view that the foreigners' arrival is part of Amaterasu's plan for a new global order; Christianity he knows better now,

44 *Ibid.*, p. 122.
45 Ōkuni's views of Christianity in this period offer an interesting contrast to those of the Buddhist world, where the anti-Christian movement was just gathering momentum. See Yamamoto Yukinori 山本幸規, 'Jakyō o miru me – bakumatsu bukkyōkai ni okeru hajaron no keisei to *Hekija gohōsaku*' 邪教を見る目 ― 幕末仏教界における破邪論の形成と『闢邪護法策』, *Kikan Nihon shisōshi* 季刊本思想史 15 (1984).
46 *Ibid.*
47 *Ibid.*, p. 124.

too. Yet, the significant shifts in his position – his greater knowledge and his silence on the question of Christianity's ethical compatibility with Shintō, for example – do not allow that Amaterasu's will might extend to permitting the practice of Christianity in Japan. In the next section, we consider Ōkuni's final thoughts on Christianity in the form of a memorial he submitted to the Restoration government in the first weeks of the new era.

'WESTERN SHINTŌ' AND THE RELIGION OF THE LORD OF HEAVEN (1867–8)

In May 1868, Ōkuni Takamasa, at the grand old age of 76, submitted to the Restoration government a detailed memorial on Christianity, 'Tenshukyō ni kansuru ikensho' 天主教にかんする意見書.[48] The occasion was the convening of an imperial conference in the Osaka Honganji 本願寺 to decide the fate of the thousands of native Christians, whose leaders had been recently arrested in Nagasaki by the newly appointed magistrate of that city.[49] The main text of the memorial is published here for the first time:

> The religion of the Lord of Heaven: a personal view[50]:
> The religion of the Lord of Heaven was known in Ming China as 'Western Confucianism' 西儒. The religion was established there by Matteo Ricci, Giuglio Aleni and others. It acquired greater popularity still under the Qing dynasty, and Emperor Dao Guang 道光 himself became a believer and churches were built throughout the empire. In Japan, in the age of Oda Minister of the Right Nobunaga, Portugal and Spain sent over many *bateren* and *iruman*,[51] with the intention of spreading the religion throughout the land. However, the sect that they sent was a sub-sect of the religion of the Lord of Heaven, the one known as Kirishitan. Kirishitan was known in the West, too, as a pernicious creed. Its priests used sorcery and, before long, it was banned. The religion of the Lord of Heaven set up just now in Nagasaki is greatly different from that of the Kirishitan sect, however. It is none other than the orthodox religion of Jesus respected

48 This is in *Kansaikō hōmu yōsho zanpen* 勧斎公奉務要書残編 (MS, Kunaichō Shoryōbu).
49 On this conference, see Breen, 'Emperor, state and religion'.
50 Ōkuni here uses 'the religion of the Lord of Heaven' to denote not Catholicism alone but Christianity in general.
51 *Bateren* and *iruman* respectively are terms for 'fathers' (*padres*) and 'brothers' (*irmao*).

in England, France and America. It never loses sight of the virtues of loyalty, filial piety, benevolence and chastity; it teaches nothing but charity and good works ... What is known in the West as the Lord of Heaven is, as it were, a shadow cast by the founder of the imperial line. He is of the order of Shang Di 上帝 in China and the historical Buddha in India. I have recently had the opportunity to read works like *Tian dao su yuan* 天道溯原 [Proof of the heavenly way], *Sheng jiao li zheng* 聖教理証 [Apologetics for the sacred teachings] and *International law*.[52] It is quite clear from these that the Christianity of today is as different from the Kirishitan of former times as clouds are from mud. It is what the English, the Americans and the French venerate as the religion of Jesus. It has, as its base, loyalty, filial piety, benevolence and chastity. It practises charity and good works. It has set up orphanages and hospitals, calling them 'holy societies' or 'benevolent societies'; they devote themselves exclusively to acts of goodness. All of this traces its origins back to some 200 or 300 years ago, as the references to orphanages in the *Zhi fang wai ji* 職方外記 [A geography of the world],[53] say, make quite clear. Thereafter, they added institutions to look after lepers; they even took care of the insane. In other words, they devoted their energies to the arts of pacifying the people ... It will be extremely difficult to reject the foreign creed in the absence of an efficient means of doing so.

Christianity is really a rather good religion,[54] but the problems regarding its practice in Japan are that its headquarters are sited overseas. If people become intoxicated with this foreign creed and invest vast sums of money in it, it may well cause great harm to Japan. Honganji Buddhism is a foreign religion, of course, but its headquarters are here in Kyōto, and so even if its sectarians invest their fortunes in it, it remains, after all, Japanese. There are major problems attached to Christianity's headquarters being sited overseas. I am in perfect agreement with the recent communication from Nagasaki in which [the magistrate] said he was resigned to meting out appropriate punishments [to the native Christians there], but that this did not constitute a lasting policy. I am in agreement, too, with the magistrate's proposal that the court establish teachings of the

52 *Tian dao su yuan* by William Alexander Parsons Martin was published at Ningpo, 1858, and *Sheng jiao li zheng* by Albrand at Shanghai, 1852; on *International law* (*Bankoku kōhō* 万国公法), see below.
53 Giuglio Aleni was the author of *Zhi fang wai ji* (Hangchow, 1623).
54 'Zuibun yoroshiki oshie' 随分よろしき教え.

Great Way for all to see, and set out basic rules for countering the foreign religion. Indeed, unless there is a single set of teachings for the entire nation, then we shall not be able to counter the religion of the Lord of Heaven. Recently, however, I have had occasion to survey those religions of ours that call themselves Shintō and the ancient way, but there is nothing remotely capable of taking on Western religion.

Ōkuni first, then, confirms the existence of different branches of the religion of the Lord of Heaven: a pernicious variety, and an 'orthodox' variety. It was the former that came to Japan some 300 years before, only to be proscribed within a matter of years; the latter, however, was regarded in China as 'Western Confucianism', and was even followed by an Emperor of the Qing dynasty[55]. Thus far, there is less development than consolidation of the position Ōkuni held in the 1860s. Next, however, he writes of the orthodox religion of Jesus, which he believed the Nagasaki Christians to be adherents of, that 'it never loses sight of the virtues of loyalty, filial piety, benevolence and chastity' and 'teaches nothing but charity and good works'. As though to emphasise the point, he repeats it several lines later. By attributing to Christianity the virtues that he earlier depicted as defining Shintō, he has effectively overcome the major ethical objection to Christianity's acceptance. The charitable works of Christianity that were, in the 1850s, 'a very bad way' have a decade later become manifestations of Christianity's ethical qualities.

Having thus pinpointed an ethical identity between Christianity and Shintō, Ōkuni proceeds to a different plane, defining the Lord of Heaven as a 'shadow' cast by Amaterasu. Previously, Ōkuni had identified the Christian creator with Amenominakanushi, but here he sees an identity between the Lord of Heaven (here meaning Jesus?) and the imperial ancestor. The Lord of Heaven is here placed in a position relative to that of Amaterasu, but unlike the earlier Amenominakanushi identification which was strictly 'theological', this Amaterasu identification, symbolically at least, brings Christianity down onto the political plane – Amaterasu is, after all, the ancestor of the imperial family. What makes this position tenable is, of course, the fact that Christianity

55 Ōkuni presumably knew of the 'Western Confucianism' tag from texts such as Nicholas Trigault's *Xi ru er mu zi* 西儒耳目資, which was published at Hangchow in 1626. Dao Guang is the reign name for the sixth Qing Emperor, Min Ning, who reigned from 1782 to 1850. Min Ning presided over the Nanking Treaty that concluded the Opium Wars in 1842, but Ōkuni's reasons for believing he became a convert to Christianity are unclear. On Min Ning, see Arthur W. Hummel, ed., *Eminent Chinese of the Ch'ing period (1644–1912)*, 2 vols. (Washington, The Library of Congress: 1943), vol. 1, pp. 574–5.

is really a 'rather good religion'. Ōkuni seems here to be denying himself all means of countering Christianity from the Shintō-ideological standpoint. Indeed, the only anti-Christian argument offered is a restatement of the objection he made in the 1860s that the headquarters were sited overseas. It is for reasons of the *fukoku kyōhei* 富国強兵 (rich country, strong army) variety, then, that Christianity is to be countered. But Ōkuni is no longer arguing that Christianity must be kept out; rather he turns his mind to ways of containing and accommodating it. The 'communication from Nagasaki' Ōkuni referred to was a report that Sawa Senka 沢宣嘉, the magistrate, had submitted after interrogating the native Christians.[56] In it, Sawa urged the government to plan for the post-proscription era. Ōkuni fully agreed with Sawa on the need to establish national teachings as the key counter to Christianity.

What Ōkuni appears to be saying here is that the religion of the Lord of Heaven was a rather good religion, ethically, theologically, and politically too, 'compatible' with Shintō. Just as Christianity was regarded in China as Western Confucianism, so too in Japan could Christianity be regarded as 'Western Shintō'. In order to make sense of the idea of 'Western Shintō', however, it was essential that Japanese Shintō be first established. It did not exist at that time, and it was thus that Ōkuni concluded his memorial by proposing that the political leadership consult his colleagues in the government Shintō office on how this might best be done. Subsequently, indeed, the government took Ōkuni's advice, and placed Fukuba Bisei and Kamei Koremi at the forefront of government Christian and Shintō policy.[57]

If the above is an accurate assessment of Ōkuni's position, then the question remains why Ōkuni's views developed in the way that they did, and why, from a position of absolute rejection in the 1850s, they arrived at one in which the accommodation of Christianity had become feasible. The fact that Christianity was currently being practised at Nagasaki was presumably of the utmost importance. We have already encountered several examples of Ōkuni's political realism, his acceptance of the realities of international politics, and this, coupled with his faith in Amaterasu, which taught him that little happened that was not in accord with her divine will, made Christianity easier to accept. But Ōkuni also cited three texts that exerted a profound influence on his thinking: Martin's *Tian dao su yuan* 天道溯原, Albrand's *Sheng jiao li zheng* 聖教理証 and *International law*. Some brief comment on each of

56 Sawa's communication can be found in *Kyūshū jiken oyobi Nagasaki saibansho karidome nikki* 九州事件および長崎裁判所かりどめ日記 (unpaginated MS in Tōkyō Daigaku Shiryō Hensanjo). See also Breen, 'Emperor, state and religion', ch. 3.

57 See Breen, 'Emperor, state and religion', chs. 2, 3 and 4.

these is called for.

Williams Martin's *Tian dao su yuan* was a highly influential text, responsible for bringing many Japanese to Christianity in the Meiji period.[58] Not only was it the most thoroughgoing handbook on Christian doctrine at the time, it sought, very much in the manner of Matteo Ricci's earlier writings, to identify areas of common ethical ground between Christianity and Confucianism. 'Confucianism talks of sincerity and a true heart. Jesus' way, too, strives for truth and correctness through prayer. Through devout prayer, truth and correctness will arise naturally in men's hearts ... The way of Confucius and that of Jesus differ in terms of their breadth, but the difference is not that between a heresy and an orthodoxy.'[59] Such passages as these are likely to have encouraged Ōkuni in his belief that Christian and Shintō ethics were similarly compatible. The Catholic Albrand's *Sheng jiao li zheng* sought to highlight theological rather than ethical common ground between Confucianism and Christianity: 'even though it is the case that the two characters for Shang Di found in the Four Books and the Five Classics are different from the characters for Tenshu, their virtue is one and the same. From this may it be known that the deity we worship as Tenshu is none other than the Shang Di worshipped by the ancients in China.' Here, possibly, was justification – if not inspiration – for Ōkuni's understanding of an essential parity between the Christian Lord of Heaven and Amaterasu.[60]

The third text cited as influential was *International law*.[61] That it inspired a tract by him called *Shinshin kōhōron* [The new true international law] is indicative of the influence it exerted on Ōkuni's thinking as a whole, but its significance for his view of Christianity is less than clear. Already in the early 1860s Ōkuni had acknowledged the importance of Christianity in the political and social development of the most powerful Western nations.

---

58 On the influence in Meiji Japan of the *Tian dao su yuan*, see Yoshida Tora 吉田寅, '*Tendō sogen* to Chūgoku, Nihon no kirisutokyō dendō' 天道溯原と中国日本のキリスト教伝道, *Rekishi jinrui* 歴史人類, 15 (1985).

59 I have used the version of *Tian dao su yuan* given in Yoshida, '*Tendō sogen*'. For the citation here, see p. 31.

60 Ōkuni's positive approach to *Tian dao su yuan* and *Sheng jiao li zheng* is in striking contrast to that of Bakumatsu Meiji Buddhists. Sōyō Kyakusui's 相陽却水 '*Doku Tendō sogen*' 読天道遡原 and Shingai Inshi's 深慨隠士 '*Kankō sango*' 寒更截語 are representative works that find especially in *Tian dao su yuan* evidence of Christianity's perniciousness. On early Meiji Buddhists' perceptions of Christianity, see Yoshida, '*Tendō sogen*', p. 64, and Yamamoto, 'Jakyō o miru me', p. 94.

61 It is not clear whether Ōkuni read Martin's translation of *International law* or whether he received information more directly from Nishi Amane 西周, who had now returned from studying international law in Holland. Nishi was an acquaintance of Ōkuni's from their days together in Tsuwano.

International law presumably taught him that Christianity operated, additionally, as the principle that guided all nations of the globe in their relationships with each other. 'This law belongs to those nations that revere or are subject to the Jesus of Europe. It operates wherever there are people who believe in the teachings of Jesus. No one else adheres to this international law.'[62] Passages like this presumably convinced Ōkuni less that Christianity was a 'rather good' religion than that it was one impossible to resist.

CONCLUSION

We have seen how, then, by a complex process, Ōkuni's attitude toward Christianity shifted over time. It was theologically capable of accommodation within Shintō, not necessarily pernicious, but still to be rejected without condition from Japanese soil in the first stage. A critical decade later there was no change to Ōkuni's belief that Amaterasu was in charge of the world. But if there was no change either to his rejectionist position on Christianity, its rationale was apparently now primarily economic. Ōkuni demonstrated a new responsiveness to 'progressive' views of the foreign religion, and discovered that if there had in the past been pernicious varieties of Christianity, there was also an 'orthodox' variety.

With the Restoration, the contradictions inherent in this position reached something of a resolution. Christianity – the Christianity presently practised in Nagasaki – was, he concluded, a rather good religion, capable of accommodation not only theologically but ethically and politically too. The outstanding objection was its 'foreign connection', and the serious economic harm implicit here. But Ōkuni was clearly under no illusions that, for this or any other reason, Christianity could – or should – be kept out of the emerging modern state. It was, thus, before a combination of political awareness and unswerving belief in Amaterasu that the contradiction in his position on foreigners and foreign religion dissolved. Once Shintō itself had been firmly established, Christianity could be – had to be – accommodated, in some as yet ill-defined fashion. Christianity could be accommodated as 'Western Shintō' in Japan, just as, in the past, it had been accommodated as 'Western Confucianism' in China.

There are three areas for further study that this exploration of Ōkuni's shifting attitude towards Christianity appears to open up. Firstly, Ōkuni offers the possibility of an alternative in bakumatsu Japan to the Ōhashi Totsuan-type

---

62 Tanaka Akira 田中彰, ed., *Nihon kindai shisō taikei* 日本近代思想体系, 1 'Kaikoku' 開国 (Iwanami Shoten, 1991), p. 476.

196

rejection of all things Western and to the 'Western techniques, Eastern ethics' approach of Sakuma Shōzan, Yoshida Shōin and Yokoi Shōnan. Ōkuni's discovery of an essential identity between Shintō ('Eastern ethics') and Christianity ('Western ethics') calls into question, for example, Maruyama Masao's bracketing of Ōkuni alongside other thinkers of the latter type in the bakumatsu period. Secondly, there are implications here for our understanding of the nature of Shintō thought in the bakumatsu-Restoration period. What Ōkuni advocated was far from religious freedom, to be sure; precisely what he had in mind for Christians, to what extent their religious and political activities would be restricted, is far from clear. Nonetheless, the accepted view of Shintōists of this period, that they 'advocated the absolute rejection of all foreign creeds', is surely no longer tenable.[63] The question remains as to whether Ōkuni was a typical Restoration Shintōist or an exceptional one. The third and final point relates to the wider state-religion question in Meiji Japan. According to the standard interpretation, there was a decisive break between the 'absolutely rejectionist' Shintō of the early period and later 'state Shintō', which 'subjected (accommodated) other religions to itself'[64] and 'found a place within itself for that modern ethical principle of "freedom of conscience" – albeit in a mock form'.[65] Our exploration of Ōkuni's thought suggests the possibility of more ideological continuity between the Shintō of the early and later Meiji periods than is usually acknowledged. The implications that this, in turn, has for our understanding of the process, the timing and, indeed, the very nature of 'State Shintō' must be explored elsewhere.

63 Haga Shōji 羽賀祥二, 'Shintō kokkyō no keisei – senkyōshi to tennō kyōken' 神道国教の形成 ― 宣教使と天皇教権, *Nihonshi kenkyū* 日本史研究 264 (1984): 2.
64 Nakajima Michio 中島道夫, 'Meiji kenpō taisei no kakuritsu to kokka no ideorogii seisaku – kokka Shintō taisei no kakuritsu katei' 明治憲法体制の確立と国家のイデオロギ ― 政策 国家神道体制の確立過程, *Nihonshi kenkyū* 176 (1977): 168.
65 *Ibid.*, p. 167.

9

Shinmeiaishinkai and the study of shamanism in contemporary Japanese life

Helen Hardacre

INTRODUCTION

Carmen Blacker's *The catalpa bow* is a morphological study of Japanese shamanism from ancient times to the present, tracing its development from its earliest manifestations to the forms seen in the new religions. This formidable work will long remain a classic among studies of Japanese religions, and its memorable prose and impressive case studies will leave a lasting imprint upon scholarly understandings of the centrality of shamanism in Japanese religious history. Blacker's work was one of the first studies by a Western scholar to signal the importance of shamanic elements among the new religions, as a part of the charismatic experience of the founders, in healing, and as an ongoing aspect of communal religious activity. Shamanic elements occupy a central place in the majority of new religions, regardless of the doctrinal origins of particular religions in any of several schools of Buddhism, in Shintō, or in the idiosyncratic revelations of founders not identified with either Buddhism or Shintō.

Observers of new religions founded, or enjoying their first major expansion, since the 1970s have identified a new development: the so-called new-new religions (*shin-shin shūkyō* 新新宗教). These organisations retain many of the features of the earlier new religions, including the centrality of shamanism. Japanese scholarship on modern and contemporary religious life is currently divided, however, on whether it is necessary or sensible to utilise the category 'new-new religion'.[1] At issue here are several complicated and

---

1 Leading sociologist of religion Inoue Nobutaka 井上順孝 takes the view that the term *shin-shin shūkyō* is ahistorical and obscures the process by which all religious movements rise and fall: *Shinshūkyō no kaidoku* 新宗教の解読 (Chikuma Shobō, 1992), pp. 160–1. Nishiyama Shigeru 西山茂, one of the first scholars to adopt the term 'new-new religions', has since rejected it in favour of a historical study that would liken this contemporary development to the appearance of occultism as a general cultural interest in the Taishō period. See Nishiyama Shigeru, 'Reijutsuteki shinshūkyō no taitō to futatsu no "kindaika"' 霊術的新宗教の台頭と二つの「近代化」, in Kokugakuin Daigaku Nihonbunka Kenkyūjo, ed., *Kindaika to shūkyō buumu* 近代化と宗教ブーム (Dabōsha, 1990).

interrelated points. First is the fact that both the terms 'new religion' (*shinshūkyō*, 新宗教, *shinkōshūkyō* 新興宗教) and 'new-new religion' were originally coined by journalists, who noticed marked upswings of religious activity, the foundation of novel religious organisations, and the participation in them of large numbers of people. It was journalists, intent upon selling popular magazines or arousing interest in television programmes about these religions and such related phenomena as the predictions of psychics, who originally popularised these terms. This is to say that the terminology has, so to speak, a life of its own outside the purview of academic scholarship.

The origin in 'journalese' of key terms in the study of modern religious life is problematic in various ways; especially important for this study is the fact that journalists do not, of course, need to concern themselves about such matters as historical process, essential (as opposed to ephemeral) differences between the 'new' and the 'established' (*kisei shūkyō* 既成宗教) religions, or between the 'new' and the 'new-new', nor what to do with problematic, borderline cases. Obviously, journalists are not well situated to investigate these matters, nor would attention to them tend to increase readership or viewing rates of their accounts of the religions in question.

For scholars, however, the matter is not so simple as adding an extra 'new-' each time the statistics on religious participation rise, or when there is a news vacuum on other fronts. For historians of the religions of Japan, it is necessary to view these contemporary developments in the context of millennia of religious history. From that perspective, the continuity with previous eras of religious history is more impressive than the discontinuities, especially as the 'new-new religions' both continue and transform earlier shamanic traditions, though departures from the past tell us important things about the present as well.

Following an introduction to the subject of the 'new-new religions', this essay introduces the new-new religion Shinmeiaishinkai 神命愛心会, founded by Komatsu Shin'yō 小松神擁 (born 1928), in which the key element is shamanic activity practised in combination with geomancy, directed principally to people in the small business sector, especially in the Ōta 大田 ward of Tokyo. Currently it claims about 50,000 members. Shinmeiaishinkai provides a good illustration of new trends in urban shamanism, as well as of the 'targeted' nature of numerous 'new-new religions', that is, their specific identification of a particular sector of the larger population as the intended recipients of the religion's message. The membership of the religion and its present concerns tell us much about the contemporary situation of this sector as a whole, and about the context in which it becomes 'available' for proselytisation by religions like Shinmeiaishinkai. Following this case study, we will return to a consideration of this representative of the 'new-new' in the light of Blacker's work on Japanese shamanism.

THE 'NEW-NEW RELIGIONS'

Religious movements all over the developed world commenced a transformation in the mid-1970s, following the economic downturns precipitated by the oil shocks of those years. In Japan, the oil shocks marked the end of a trend towards rationalisation and the beginning of the appearance of self-consciously irrational, occult phenomena in religion, an end to utilitarianism and a move towards expressivism. There began a boom in spiritualism and magic, of which youth have been the chief consumers. All national surveys found increased interest in religion, as well as rising incidence of such traditional observances as seasonal grave visits and tending domestic altars for the ancestors or the *kami*. New religious groups appeared, with rapidly growing membership. Intense media attention to the spirit world, astrology, and spirit possession flooded the marked with magazines, books, and television productions. The resulting popular interest has been quickly commercialised, especially in publishing, and the works of Krishnamurti Rajneesh, Shirley MacLaine, Carlos Castaneda, and Rudolf Steiner rapidly became bestsellers, as did thousands of books on astrology, new science, transpersonal psychology, channelling, life after death, and new age phenomena of all kinds.

The largest of the 'new-new religions' founded as part of this general 'religion boom' are Glad Light Association, Agonshū 阿含宗, and Mahikari Bunmeikyōdan 真光文明教団 and its offshoots, but there are also many smaller, possibly more ephemeral, groups sharing many of the same characteristics. Some, like Yamagishikai and Ōmushinrikyōdan オウム真理教団, tend to be esoteric, their members hidden from society, while others like Agonshū and Ōyamanezu no Mikoto shinji kyōkai 大山祇命神示教会 make frequent, skilful use of print and broadcast media to become better known. Agonshū, for instance, has national television coverage of its annual Hoshi matsuri 星祭 and has hosted the Dalai Lama at its Aura no saiten オーラの祭典, held at a huge Tokyo public hall, the Budōkan.[2] The new-new religion Science of Happiness (Kōfuku no kagaku 幸福の科学) hosted a birthday celebration for its founder at the Budōkan, an event covered by all the major television networks.

2 Inoue Nobutaka, *Shinshūkyō jiten* 新宗教辞典 (Kōbundō, 1990), pp. 205–6; Numata Ken'ya 沼田健哉, *Gendai nihonjin no shinshūkyō* 現代日本人の新宗教 (Sōgensha, 1988), pp. 57, 82; Shimazono Susumu 島薗進, *Gendai kyūsai shūkyōron* 現代救済宗教論 (Seikyūsha, 1992), pp. 221–32.

The 'new-new' in religion is distinguished from the merely 'new' by several characteristics, not all of which are necessarily present to qualify a particular organisation for the designation 'new-new'. The new-new groups have a younger membership, and they are, from one point of view, a part of contemporary youth or adolescent culture and represent an experimentation with the spiritual dimension of life. As such, from a youthful participant's point of view, they can provide a haven or respite from the demands of study and work. Some new-new religions are targeted directly at youth and are said to have as many as sixty per cent of their members in the under-thirty age group.[3]

Older generations of new religions relied heavily upon frequent congregational meetings and smaller counselling sessions (such as the often-studied *hōza* 法座 of Reiyūkai Kyōdan 霊友会教団 and its offshoots) to provide a basic 'glue' of relationships among the members and between members and leaders. These face-to-face encounters, often given a tone of deep existential significance when members seek to resolve some personal problem through the aid of fellow members and the counsel of leaders, are the heart and soul of the new religions. The fellowship and friendships engendered by these frequent assemblies are a major venue for the transmission of the lived teachings of these religions, and the religions themselves are constructed and perpetuated through them as their basic organisational units.

In the new-new religions, however, it is frequently the case that the religion's teaching is transmitted principally through publications, audio tape recordings of sermons and testimonies, and videotapes.[4] For example, in such religions as the Science of Happiness, novice members can *only* become eligible for full membership by passing examinations on ten of the founder's books. The founder Ōkawa Ryūhō 大川隆法 was a publisher before his revelations, and the religion's publishing business is a major source of its financial support. In some cases isolated reading and study can substitute to a

---

3 Nishiyama, 'Reijutsuteki shinshūkyō', p. 202, cites the figure of 60% youth membership for Sekai Mahikari Bunmei Kyōdan, but the trend toward a high proportion of young members has been widely reported by virtually all scholars of the new-new religions. One study focusing on this aspect of the new-new religions is Murose Tadashi 室生忠, *Shinjinrui to shūkyō – wakamono wa naze shin–shin shūkyō nihashiru no ka* 新人類と宗教 – 若者はなぜ新新宗教に走るのか (Shin-chōsha, 1986). On the other hand, more recent studies cast doubt on such high estimates, pointing out, among other things, that the 'youth' category employed by the religions themselves can sometimes include people up to the age of 35: see Tani Tomio 谷富夫, 'Shinshūkyō seinensō ni okeru jujutsutsei to kyōdōsei' 新宗教青年層における呪術性と共同性, *Academia* 57 (1993):163–4, 171.

4 Numata, *Gendai nihonjin no shinshūkyō*, p. 82.

large extent for the communal interaction so central in the older new religions.[5] Membership is generally more 'privatised' or 'individualised', making fewer requirements for communal activity upon followers. An individual who wishes to follow the religion principally as an intellectual pursuit, without necessarily disclosing to fellow members the details of his or her personal life, is much freer to adopt this approach than in the older new religions. Neither do the new-new religions place such a premium on making members go out and proselytise as proof of their commitment; if a person prefers that religion be principally a matter of the interior life, a private experience, that orientation finds affirmation much more frequently in the new-new religions than in the new religions. These tendencies may flow in part from the dislike many young people have of group activity that requires them to suppress their individuality in order to harmonise with the group, and from the increasing preference of younger, more highly educated sectors of the population to privatise religion, to be embarrassed and repelled by public displays of emotion in the confessional mode so common in the new religions.[6]

By comparison with the new religions, the new-new religions sometimes adopt a distinctly intellectual approach, one that privileges the printed word over the spoken, and clear articulation of doctrine over communal participation. The older new religions typically put great emphasis upon communal participation in their evaluation of the commitment level of a member and relatively less (if any) upon the intellectual mastery of abstract doctrines. By contrast, the examination format for assessment of members' intellectual grasp of the religion's teaching seems to be becoming a hallmark of these organisations. This format is one probably all too familiar to young members just emerging from or still in the throes of the educational system. It represents a variety of the credentialising function of the educational system, widely taken to be synonymous with education itself: to be educated, or, in this instance, to have mastered the religion, thus becomes a matter of passing an examination on its doctrinal component. While communal activity is certainly not absent in the new-new religions, this balance of group participation and an intellectual approach seems to be reversed in the new-new religions.[7]

The older new religions that succeeded well enough to perpetuate them-

5 Examinations on group doctrine have not been absent among the older generation of new religions. Indeed, they are standard fare in such well-established organisations as Sōka Gakkai 創価学会. The difference is that in older groups the examinations were supplemental to but not by any means a substitute for frequent, intense, communal activity, as seems to be the case in at least some of the newer groups.

6 Tani Tomio, 'Shinshūkyō seinensō ni okeru jujutsusei to kyōdōsei', pp. 149–271, *passim*.

7 Shimazono Susumu, *Gendai kyūsai shūkyōron*, p. 228.

selves for a second and succeeding generations usually presented themselves as universal religions. Under this general universalist umbrella, a special meaning was sometimes reserved for Japanese ethnicity, so that, for example, in Reiyūkai Kyōdan the religion might hold that the Japanese people share a special mission, or that the Japanese language is essential to unobstructed communication with the sacred. Even those which provided a special interpretation of Japanese ethnicity did not, however, usually identify and target a specific audience as the particular or limited reference group for the religion. Among the new-new religions, however, one can see explicit targeting of such groups as teenage girls or people in the small business sector, and a more prominent emphasis upon catering to that audience rather than upon a self-presentation as a universal religion. This is the case, for example, in Shinzankai 神山会, founded by comic book author-illustrator Yamamoto Suzumiko 山本鈴美香, a new-new religion which has its core membership in Yamamoto's teenage girl readership, who became her converts following her revelations.[8] Later sections of this paper will show how Shinmeiaishinkai focuses upon small business people as the group for whom the religion's message is mainly intended.

We can identify an ethos distinctive of the new-new religions, if not necessarily universal among them, which represents a departure from the basic optimism of the preceding generation of new religious movements. It would be putting the matter too strongly to say that the new-new religions are, without exception, pessimistic, but it is common to find a sense of uncertainty, contingency, and anxiety about the future. It goes without saying that the timing of the founding of these religions is intimately related to their ethos; its *fin de siècle* character is fairly clear-cut. The oil shocks of the 1970s, after which most of them were founded or experienced their first significant growth, marked the stabilisation and decline (relative to the previous era of 'high economic growth') of the Japanese economy, leading to the recession of the early 1990s, called the 'burst bubble' economy, leaving many people's confidence in the economy badly shaken. In the case of those most directly aiming at youth and small business, however, there is in addition a relationship to be drawn between their members' economic vulnerability or uncertain future and their *attraction* to a religion with a world view which reflects their own sense of uncertainty.

The new-new religions feature spiritualistic or occult phenomena

---

8 A similar case is the new-new religion Suhikari Kōha Sekai Shindan ス光光波世界神団, founded by comic book author Kuroda Minoru 黒田みのる. See Andō Naohiko 安藤尚彦, 'Kyōso ni natta mangaka, tenshi to kashi suru SF sakka' 教祖になったマンガ家、天使と交信するSF作家, in *Imadoki no kamisama* いまどきの神サマ, Bessatsu Takarajima 114 (JICC Shuppankyoku, 1990), pp. 231–2.

prominently: astrology, divination, onomancy, and geomancy. These elements generally have a basis in the initiatory experience of a charismatic founder, and the founder takes on the character of, among other things, a skilled technician of these prognostic 'technologies'. Founders and their sub-leaders further down the organisational hierarchy use these technologies to counsel members seeking an indication of future events or trends to counter a sense of life's basic unpredictability and the unreliability of luck or personal effort for bringing about the results they desire. The technologies of future knowledge introduce systems of regularities and rules in a loose sense and thus provide some assurance, if only temporarily. Besides techniques such as divination and geomancy, both founders and congregants emphasise the development of spiritual faculties (*reikan* 霊感, *reinō* 霊能, and other terms). Techniques for identifying and communicating with individual 'protective spirits' (*shugojin* 守護神 and other terms) provide a central focus for group activity and individual devotion. Believers apparently hope that direct insight into the spirit world, sometimes aided by helping spirits, can, like astrology and so on, provide a hedge against uncertainty.

One distinctive feature of some groups is a founder who has neither practised ascesis (*shugyō* 修業) nor taken part in organised religion of any kind prior to an experience of possession or election by a deity. This is true, for example, of the founders of Glad Light Association, the Science of Happiness, and Shinmeiaishinkai. In the case of Komatsu Shin'yō, founder of Shinmeiaishinkai, revelation was a completely unprecedented bolt from the blue. By contrast, Takahashi Shinji 高橋信次 (1927–76), founder of the Glad Light Association, had had unexplained out-of-body experiences since childhood, but had not attempted to interpret them in terms of any religious organisation.[9]

In earlier generations of new religions, stories of founders suffering bitterly on the road to religious insight were at the core of virtually all their hagiographies. Their suffering constituted a sort of proof of the value of the teaching they propounded, and the proposition that this truth was won with the founder's sweat and tears greatly elevated the value placed on the teaching by followers. In this way, the idea that a founder had trained and suffered in the course of finding the ultimate path provided a central element of legitimation. In its absence, prospective founders might simply have been dismissed as mentally ill and never have found a hearing at all. If ultimate truth is the sort of thing that simply drops one day from the sky, why exert oneself in its pursuit? Why devote oneself to a group expounding such nonsense? These sorts of questions might arise for members of the older new religions if confronted by tales of the founders of new-new religions who

9 Inoue Nobutaka, *Shinshukyō jiten*, pp. 888–9.

have not had to struggle. In the context of new-new religions which promote the idea that anyone can cultivate spiritual powers, however, the absence of long training as a prelude to the founder's acquisition of such powers may stand as proof that such powers truly are available to all. It remains to be seen whether founders of the new-new religions lacking a history of ascesis can find an equally powerful basis of legitimation that can endure through time.

Studies of the new and new-new religions in Japan are now at an important turning point. The appearance of the new-new makes it clear to virtually all scholars that there is a need to rethink the historiographical presuppositions of work in this field in a fundamental way. The 'new' were previously contrasted with the 'established' religions, by which was meant temple Buddhism and shrine Shintō. Both 'new' and 'established' have tended to be treated as static and mutually exclusive categories. Because categorisation was basic to the exercise, and because the categories themselves obscured the process of creation, development, and institutionalisation by which *all* religious organisations come into being, the appearance of the 'new-new' compounds an absurdity. It is abundantly clear to most scholars, it is safe to say, that we must identify long-term processes of religious change as the basic framework for understanding Japanese religious history and move beyond our former lepidoptery.[10]

In the service of such a reorientation for religions of the modern period, it is useful to take account of historical changes in Japanese shamanism which align it with the growth of spiritualism and occultism in the West. The travels to Japan of Madame Blavatsky and the widespread influence of her works in translation, the residence in Meiji and Taishō Japan of numerous Western spiritualists, and the institutionalisation within the new religions of the Meiji and Taishō periods of spiritualists who had absorbed the occultism of the West have played important roles in the formation of lay religious organisations in Japan.[11] Likewise, Indian independence movements drew Indian philosophers and religious leaders to Japan, and their influence has been felt as well. The flight to Japan of White Russians after the 1917 revolution came together with these trends, as did the cultural influence of

10 See Inoue Nobutaka, 'Shūkyōshi no ashimoto', in *Kindaika to shūkyō buumu.*

11 Asano Wasaburō 浅野和三郎, an intellectual leader of Ōmotokyō 大本教 during the late Meiji and Taishō periods, is an important example of this type of individual. He read widely in Western spiritualist literature, originally under the tutelage of Lafcadio Hearn, and was an enthusiastic follower (up to a point) of Madame Blavatsky and the Theosophical movement; see Matsumoto Ken'ichi 松本健一, *Kami no wana – Asano Wasaburō kindai chisei no higeki* 神の罠 一 浅野和三郎近代知性の悲劇 (Shinchōsha, 1989).

figures like Lafcadio Hearn and others who encouraged the preservation of shamanic, ghostly, and other religious elements within the state-sponsored cultural transformation to a 'modern', secular society. If we take account of the significance of a spiritualist element in Japanese shamanism in the twentieth century, the present situation can be seen to be directly continuous with this earlier history, and it is not necessary to appeal to a category like 'new-new religion' to reach an understanding of the appearance of the religions in question.[12]

As in the earlier new religions, shamanism occupies a central position in the new-new religions, but we can see many significant changes as well. For example, shamanic experience in the form of possession (*kamigakari* かみが かり) or direct communication with supernatural beings remains a central feature of the life stories of the founders, and many appeal to divine inspiration or the ability to communicate with spirits as the basis for guidance of their organisations or for counselling their followers on specific problems. Shamanic healing by founders and followers alike continues to provide a major activity, but its pre-eminence is less marked as the concern with ongoing guidance in an uncertain world (through astrology, geomancy, and other prognostic technologies) assumes greater importance. Followers of the new-new religions are less often originally motivated to join these groups because of the desire to be healed than in the case of the new religions.[13]

Japanese shamanism has traditionally maintained its own institutions of 'ordination' in a loose sense. Where the individuals concerned have been ordained as Buddhist clerics, for example in the Nichiren 日蓮 school, the matter is clear-cut: their clerical ordination serves in the eyes of clients to validate and legitimise their shamanic activity of the kind described in *The catalpa bow*. Ranks, titles, and certificates are held by persons purveying shamanic services like healing in the Shugendō tradition as well, and in such confraternities related to the cult of sacred mountains as the Ontake *kō* 講. *Miko* 巫女 affiliated with Shintō shrines have usually likewise gone through a period of study, training, and apprenticeship, to emerge with some sort of certificate. Similarly, the practitioners of such regional varieties of Japanese shamanism as the *itako* イタコ, *kamisan* カミサン, and *gomiso* ゴミソ of the north-east, and the *yuta* ユタ and *noro* ノロ of Okinawa have traditionally been trained by an older generation, validated by them, and have then passed their skills on to a younger generation, as have shamans among the Ainu.

Shamanic figures among the older new religions have sometimes had a formal initiation or ordination in sectarian or regional varieties of shamanic

---

12 See Nishiyama Shigeru, 'Reijutsuteki shinshūkyō'.

13 Inoue, *Shinshūkyō jiten*, p. 206.

practice, but more often they, especially the women among them, have had some experience in the established religions before their revelations, to which was added a protracted period of trial and suffering in ascetic practices (sometimes of their own devising), and it was the combination of these formal or institutional experiences plus their own ascetic experience on the basis of which they claimed religious authority for their revelations and for founding religions.

One highly distinctive characteristic of some of the new-new religions is the absence from their founders' life stories of any basis in the ordaining structures of sectarian and regional varieties of shamanism. This is the case in the life of Komatsu Shin'yō, founder of Shinmeiaishinkai. In her case, we find a continuing appeal to revelation, but with no basis in prior ascetic experience, nor any link whatsoever to traditional institutions of shamanic ordination or initiation. Instead, she has come to present herself as a technician, a professional of the sacred with a mission to small business. Because Komatsu and the founders of other new-new religions lack the authorisation of 'ordaining' institutions *and* the legitimation of long *shugyō*, they must rest their claim to religious authority on some other basis. That basis may be composed of both religious and secular elements, combining revelation or continuing communication with spirits, skill in one or more of the prognostic technologies, and, as is the case with Komatsu, accreditation as an accountant and small-business consultant.

Shamanism in urban Japan, whether or not affiliated with the founding of a new-new religion, is changing, breaking out of the old structures of sectarian ordination or ascetic validation and taking a more 'entrepreneurial' approach, often identifying a target 'market' narrowly and then 'marketing' the religious services most directly relevant to the social and economic circumstances of that market. One has only to read the Yellow Pages of the telephone directories of any Japanese city under *uranai* 占 (divination, fortune-telling) to see page after page of illustrated advertisements for shamans and psychics offering consolation for aborted foetuses, remedies for disappointments in love, assistance in attracting good luck, or general increase of good fortune.

While some of these shamans have undergone some sort of sectarian training or ascetic discipline, this is not necessarily the case, and more and more it is becoming possible to have a profession as a shaman or diviner without any such background. While a full explanation of the reasons behind this phenomenon are beyond the scope of the present study, it may be useful to mention one factor of widespread influence: the popularisation of that variety of divination called Takashima Ekidan 高島易断. Developed by Takashima Kaemon 嘉右衛門 (1832–1914), the Takashima method of

207

divination draws on the *I ching* 易経 and other Chinese classic texts of divination but in a simplified form. There are at least five educational institutions in Japan which provide instruction in divination by this method, and it is common to see shamans and diviners who operate independently claiming the general authorisation of Takashima Ekidan.[14] Several different, competing claims to the official succession of Takashima Kaemon have splintered the tradition, allowing more or less anyone who claims the mantle to wear it.[15] No authorising body stands behind a shaman's or a diviner's claim to practise Takashima Ekidan, which makes the label ideal as a masthead for enterprising individuals wishing to set up independently.

I will turn now to a description of Shinmeiaishinkai and its founder, returning in the final section to a consideration of the significance of this religion from the perspective of the history of Japanese shamanism and its significance within the new-new religions.

SHINMEIAISHINKAI[16]

Born in 1928 in Yokohama, Komatsu Kiyoko 清子 experienced her first revelations in 1976. Komatsu experienced a visitation from the bodhisattva Kannon, popularly regarded as a goddess of mercy, who was acting as a messenger from the Sun Goddess, Amaterasu Ōmikami 天照大御神. Komatsu changed her name to Shin'yō at the time of this first revelation. This occasion is recounted in Komatsu's autobiographical *Kannon-sama no otsuge* (pp. 38–46), and there both goddesses address Komatsu, saying that she must act as their mouthpiece and human messenger, to save the Yamato people (the Japanese) from a coming apocalypse. When Komatsu protested that she was unfit for this mission because she had never experienced religious training of any kind, the goddesses replied that such observances were unnecessary in Komatsu's case.

14 Hara Hidejirō 原秀次郎, 'Eki no hon no mise' 易の本の店, *Nihon kosho tsūshin* 日本古書通信 47 (1982): 10–11.

15 Sugata Masaaki 菅田正昭, *Fukugan no shintōkatachi* 複眼の神道家達 (Hachiman Shoten, 1987), pp. 208–33.

16 The discussion of Shinmeiaishinkai that follows is based mainly upon a book by the founder titled 'Revelations from Kannon; destroying evil spirits and acquiring protective spirits' (*Kannonsama no otsuge – akurei o hakai shi shugorei o mote* 観音様のお告げ ― 悪霊を破壊し守護霊を持て) and upon a two-hour management seminar in February 1993, a tape recording of which was obtained for me by a research assistant.

'No, no', said Amaterasu, 'your entire life, every single day of it, has been your training (*gyō* 行). Holding back your tears though you were in pain, crying only into your pillow, those times were your training'. (p. 42)

In subsequent visitations, Komatsu received many messages from Kannon and Amaterasu which enabled her to counsel the followers who soon came to her. Because of her location in Ōta ward, the most densely populated area of Tokyo, a district filled with small businesses and factories, Komatsu has concentrated on this sector of the population. Businessmen come for consultation on a variety of highly technical matters, and Komatsu counsels them on the combined bases of divine inspiration, her own secular credentials as an accountant and small-business consultant, and through the application of geomancy (*hōigaku* 方位学). (See the two testimonies appended at the end of this essay for a sample of Komatsu's technical consultations.)

A major activity of Shinmeiaishinkai is seminars devoted to small business concerns. Twelve such seminars are offered annually, six in Tokyo and six in Kōbe, held in a rented hall of the Ōkura Hotel. Admission to each seminar costs 20,000 yen. Advertised by flyers and posters in the trains and train stations, the seminars are called 'Spiritual management seminars', with the subtitle, 'The kingly way lies in gaining divine power'. The text of the advertisement for the 1993 schedules reads as follows: 'This is a certain opportunity to make a solid recovery from the violently changing conditions caused by the burst bubble economy, by gaining divine power!' Komatsu is introduced in the flyer as having a combination of religious and secular qualifications to address small businesses:

Komatsu Shin'yō Sensei has been providing guidance to people from across the nation through her communications with the spirits of the great gods, to break through their predicaments and anxieties since July 1976, when Amaterasu Ōmikami descended to her ... Komatsu Sensei holds qualifications as a management consultant and diagnostician of small- and medium-scale business (*chūshō kigyō shindanshi* 中小企業診断師). She has counselled tens of thousands of people, especially famous people in the political and economic worlds. She also manages four companies, of which Komatsu Consulting is one, and is the high priestess of the Shinmei Shrine 神命宮.

The seminars are advertised as taking up the following topics: 'What to do in order to be blessed with good connections', 'How have managers who are suffering today departed from the will of the gods?', 'Analysing the news and technology according to divine inspiration', 'What is going wrong from the gods' point of view when someone works and works without success?', 'The gods' view of bankruptcy', 'The gods' view of betrayal of management by their subordinates', 'Why management must be virtuous', 'How to raise capital', 'The required conditions for success as a businessman', 'The kind of manager the gods love', 'Why the bubble burst in the Japanese economy', and 'Quick recovery from the burst bubble economy'.

The following is a condensed report of the Tokyo seminar on 8 February 1993, which was attended by 220 persons, (128 men and 92 women; that is, 58 per cent male and 42 per cent female). The two-hour address by Komatsu was divided into two parts, a general prediction of events and the economy for 1993 during the first hour, and in the second hour a detailed explanation of geomantic forces in accord with which small-business people should construct their homes and businesses. The first hour can be paraphrased as follows.

> 1992 was a very bad year, but now we are at a turning point. In 1992 all evil things were brought to the surface and became apparent, but the world is now under control and set upon a better course. If you made a plan last year, this is the year to implement it. At the last seminar, I asked you to make a plan for change, and I believe that you have come here today with that plan. You have invested time and money in this seminar, but your investment will be meaningless unless you make plans and act on them. Last year was very severe, but this year we can grasp the results of effort. This year the conditions for achieving peace are favourable, because the friction between the United States and the former Soviet Union has ended. With this, the results of the past have become visible, and we can now see the real character of the Soviet Union, its problems of food supply, and so on. There may be problems in Japan's relations with other countries, but prospects for business with south-east Asia are good. Already many foreigners come to work in Japan. The Japanese now all go to college, and they dislike work like labouring on construction sites. Thus many employers have to hire foreign workers, even though they know that they may be illegal workers. It is fine for them to be in Japan as long as they obey the law, but the government must give more attention to this area. The export sector will do well this year. There will be more activity in the stock market, but prices will not rise. This is a good year to invest in long-term stocks, while the price is low and stable. This is not a year to sell. Avoid doing

business transactions other than in cash; stay away from cheques, bank drafts, and bills of exchange. In particular, avoid non-cash transactions located to the west of the company president's residence. Even worse are such transactions located to the east; these are not to be entered into, as they will definitely cause trouble. In any non-cash transactions check your partner's credit in advance. Pay special attention to your home, and calculate the direction of business transactions from your home, not from the business. The basis of the company president's fortunes lies in the home, not the company. Last year was the worst, for the manufacturing sector, and the first half of this year won't be much better. Things will not be really good again until 1997, so the key to this sector is to hang on until then. Concentrate on what you must do to survive until 1997. This is a year in which to train young workers. The big companies aren't hiring, so there will be a lot of well-qualified new graduates who can be snapped up by small- and medium-sized business. This is an employers' market. Find good workers and train them so that they will be able to take advantage of good conditions in 1997. Don't wait until then to look for good workers, or it will be too late.

The seminar included a set of predictions about the likely fortunes of various business sectors during 1993.

The auto industry should do well, especially exports. Agriculture will continue to suffer from a labour shortage, and it will be difficult to find young men willing to succeed to the headship of agricultural families. To ensure the future, it is important to create a stable life for these men. It would be a good year to have them marry. Fishing will be a little better this year. 1992 was a horrible year for construction and real estate. People in this sector should look for a new beginning and prepare to start again from scratch. Most working people know that they will never be able to buy a house of their own and they are in a sour mood of resignation. The industry should provide housing that they can afford; this is the key to the future of these linked industries. New ventures in food processing will either be great successes or complete failures. A focus on 'instant' foods that are easily prepared and fun to eat will definitely succeed. Sports and dancing will be popular this year.

Besides general business predictions, the audience was advised to beware of danger.

211

Traffic accidents will decrease, but sickness is on the rise. Know your body's limits and do not overstep them. Blood disease is a big danger. AIDS is a threat, of course, so be careful. It comes from the third world. Kidney disease will increase. It will be necessary to clean the blood. Exercise to stimulate the circulation and to create physical strength capable of resisting disease.

On the whole, the oracles of most varieties of Japanese shamanism have tended to report events taking place in an unseen spirit world rather than predicting the course of secular affairs. Predictions relating to agriculture and fishing may be a partial exception to the trend, but even there the emphasis has been on the control of plant and piscine worlds by divinities resident among the spirits. Traditionally, shamans would have avoided secular speculations, because their qualification to act as mouthpieces for the gods rested precisely on their separation from ordinary society, self-consciously purifying themselves of the desires and ambitions of the world. They could, ran the internal logic of the system, open a channel of communication with the sacred precisely because they held themselves aloof from secular pursuits. Seen in this light, Komatsu's brand of oracle represents a distinct departure from historical shamanic traditions.

Komatsu's prognostications show a keen awareness of the concerns of the small-business sector and an ability both to gather and to analyse information on the economic trends most likely to affect it directly. Small-scale manufacturing, for example, is an area hard-hit by the so-called labour shortage of the 1980s, a shortage, that is, of male middle school or high school graduates seeking factory jobs. As more Japanese youth go to college and spurn the 'three Ks', work that is dirty (*kitanai* 汚い), physically taxing (*kitsui* きつい), and dangerous (*kiken* 危険), more small-scale factory employees look to foreign workers. They do so reluctantly, however, knowing that this course is fraught with difficulties precipitated by cultural and linguistic differences, and by legal liabilities that may attend the hiring of illegal immigrant workers. That many foreign workers are in Japan illegally, having overstayed a tourist visa, is an open secret. Komatsu calls attention to these anxieties of small business explicitly.

She rings a note of optimism in an otherwise gloomy picture, however, when she says that although manufacturing will remain in the doldrums until 1997, until which time many businesses will do well merely to survive, the big companies are not doing much better, and there is a way for small business to benefit from their misfortune. That is to recruit from the pool of well-qualified Japanese college graduates who in better times would have been snapped up by the big companies. This skilled workforce should be trained diligently, so that they will be well positioned to go forward after 1997.

QUESTIONS AND PREDICTIONS

As the final part of the seminar, Komatsu entertained questions from the floor, sometimes responding immediately, and sometimes only after 'consulting' the gods (*ukagai o tateru* 伺いをたてる). In these consultations she would pause, and the master of ceremonies would request that everyone bow their heads for about two minutes, during which time Komatsu would begin to deliver an oracle through the microphone. These words were to be taken as the deities speaking through Komatsu. The linguistic style of the oracle is distinctive, occasionally employing archaic verb forms to distinguish it from ordinary speech. The responses to audience questions very frequently incorporated a recommendation that the questioner make a further appointment with the consultation staff of Shinmeiaishinkai, as in the following interchange.

> *Questioner*: How should the third-generation president of a corporation conduct business?
> *Komatsu*: The appearance of the third-generation president means that the business will continue in perpetuity. He should protect and exchange the old workers for new ones, skillfully. Do you live with your mother?
> *Questioner*: No.
> *Komatsu*: Do you visit her?
> *Questioner*: About twice a month.
> *Komatsu*: Since that is the correct attitude, your employees will follow you in having correct attitudes. In your residence do you occupy the 'president's place' (*shachō no za* 社長の座) [in the north-west]?
> *Questioner*: No, the north-west is occupied by a closet.
> *Komatsu*: Please move that closet, but not too quickly. Move it in accordance with the advice of a counsellor. Since the appropriate day for such a move differs from case to case, I will instruct you later.

This interchange incorporates both praise for the questioner as a filial son and the suggestion that his fortunes could improve further through altering the geomantic conditions of his dwelling so that he comes to occupy the space properly reserved for him as company president. Sometimes, however, it is not a question of improving future prospects so much as salvaging from disaster, as the following interchange makes clear.

> *Questioner*: I went bankrupt when the bubble burst. I have about one hundred million yen worth of products still on hand, but I have been unable to sell them. My company was shut down in February, 1991.
> *Komatsu*: I wish to consult the gods.
> *Master of Ceremonies*: Everyone, please bow your heads.
> *Komatsu*: Walking the road to Seto is a path strewn with many difficulties, but it is this rocky way that avoids disappointment. Offer *sake* to the south-west. There is a place in that direction like a swamp. Be guided there, and take a branch from a pine tree which you will find there. Put it in water and offer *sake* beside it, and then return home. At a certain house on the way, there is an altar to Inari. Apply to your situation a hint that you will find there. Do you worship Inari?
> *Questioner*: No.
> *Komatsu*: There is a pine tree near an Inari shrine by a river. Put a branch from this tree in water and offer *sake* [to the gods].

Here the questioner is already beyond the help of business tips or conventional ethical guidance about filial piety, and he has exhausted the legal means open to protect himself and his company by going bankrupt. This situation elicited a kind of response much closer to traditional shamanic oracles, in that the prescription about rocky roads and a swamp vaguely mirrors the questioner's difficulty in unloading the last of his company's assets, but holds out only the dim hope that a hint may be gained by worshipping a traditional patron of commerce, Inari. While this consultation dealt with a personal problem, questions sometimes touch on national events thought to have some implication for everyone.

> *Questioner*: What is the significance of the marriage of the crown prince for the people of Japan?
> *Komatsu*: Last year was an unlucky year (*yakudoshi* 厄年) both for the emperor and the crown prince, but now they have both emerged from that. The wedding will augur a bright year. The emperor and crown prince can live in peace of mind. The Shōwa emperor inaugurated monogamy [within the palace]. He was a model for the Japanese family. He was pressured to take a concubine when no

male issue was born, but he resisted, knowing that to take a concubine would sadden the empress. Then the next year a son was born, and later a second son. Thus he reigned a full sixty years.

Here again, the answer bears little relation to the question, which merely serves as a platform from which to launch an endorsement of trends that originated with the Shōwa emperor for the imperial house to adopt monogamy, for increasingly visible representation of the figure of the empress alongside the emperor, and for the rejection of concubinage. The reason advanced for the latter, that it 'would sadden the empress', seems to rest on an image of the imperial couple as essentially like the ideal conjugal pair of a Japanese middle-class nuclear family, thoroughly de-divinized and domesticated, mirroring the ordinary citizenry in its social relations.

GEOMANCY

Shinmeiaishinkai is distinguished from other new-new religions by a focus upon geomancy, that is, the principles of locating a dwelling in relation to the four directions in such a way that maximum benefit is derived for the inhabitants, and so that harm is avoided. Geomancy is, of course, a hallmark of Chinese popular religion. It has historically tended to be less developed in Japan, probably due to different settlement patterns and a scarcity of arable land. In these circumstances, the sort of elaborate geomantic considerations given to grave placement in China, for example, have never had much scope to develop, and instead, in urban Japan during its modern history geomancy has been much attenuated. If people attend to it at all, concern has tended to focus on the placement of toilets.

Geomancy in Shinmeiaishinkai revolves around a small number of relatively simple principles and apparently originates in Komatsu's revelations rather than deriving from Chinese systems or traditional Japanese geomantic lore. The first principle is that a spot in the north-west of the dwelling should be designated the 'president's place', and all geomantic calculations about a business should take this spot as their epicentre. Ideally the *tokonoma* 床の間, or recessed alcove, of the main living room should be located there. Thus if a prediction is made that new deals from the east are favoured, the location of the 'east' should be calculated from the 'president's place' in the home, not from the location of the business.

Komatsu links the necessity of the 'president's place' with male authority. The existence of the 'president's place' expresses the husband's authority within domestic space, it being taken for granted that the 'president' is the

215

husband, in relation to whom all co-resident males are junior in authority and all females subordinate. The seat of male authority should, first, be created architecturally in the proper (north-west) space of the residence, and the man alone should occupy it. If the 'president'/husband does not occupy this space, his wife's authority will begin to rival his own. The image here is of the man seated with his back to the *tokonoma*, thus occupying the traditional seat of honour within the household. Without this, relations between husband and wife will be jeopardised by this disturbance to the man's rightful hierarchical superiority over the wife. Operating on the model of a zero-sum game, Komatsu repeatedly says that a rise in women's status is equivalent to a decrease in men's status, and that men are made effeminate and weak by any strengthening of the position of women. In this she expresses the casual sexism and misogyny to be seen in many contemporary religious groups, coupled with indifference to the irony of this view in her own case, given her headship of four companies and divine election while married to a small-business man. We have no evidence revealing the reaction of either male or female audience members at the management seminars to this sexist rhetoric, but the suggestion that women are to blame for any troubles men may have is standard fare in much contemporary Japanese popular culture, including religion.

In an area like Komatsu's home ground of Ōta ward, probably some significant proportion of the adult male population, – running a small factory or shop of some kind – could be called a *shachō*, 'company president'. This title lends dignity to a mode of subsistence which may otherwise be more notable for its absence of that quality, however, especially in economic hard times. The testimonies appended to this essay give some insight into the life of the small company 'president', an existence for which the title of a highly popular, long-lived, sentimental movie series is quite appropriate: 'Otoko wa tsurai yo' (男はつらいよ, 'It's a rough life for a man'). The testimonies show us men who work long hours alongside their employees, a category typically including non-salaried family members, mostly performing menial, manual labour for poor returns. More often than not, the family resides above or adjacent to the factory floor. Frequently, as in one of the testimonies presented here, they are small-scale manufacturers producing parts or materials as subcontractors to large firms, and they produce at the whim of these larger firms, dependent upon them, mercilessly squeezed by them, desperate to please them. The small firms operate with little capital and no access to technical assistance beyond their own inventiveness. In an economic recession, their vulnerability is nakedly exposed, and they must struggle with their every resource simply to stay afloat. As is the case with Tako ('Octopus', タコ), the *shachō* of a print shop in 'It's a rough life for a man', the title *shachō* is largely honorary and is applied with more than a little irony, honouring effort while turning a blind eye to the absence of substantial achievement or wealth.

Komatsu's geomancy seeks to create in domestic space a haven of respect and dignity for men like Tako, who may not get much of either in the business world. Her creation elevates men by suppressing women, leaving women's roles in support of this construction of the home invisible. To make their roles in unpaid labour in the factory and in the homes of small business too clear would make all too obvious, of course, men's dependence upon women, detracting from the desired representation of men as powerful, prideful, and independent.

Komatsu's geomancy as expounded in her management seminars has a further didactic purpose: to show how the wicked are eventually brought down by poor geomancy. Her favourite example is the house of Kanemaru Shin 金丸信, former vice prime minister accused in a bribery scandal in early 1993. Kanemaru's Tokyo residence is a two-storey dwelling in which much of the ground floor is occupied by a garage. The dwelling is entered by climbing stairs to the second storey and passing through an entryway located almost at the centre of the building. That is, a central space is cut away to make room for stairs and this entryway. The house lacks a straw-mat-floored (*tatami*) room as the main living space, and thus it is missing the *tokonoma*. Therefore, it is missing the 'president's place', a sure recipe for disaster. The cut-out central space and the absence of the 'president's place' are, in Komatsu's view, geomantic suicide. A house is analogous to the human body, and it should be kept whole and in one piece. The hollowing out of a central space seen in Kanemaru's residence is equivalent to an eviscerated, disembowelled body, one which has had its middle cut out. Living in a place like this could not fail to bring disaster to the residents. The first evidence of this was that Kanemaru's wife died after moving to this dwelling, and the second, apparent only after the seminar was concluded, was Kanemaru's own arrest and political downfall to become a figure of infamy.

Returning finally to *The catalpa bow* and to whatever conclusions can be drawn from an examination of Shinmeiaishinkai in the light of Blacker's study, I offer a single observation only. *The catalpa bow* frequently points out that the world view which sustained traditional forms of Japanese shamanism is disappearing, and the reader senses the author's passion to record all the varieties of shamanism before they vanish. It seems to me, however, writing eighteen years after the publication of *The catalpa bow*, that Japanese shamanism is undergoing transformation rather than extinction, and that alongside the relentless rationalisation and secularisation of publicised representations of Japan, the quest to anchor shifting material fortunes in an unseen, unchanging world of unassailable and absolute meanings is equally and increasingly strong.

By comparison with the traditional shamanic forms Blacker documents, Komatsu Shin'yō differs in the absence from her life before her revelations of any systematic ascetic training or experience of apprenticeship and ordination under a senior shaman. This means that the basis of religious experience for her shamanic practice is thin by comparison with more traditional forms of shamanism. Lacking the recognisable 'credentials' of ascesis and initiation, her authority relies heavily on secular credentials as an accountant and business consultant, and on the ability to use the technical jargon of economics and business in a way that appeals to the small business sector. These secular credentials are further bolstered by her use of a distinctive prognostic technology, geomancy. Revelation, business consulting, and geomancy provide for Komatsu three different bases from which to claim the right to speak and to be heard. The overall persona she has constructed has a major component in which she presents herself as a technician speaking on divine authority. Here she differs from more traditional shamans in being a medium whose prior experience and present qualifications in this-worldly terms apparently nuance the content of her message and appeal significantly. Indeed, since she cannot claim the purity of the celibate or otherwise ascetic shaman, she *must* rely on technique and secular credentials. To the extent that Komatsu typifies a broader change in the character of contemporary Japanese shamanism, it may be that the future of the phenomenon will see an increasing number of women practising shamanism as independent religious entrepreneurs, marketing targeted expressions of a variety of prognostic technologies to a variety of clienteles.

APPENDIX: TESTIMONIALS

Arai Kunihito 荒井国人, President and General Manager, Shinwa Birudo Kabushiki Kaisha 新和ビルド株式会社, Kawasaki City

My business is mainly concerned with general construction and trade with China. Since August 1985, I have been receiving Komatsu Sensei's management consulting. In setting up a joint Japanese–Chinese corporation for the production of non-combustible insulation products, we were unable even after years of research to decide among a number of possible ingredients and had come to a halt. But through Komatsu Sensei's guidance, the correct formula became clear, and we were able to proceed to production. Now our product is in use by the construction industry, and I am certain that it will enable the improvement of insulation materials to make great progress. I encourage everyone to receive Komatsu Sensei's guidance and to develop your business on that basis.

Inoue Ichizō 井上一二三, President and General Manager, Muffler Technology, Tokorozawa City

I was under orders to improve a muffler I produce as a subcontractor to a large corporation, to make it smaller and lighter, but with two days to go before my delivery deadline, the product's efficiency rating still wasn't good enough, in spite of repeated efforts.

I had been in the muffler design and installation business for ten years, and there had never been a claim of customer dissatisfaction with my products, so to have [to remake my product like this] was nearly a matter of life and death to me. I couldn't say I wasn't ready, so I went at the remake with all my determination to use my knowledge to the fullest, but for all that my unease wouldn't go away. So I decided to consult Komatsu Sensei to receive a divine judgement on my blueprint for the remake.

Although she is so busy, Komatsu Sensei agreed to receive me, and I am so grateful for the oracle she gave me. I read and re-read the words of the oracle again and again, it goes without saying. The oracle revealed a method unknown to me in my previous experience, but I resolved to buy the parts as indicated in the words of the gods. I installed a test model for my customer, and the result was exactly fitting their specifications. In order to get the job right, I put aside all my other duties and returned to being a technician. I became one with my factory workers, using all my spiritual and physical strength. Finally, through constant stress and perseverance, we succeeded in finishing the improvement and production of our new product. Even if our spiritual, intellectual, and physical strength had been sufficient to the task, we couldn't have done it without the gods' words. As I express my gratitude for being able to borrow the power of the great gods, and for being able to know Komatsu Sensei, I pray for ever greater development.

10

The Ainu *iyomande* and its evolution

Fosco Maraini

The word *iyomande* (or *iyomante*, there are a number of local variations) means, according to Kayano Shigeru, simply 'to send off that (animal or object)'.[1] This is the widest sense of the term, and it refers to the Ainu custom of 'sending off' animals to the world of their ancestors, generally by killing them, though a small-scale *iyomande* may be performed for an animal that has died naturally. Sometimes a brief *iyomande* is performed to dispose of inanimate objects toward which one owes a debt of gratitude. This special case makes one think of the Japanese custom of disposing ceremonially of old needles (*hari kuyō* 針供養), or other objects, for instance *obi* 帯. The idea, however, which the word *iyomande* evokes in the mind of most northern Japanese, and of many foreigners, is the specialised and very important case in which the animal 'sent off' is a bear cub. I shall here use the word *iyomande* only in this particualar sense, referring to the ritual sometimes rather roughly translated into English as 'Bear Festival', and into Japanese as 'Kuma-matsuri' 熊祭.

As Batchelor put it, the *iyomande* is 'the greatest racial religious act of ceremonial worship of the Ainu brotherhood'.[2] Put more simply, it certainly is, or was, the main social and religious event in any Ainu community. It generally took place once a year, in winter, but this depended very much on the supply of bear cubs available after hunting expeditions in the mountains. The ritual appears to be a very ancient one. The earliest mention of it is a Japanese description of 1652, translated into French in 1814.[3] A large number of Japanese paintings, prints and designs of the eighteenth and nineteenth centuries show various moments during the *iyomande* ritual.[4] It is very

1 Kayano Shigeru 萱野茂, *Shashinshū Ainu: Niputani no Utonmunukara to iyomante* 写真集アイヌ二風谷のウトンムヌカラとイヨマンテ, photographs by Sutō Isao 須藤功 (Kokusho Kankōkai, 1979), pp. 90–1. The wedding ceremony took place on 10 April 1971, the *iyomante* on 3–7 March 1977.

2 John Batchelor, 'The Ainu Bear Festival', *Transactions of the Asiatic Society of Japan*, Second Series, 9 (1932): 37–44.

3 J. G. Frazer, *The golden bough*, Spirits of the corn, vol.2 (London: Macmillan, 1912; reprint, 1933), p. 187.

4 Except for the early work of MacRitchie, there does not seem to be any study in Western languages reproducing even part of the large corpus of Japanese paintings, prints, and designs concerning the Ainu: David MacRitchie, *The Ainos*, supplément

220

important to remember that the *iyomande* is not a ceremony belonging exclusively to the Ainu: various neighbouring people, especially the Gilyaks, the Oroks, and the Golds, who occupy territories to the north of Hokkaidō, in Sakhalin or on the mainland near to the mouths of the Amur river, have ancient traditions which, though showing variations from group to group, are fundamentally expressions of similar beliefs, and develop along similar ceremonial lines. I shall not deal with this extremely interesting side of the picture, because it has been dealt with masterfully in two works already.[5]

I propose here to relate my experiences of two *iyomande* I happened to witness, the first in the village of Kotan, on the shores of Lake Kutcharo in eastern Hokkaidō, during March 1954, and the second in the village of Nibutani, in the southern part of Hokkaidō, at the end of February 1971. Someone may perhaps ask why, in the mid-nineties, I should write about these long-past events. The more time passes the more I realise that the *iyomande* of 1954 belonged to another age; I will not say it was the last genuine *iyomande*, but it was certainly one of the last. The Ainu elders or *ekashi* of that period belonged to a surviving Ainu culture; with their demise, which took place shortly afterwards, most links with the past were broken, severed by the onslaught of another, different way of life, bringing along new values, attitudes, conceptions, and religious or non-religious ways of thinking. The *iyomande* of 1971 was quite different, and now, it seems, we have reached a third period. So this is the moment to draw upon old notes, old photographs, and recollections, trying to trace the steps of an evolution which has been taking place during all these years.

When I first visited the Ainu in 1939, the culture of the Ainu was still partly alive. Ainu villages were formed by rows upon rows of traditional

au tome IV des Archives Internationales d'Ethnographie (1892). The following pictorial sources are available: *Ainu fūzoku* アイヌ風俗 (Noboribetsu: Yoshikawa Tanseido, n.d. [probably early 1930s]), a small album with reproductions of 53 paintings executed by Nishikawa Hokuyō 西川北洋 around 1870 and now in the Museum of Hakodate, which are among the most interesting documents on Ainu ethnography; Koshizaki Shūichi 越崎宗一, *Ainu-e* アイヌ絵 (Sapporo: Nakanishi Shashin Seihan, 1959); Izumi Seiichi 泉靖一, *(Kinsei no wajin gaka ni yotte egakareta) Ainu no sekai* 近世の和人画家によって描かれたアイヌの世界 (Kajima Shuppankai, 1968); Takakura Shin'ichirō 高倉新一郎, *Ainu-e shūsei* アイヌ絵集成 (Banchō Shobō, 1973), 2 vols. (with good colour illustrations and extensive English summary by H. Stewart); *Ezo fūzokuga ten* 蝦夷風俗画展, catalogue of an exhibition at Riccar Art Museum, Tokyo, 1980; *Ezo no fūzokuga – Kodama Teiryō kara Hirazawa Byōzan made* 蝦夷の風俗画 一 小玉貞良から平沢屏山まで, catalogue of an exhibition held at Asahikawa Museum of Art and Hokkaidō Museum of Modern Art in 1992.

5 J. G. Frazer, *The golden bough*; and A. I. Hallowell, 'Bear ceremonialism in the northern hemisphere', *American Anthropologist*, New Series, 28.1 (1926): 2–175.

Ainu huts of wood and reeds – now completely disappeared; inside the huts the Ainu, especially the women, spoke their own language (now dead), and the ancestral religion was still followed, at least by elderly men (*ekashi*). I also had the signal fortune of becoming a friend of Dr Neil Gordon Munro, a Scotsman who had retired in old age to a house in the village of Nibutani, with the purpose of studying the Ainu at close quarters. Dr Munro and his wife, Chiyoko, gave me many times the most generous hospitality in their home, and I was able to learn a great deal from them concerning Ainu society and religion.

On the other hand, this period, just before the Pacific War, had some distressingly negative aspects. All foreigners were considered at least potential spies by the military police (*kenpeitai* 憲兵隊), and our movements were very much restricted: this applied particularly to the Americans and the British, but belonging to an Axis Power, as I did, made practically very little difference. Dr Munro had become a Japanese citizen, which was not a positive asset in the eyes of the fanatical 'double patriots', to use Richard Storry's expression. Whenever I moved around Hokkaidō I was followed, visibly or not, by the eyes of the police, and this not only made us nervous, but discouraged the Ainu from becoming friends with a foreigner and giving him even innocent information about their customs and religion. Though I heard and read a lot about the great *iyomande* ritual, the so-called Bear Festival, I was never able to see one during the years 1939–41, when I lived in Hokkaidō. One *iyomande* ritual seems to have taken place in 1939, but for various reasons it was kept secret, and I received no information about it. There may have been other performances, though they must have been much simplified and reduced, because of the prevailing political conditions, and because of restrictions becoming harsher every year, in every direction.

During the suffocating years of the war, my movements became more and more restricted; on 8 September 1943, when Italy was divided in two, the south passing to the Allies and the north remaining stubbornly attached to Germany, my family (myself, my wife, and three children) became officially enemies of Japan and we were confined in a concentration camp at Nagoya. There we remained until 15 August 1945.

At the beginning of April 1942 (that is, well before our internment), Dr Munro sent to me in Kyōto, where I was then residing, a most pathetic note (later taken away from me by the police) in which he said something like: 'I would be immensely happy if you could come to Nibutani . . . I am very ill . . I would like to see you briefly before "all is silence" . . .' Most fortunately, the chief of the foreign section of the Kyōto police was a very friendly and liberal man who spoke excellent French. Somehow or other a miracle took place, and I got a special pass allowing me to go to Nibutani. For a foreigner to cross most of Japan at that crucial period was something quite unusual; I was stopped, and my papers were examined, dozens of times. But I finally made it. Dr Munro was in very bad shape; he had an intestinal occlusion, and as a doctor he knew how dangerous this was. Good medical attention would have saved him, but there was none. Day by day he got worse, and he died on 26 April. The day after I was able to witness how dearly he was loved by the Ainu. A stream of hundreds of people, not only from Nibutani, but from many other villages along the Saru valley, came to give their last salute to their benefactor. It was a most moving scene.

Let me now turn to 1954, some twelve years after that very sad visit to Nibutani. Fortunately even the deepest sorrows are forgotten, the dead are buried, and the spring comes forth once more. I still remember the joy, the exhilaration, with which I moved then about Japan. For years and years during my earlier stay in Japan, I had obtained mere glimpses of the country, through the tight net of suspicions and prohibitions which imprisoned us. Now I could go wherever I liked, speak with absolutely anybody, visit the most remote corners of a vast archipelago. It was wonderful, a season of unbounded joy.

One of my first thoughts was about Hokkaidō and the Ainu. So I travelled to Nibutani. Would it be possible, at last, to witness a genuine *iyomande*? The situation looked very grim; the Ainu there had suffered painfully during the war from hunger, cold, and indescribable misery. Most of the elders had gone, the younger people had no vitality left, and no interest in their cultural heritage; they were barely starting to make a living by carving little wooden bears and trays for export and for sale to tourists.[6]

Upon returning to Sapporo I had the good chance of running into two men with clear ideas and exceptional enthusiasm: the first was Professor Kōno Hiromichi, then a teacher at Hokkaidō University, the second was Sarashina Genzō, a freelance writer and journalist, who had dedicated his life to research on Ainu folklore and Ainu oral literature. Both advised me to go to the village of Kotan, on the shores of lake Kutcharo, in the far eastern portion of Hokkaidō, where traditions had not entirely died out, and where some eminent *ekashi*, with deep knowledge of ancestral traditions, were still alive.

Professor Kōno and Sarashina Genzō were so enthusiastic about the idea of organising a genuine *iyomande*, of which I proposed to shoot a brief film, that they accompanied me personally to the town of Teshikaga, and then to the village of Kotan. Professor Kōno was on intimate terms with the director

6 On the loss of interest in their traditions among young Ainu during these years see Kayano Shigeru's courageous autobiography, *Our land was a forest: an Ainu memoir* (San Francisco: Westview Press, 1994), p. 99.

of the museum of Kushiro, which owns a substantial collection of Ainu material, and persuaded him to loan to the Ainu of Kotan some 20 gowns for the women to wear, as most of the people had sold their heirlooms to passing American soldiers during the first months after the war. At first the reception of my plan, which happily had now the full support of the two well-known authorities from Sapporo, was at most lukewarm. Also, the people of Kotan had passed through very grim years during the war; food was scarce, wood had to be delivered to the government, shoes were made with scraps of animal skin, or with old tires. The unending fight to survive had drained them of all interest in anything so useless as 'traditions'. Then slowly some of the *ekashi*, and some of the older women, most of whom still had large blue tattoos around the mouth, began to take an interest. They saw that we were proceeding in earnest with the preparations; they were also impressed by the fact that I had brought with me four technicians from Tōkyō to help me shoot the film. After a few days the old men and women were asking with real glee in their eyes: was it really true, were they really going to have an *iyomande*? After dark, when we all gathered in the house of Yanaka Torizō, the local *ekashi*, there were drinks of *kamui-ashkoro*, millet beer, or Japanese sake, and songs. The atmosphere was changing completely. The entire village seemed inebriated by the plan to hold an *iyomande*.

The season was ideal: March in Eastern Hokkaidō is still quite cold, but the sun was very often visible. Kotan consisted of some twenty houses built along the shore of Lake Kutcharo, the largest body of fresh water in Hokkaidō, some 8 miles long and 6 miles wide. Now it was completely frozen, and offered a splendid background for all the main scenes of the ritual.

An *iyomande* can be fairly complex, or less so, according to a number of variables. In our case both my mentors, Kōno and Sarashina, and the village elders all wanted it to be as perfect as possible. One serious problem we had at Kotan was the lack of a bear. Usually every Ainu village had more than one in a wooden cage, slowly growing up to be ritually dispatched at the age of three or four in the course of an *iyomande*. The fact that the village of Kotan, fairly large for that remote district, had no bear was a clear sign of the general destitution and enforced loss of interest in all ancient traditions. Fortunately for all of us, the traditions may have been put aside, but they were not forgotten; the older men, and the middle-aged ones too, were still entirely conversant with their past. Someone remembered that a village not far from Bihoro owned a bear; so a truck was sent with a couple of men from our group, with orders to buy it whatever the price.

When the truck came back with the bear, there was an enthusiastic reception by the people of Kotan. It was a truly moving scene. I realised then, for the first time, how much that animal meant for the Ainu. Women had tears in their eyes, children were beside themselves with joy. Unfortunately, the only bear to be found in this part of Hokkaidō was slightly too young (two and a half years, instead of the canonical three or four), and therefore rather small for its role. But we had to accept it as it was. A very handsome cage had been built near to the shore of the lake, by a group of men working tirelessly for a whole day. The bear was put inside the cage, and a number of women came along bringing choice morsels of food (dried fish, rice dumplings, and so on) for the 'little god'. Then they started dancing around the cage, singing the praises of the sacred animal, and rhythmically clapping their hands.

Preparations for the *iyomande* were going on at full speed all over the village. An extra hut was built in no time to house some of the rituals, without inconveniencing Yanaka and his family too much. Girls, outside in the open, started pounding rice and millet in large, wooden mortars (*nisu*), with strong poles (*yutani*) in their hands; the pounding was accompanied by a very pleasing rhythmical song, sung with great gaiety. In Yanaka's home older women were preparing millet beer (*kamui-ashkoro*), a milky liquid with a pleasant taste, but very low alcoholic content.

People were miraculously appearing out of nowhere, on large sledges pulled by horses. A formidable addition to the party was represented by the arrival of a hefty elder (*ekashi*) from the village of Bihoro, some 40 miles away. Kikuchi Ginosuke, to use his Japanese name, though 77 years old, appeared to be in excellent health and in very high spirits. Both Professor Kōno and Sarashina Genzō referred to him all the time as a precious source of information on the correct procedures for the *iyomande* ritual. Photographs reveal his extraordinary personality better than any verbal description could do. He could be very serious, expressing authority with full dignity, or religious concentration, even mystical devotion; he could be the happy patriarch among a swarm of kindred villagers, though perhaps the best images were those that caught him in a faunesque mood of blissful gaiety.

The two principal *ekashi*, Kikuchi and Yanaka, became immediately busy preparing the numerous *inau* required for a complete *iyomande*. *Inau* (or *inao*) have been defined by Batchelor as 'whittled pieces of willow, lilac and other wood, which are stuck in the ground as offerings to the gods'.[7] As we shall soon see, many *inau* are not stuck directly into the ground, but fastened to tall poles which are then stuck in the ground. *Inau*, Batchelor adds, 'are supposed to have special magical power. Some are regarded as gods, some as offerings to the gods, and others as simple charms.' *Inau*, he concludes, 'bear some mark or sign by which the gods may know who is the

7 J. Batchelor, *An Ainu–English–Japanese dictionary*, fourth edition (Iwanami Shoten, 1938), p. 191.

offerer. In the Ainu idea, no greater sin can be committed than stealing and hiding the *inau* of another person, the idea being that the gods, finding themselves without them, will withdraw their favour from those who ought to have offered them. No worse name can be given to an Ainu than *inau sak guru*, the man without *inau*.' Each *inau* bears a special sign, a sort of signature, of the person who offers it; such signs are called *itokpa*, or *itoppa*.

Inau do not belong exclusively to Ainu culture. Similar whittled wooden objects are known all over Japan, but especially in the north (the Tōhoku district), where they appear both as toys and as wands with a religious meaning. The similarity between *inau* and the *nusa* 幣 wands universally used in Shintō rituals is more striking, even if the *nusa* in its present form does not have shavings as a crown, but strips of paper.[8] Whittled wooden sticks appear also among objects (religious or otherwise) belonging to some northern neighbours of the Ainu, especially the Gilyak and Orok tribes of Sakhalin; but similar sticks have been noticed in many places as far apart as Wisconsin in the USA, Malaysia, Australia, Yunnan (China), the Chittagong Hills (Bangladesh), Assam (India), and especially Borneo, with numerous and striking examples.[9]

The *inau* required for the *iyomande* ritual are many, and of different types and designs. Over 30 were prepared by Kikuchi and Yanaka, a task which took the afternoons of a couple of days before the main event. The job was also interrupted a number of times to perform *kamui nomi* for various gods, especially for Abe (or Ape) Kamui Fuchi, the mother goddess of the hearth, the household, and the Ainu people.[10] A *kamui nomi* rite consists essentially in offering a few drops of *kamui-ashkoro* (milky millet beer), held in a lacquered Japanese cup (generally an ancient heirloom of the family), of the type called *tenmoku-dai*, lifting and sprinkling the liquid by means of an

8 The similarities between Ainu *inau* and Shintō *gohei* 御幣 were noted by Aston in 1900: W. G. Aston, 'On the Japanese Gohei and the Ainu Inao', *Report of the British Association for the Advancement of Science* 1900: 900–1, and 'The Japanese Gohei and the Ainu Inao', *Journal of the Anthropological Institute of Great Britain and Ireland* 31 (1901): 131–5.

9 The subject has been examined extensively by Carl Schuster, 'The Ainu Inao; some comparative considerations', *Proceedings*, VIIIth International Congress of Anthropological and Ethnological Sciences (Tōkyō and Kyōto, Science Council of Japan, 1968), vol. 3, pp. 86–99.

10 The sex of Kamui-Fuchi does not seem to be firmly or always established; he/she may be thought of as sexless, a case somewhat similar to the one of Avalokiteśvara/Kannon (or Kanzeon) in Japan. See Katarina Sjöberg, *The return of the Ainu* (Chur: Harwood Academic Publishers, 1993), p. 60 (interview with Hidaka, an Ainu *ekashi*, in 1988).

iku-bashui, a decorated libation wand. These sticks are sometimes called in English 'moustache-lifters' after their secondary employment: when the offering of beer has been made, accompanied or not by prayers or announcements, the *ekashi* partakes briefly of the drink, and at that moment the stick may be used to lift his abundant moustache. In the first case the use of the *iku-bashui* is highly liturgical – it is often said that these wands were originally simplified images of birds, symbolising their function as messengers of prayers from the human to the divine level or sphere; in the second case the use is purely practical, cosmetic. *Iku-bashui* should therefore be called in English 'libation wands', and never 'moustache-lifters'.[11] In the case of *kamui nomi* on behalf of Abe Kamui Fuchi (the hearth goddess), one or two small *inau* of a special type are stuck in the bed of ashes at the north-east corner of the hearth; once set in place they can serve for many *kamui nomi* rituals.

A most important operation, which must be completed before the actual *iyomande* starts, consists in the construction of an appropriate *nusa* or *nusa-san*, not too far from the eastern window (*rorun puyara*) of the bear owner's house, or the village chief's house. The *nusa* is formed by a range of poles with new *inau* fastened to them, dedicated to various gods. It is well to remember that the relationship between *inau* and gods may be in many cases (and this is one) ambiguous; *inau* are offerings, but also somehow (like the Japanese *shintai*) objects on which the gods descend, therefore at least briefly gods themselves.

The *nusa* is draped with decorated mats (*inauso*), which, in our case, were hung at the last moment because the place was very windy, and sudden gusts might have destroyed them. A number of gifts were hung on the mats. First of all foodstuffs, rice dumplings (*shto*, or *shito*), dried fish, and dried seaweed. A second type of gift varies according to the sex of the bear which is honoured during the *iyomande*; if, as in our case, the animal is male, gifts will include swords (*emush*), with their typical sashes (*emush-at*), arrows (*ai*), bows (*ku*), quivers (*ikayop*), and other similar objects; if female the gifts will be quite different and may include necklaces (*tamasai*), embroidered gowns (*kaparimip*, *attush*), ear-rings (*ninkari*), embroidered muffs for the hands (*tekumbe*), and so on.

More mats were placed on the ground, or on the snow, in front of the *nusa*. After the animal has been 'dispatched', its carcass will be reverently arranged there, together with many more offerings of food and of objects pleasing to the bear, according to its gender. It is there that the main officiating *ekashi* will take their seats for the adoration of the 'little god'. A *nusa* could

11 On *iku-bashui* see F. Maraini, *Gli Iku-bashui degli Ainu* (Tokyo: Istituto Italiano di Cultura, 1942).

therefore be called an 'altar', extending rather arbitrarily the meaning of the word, though it certainly does function as one.[12]

Nusa, though fundamentally similar in structure, seem to have changed in detail, both during the course of time and from district to district in Hokkaidō – leaving out of the picture possible variations in Sakhalin (Karafuto) and the Kurile islands (Chishima). Japanese paintings of the early nineteenth century show *nusa* as a well-built recess draped with coloured mats. This is not the place to trace a history of *nusa*, but I would like to mention a few cases to show how varied the picture can be. One should not apply to the Ainu religion the conceptual and liturgical rigidity of highly developed faiths, such as Christianity, Judaism, or Buddhism. There has never been among the Ainu a religious centre, or a religious authority of such importance as to be able to impose on the entire culture and its territory definite conceptions and homogeneous ritual rules. *Nusa*, therefore, vary not only according to the relative importance of local gods (*kamui*), depending on local conditions and traditions, but also in harmony with family records, or even according to the tastes of single influential *ekashi*.

A few important documents, dating from the 1930s, when traditions were still vigorously alive, give images of *nusa* with striking differences distinguishing one from the other. The two examples on the following page come from a famous work by Kindaichi and Sugiyama.[13]

These two *nusa* obviously inspired a somewhat simpler *nusa* put up for an *iyomande* performed at Nibutani at the end of February and the beginning of March 1977, that is, in the third wave of the history of the *iyomande*, that of the modern revival period. Money and time were then no more a problem, and everything was done on a most splendid scale. Mr. Kayano Shigeru, an acknowledged authority on Ainu culture and religion, directed the event. Two years later he published a book with complete photographic documentation, in black and white and in colour, of the entire ritual, from the earliest preparations to the very end.[14] It is difficult to say how much living tradition there is in these latter-day *iyomande*, and how much they are the result of eager research done in libraries and museums. Possibly the most complete old description of the *iyomande* ritual is due to Natori Takemitsu,

---

12 The term *nusa* offers another example of the important common ground existing between Ainu and Japanese religions. In Ainu *nusa* refers to a row of sacred *inau* wands arranged in various ways; in Japanese it indicates a particular type of *gohei* used in purification rites. See entry 'Gohei' in *Kodansha encyclopaedia of Japan* (Tokyo: Kodansha International,1983) vol. 3, p. 40.

13 Kindaichi Kyōsuke 金田一京助 and Sugiyama Sueo 杉山寿栄男, *Ainu geijutsu* アイヌ芸術 (Daiichi Seinen-sha, 1941), fukusōhen 服装篇, pp. 1–5.

14 See note 1 above.

based on information gathered during the late 1930s from reliable *ekashi* of various districts in Hokkaidō.[15] A schematic plan of the Nibutani *iyomande nusa* of 1977, as given in Kayano's book is shown in Fig. 3.

Fig. 1

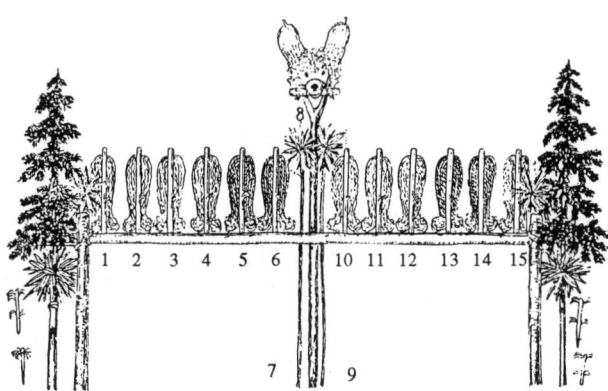

Nusa for an *iyomande* performed in the village of Hamamasu on the west coast of Hokkaidō (Ishikari district), during the late 1930s(?). The pantheon is quite different from the well-known one from the Hidaka district: sea gods and river gods are here very important.

The numbered *inau* were dedicated as follows:

1 god of upper valley of the bear
2 god of lower valley of the bear
3 local river god
4 local male and female mountains
5 bird gods
6 the protector of the village (*Kotan koro Kamui*)
7 & 9   *tagusa*, sticks with bunches of bamboo-grass leaves
8 *kiraunsapa-ni*: forked pole for bear's head
10   local river gods
11   local river gods
12   god of the bay
13   god of the sea floor

---

15 The work appeared originally under the names of Inukai Tetsuo 犬飼哲夫 and Natori Takemitsu 名取武光 in *Hoppō bunka kenkyū hōkoku* 北方文化研究報告, vols. 2 and 3 (1939 and 1940). It has been reprinted as 「イヨマンテ（アイヌの熊祭）の文化的意義とその形式」 in *Natori Takemitsu chosakushū* 名取武光著作集 (Sapporo: Hokkaidō Shuppan Kikaku Sentā, 1972), vol. 1, pp. 246–330.

14   grampus, *Rep un Kamui*, god of the sea
15   gods of the local coast
The *inau* seem to be fixed directly to the strong transverse pole; only the *tagusa* sticks and the *kiraunsapa-ni* pole appear to reach the ground. The presence of two young fir trees at both ends of the *nusa* is an interesting detail.

Fig. 2

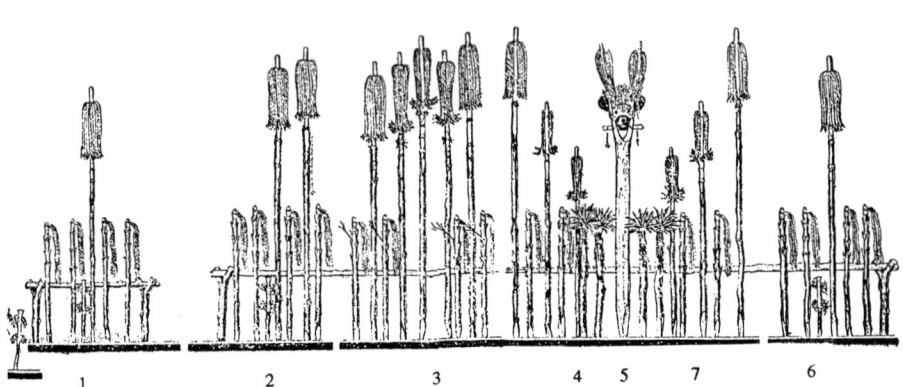

Highly complex *nusa* as seen at Nibutani (Hidaka District) by Kindaichi and Sugiyama during late 1930s(?).
The numbered *inau* were dedicated as follows:

1   *Nusa koro Kamui*, gods of the *nusa*, protectors of the Ainu people, and of agriculture
2   *Shiramba Kamui*, gods of trees, woods, plants in general
3   *Hashinau Kamui*, protectors of hunters and animals
4   *tagusa* sticks (sticks with tufts of bamboo-grass)
5   *kiraunsapa-ni*, thick forked pole for bear's head decorated with *inau*, and *inau kike* (*inau* shavings).
       The bear's head is called *Metok Kamui* (or *Marapto Kamui*)
6   *Wakka ush Kamui*, god of waters (rivers, sources, lakes)
7   *Shinnurappa ush Kamui*, special *inau* for spirits of ancestors

Fig. 3

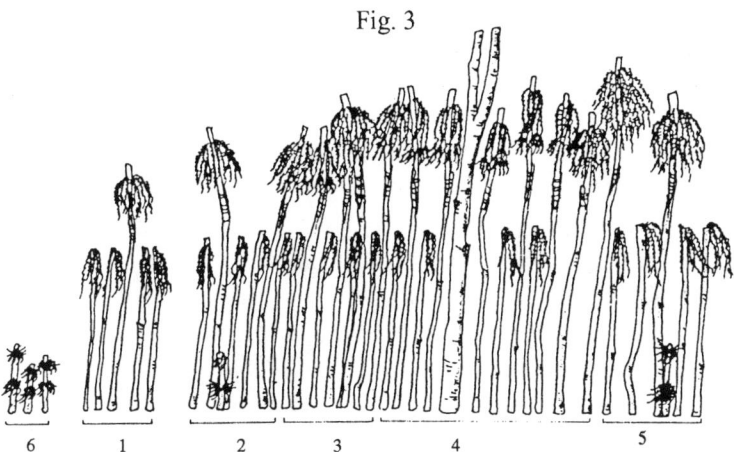

1 *Nusa koro Kamui* (god of the fields)
2 *Shiramba Kamui* (god of trees and vegetation)
3 *Hashinau Kamui* (god protecting hunters)
4 *Metot Kamui* (the actual bear 'sent off' during the *iyomande*)
5 *Wakka ush Kamui* (god of water, rivers, springs, lakes.)
6 *Shinnurappa ush* (kamui) (spirits of the ancestors)

Fig. 4

The bear's head as decorated and set up on the central pole of the *nusa*:
    1   at Hamamasu, in the Ishikari district
    2 & 3   at Nibutani, in the Kidaka district
(from Kindaichi and Sugiyama, *Ainu geijitsu* [Tokyo, 1942]).

Our *nusa* in 1954 was fairly simple, consisting of only six main *inau* and a couple of *tagusa*, as shown in Fig. 5.

Fig. 5

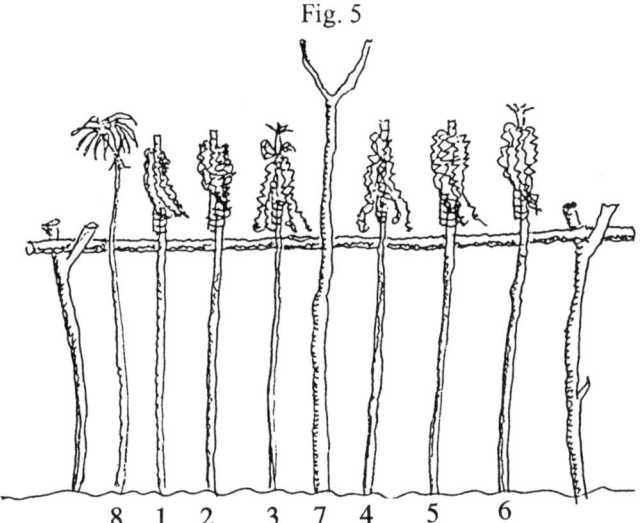

The numbered *inau* were dedicated as follows:

1   to the parents of the bear which was being 'sent off'

2   to *Kim un Kamui*, the great 'Spirit of the Mountains', personified by bears

3   to the owl god, protector of the village

4   to the bear which was being 'sent off'

5   same

6   to the Protector of the Village (*Kotan koro Kamui*)

7   in the middle stood a tall forked pole (here called *yuppaoma-ni*), where, at the end of the ritual, the decorated bear's head would be arranged.

8   some *tagusa* (sticks with tufts of bamboo-grass) were added at various moments of the ritual

Four or five old bear skulls, quite dry, had been added by one of the *ekashi*, who told me this made the *nusa* look 'more ancient'.

Our *nusa*, on the whole, seemed to be very similar to the one which was set up for a *iyomande* performed at Piratori on the unusual date of 3 August in 1958, and which has been accurately described by Professor Joseph Kitagawa.[16]

16 Joseph Kitagawa, 'Ainu Bear Festival (*Iyomante*)', *History of Religions*, 1 (1961): 95–151.

There is one point I would like to mention here, and to which I will return later on. All the laborious preparations for the *iyomande* produced at Kotan in 1954 were undertaken by the *ekashi*, by women and children, without ever mentioning the word 'work', or any compensation thereof, in a spirit of pure enthusiasm. After the uncertain moments at the beginning, when the very idea of an *iyomande*, following years of misery, seemed inappropriate, perhaps even annoying, there had been an extraordinary turn in the opposite direction, and all those engaged in the project had become enthusiastic about it. Naturally, the building of the extra hut, the bear's cage, the bear itself were all paid for, but nothing was asked for the preparation of the many *inau* necessary for the ceremony, or for kneading and cooking hundreds of rice dumplings. We provided the rice, the millet, and so on; the Ainu women did the rest.

THE SPIRIT OF THE *IYOMANDE*

At this point something should be said about the spirit of the *iyomande*, what it may have meant for the Ainu, though it should be remembered that this certainly varied from place to place, and from time to time. Possibly the main ideas are, or were, clear in the minds of the *ekashi*, especially Kikuchi Ginosuke, whom I questioned a number of times, and whom Kōno and Sarashina took as their guide, but Ainu old men were not used to verbalising their knowledge, thoughts, imagination, or emotions. Finally there remains the question of translation, both from the Ainu (for some main concepts) and from the Japanese (for descriptions and explanations) into English, a long and roundabout path with the possibility of many pitfalls. With these caveats in mind, we may attempt a summary of what the *iyomande* may have meant to the Ainu.

The Ainu seem to have visualised the universe as composed of three worlds, superimposed one on the other. The present world in which we all live is *Ainu moshiri* (Ainu-land; remember that 'Ainu' means human being); somewhere, possibly above, there exists a *Kamui-moshiri*, a land of the gods; more vaguely still, an inferior and dark world, *Pokna moshiri*, was sometimes referred to. The arrangement is similar to the ancient Japanese scheme of things, and has parallels among many ethnic groups, especially in northern Asia. A basic point seems to be that very little difference was felt to exist between animals and human beings. In some cases the animals seem to have had a place of their own in the *Kamui-moshiri*, the divine world; other utterances seem to imply that gods, living in human form in their upper world, took an animal disguise when visiting *Ainu moshiri*.

The important point is that bears are considered to represent the main and most awesome god of the mountains, *Kim-un-kamui* ('in-the-mountains-god'). It should be made clear from the start that the *iyomande* ritual is totally free from the idea of sacrifice. The bear is not to be 'offered' to the gods – and, someone has shrewdly observed, to whom could he be offered, being the highest of all the gods? The Ainu conception is quite different, and perhaps rather startling to someone who hears about it for the first time.

The young bear, generally the cub of a female bear killed on a hunting expedition, is taken with great care, and with signs of particular respect, to the hunter's village, put in an appropriate wooden cage (*hepere-set*), and reared for a couple of years, or more, with the greatest affection. The cub receives the best food available, sometimes better than the fare of his hosts, placed on a wooden platter, and is in all substantial and formal ways considered a highly honoured guest. The 'little god' receives offerings of sacred millet beer, and prayers. In times gone by, if the animal was very small and toothless, one of the village women would become its 'foster mother', and milk it from her breasts. This custom has long since disappeared, but it was clearly illustrated in Japanese paintings and prints of the eighteenth and nineteenth centuries.[17]

A very important idea, at the back of these customs and of the entire *iyomande* ritual, is simply that the bear-god (as well as the other gods of the Ainu pantheon) enjoys the same things that human beings do. A human guest would greatly rejoice at being honoured with much respect and many ceremonies, receiving the best food and drink in sincere gaiety, being offered fine and costly gifts: it is surmised that the same applies to the bear, and to other Ainu gods. It is interesting to remember that the same principle is valid for many Shintō gods, in a Japanese context: a full blown *matsuri* is often an uproarious entertainment meant to please both gods and human beings.

The *iyomande* ritual, the little god's 'send-off', is seen entirely in this light. Somehow or other there is what could be called a moment of numinous blindness: the fact that the poor bear is killed not only does not trouble the participants in the least, but is hardly mentioned. I had the firm impression that, though the action took place, it was not so to speak mentally registered. The accent is entirely set on the 'splendid send-off', the royal dispatch of the beast as a spiritual entity, loaded with gifts for his ancestors in the mysterious mountain world, the bearer of prayers from his devoted friends, the Ainu.

There occurs here a most interesting and curious psychological somersault, for the entire event is seen from the imagined point of view of the bear. The animal-god is supposed to be pleased, happy, fully satisfied, by how the Ainu treat it, how they 'send it off' with ceremonies, songs, and gifts that he may take back to his parents and ancestors, giving them pleasure and prestige. The fact of being killed is entirely overlooked. So much so that the bear, if

17 The practice was also witnessed by John Batchelor: see his *The Ainu and their folk-lore* (London: Religious Tract Society, 1901), p. 484.

fully pleased by the richness and splendour of the 'send-off', will come again and again among men, to be newly 'sent off' in the same way.

This somewhat involved psychological process (which has parallels in other ethnic contexts), is nowadays, even if well known and often explained to interested visitors, a relic of the remote past, most probably on its way to extinction. There are some extraordinarily explicit documents, collected by Japanese scholars such as Kindaichi Kyōsuke and Kubodera Itsuhiko during the 1930s, when Ainu culture was waning but still alive in some districts, that give us an intimate, and very clear, vision of the thought processes behind the bear hunt and *iyomande* rituals. I am thinking, for instance, of the splendid 'Song of a bear', recited in 1932 by Hiraga Etenoa and recorded by Kubodera Itsuhiko. Later on this song was translated into English by Donald Philippi, who wrote that, 'the song gives the whole scenario for human–bear relationships'.[18] The poem is much too long to be quoted in full, but a summary is certainly necessary here.

The song is presented as if narrated by the bear himself. He was moving around a valley in the wilds, when 'from behind a tree the top of a bow could be seen protruding. Overjoyed I rushed toward it. A pretty little arrow lodged itself with a thump in my body'.[19] As can be immediately seen, the bear's imagined reactions are exactly the opposite of what a real animal might be supposed to have felt on such an occasion: first fear at the sight of the bow, then pain at the thrust of the arrow in his flesh. The bear notices two young men running away. He starts to chase them. But the 'pretty little arrow' had been loaded with aconite poison (*shurku*), which soon causes loss of consciousness in the animal. In this new dreamy state, the God of Aconite Poison (*Shurku Kamui*) delivers to the bear a message from the fire goddess of the humans, *Abe-Fuchi Kamui*: 'O weighty deity, please come to pay me a peaceable visit, and let us meet to enjoy peaceful conversation!' The God of Aconite Poison wraps himself around the bear and seizes him with his powerful hands: 'I tumbled down and lay outstretched majestic and godlike. I lost all consciousness of what was happening.' After sleeping for a while, the bear opens his eyes, and finds himself lying on the branch of a tree, 'with my hands and legs hanging down limply'. Philippi adds a note here to say that this is a conventional formula applied to a soul after it has left a corpse. The soul of the bear now looks down uncomprehendingly on the carcass he has just abandoned, not recognising it as his own. Soon the bear, as a disembodied soul, notices that the young hunters have returned. He sees them picking up

---

18 Donald L.Philippi, *Songs of gods, songs of humans; the epic tradition of the Ainu* (University of Tokyo Press, 1979), pp. 115–25.

19 *Ibid.*, p. 118.

the bear's cub. He also notices them preparing the carcass of the adult beast, killed by the poisoned arrow. 'The brain and eyes are removed from the animal's head, which is then stuffed with wooden shavings.'[20] *Inau* are prepared and stuck in the ground next to the carcass. The young men worship the beast which they have slain, as God of the Mountains (*Kim-un-Kamui*). The *inau* are made according to a special model called *shutu-inau*. The young hunters rub their hands together in ritual fashion, while paying their respects to the bear-god.

The *shutu-inau* are considered to be minor deities. Taking this fact into account, the prayer which the young men offer to the carcass of the bear becomes intelligible. 'Do you deities enjoy yourselves by conversing together! It has already become dark by now, and since it is too late to move the bear, we will leave him here. When morning comes, we will come back. Then we will bring the weighty deity (the bear) down to the village. Do you deities both watch over each other!' The young men leave for the village, taking the cub with them. Somehow, one young man comes back, lights a fire and keeps guard on the carcass of the large bear killed by the poisoned arrow. The young man looks up to the tree above the fire and says: 'O weighty deity, come down beside the fire, and let us enjoy ourselves in conversation!' The bear's soul resting on the tree accepts the invitation. 'Thus did he speak, therefore I went down beside the fire and we began to engage in pleasant conversation.' During the night, the young man is busy most of the time chasing away with a club other beasts, foxes, wolves, and eager birds, all attracted by the meat of the bear's carcass. When morning comes, the young man disappears, and the bear's soul climbs up to his branch on a nearby tree. After a while the soul sees a crowd of Ainu coming up the mountain. Some of the men skin the carcass of the bear lying on the snow, carve the meat into pieces and finally carry it all down to the village, arranged in parcels on their shoulders. The bear's soul sees all these details, describes them in its song; then joins the men. 'We walked down the hill until we came upon a human village, a populous village. At the centre of the village an immense house was seen standing majestically. I was seated in the middle of the spirit fence [the *nusa*], the *inau* fence just east of the house.'

After a while the Fire Goddess, 'wearing sixfold layers of magnificent robes fastened under her girdle and sixfold robes hanging loosely', comes to invite the bear's soul inside. 'I thank you [she says] for having come to pay me a peaceable visit, for it is just such conduct for which a weighty deity wins praise!' The bear's soul then enters the house and is invited to take a seat at the *ror*, to the east of the fireplace, the most sacred and honoured place in the house. In the meantime everybody in the village is busy with

20 *Ibid.*, p. 120.

preparations for 'my ritual dismissal (*hopunire*)'. The *hopunire* is not an *iyomande*, but a minor ritual to please the slain bear's soul. An *iyomande* will undoubtedly be performed, after two or three years, to 'send off' the bear's cub, which has been brought down from the mountain and will be reared in a *hepere-set* cage.) After the *hopunire*, the bear's soul goes back to his mountain haunts heavily laden with food, wine, gifts. Also his bear wife, who seems to have been killed previously, returns as a soul to their home in the hills charged with gifts received from human beings, from the Ainu. The bear-family is now in a most favourable position; they have abundance of everything, and are therefore able to send out invitations to all gods, near and far, to join them for 'a delightful banquet'.

Some time passes. Finally the family cub returns home, as a soul. 'Our dear little child came back from the humans carrying on his back much wine and many *inau*.' Obviously he had been 'sent off' with a resounding *iyomande* by the people of the village at the feet of the mountain. The song ends with an expression of delight by the bear's soul. 'Once again we invited the gods dwelling nearby and the gods dwelling far away. The invited guests were shown in with much ceremony. After that, the peerless feast went on magnificently.' The divine community of bears, in the Ainu view, depends on human beings for their happiness, pleasures, and satisfaction.

The extraordinary counterpoint of different existential planes in the 'Song of a bear' – on one hand the actual, real, material world, in which the actual, real, living society of humans and animals interacts, on the other hand the dream-like parallel plane of imagined visions – reaches unheard of shades of refinement, overcoming with ease and elegance barrages of possible contradictions. But these are ignored, or, if pointed out, simply make the informer nervous. 'Such questions are never asked when listening to a story!', exclaimed a Formosan native answering an anthropologist who had put such questions to him.[21] A complete imaginary bear psychology is created out of nothing, entirely forgetting the fact that, if the animals had words, they might tell a completely different story. The poor bears, however, have no words, while the Ainu express themselves admirably. In this case it is their story which arouses our interest, and explains many details of their prayers, as noted down by Batchelor, Kindaichi, Natori and many others, prayers which otherwise would hardly make sense.[22]

21 Dezso Benedek, *The songs of the ancestors*, Taiwan Aborigine monograph series 2 (Taipei: 1991), p.167.

22 Sixty-six prayers (some quite long), uttered during the entire *iyomande* ritual, as performed by the Ainu of the Saru valley (Piratori, Nibutani, etc.), were taken down from the mouth of the famous *ekashi* Hiramura Kotampira, during the late 1930s by Natori Takemitsu. See 'Saru ainu no kuma-okuri ni okeru kamigami no yurai to nusa'

Here, for example, is a preliminary prayer pronounced at the outset of the *iyomande*, as taken down at Piratori by Batchelor some time during the latter part of the last century.

> O thou divine one, thou didst come into this world for us to hunt. O thou precious little one, we worship thee; pray hear our prayers. We have nourished thee and brought thee up with great pains and care, and all because we loved thee so much. Now, as thou hast grown big, we are about to send thee to thy parents. When thou comest to them, please speak well of us and tell them how kind we have been to thee. We beseech thee to return to us once more, that we may again entertain thee.[23]

When the *ekashi* says, 'We beseech thee to return to us once more, that we may again entertain thee', the phrase, read in the light of the 'Song of the bear', makes perfectly good sense, instead of sounding ironic, grotesque, or simply impossible to understand.

Professor Kindaichi Kyōsuke, the illustrious recorder, and translator into Japanese, of a vast collection of Ainu *yukara* poems, fills in the picture with other details. Men and gods live in two distinct but somehow very similar worlds; both worlds are beautiful and desirable; both have huts, villages, seasons, forests, rivers, seas, and so on. When gods visit the human world they take on animal *hayokpe* (or *hayokube*), more exactly animal garments (according to Batchelor the word means 'armour'), with furs if appearing as a bear; with feathers in the case of an owl, or other birds; with scales in the case of a fish, and so on. Men, in this particular range of ideas, do not 'kill' the animals they feed upon, but simply free them of their *hayokpe*, and send their spirits back to the world of the gods. '*Kamui* gain esteem in the kingdom of the gods', Kindaichi explains, 'by being well thought of or by being respected by men, because when people think well of them they will often hold festivals, distribute wine, and make offerings to the gods. These offerings, it is said, will be manifold when they reach the kingdom of the gods, where the gods can invite neighbours to their houses to eat. On the contrary, gods who are not well thought of by men and who are given no festivals, are

---

沙流アイヌの熊送りに於ける神々の由来とヌサ, *Hoppō bunka kenkyū hōkoku*, 4 (February 1941), pp. 77–112 (Natori gives Japanese translations). For a more recent work, which gives a dozen prayers, with Japanese translations, see *Iyomante – kuma no tamashi-okuri hōkoku-sho* イヨマンテ ― 熊の霊送り報告書 (Shiraoi: Ainu Minzoku Hakubutsukan, 1991), p. 112.

23 J. Batchelor, *Ainu life and lore* (Kyobunkwan, 1939), p. 207.

miserable, for they are short of money and very poor in their country'.[24] In other words, men and gods live in distant and separate worlds, but are deeply dependent on each other; and not only in one direction (men upon gods), but also in the opposite direction (gods upon men). Therefore, Kindaichi observes, when bear or other animal meat is eaten gaily by the Ainu, the occasion is called a 'banquet' as seen from the viewpoint of man, but 'an entertainment' as seen from that of the gods. Men rejoice in honouring the animal's *hayopke* ('armour') of meat, and partaking of its bounty; the god, on the other hand, is on the receiving end too: as a most honoured guest he is given prayers, food, wine, gifts of all sorts. Therefore, quite reasonably, the beast wishes to 'come again', to be 'sent off' again. Being killed by man, Kindaichi concludes, is an event for which the bear must feel deeply grateful. The entire cycle achieves a strange, subtle, fairy-like logic of its own.

THE *IYOMANDE* RITUAL

Let us now return to Kotan. Those last days of March were generally fine. The place had then a legendary, most privileged beauty of its own. Imagine a small group of low wooden huts practically hidden in a grove of very large deciduous trees, near to the lonely shore of an immense frozen lake, lake Kutcharo, hemmed in at a distance by solemn hills covered with forests and snow. No sign of human habitation was to be seen, and the vast expanse of ice covering the lake gave extraordinary nobility to anything taking place here, on the shore.

The last, and most important, day of the *iyomande* ritual had arrived. From early morning groups of women were seen dancing around the *hepere-set* (the bear's cage), clapping their hands rhythmically and singing praises to the 'little god'. More than once, two or three *ekashi* came down from the village and offered drops of *kamui-ashkoro* (millet beer) to the bear, uttering words of praise and prayers. The *ekashi* held in their left hands a *tenmoku-dai* Japanese lacquered cup filled with milky beer, while they repeatedly dipped an *iku-bashui* (libation wand) in the liquid, then scattered drops of it toward the bear in its wooden cage. Somehow or other the *ekashi* had come upon some ancient Japanese red samurai coats (*jinbaori*), most probably received by their ancestors in exchange for bear pelts, eagle feathers, or dried fish. The bright splashes of red against the white snow and blue sky were excitingly beautiful. I feel sure that very few *iyomande*, at least in these latter years,

---

24 Kindaichi Kyōsuke, 'The concepts behind the Ainu Bear Festival', *The South-Western Journal of Anthropology*, 5 (1949): pp. 345–50.

have ever reached such a high aesthetic pitch as this one performed at Kotan. The *iyomande* witnessed in 1958 at Piratori by Professor Joseph Kitagawa seems to have been by comparison a much more prosaic affair.[25] One should also remember that the summer (the ritual in 1958 took place on 3 August) is, according to all Ainu traditions, a most incongruous season for a proper 'send-off'. Winter is generally chosen for many reasons, among them the fact that the bear's fur is at its finest, and bear meat at its best because of abundant fat under the skin. The presence of snow and ice on the ground and on the nearby forest trees is somehow felt to offer the proper climatic and emotional background for the ritual.

Around eleven in the morning all those taking part in the *iyomande* gathered around the bear's cage, which on this and other solemn occasions is called the *peurep-chise*, the 'bear's home'. The chief *ekashi* pronounced the *hepere-kashpaotte*, a special goodbye prayer (literally 'the bear's command'), giving instructions to the 'little god' for his return to his parents and ancestors. A special *inau*, called a *shutu-inau*, and representing the *Shutu-inau-Kamui* ('the ancestor-*inau* god'?), is presented to the bear as a protection against demons and evil beings during his return home.

By this time everything was ready. Two sturdy young men, holding a rope in their hands, climbed onto the bear's cage, and performed a vigorous dance, with bear-like movements, called *set-kata-tapkara* ('dance upon the cage'), accompanying it with a song. This is a moment of great gaiety; while the men dance, the circle of women around the cage moves with renewed vigour, children lift their arms and shout. After a while, the dance on the cage stops, another man climbs up; the three uncover the cage and, with some difficulty, fasten a lasso around the bear's waist: this moment is known as the *tush-kore*, 'the rope-fastening'. Then, all of a sudden, the 'little god' is pulled up and out, and falls on his feet on the ground next to the cage. Naturally the animal is bewildered by this sudden change, and possibly frightened by the crowd which immediately retires to a certain distance. The men jump down from the cage, and in a few seconds everything is again in order. The bear is bound by ropes around his body, the ends of which are held firmly in the hands of two strong Ainu, who can easily control every movement of the beast, and direct its steps in any desired direction. The women have by now left the cage, and form a very large loose circle around the central ground of the village, continually singing, and clapping their hands.

The bear is now gently directed toward the *nusa* altar, with its mats and tall range of *inau*, to pay his respects to his ancestors. The beast is also decorated with some bits of coloured cloth and given ear-rings, a moment of

25 See note 16 above.

the ritual called *pon-pake-imire* ('little-head-clothing'). As noticed previously, our bear was young and small; a fact which did not give the *iyomande* that fearsome aspect it must have had when dealing with a large and powerful beast: on the other hand all phases of the ritual were made easy and playful. The 'little god' ran, or rather romped gaily, toward the symbols of 'his ancestors', possibly attracted by the many rice dumplings (*shito*) decorating the altar.

The cub was then led to the house of the village *ekashi*; suddenly a strong and daring man grabbed the animal by the skin of its neck and lifted it to the sacred eastern window (*rorun puyara*); the bear was cuddled to pay its respects to the Fire Goddess, *Abe-Fuchi Kamui*, who dwells in the hearth. The 'little god' did not seem to appreciate very much this pious homage to the fire goddess, and he continued to growl fiercely till let down again on the snow.

These salutations were only the preliminary stages to the main act of the day, to the core of the ritual, the *hepere tukan* ('the bear hunt', 'shooting at the bear'). During this part of the ritual, the bear is paraded round the village, while a sort of mock hunt is enacted: Ainu men, first the *ekashi* wearing their red *jinbaori*, sometimes with *sapaumbe* crowns on their heads, then younger men, shot from their bows blunt decorated arrows (*hepere-ai*) toward the beast. These arrows cannot injure the bear, but they may arouse its rage. The *hepere tukan* can last a long time, and it is one of the highlights of the ritual. There may be slack moments, but then suddenly the bear reacts fiercely to one or more of the *hepere-ai*; the men shout as if the hunt were real; the women come out with gales of laughter, clapping their hands with renewed vigour; children run here and there shrieking. These rowdy moments of the *hepere tukan* are considered the spice of the ritual; the livelier they are, the greater the success of the *iyomande*. Some of the men also hold in their hands long poles with tufts of bamboo-grass tied on at the end, and with these may dance, prodding the bear from time to time, or pushing it in the desired direction: these poles with bamboo-grass are called *ragusa*.

In the meanwhile not far from the *nusa* altar, a strong, tall, wooden pillar (*tush-op-ni*) with a crown of bamboo-grass leaves on top, was driven into the ground (in some cases the *tush-op-ni* is prepared the day before, when the *nusa* altar is put in place). By and by the bear becomes weary; its reactions to the mock hunt appear to be weaker; the beast is losing interest or simply getting tired. The moment for the real 'send-off' has come. One of the Ainu fixes the ropes tied on the bear to the *tush-op-ni*, and an elder offers to the 'little god' drops of sacred beer, with new prayers.

The actual dispatch generally takes place when four or five strong young Ainu grab the beast by its front and rear legs, while five or six other men manage to get its neck inserted between two thick wooden poles, pressing on them with the weight of their bodies; in a few seconds the animal is choked to death. There is no doubt that this procedure, which was followed at Kotan, is traditional. Any number of old Japanese paintings and ukiyo-e prints show a ritual 'send-off' of this type quite clearly. There is, however, mention of the bear being dispatched by means of one or more arrows shot at its heart. This seems to have been the case during the *iyomande* witnessed by Professor Kitagawa in 1958. Professor Kitagawa's description seems to imply that both methods of 'sending off' the bear were used. Arrows were shot 'not once but two or three times' to dispatch the animal. He also adds that the blood was caught carefully and drunk. 'Those who drink fresh bear's blood at *Iyomante*', he wrote, 'have to stay away from women until the coming of the new moon. If they do not do so, it is believed that they will die. For this reason only the elders are urged to drink the bear's blood warm.' After this ordeal, the bear seems to have been throttled between two poles, in the traditional way. It is not clear from the description if the animal died from the arrow shot at its heart, or was simply wounded and then killed by being throttled between the two poles. Killing the bear with one or more arrows shot from close quarters seems to have been the method followed also during the elaborate *iyomande* performed in 1985 at Chikabumi, near Asahikawa, in central Hokkaidō.[26]

As soon as the bear is dead, the carcass is carefully carried to the *nusa* and properly displayed there in a prone position. Many gifts are displayed around the bear, and under its head. If the bear is a male, as was the case at Kotan, the main gifts consist of swords, with their typical Ainu sashes, bows, arrows, and quivers; gifts proper for a male are also hung on the screen of mats which forms a main part of the *nusa* altar. If the bear is a female, as was the case for the *iyomande* performed at Chikabumi in 1985, the gifts consist mainly of necklaces, *attush* gowns and other clothing items, plus a bundle of *inau*. Ear-rings are also considered proper. Both male and female bears are offered presents of food: round rice dumplings (*shito*) generally skewered in groups of five, seven or eight on sticks; cooked rice in Japanese lacquered cups; dried fish, dry seaweed, and other delicacies.

This is an important moment. The main officiating *ekashi* come and squat on the mats at the feet of the *nusa* and start a *kamui nomi* worship, offering drops of milky beer with their *iku-bashui*, while reciting prayers to the 'little god', now considered to be exquisitely divine, a full spiritual entity. The prayers are recited in a very deep guttural tone of voice.

The small crowd of people from neighbouring villages, from the town of Teshikaga, who had come to witness the *iyomande*, by now had left us; and

26 Sōga Tetsuo 相賀徹夫, ed., *Iyomante: Kamikawa chihō no kuma-okuri no kiroku* イヨマンテー 上川地方の熊送りの記録 (Shōgakkan, 1985).

we remained completely alone, in front of the *nusa* and the *ekashi*, on the windy shore of lake Kutcharo, with its endless expanse of ice and snow, under a blazing spring sun. The three old men (Kikuchi Ginosuke, Yanaka Torizō, and Maeda Sentarō) could have returned to the village for lunch, but something magical, a mysterious inebriation, kept them there while they delivered an unending series of prayers and songs in honour of the bear's spirit, ready to depart for 'the land of its ancestors'. In this sense I believe that the *iyomande* of Kotan in 1954 was really one of the very last genuine rituals to be held by the Ainu, and this was due of course to the presence of a number of extraordinary elders who soon afterwards died. The three *ekashi*, and a group of women nearby, who went on tirelessly singing and clapping their hands, quite evidently found deep consolation simply living through their ancestral rites, using their ancestral language, letting themselves become submerged by ancestral beliefs, metaphors, symbols, forgetting their present plight, the domineering presence of *shamo* people (the Japanese) on their beloved Ainu Moshiri (Ainuland). Even a foreigner from far away (or, perhaps, just because he came from another planet) felt suddenly part of an emotional and religious world he had looked upon, until then, with much sympathy, but inevitably from the outside.

Slowly, as happens in March, the weather changed. The morning had been splendid; after midday, gusts of strong wind came from the lake; then a grey and dreary mist covered the sky and it became very cold; from time to time some flakes of snow drifted through the air, covering the bear's fur with white spots.

The bear was offered a 'banquet' before its spiritual departure for his ancestors' land. Three or four lacquered bowls of rice were set in front of the snout of the carcass; soups with vegetables and fish were provided in other cups; someone came along with dried fish and dried seaweed. Sake and millet beer were offered again and again, sprinkling drops of the liquid on the bear's head with *iku-bashui*.

Finally the moment came for cutting the carcass to pieces, a long and laborious operation performed with great attention by Yanaka Torizō, with the assistance of other local men. This part of the ritual, which lasted for over an hour, made me think of certain remarks by John Batchelor in which one senses a certain Victorian aversion to the more animal aspects of the 'festival'. The main point is that a bear, when opened and sectioned, has a painfully human aspect; the paws, especially, look frighteningly like the hands and feet of a child.

The Ainu gave much importance to the operation, and followed detailed rules, of which Yanaka and the other two *ekashi* were perfectly aware. The bear was turned around on the snow, with its belly upward. A deep and

244

straight incision was made with a short and sharp knife, from the throat all the way to the crotch of the animal. Other incisions were made around the skin of the legs and arms of the beast, and the fur was torn away. The choice meat under the palms of the paws was very carefully scraped away and stored on a dish as a special delicacy. Then most of the fur (except that on the head) was ripped off. The abdomen was opened and all the internal organs were taken out one by one. Old Yanaka worked with the swift precision of an anatomical technician in a medical school; the liver was tied with cord to keep the bile from flowing out. Heart, lungs, liver, stomach, spleen, kidneys, and finally the intestines were put on different trays. The blood had been carefully collected in a couple of lacquered cups and was now drunk very solemnly by the three *ekashi*, a communion with the mysterious powers of the mountains and the forests, represented so impressively by the bear.

In some *iyomande* the bear's meat, cut into pieces, is tied bit by bit to a small tree deprived of all its leaves (*kamushke-ni*),[27] but this was not done at Kotan. All the meat, plus the skin with its fur, and the head of the beast, was put with order and care on a series of six lacquered trays (old Japanese objects, belonging for generations to the Yanaka family). The trays were then picked up by a group of six Ainu who solemnly walked in procession passing by the bear's cage, up to the chief's house. The trays were finally passed inside the home through the sacred eastern window (*rorun puyara*), and deposited at the head of the hearth. By this time it had grown dark and very cold.

During the evening of the main day in the *iyomande* ritual, all those who had taken part in the event gathered in Yanaka's house, to pay their respects to the 'little god', represented by the bear's head and skin neatly folded, displayed at the place of highest honour, on the eastern side of the hearth, under the sacred window. Many gifts were arranged around the trophy; the fundamental ones for a male bear (swords, bows, arrows, quivers), plus much food, rice, millet dumplings, dried fish, and cups full of millet beer. The atmosphere was totally relaxed, though one by one the men, in order of importance and age, performed a *kamui nomi* rite in front of the bear's head and fur, uttering traditional prayers of farewell. The day had been long; most elderly people, both men and women, were tired. There was some dancing and singing, but nothing very rowdy. A couple of hours after dark most guests were lying down wherever it seemed convenient, and were snoring.

The third day of the great *iyomande* ritual was particularly happy and relaxed. The breakfast was late, leisurely, and abundant; a mixed fare of Japanese and Ainu food, with lots of *misoshiro* soup, boiled rice, and dried

27 For pictures of this rather gruesome part of the *iyomande* see the photographic album referred to in note 1, above.

245

fish; some of the boldest men had already started drinking millet beer and even sake. The younger crowd gathered outside for various games. There was for instance the 'dance of the tray', in which a boy and a girl danced to the song of a crowd around them; one of the couple held in his hands a wooden tray, then as suddenly as possible he or she threw the tray to the other dancer: if the object was caught flying in the air, very good, the prospects of marriage during the course of the year were excellent; if the tray went flying in the snow, too bad, the hopes of future happiness were slim.

Another very popular game was a tug-of-war on that ideal field, the infinite expanse of ice and snow covering lake Kutcharo. A long rope was made by tying together the many fragments found around the village, and the boys took hold of one end, while the girls went for the other. The tug was repeated three or four times without a decisive victory on either side. Then finally the boys managed to make the girls skid on the ice, and in a few seconds they had won – though they were falling on the snow one after the other. Most popular with the children was a game in which old uncle Kikuchi came out on the snow and started throwing walnuts all around, of which he had a bagful: now and then he stopped, and the children counted how many nuts they had gathered; the one with most had won – and the event was followed by gales of laughter and the wildest screams. There was also some wrestling, not among boys, but among girls. Ainu girls showed a most extraordinary grit, only allowing their shoulders to be forced down on to the snow after terrific fights.

These and other games went on for the whole afternoon. Meanwhile the older women, inside Yanaka's home, were preparing the bear stew, of which everybody who had taken part in the ritual, plus a number of outside guests who had turned up at the last moment, would be allowed to have at least a mouthful on his or her rice. The bear's meat is considered not only a real delicacy, but is said to keep the younger ones healthy for the entire year, and to prolong the life of the elderly. There is also the deep, unexpressed feeling that eating the sacred bear is a form of communion with the gods, a way of appropriating in one's body and soul some of the mysterious forces hidden in the mountains and forests of Yezo. I think that when it comes to this point even the disillusioned Ainu of today are deeply moved; in 1954 much of the traditional world was still alive, and one could sense immediately how emotionally involved every one was with the preparation of the evening 'banquet'.

Meanwhile a small group of men, led by Yanaka who knew exactly the complicated procedure, were preparing the head of the bear for its insertion at the centre of the *nusa*, which would be its final destination. In the old days, as witnessed by Sugiyama Sueo both in the Ishikari district (not far

246

from Sapporo) and in the Hidaka district, the result was a work of great elaboration, but at Kotan it turned out to be simpler: the skull was cleaned of its flesh and then decorated with *inau-kike*, curly shavings of willow wands. At this stage the bear's head has a special name, *marapto-sapa* or *maratto-sapa*. When put on the special pole at the centre of the *nusa*, the *yuppaoma-ni*, the *ekashi* gathered in front of it and performed a long and very devout *kamui nomi* in its honour, singing again prayers and salutations.[28]

Finally, all of us, young and old alike, gathered in Yanaka's home for the final festive moments of the ritual. Prayers were said by the host to *Kamui Fuchi*, the hearth goddess, to *Chise-koro-kamui*, the protector of the house, and to the departing bear, then Japanese cups were filled with rice; selected guests received also a small dish of the bear stew, others had a spoonful poured on their rice. Soon cups and glasses of millet beer had their effect. Some of the younger ones got up and started dancing, singing, clapping their hands rhythmically. The house was on the whole rather large, but with such a crowd it was cramped. I sat near old Kikuchi *ekashi* who was beaming with delight: 'to think we wavered at the beginning! Things had been hard on us for too long. We had forgotten how to be happy!' A couple of hours later the confusion was total. Some of the older guests were sleeping and snoring in their corners, the younger ones were dancing and singing, the bear stew had long been finished, other dishes were offered to those who were still hungry.

I happened to go outside for a few moments. The weather had cleared; a sky full of fierce stars covered the frozen desert of lake Kutcharo. Suddenly I found one of the Ainu elders next to me. I looked at him; he had tears in his eyes. 'For an hour we can be happy again,' he muttered, rather vaguely because he had drunk too much millet beer. 'This is *Ainu moshiri* as we could only dream of it.'

EPILOGUE

Some seventeen years later, in 1971, I was in Tokyo and a group of film-makers working for Italian television asked me if it would be possible to organise an *iyomande* for them to film. I thought it might be possible, and we left for Hokkaidō. There we visited various locations; but unfortunately the *ekashi* of

28 The *yuppaoma-ni*, as witnessed by Kindaichi and Sugiyama during the thirties (see Fig. 4), was an extraordinarily elaborate construction, to which an *attush* (gown) had been added, giving the 'being' a prehistoric man-beast appearance. Our *yuppaoma-ni* was simpler; rather like No. 2 of Fig. 4. The two pendants beneath the bear's skull hold (left) the beast's eyes, and (right) its penis and testicles.

1954 that I had known so well had all 'joined their ancestors'. Finally we met with a good reception in the Saru valley of Hidaka, in the well-known Ainu centre of Nibutani. I will say straight away that the programme came off fairly well. The season (late February) was good, with much snow on the ground. I will not describe again the *iyomande* ritual, which more or less followed the traditional pattern. I would only like to recollect some important differences which I was forced to notice, when comparing this new edition of the ritual with the old one.

As soon as mention was made of the word *iyomande*, the response was clearly positive, with one great difference from 17 years earlier: we were told that they would be happy to organise the ritual, but they wanted to know how much we would pay for it. At Kotan the first reactions had been negative, but once the idea had been taken up, the enthusiasm for the ritual had become contagious, and everything worked on a purely idealistic line; people were paid, of course, but this was, so to speak, an afterthought, and never became a condition for moving on the organisation. I am not blaming the new group; things had radically changed since 1954: we all lived in a world where every step, every movement, was valued on a monetary scale. It was most noticeable, however, that interest in realising a vast, complex social and religious event, which had been so clear and touching in the case of Kotan, was entirely forgotten; an *iyomande* had become, like an engraved tray, or an embroidered *attush* kimono, an object for sale to tourists.

This purely mercantile vision of the event was reflected in many subsequent details. Only one *ekashi* knew anything about the complex procedures regulating the ritual, and even he mumbled the prayers with none of the assuredness and clarity which were so characteristic of Kikuchi or Yanaka *ekashi*. As for the younger people they were just performing a play: all true religious meaning had disappeared long ago; some puffed at their cigarette stumps while herding the bear around the pseudo-village, made entirely of huts built for tourists, in which nobody now lives, every sane Ainu preferring a warm Japanese house to the rickety shacks of the old days. Let me repeat that I am not criticising the Ainu of a new generation; I understand their position entirely; but I was forced to register in my heart these epochal changes. Kotan had been a deeply moving experience; this latter-day *iyomande* was a fine show but a cruel disappointment.

More years went by. As everybody knows, since 1968–70 the small, but very sensitive, Ainu world has undergone a new and important transformation. For some 20 years (let us say 1950–70) most young or middle-aged Ainu were uninterested in their store of ancient traditions. Most of them were busy participating, even if in a marginal way, in the extraordinary Japanese boom of those years. Many just stopped thinking about an Ainu identity; they were happy to merge into the mainstream Japanese current. Then a wind of change came upon Hokkaidō. Young Ainu people started taking an interest, which became progressively deeper and livelier, in their ethnic, religious, cultural identity. Unfortunately there had been a gap of a generation between the last *ekashi* and *fuchi* (old men and women) who knew the traditions, who had them in their souls and their blood, and their grandchildren. Rituals were taken up again, but for instruction one had to look for some rare survivors, or one had to read books in libraries. In other words, there was a certain danger of artificiality hovering over this renaissance.

The *iyomande* ritual has been no exception. It is now revived from time to time, but it is a 'third-generation' ritual. The first generation had been the old, spontaneous, and genuinely traditional ones, bringing a deeply religious experience to the people. Then the shows for tourists had come, devoid of all spirituality, mere ballets undertaken to earn money. More recently an *iyomande* has become a means by which the Ainu assert their ethnic identity; though one may wonder if the genuinely religious feeling has managed to survive, or if it has not been replaced by more worldly, even political, considerations. Certainly these latter-day *iyomande* have been distinguished by great richness, splendid display, most fussy attention to every detail. The guides, one suspects, have been old books and journals consulted in libraries, rather than living people's memories.

The elaborate *iyomande* performed at Nibutani in 1977 was certainly inspired by the descriptions and illustrations appearing in the book by Kindaichi and Sugiyama; at the end of the ritual the bear's head, crowned with *inau* wands and *kike* curly shavings, was fixed to the *yuppaoma-ni* forked pole, and draped with a *kaparimip* gown, giving the vaguely human mannequin a mysteriously terrifying aspect. The Chikabumi *iyomande* of 1985, also very gorgeous, ended on a simpler tone – at least judging by the published photographs.

These developments are certainly welcome; one likes to see the Ainu reasserting their culture, their identity. But how much of the genuine spirit of the ritual is still there? This is a question we shall have to leave to a new generation of observers and interpreters. Personally I feel immensely happy, and grateful to all the Ainu *kamui*, that I was able to witness that poor, simple, homely, unpretentious, imperfect *iyomande* on the shores of lake Kutcharo in 1954, so rich in human warmth and genuine religious feeling.

11

Mizuko kuyō: the re-production of the dead in contemporary Japan[1]

Elizabeth G. Harrison

INTRODUCTION

Despite claims to a long history, the phenomenon of *mizuko kuyō* 水子供養, the performance of memorial services (*kuyō*) for dead children (*mizuko*) in Japan, appears to have become a public phenomenon during the late 1960s or early 1970s.[2] Since that time, visitors to temples and shrines throughout the country have frequently encountered rows of identical carved or moulded figurines hung with cloth bibs and hats, decorated with flowers or pinwheels, and surrounded by all manner of toys and food set within easy reach. These figures are usually associated with the bodhisattva Jizō, the Buddhist deity who has come to be seen in Japan as the protector of dead children and to whom parents may address prayers for the care of a dead child. At many religious places (both sites established through association with a religious institution, such as shrines, temples, churches, and meeting houses, and non-institutionalised sites) one can request that a memorial service be performed for one's dead child and one can participate in the service, although direct participation is not required. All that is required is that one pay the appropriate fee, whether in person or by mail. It is mostly women who can be seen at mizuko kuyō services, many of them women in their sixties and seventies who lost children soon after World War II. Some people see this as a one-time duty, but many speak of this practice as a lifelong commitment.[3]

The focus of these activities is primarily children who were aborted or who miscarried, or those who died while still very young.[4] Until mizuko

---

1 This paper is based on fieldwork conducted in Japan from 1984–9 in collaboration with Professor Bardwell L. Smith of Carleton College, Northfield, Minnesota, USA.

2 The word *mizuko* (sometimes pronounced *mizugo*) is most commonly written with the characters for 'water' and 'child'. Written in a different way, 不見子, the word can also be construed as 'unseen child' or 'unseeing child'. *Kuyō* is the standard Buddhist word for what Americans would call a memorial service.

3 For a more detailed examination of the various elements of this practice in English, see Anne Page Brooks, '*Mizuko Kuyō* and Japanese Buddhism', *Japanese Journal of Religious Studies* 8, No. 3–4 (1981): 119–47.

4 Japanese consideration of an aborted 'child' as a 'child' does not hinge upon an argument concerning when or whether an embryo or foetus is human. Rather, and

250

kuyō, all of these had been 'left out of' the usual Japanese Buddhist funeral and memorial services for the dead.[5] Through the performance of a mizuko kuyō service, such children may be given a name or a form, brought to the attention of a deity, and provided with various sorts of 'nourishment' (one sense of the term *kuyō*), including offerings of money, food, flowers, prayers, incense, and the reading of religious texts, in the hope that they will not suffer greatly wherever they are, that they will soon be reborn into a good life, and that they will stop creating problems for their living families, if they are perceived as doing so. Through advertising and by word-of-mouth the public is encouraged to take part in these services regularly so as to ensure the well-being of the child. The media in Japan have dubbed this practice a 'boom', portraying it as a money-making venture by Buddhist clergy which preys upon the guilt of women who have lost a child. This approach has effectively blocked public consideration of mizuko kuyō as anything other than a meaningless fad and a scam.

Upon close examination, however, mizuko services appear to play a constructive role for the people who participate. The services address their immediate experience of daily life: the loneliness of post-war family life, of child-bearing and child loss, and of mothering.[6] It is tempting to view the practice as emerging naturally from the stream of Japanese religious tradition in response to the perceived personal and social problem of how to deal with the loss of a child. Such a view would stress the continuity of the practice of mizuko kuyō with other Japanese religious practices, both contemporary and historical, and would situate it within an ahistorical context of death and mourning and ritual. This is a metonymic approach in which each individual

much more simply, Japanese society allows anything that might have been a child to be called one.

5 It is often explained by both clergy and lay people that traditionally children who died at a very young age were not acknowledged in Buddhist funeral and memorial services in Japan. This may be because very young children were not considered to be individuals distinct from their mothers. As with most other religious practices in Japan, however, we find a great disparity in funeral practice: funerals were performed, and graves and memorial tablets created, for some children. In his 1963 survey of ancestors, Robert J. Smith found a large number of memorial tablets for children who died before the age of ten. See his *Ancestor worship in contemporary Japan* (Stanford: Stanford University Press, 1974), p. 179.

6 This paper will focus mainly on women and mizuko kuyō, because they represent the overwhelmingly larger portion of lay people who take part in the practice. But certainly no study of the phenomenon would be complete without a close look at the participation of fathers and their sense of relationship with what, for them, can only be an imaginary child. Imaginary is used here in a Lacanian psychoanalytic sense; I do not mean to belittle a father's feelings of 'fatherhood' toward such children in any way. I would also call a mother's relationship to her dead child an imaginary one.

251

experience of child loss is seen as always already representative of the universal human experience of death, and each ritual or organised practice as representing the role of religion in addressing human suffering. While this kind of view may be useful and even unavoidable, it is also problematic. When read metonymically, the experience of each individual becomes lost in the universal, and the significance of specific ritual constructions is easily lost when seen as part of the spectrum of religious responses to a common human problem. A metonymic approach ignores the historicity and singularity of individual response as well as the creative and transformative properties of language and ritual.

This paper is an attempt to rethink the singularity, or the discontinuity, of mizuko kuyō as a socio-religious phenomenon, to see it as it may allow contemporary Japanese to re-produce their dead, and thus their individual past, in a post-war Japan cut off from its national past. Gluck has spoken of the Japanese perception of the post-war era as completely separate from the pre-war era of the Shōwa period. She treats this perception as myth, since 'common sense attests to the contrary, knowing that, personally, socially, or nationally, history does not begin again ...'[7] But regardless of the physical continuity which we so often choose to construct in the trails of time, I think we must recognise that history does begin again cognitively whenever received elements are recombined into a new vision of the world.

In this paper I will suggest that the discontinuity in national consciousness felt by Japanese after defeat in the Second World War is echoed by the discontinuity in individual consciousness engendered by the loss of one's child. From this point of view, the public practice that is mizuko kuyō accomplishes a re-production of the dead in everyday life at both the national and the individual levels of experience. This is not simply a case of the production or creation of something new, for the spirit world played an active part in Japanese constructions of reality before the war as well, in the work of Hirata Atsutane 平田篤胤 in the nineteenth century and Yanagita Kunio 柳田国男 in the twentieth. And it is not a reproduction in the common sense of the word, a copy. It is a *re-production*: mizuko kuyō brings the dead to a new life in a new post-war world. In the course of this study, we shall recognise elements received from other times (which usually leads to comfortable narratives of continuity) as they are used to define this new vision, a re-vision based on the concerns of immediate everyday life and articulated in part through a re-configuration of received ritual elements. Many usually unhyphenated 're-' words are hyphenated here to emphasise the possibility of seeing this continuity and discontinuity simultaneously.

7 Carol Gluck, 'The idea of Shōwa: the idea in present perspective', *IHJ Bulletin* 9, No. 4 (1989): 9.

RE-PRODUCING JAPAN AFTER WORLD WAR II

Let us consider mizuko kuyō at the national level as an attempt to reclaim modern, post-war dead into the lives of contemporary Japanese, to re-produce the dead after the rupture that was World War II. Adult war-dead have been 'recognised' and 'remembered' through both private rituals in the home and at Buddhist temples, and in public rituals at shrines and temples such as Yasukuni Jinja 靖国神社 in Tokyo and the Reizan Kannon 霊山観音 in Kyōto; although they date from different times, both of these places were created specifically to remember the adult war-dead.[8] The promulgation of the Eugenics Protection Law in 1948 made abortion legal and gave public birth to a new class of war-dead: young children, whose birth would have threatened the lives of those already struggling to survive immediately after the war.[9] The model for remembering dead children through mizuko kuyō is ancestor worship, the collection of practices and religious rituals through which dead adults are retained as family members for as long as someone remembers their distinct personalities, and through which the connection of living members of a family to a continuous line of those-who-came-before is regularly reestablished. This ancestral narrative recognises and celebrates continuity; any break in that continuity, signalled by failure to continue the ancestral rites, is potentially dangerous to the individual, to the family, and ultimately to society.

If we are to grant the war the status of having created a rupture, however, maintaining continuity with what came before would seem to be impossible. Although it is common to understand post-war Japanese as striving to rebuild their nation and to reclaim their past, what has emerged after the war is 'invented traditions' in the Hobsbawmian sense, myriad attempts to re-cognise, to *create* continuity.[10] In the religious sphere, the newness of mizuko kuyō as a public and formalised practice contrasts vividly with attempts to portray

8 Yasukuni Jinja was constructed in Tokyo in 1869. See D. C. Holtom, *Modern Japan and Shinto nationalism* (Chicago: University of Chicago Press, 1947), p. 45ff. The Reizan Kannon, overseen by Kenninji 建仁寺 in Kyōto, was erected in 1955 to memorialise the Japanese troops who died in the two world wars.

9 The Eugenics Protection Law passed in 1948 made abortion legal when the family suffered from hereditary mental disorders or leprosy, when the pregnancy endangered the life of the mother, when the pregnancy or birth would severely harm the mother either physically or economically, and when the pregnancy resulted from rape or incest. See Uchida Masa 内田真砂 and Akamatsu Keiko 赤松彰子, *Onna: kokoro to karada* 女・心とからだ (Sōgensha, 1984), p. 59.

10 This is not meant to imply that traditions at other times in Japanese history were not also invented. See E. Hobsbawm and T. Ranger, eds., *The invention of tradition* (New York: Cambridge University Press, 1983).

it as having emerged from the body of religious tradition. The newness of recognising unborn dead children ritually, especially those who never saw this world and were never seen in it, becomes lost in recent attempts to redefine such children as ancestors, thereby locating them within the 'continuous tradition' of ancestor worship in Japan.

Yet if the war was a rupture, the central post-war question was how to (re)constitute Japanese experience, not how to continue what was done before. The US Occupation sought to realign Japanese political space, and one aspect of that programme was the separation of church and state which left the emperor a human head of state, symbolic of little more than the existence of a Japanese nation. With the emperor no longer divine, no longer a link between this world and some other which stretched back to the beginning of the land, living Japanese were set adrift conceptually in much the same way that mizuko were sometimes depicted several decades later: floating in a kind of midnight limbo, with nothing to support or ground them.[11] The only possible help for the living lay in daily life, for that was all that was left. Production became the goal, and today most of the world acknowledges what Japanese workers – the usual image is of male workers – have accomplished. Although women were also involved in creating Japan's so-called post-war economic miracle, most were concerned primarily with production of a different sort: of families and children needed to support the work force.[12] Indeed, the Eugenics Protection Law under which abortions are performed today was instituted in 1948 as a measure to hasten the re-production of a healthy and strong national polity.[13] But while men's production had gained the attention of the world by the 1970s, women's had not.

RE-CONSTRUCTING A TIE BETWEEN LIVING AND DEAD

One of the most striking aspects of mizuko kuyō is the reversal of concerns that its practice implies: participants assume that the cause of unforeseen difficulty in their daily lives lies not in something visible or correctable in this world, but in the heretofore unacknowledged, yet continuing, existence

11 This is the image often described in religious literature about mizuko kuyō and depicted in comic books. It can also been seen in an Ōe Kenzaburō story entitled 'Aghwee the sky monster' in the English translation. See H. Hibbett, *Contemporary Japanese literature* (New York: Charles E. Tuttle Co., 1984), pp. 412–34.

12 See, for example, the video documentary entitled 'The Yamaguchi story: Buddhism and the family in contemporary Japan' (J&M Information Systems) for a first-hand narration of the post-war roles of both men and women and the frustrations which accompanied each.

13 Uchida and Akamatsu state that the law was last revised in 1952: *Onna: kokoro to karada*, p. 59.

of one or more mizuko related to them. That is, the practice of mizuko kuyō re-constructs a direct tie between the daily affairs of the living and a continued existence, after their death, of spirits of the dead. While in theory dead spirits of any age should be 'available' to such a relationship, in practice it is dead children who are the focus of attention in Japan today. Thus, women who perceive their lives to have changed suddenly due to illness (of their own or a family member), bad fortune in the family business, or unexpected and unmanageable changes in their living children or their marriage are likely to associate that change first with an unborn child who has not been treated properly, who may have remained unheard and unattended for days, or even for decades in the case of abortions which took place soon after the war. The solution to such problems is seen to be the nurturing of the unseen child or children through the performance of mizuko kuyō.

Hashimoto Tetsuma 橋本徹馬 was among the first to expound publicly the need for this practice by building a temple, completed in 1971, dedicated exclusively to mizuko kuyō.[14] He states that over 60 per cent of the people coming to him for free consultations about family problems had had an abortion experience within the family. It was this realisation, he says, that made him aware of all the unacknowledged dead children produced by the Eugenics Protection Law, and he began to think about the existence of these spirits and their effect on the living members of their families. He came to see many of the major social problems in Japan after the war, including defiance and neurosis among children and adolescents, delinquency and adolescent violence, terrorism, the formation of gangs (*bōsōzoku* 暴走族) and arson, as caused by the children of parents who had aborted a child. Such problems could only be cured on both a personal and a national level, according to Hashimoto, by recognising the existence of one's mizuko and caring for it through kuyō.[15]

At first glance, Hashimoto's personal history as a politician makes this a rather startling, and indeed suspicious, construction. Born to an extremely poor family in Tōhoku in the late Meiji period, he followed a boyhood dream of becoming a politician in order to change society so that no one would ever have to live in such poverty again. He left elected political life when he became disillusioned with the amount of time necessary for campaigning and established himself instead as a self-styled political commentator and consultant

14 'Shinshū no tachiba kara mita "mizuko" mondai' 真宗の立場から見た「みずこ問題」, in Dendōin Tokutei Kadai Kenkyūkai 伝道院特定課題研究会, ed., *Nyonin ōjō* 女人往生 (Kyoto: Honganji Shuppanbu, 1988), p. 74.
15 Hashimoto Tetsuma, *Mizuko Jizōji reigenshū* 水子地蔵寺霊験集 (Shiunsō, 1978), chapter 22 on the founding of the temple. Also in a personal interview at Shiunzan Jizōji, 3 December 1986.

for the poor, whom he saw as having been abandoned by society. His 'discovery' of the influence of mizuko on people's lives led him to examine religion as another way to change the world (along with politics), and after extended consultation with the most successful of his political cronies, then prime minister Satō Eisaku 佐藤栄作, Hashimoto founded his independent temple, Shiunzan Jizōji 紫雲山地蔵寺, in rural Chichibu, to the west of Tokyo.

Hashimoto's temple is commonly used by the Japanese media as an example of mizuko kuyō as big business: the thousands of stone statues of Jizō which line the slopes of the hills surrounding Jizōji (13,600 in the summer of 1992) are perhaps too easily seen merely as sources of income. He is soundly criticised by the established Buddhist sects for imitating with intent to deceive and by Japanese feminists as extorting money from women.[16] In his rather simplistic use of the familiar Buddhist images of Jizō and the six realms of existence (rokudō 六道), his vision may be seen to lack a compelling cosmology. But, on the other hand, Hashimoto's intent was to clarify and speak to one particular, overarching aspect of people's lives in contemporary Japanese society: the relationship he saw between problems in daily life and the existence *somewhere else* of unacknowledged (dead) children.

This location of the cause of discomfort in another realm, a place distinctly outside the visible and the everyday, yet connected directly to it, provides a basis for a new grounding for society. In a post-war Japan cut off from its past, the acknowledgement of a 'living' spirit world populated by mizuko (over 30 million, according to Hashimoto's estimate in a 1978 publication) reweaves the temporal thickness of daily experience, of past and future intertwined with today. In Hashimoto's scheme the dead continue living as spirits without bodies, and the connection between child and parent that is re-cognised in mizuko kuyō is both natural and continuous. The problems afflicting the lives of those who have had abortions are the cry of the unseen child for the attention of its parents. If the child is nourished through the performance of kuyō, it will no longer need to speak out, seemingly unsolvable problems will disappear, and daily life will be predictable.

This continuity is not an attempt to re-tie the present to the pre-war past, to pick up once again the strands that had fallen loose during the war. Rather, it is a re-cognition of the myriad personal productions and losses since the war. Mizuko kuyō invites each individual to speak her (or his) experience through the performance of ritual, that is, in a public mode, and, through

---

16 In all major ways, including priestly garb and elements of ritual, Jizōji looks and feels like a Japanese Buddhist temple. But Hashimoto's critics stress that he has no Buddhist training and that the 'temple' is registered with the government as an independent religious organisation and is not affiliated with any recognised Buddhist group.

such performance, to listen to and answer the speech of her child. What is continuous is the re-enactment of the parent–child relationship which is the basis of immediate daily life. Hashimoto suggests reading the 'Heart Sūtra' and his *Chichibu reichi Jizō wasan* 秩父霊地地蔵和讃, copying the 'Heart Sutra', and offering ¥100 to each mizuko every day, all to aid the spirit in transition to buddhahood.[17]

Archbishop Miura Dōmyō 三浦道明 of Enman-in 円満院, an independent Buddhist temple in the city of Ōtsu that was formerly affiliated with the Tendai sect, is often cited as the first person to advertise mizuko kuyō nationwide in the early 1970s. Trained as a Tendai Buddhist priest, Miura's formulation of the relationship between parents and mizuko is centred in the cosmology of karma. Through his counselling activities, Miura found that 98 per cent of the people who came to him with problems and 'seemed as though they shouldn't have any' had an unacknowledged mizuko in the family.[18] But unlike Hashimoto, who emphasised in an interview in December 1986 that the well-being of the dead child was his paramount interest, Miura speaks to the lives of the parents. It is the parents, he says, who are responsible for bringing into existence their mizuko through an evil act which, by the laws of karma, can only lead to an evil result.[19] That evil result, the malevolent influence (*tatari* 祟) of mizuko on the lives of the living, may immediately affect the mizuko's family (it is most often visited upon living siblings, but sometimes on parents) or be delayed until future generations.[20] To correct the problem, parents must perform kuyō for their dead child or children; when this is done, mizuko will become guardians of the family, the parents will have worked off their bad karma, and their lives will return to normal, which Miura defines as a state of good health and good fortune.[21] Although on the one hand Miura has constructed a relationship which appears to manipulate parents into performing mizuko kuyō for the sake of their own material and psychological comfort, on the other he has effectively re-woven the dead – and especially the unacknowledged dead, young children – into the daily lives of their parents.

Many individuals and groups involved in the performance of mizuko kuyō find it necessary to give mizuko a 'real' existence in this world in some way; lack of visible form is seen as one reason for the earlier lack of attention

17 *Ibid.*, p. 199.
18 Miura Dōmyō, *Senzo kuyō o shinasai* 先祖供養をしなさい (Nisshin Hōdō, 1983), p. 92.
19 Here Miura is speaking specifically about the case of abortion. *Ibid.*, pp. 87–9. However, in Japan it is common to consider even the unintentional loss of a child as the responsibility of the mother.
20 *Ibid.*, pp. 96–8.
21 *Ibid.*, pp. 90–1, 94–6.

to mizuko. Miura has parents give their mizuko a *kaimyō* 戒名, the type of Buddhist name commonly given an adult after death to identify the spirit as a follower of the Buddha, and erect an ihai 位牌, a memorial tablet, to provide the spirit a place to dwell.[22] Hashimoto asks parents to place a small statue of Jizō on the family altar in the home and to erect a larger, stone Jizō in the precincts of his temple as a gravestone. Nikō-sama 尼公様, foundress and leader of the forty-year-old new religion known as Kihōkyō Sōshin'en 鬼法 教総神苑, gives each mizuko a body in the form of a small plaster figure of a temple acolyte, holds a funeral and cremation for large numbers of these bodies at once, then inters the ashes in a large crypt in the mountains north of Kyōto. She also plants a young cedar tree for every mizuko.[23] With a name, a mizuko becomes a real person, with a visible form or place to be, a real existence, and through this action the invisible (the unnamed and unplaced) become a part of the daily world.

In this way, the re-cognition of mizuko introduces a new multivocality into the texture of post-war Japanese experience. Almost any event related to the family can now be heard to contain the voice of a mizuko in addition to the voices of the living, and any consideration of the future of a family will count among its members even those who are unseen. If this were simply a renewed concern for the family dead, one would expect that 'regular' ancestral rites also would have experienced a 'boom' in recent years, but this does not appear to be the case. Indeed, while mizuko kuyō serves to bring dead children back into the everyday life of their families, ancestors as they were formally acknowledged during the pre-war period are more and more often being sent out of the family, to take up residence in large, library-style repositories where they are cared for by a permanent staff of clergy. Thus, despite the title of this paper, it is not the dead in general who are being re-produced through the performance of mizuko kuyō. It is rather dead children, whose umbilical tie to their mothers has become the tie between this world and the other.

The newly re-cognised voices of mizuko are answered by their mothers or their parents through performance of a mizuko kuyō ritual. While not all those who have had an abortion or lost a very young child since the war choose to participate, many women, and, increasingly, many families, take part in regularly scheduled services at religious centres around the country. Some go to such services once; some go repeatedly; some say they will

22 *Ibid.*, pp. 92–3.
23 Personal interview at Kihōkyō Sōshin'en main temple, 1 December 1986, in Kyōto. Jizō is the most common form I have seen given to mizuko, however, perhaps because the shaven head and simple priest's robe of his traditional iconography make him easily identifiable with the child itself.

continue to do kuyō for their child or children as long as they themselves are alive. Some request a private service from a member of the clergy. Others never attend themselves but send money for a service in response to a newspaper advertisement or poster. And very often, clergy are approached, by mail, telephone, or in person, for counselling regarding problems in daily life which are now associated with the existence of a mizuko.

The performance of mizuko kuyō by clergy and the participation of parents in it serves as a public acknowledgement of women's invisible contribution to the national drive toward production. This, I think, is one reason for the popularity of the practice: women's lives in post-war Japan are finally being noticed. Yet this is not a laudatory acknowledgement. At the same time that it recognises women's production of children, mizuko kuyō also publicly acknowledges women's failure to care for their children properly, both because the children were not given a chance to live in the first place and because the mothers never did anything for the children after their death. Women's production of unseen children is recognised in mizuko kuyō because, although they have been successful at producing, they have failed at carrying through, at mothering. We can see the mothers' sense of this in the inscriptions on *ema* 絵馬, votive plaques, which address mizuko with apologies (I'm sorry, I wouldn't have been able to take care of you) and pleas (Please be reborn to me when I'm ready, and I'll take good care of you).

Yet rather than simply bowing to the implied criticism inherent in the public image of mizuko kuyō, Japanese women who participate in the practice do so for their own reasons. In the remainder of this paper, I will explore the role of mizuko kuyō in the lives of women in contemporary Japan through three issues: the concern for mothering a dead child wherever it may be after death; the role of the practice in allowing the mother to re-conceive herself as the mother of the child-who-never-was; and the mothering of dead children as one way to mother better those who are living. We shall see that the practice speaks directly to the primary identification in Japan of women as mothers, providing them a constructive way to mother *all* their children in a society in which to be a woman is to be a mother.

THE RELATIONAL EXISTENCE OF MIZUKO

When one begins to inquire into the meaning of the figurines lined up at temples and other religious sites to commemorate dead children, a kaleidoscope of images emerges. The figures represent dead children; the same figures may be said to be the bodhisattva Jizō or any of several other special personalities who have come to be associated with mizuko kuyō.[24] Some figures are not human in form, but are representations of a womb containing a child or Jizō. At some sites other objects are used instead of such human images, objects which are often commonly associated with ancestral rites in Japan (*ihai*, lacquered memorial tablets; *mizu toba* 水塔婆, thin, wooden funeral tablets). Offerings made to any of these images appear to be dual-purpose. They are made to the deity and to the child as they are both represented by the figure, suggesting that no matter what the figurine *looks like*, it serves as a nexus for the identification of a spirit who is construed as needing help and pacification with a caring deity. The image, whether large or small, expensive or cheap, provides a place for both the child and its protector, to whom the mother or both parents pray.

The spirit of the child is often spoken of as being somewhere else as well. It may be on some variously described spiritual plane, suffering in the shadow of other, more fortunate (more cared-for) spirits as described, for example, by the founder of Kihōkyō Sōshin'en. It may also be 'playing' dejectedly along the banks of the Sai-no-kawara 賽の河原, the river boundary of the Buddhist hells, harrassed by demons until protected by Jizō, as can be seen in many representations of mizuko in pictorial form. The spirit is at the same time here in this world, for it is often the visitation (either benevolent or malevolent) of such a spirit to its living family that convinces families that they need to take care of the child even though it may be dead and unseen. The spirit may also be present at formal religious services when they are performed for it. And some spirits will have moved on to another rebirth, even as their families continue to speak to them as babies through mizuko kuyō services.

There might at first sight seem to be no logic to this array of mizuko existences, except perhaps to call such spirits either extremely versatile or wildly schizophrenic. And yet there is an exceedingly simple logic at work here: the existence of a mizuko is defined in relation to its living family. While this is, perhaps, obvious, it is important. A mizuko does not exist in and of itself, but only 'in relation to'. Just as the child could not have been conceived without mother and father, so, too, the mizuko does not exist without a living family. If it had its own existence as an unanchored, wandering spirit, it should have been served by the rituals, offerings, and stupas provided for *muenbotoke* 無縁仏, those dangerous yet pitiful spirits who are acknowledged by the Japanese Buddhist community at large because they have no living descendents to take care of them. But although some *muenbotoke*

---

24 I have also heard figures identified as the bodhisattva Kannon or as Myōtoku-sama 妙徳さま, the mother of the eighth-century monk Saichō 最澄 and the laywoman who is reputed by one temple to have begun the practice during the Heian period.

stupas might be construed, from the offerings found there, to include mizuko, they seem to do so only insofar as some relative of a mizuko has chosen to identify the spirit with that place.[25]

The existence of a mizuko is thus a social existence, defined in relation to its family. Yet despite the usual location of figurines in a crowd of similar figures, suggesting interesting possibilities for sharing and mutual support among the families of these children, if not among the mizuko themselves, and despite the group character of many of the kuyō services, the experience of mizuko kuyō remains a personal, private one; one person's mizuko is literally nothing to someone else. And although it takes only one living descendant of any genealogical relationship to the child to give rise to the need for mizuko kuyō, the focus of the existence of the child will always be the mother as the 'place' in which its existence came to be and the person with the deepest responsibility for that existence; the father shares the responsibility for the conception of the child, but after conception and before birth his relationship to it can only be mediated by the mother.[26] It is, after all, something which occurred to the body of the mother that has resulted in the birth of a mizuko rather than a living child who will grow into adulthood in this world. When the mother is dead or unresponsive to the call of her dead child, a descendant can take her place as the mother, that is, as the person in this world who will mother the child. Participation in mizuko kuyō acts as an acknowledgement that there *was* (by virtue of its conception), *would have been* (in that a child conceived is the seed of a child born), and still *is* a child, even though that child is not now present in the mundane sense of the word.

BECOMING THE MOTHER OF THE CHILD-WHO-NEVER-WAS

It is not only the child's existence that is re-constructed through the performance of mizuko kuyō, however. In acknowledging the existence of the child, the woman reconceives herself as the mother of that absent child. Mizuko kuyō allows her to re-cognise an absent part of herself, the part of her that would have been the mother of this particular child; with the death of the child, the mother-of-that-child, too, ceased to be. I think the logic of this is clear in the

25 By contrast, in Taiwan, where the practice of mizuko kuyō has appeared recently based on the Japanese example, mizuko are thought to have their own independent existence and can be marshalled into evil armies at the beck and call of their spiritualist 'trainers'.

26 One could perhaps argue that in Japan, the father's relationship to his children often continues to be mediated by the mother even after they are born and grow older.

case of the death of a wanted child (miscarriage, stillbirth, neonatal death or death of an older child), where the mother will already have seen herself as the mother of the child. But I think the same logic holds true for the case of the abortion of an unwanted child. In order to make the choice to have an abortion, a woman must have known she was pregnant, which means she knew she was about to become a mother in the ordinary course of events. Yet even if she makes the choice not to be that mother, and even if her life goes on in the way she wants it to afterwards, that child and its mother, although absent, will always be a part of her life: her life *is as it is* in part because the child *is not* there and because she *is not* its mother.

Thus, we can see the existence of the woman-who-would-have-been-a-mother as always related to the child-that-never-was. By giving that child a concrete existence through mizuko kuyō, the woman becomes, once again and this time more or less publicly, its mother. In Japanese society, where a woman's value is defined by her ability to mother (that is, to produce and take care of children), this can be seen as a terribly important opportunity for women who did produce (conceive) children but were unable to care for them.[27] Mizuko kuyō gives such women a way to mother their 'unseen children'.

This task is easily accomplished in the hybrid Buddhist culture of Japan, which allows for both the continued existence of sentient beings after death and a continued, active relationship between the living and the dead. By performing mizuko kuyō or having it performed, the mother can be a mother to her child no matter where it is. The most direct articulation of this that I have encountered is the *ryūzanji* 流産児 *kuyō* service held by Seichō no Ie 成長の家, one of the so-called new religions in Japan that was founded early this century.[28] In the monthly service that was begun at the Kyōto headquarters in 1987, participants dressed in short white jackets fill out two identical paper amulets (*kami ofuda* 紙お札) with their name and age and the name and age of their mizuko. Where the child did not have a name, the mother gives it one; if the loss of the child occurred before it was possible to know its gender, she chooses a name according to the gender she thinks the child was. One of these amulets is offered at the altar, presumably as a way of bringing the mizuko to the attention of the central deity, Kannon. The other is held by the women until, at a certain point during the service, the curtains

27 Helen Hardacre made the point that to be a woman in Japan is to be a mother in a paper she delivered at the 'Rethinking Japanese Religion' Workshop at Cambridge University, 3–7 April 1991.

28 Literally, kuyō for a miscarried child or a child who has flowed away. This is one of a number of variant names for what is referred to throughout this paper simply as mizuko kuyō. Some religious establishments have felt the need to create their own name for the practice because of the negative press surrounding it.

are drawn and the lights put out in the room. Each woman is then asked to open her clothing, place the amulet directly next to her chest, and restore her clothing to its normal order. The women are instructed to carry the amulet in this way for a month, *as if it were the child*, treating it in the same way they would any other child of that age in their family. They are to speak to it, hold it, and feed it (although the latter would be done in the form of offerings of food placed in front of it rather than real feeding). They can also take it into the bath with them as they would any young child, if they wrap it in plastic first. Later in the same service, the women are helped to prepare trays containing plastic children's dishes filled with sweet crackers and, in a cup, sugar-water. Each mother carefully prepares her own child's tray, then solemnly offers it at the main altar by following the ritualised actions of the women before her and finally placing it in one of the rows of racks for that purpose.

A large part of the Seichō no Ie *ryūzanji kuyō*, like mizuko services at other places, consists of the chanting of religious texts by the clergy leading the service as well as, at certain times, chanting by the participants. Incense, money, and the first paper amulet are also given as offerings in the hope that each child will receive what it needs to nourish or support it wherever it is. In this way the child, conceived as being somewhere else and in need of care, is 'mothered' through the use of a substitute which brings the child, in the form of the paper amulet, into its mother's arms. The women at the service are told to live with their 'amulet-child' for one month, then to bring it back to the meeting place for the following month's kuyō service. If, at that time, they feel that everything is settled and all is well, they can offer the second amulet at the altar and continue to participate in the more usual portions of the service as regularly as they like. If, however, they feel that something remains unsettled with regard to the child, they can continue to live with the 'amulet-child' for another month, or for as long as it takes to feel at peace, after which the amulet will be given up at the altar.

It is never explained just what might remain unsettled or what the nature of the comfortable or peaceful state each mother is supposed to reach might be. The implication, from the context, is that both child and mother need the time together to establish beyond any doubt that each is still there for the other. In being given her child, the mother once again becomes its mother and is able to actually play out that role with the amulet. It would seem that she no longer needs the substitute after she has come to recognise that the child will always be (and has always been) a presence in her life even in its physical absence. The mother's participation in Seicho no Ie's version of mizuko kuyō rituals from that time on becomes a way for her to continue mothering her child.

I would suggest that the creation of a mother and a child in close relationship to each other which is accomplished through this graphic playing out of roles can be seen as the paradigm for all observances of mizuko kuyō.[29] An unseen child, a child-who-never-was is acknowledged *to be*, by giving it a name or a form. And by virtue of that child's 'existence', the woman-who-never-was-its-mother *is*. With its existence established, the child can then be addressed in much the same way in which Japanese people address any 'unseen presence' such as ancestors or *kami*, through rituals which are already well articulated within the various religious institutions. Indeed, in overall form there is little difference between most mizuko kuyō services and a service for ancestors (*senzo kuyō*) in its current Japanese Buddhist manifestation. The service allows the woman to carry out her role as a mother as it has been defined in Japanese society. Many women say that they have never forgotten the child that they conceived and have always wanted to have some way to take care of it. Mizuko kuyō speaks to that desire.

TO MOTHER ALL ONE'S CHILDREN

Yet it is not only dead children who are served by the practice. Many women see mizuko kuyō as a way to mother their *entire* family better. A mizuko may be welcomed into the living family like a long-lost relative, and living children may accompany their parents to a religious site to take part in mizuko kuyō for their dead sibling(s). By acknowledging the existence of and caring for her mizuko, a mother and her living family can, in one common explanation, avoid malevolent intrusions of the child into the family's life. In another view, proper attention to one's dead child or children will encourage them to take on the role of protective deity (*mamori-gami* 守り神) for living members of the family, helping to ensure their continued well-being and success in this world. A more Buddhist formulation of this makes use of the concept of transfer of merit (*ekō* 回向), suggesting that the merit earned on behalf of the dead child will not only help its situation wherever it may be,

29 There are, of course, exceptions to this. For example, the Jōdo Shinshū sects do not officially perform mizuko kuyō, as it would be an acknowledgement that Amida does not already watch over all mizuko. However, Shinshū priests with whom I have spoken admit that when they are approached by a distressed parishioner asking for a service for his or her mizuko, they will usually perform one. This kind of response by Shinshū clergy is suggested in sectarian publications such as *Nyonin ōjō* and Kitazuka Mitsunori 北塚光昇, *Shinshū to mizuko kuyo* 真宗と水子供養 (Kyōto: Nagata Bunshōdō, 1988). The thrust of the service, from the priest's point of view, is to convince the parent that she need only believe in Amida. That is not necessarily what she sees happening, however.

but will also be reflected back to improve the lives of living family members. In this sense, the performance of mizuko kuyō provides women with a way to mother all their children better.

This paper has been an attempt to look at the religious practice known as mizuko kuyō as a social and a personal phenomenon specific to post-war Japan rather than as a practice emerging from a continuous Japanese religious tradition. Certainly many of the elements of mizuko kuyō will look familiar to the student of Japanese religion: the concepts of *kuyō* and *tatari*, the sites and ritual implements and movements, images such as Jizō and Kannon. But these elements have been recombined to address newly perceived problems, and in their combination a new view of the world is spoken. For example, Jizō is no longer simply an all-purpose protector of children and travellers, one who wanders freely elsewhere, through the six realms, helping those who are deserving. Now he is also the intermediary who brings together the worlds of parents and mizuko, the worlds of the living and the dead. His shaven head, peaceful, childish countenance, and simple robe encourage family members to treat him as the child he is to watch over, and in a curious way he becomes that child. This identification is so strong and 'natural' that scholars and those associated with the performance of mizuko kuyō are now beginning to look for Jizō's relationship with unborn children at other times in Japanese history. We are beginning, in effect, to rewrite Jizō's place in the past so that it will conform with his role today.

Ancestor worship is another element in the traditional picture of Japanese religion which is being reworked in relation to the 'discovery' of mizuko. A general understanding of the ancestors in Japan has, until recently, excluded babies and miscarried and aborted foetuses from funerals and memorial services; very young children were not defined as full-fledged members of society and hence could not be ancestors. But now, as a part of mizuko kuyo, graves and memorial tablets are being prepared for such young children. Precedents for these moves are being 'found' in earlier times. For example, carved wooden *kokeshi* 小芥子 dolls, formerly described as a traditional folk-craft of northern Japan, have acquired a new history: they are now seen by some as attempts to give a 'real' existence in the family to children who had been the victims of infanticide (*mabiki* 間引) during the seventeenth and eighteenth centuries.[30] And historical religious texts and rituals are being re-read to see how they 'have always spoken to' mizuko kuyō.[31]

This is one sense, I think, in which history has begun again in post-war Japan. Women's lives and their personal relationship with their children have become a part of public religious practice, and thereby of national life. Their concern for mothering even their dead children is now a focus of public and private attention to the extent that mizuko kuyō is performed across Japan and discussed widely in the media; the 'boom' effect of the spread of the practice has served to heighten awareness of that relationship. Full consideration of the phenomenon of mizuko kuyō will need to include consideration of the ways in which it draws upon historical elements of Japanese religious life as well as serious examination of the manipulative aspects of the practice as it has been developed within structured religious settings. But at the same time that we consider those issues, I believe that we must not lose sight of its constructive aspects, of the ways in which it accomplishes a new view of women and children in contemporary society through the re-production of the dead.

30 The identification of *kokeshi* dolls with mizuko is suggested not only by their shape and their origin as a household craft, but also by a possible alternative writing for the word kokeshi which means 'do away with a child': see, for example, the mizuko kuyō registration form entitled '"Kokeshi Jizō" mizuko kuyō shuisho' 「こけし地蔵」水子供養趣意書 distributed by Tandenji 単伝寺, Yawata City, Kyōto Prefecture. Mabiki was the Japanese practice during the Tokugawa period of 'weeding out' unwanted children by killing babies immediately after birth. Scholars are in disagreement as to whether the practice was common or limited to certain places and certain times of extreme economic hardship: see Chiba Tokuji 千葉徳爾 and Ōtsu Tadao 大津忠男, *Mabiki to mizuko kuyō* 間引と水子供養 (Nōsan Gyōson Bunka Kyōkai, 1983).

31 An example of this is *segaki* 施餓鬼 *kuyō*, memorial services for the dead who have no living relatives, which are traditionally performed as part of the yearly Obon services in Japan. *Segaki kuyō* or *segaki-e* are now defined by one Nichiren Buddhist priest as the historical manifestation of mizuko kuyō: personal interview, Kyōōji 経王寺, Miyazu, Kyōto Prefecture.

12

Pilgrimage as cult:
the Shikoku pilgrimage as a
window on Japanese religion

Ian Reader

INTRODUCTION

Pilgrimage is one of the most universal of all religious phenomena, and there are few religions or cultures in which it is not found in some form or other. As such pilgrimage has rightly been analysed and discussed in universal terms by those interested in the comparative study of religion and of ritual processes, and numerous attempts have been made to formulate overarching theories that encompass the multiple manifestations of pilgrimage across the globe and to draw out points of similarity between different religious cultures through an understanding of the pilgrimages they have given birth to. Because the study of pilgrimage has been pursued by academics from a variety of disciplines, in particular theology, history, religious studies, social geography and social anthropology, perhaps more dispute than consensus has arisen over the possible universal modes of interpretation that can be applied to this subject.[1]

I would like to thank the Leverhulme Trust and also the Japan Foundation Endowment Committee (Grant No. 597) for their financial assistance which enabled me to carry out some of the fieldwork on which this essay is based in Japan from September 1990 to March 1991.

1 A. Morinis, *Pilgrimage in the Hindu tradition: a case study of West Bengal* (New Delhi: Oxford University Press, 1984), pp. 233–75, provides a detailed discussion of these issues. Besides the differing theories and interpretations that are held by different scholars, there have in recent years been implicit, and at times overt, conflicts between those in different academic disciplines, who are naturally interested in different elements within pilgrimage culture. If one can be permitted to simplify this issue, historians have been more concerned with understanding the processes of development and change at pilgrimage sites; theologians with the ways that pilgrimages relate to questions of belief and to interpretations of deities; and anthropologists with analysis of the social processes expressed in pilgrimage. In particular the anthropologists, who consider that they alone are attempting to analyse, interpret and formulate theories about pilgrimage, have been critical of the other disciplines for what they see as a failure to seek analytical perspectives: of course, this attitude has not always endeared

What is of greater concern to me here, however, is that, besides their potentially universal dimensions, pilgrimages also act as important reflections of the cultures from which they emerge. Thus Jonathan Sumption, in his discussion of pilgrimage in medieval Europe, has suggested that through the study of pilgrimage one could gain insights into the nature of medieval religion, for it 'affords a unique reflection of medieval religion at every stage of its complicated development'.[2] Morinis has reiterated this point in his discussion of West Bengali Hindu pilgrimages, commenting that 'the unique character of a place of pilgrimage emerges as the creation of the local forces of religion, history, economics, politics and geography'.[3]

It is from this perspective that this chapter is framed. Since I have discussed the universal and potentially universalising aspects of pilgrimage at length elsewhere, it is not my intention here to go further into comparative discussions of pilgrimage.[4] Rather, I shall be concerned to draw out some of the main religious themes that are expressed in Japanese pilgrimages and to suggest what Japanese pilgrimage can tell us about Japanese religion. In so doing I shall be seeking to use the medium of pilgrimage – and in particular the Shikoku pilgrimage, which is perhaps the best-known and certainly one of the most widely performed of all Japanese pilgrimages – as a window and lens through which to view Japanese religion. Although it would, in the context of one paper, be impossible to illustrate and discuss all the themes of pilgrimage and Japanese religion fully, I will examine a number of interrelated themes that are central to, and prominent in, both. These themes are, broadly speaking, the individual drive towards transcendent salvation coupled with the seeking of this-worldly benefits (*genze riyaku* 現世利益), two issues that often go hand-in-hand; the concept, nature, incidence and interpretation of miracles; and the role of charismatic and inspirational holy figures who serve as mediating agents between ordinary people and the spiritual world. Underlying these themes are the importance of personal verification and

anthropologists to those in other disciplines! For some views on these issues, see my comments in I. Reader, 'Introduction', in I. Reader and Tony Walter, eds., *Pilgrimage in popular culture* (Basingstoke: Macmillan, 1993), esp. pp. 10–15, where I also give a general synopsis of contemporary debates about the analysis of pilgrimage; G. Bowman, 'Pilgrimage conference report', *Anthropology Today* 4/6 (1988): 20–23, and J. Eade and M. Sallnow, *Contesting the sacred: the anthropology of Christian pilgrimage* (London: Routledge, 1991), pp. 1–29, provide further angles on these questions from an anthropological perspective.
2 Jonathan Sumption, *Pilgrimage: an image of medieval religion* (London: Faber and Faber, 1975), p. 307.
3 Morinis, *Pilgrimage in the Hindu tradition*, p. 236.
4 See I. Reader, 'Introduction' and 'Conclusion', in I. Reader and Tony Walter, eds., *Pilgrimage in popular culture.*

interpretation of religious issues and experiences, and the preference of Japanese people for proximate and tangibly verifiable figures of veneration who are close to, or part of, the human world, over and above more distant spiritual entities.

JAPANESE PILGRIMAGE CULTURE:
SHIKOKU, SPIRITUAL SALVATION AND WORLDLY BENEFITS

Japan has long had a rich and varied pilgrimage culture whose roots are closely intertwined not only with aspects of popular devotion, piety and religious mobility, but also with more secular issues such as social change and the development of economic infrastructures and transport communications.[5] The wide variety of Japanese words such as *mōde* 詣で, *sankei* 参詣, *mairi* 参り, *meguri* 巡り, *sanpai* 参拝, *junpai* 順拝, *junrei* 巡礼 and *henro* 遍路 that may be used in varying contexts to describe the phenomenon of pilgrimage and visits to religious sites, may in itself be taken as evidence of a strong and diverse pilgrimage culture in Japan.[6] The varieties, forms and levels that such travel and visits may take further indicate a rich tradition of religious travel ranging from circuits of a number of temples such as the Shikoku *henro* or pilgrimage encompassing 88 sites, and the Saikoku 西国 *junrei* or pilgrimage to 33 sites dedicated to the Bodhisattva Kannon, to the vast numbers of smaller routes that copy their basic format; according to recent calculations and compilations of such routes, there are over 300 small-scale and localised versions of the Saikoku, and over 120 versions of the Shikoku, pilgrimage in Japan.[7] Besides these there are numerous other pilgrimages that incorporate a number of temples (and shrines) enshrining one deity in a wider group such as the *shichifukujin* 七福神 *meguri*, the

5 Although the economic and social aspects of pilgrimage are intrinsic and important themes in the study of Japanese pilgrimage, space does not permit discussion of these here. For fuller discussion of these issues, one can do no better than to look at Shinjō Tsunezō 新城常三, *Shaji sankei no shakai keizaishiteki kenkyū* 社寺参詣の社会経済史的研究 (Hanawa shobō, 1982), which is an expanded version of Shinjō's original edition of 1964. This comprehensive account of the social, economic and historical dimensions of religious travel in pre-modern Japan has formed the source for virtually all subsequent discussions of these questions.
6 Hoshino Eiki 星野英紀, 'Junrei to seichi' 巡礼と聖地, in Kanaoka Shūyū 金岡秀友 and Yanagawa Keichi 柳川啓一, eds., *Bukkyō bunka jiten* 仏教文化事典 (Kōsensha, 1989), p. 731.
7 Tsukada Yoshio 塚田芳雄, *Nihon zenkoku sanjū sankasho hachijūhakkasho shūran* 日本全国三十三所八十八所集覧 (private publication, 1981).

pilgrimage to the seven gods of good fortune. Furthermore, there are countless other pilgrimages centred on one holy site, such as those to sacred mountains like Ontake 御岳 or Ishizuchisan 石鎚山, performed by religious con-fraternities (*kō* 講) whose focus of attention is the veneration of these sites and their deities, and to holy centres specific to particular religious groups, such as organised pilgrimages to the head temples (*daihonzan* 大本山) of specific Buddhist sects, a practice widely encouraged in the Jōdo Shin 浄土真 and Sōtō Zen 曹洞禅 sects, and to the headquarters or sacred centres of new religious movements, a practice widely followed in, amongst others, Tenrikyō 天理教 and Sōka Gakkai 創価学会.

Of all these pilgrimages, probably the most widely known in Japan, and certainly the most atmospheric, and the one I shall focus my attention on here, is the route that circles the island of Shikoku, taking the pilgrim on a journey of some 900 miles and a circuit of 88 temples.[8] This pilgrimage, focusing as it does on the holy wandering folk Buddhist saint Kōbō Daishi 弘法大師, who is believed to travel with all pilgrims, watching over them, helping them to attain their wishes and showing them a path to salvation, has become something of a cult in its own right.[9] Although the various temples along the way have, as their main images of worship, one of the many Buddhas and Bodhisattvas venerated in Japan, they also all have a Daishidō 大師堂 or hall of veneration to Kōbō Daishi, which for many pilgrims serves as their primary focus of worship at the sites. Many pilgrims become so involved in the Daishi cult that they perform the pilgrimage many times; indeed, some I have interviewed have performed it more than one hundred times, spending several months a year on the road and making the pilgrimage the centre of their lives.[10]

8 For pilgrims who follow standard pilgrimage customs, the number is actually ninety, for it is normal to return to the temple one started at, to give thanks for a safe completion, and to visit the mausoleum of Kōbō Daishi at Kōyasan 高野山 to pay homage there.

9 Although Kōbō Daishi is the posthumous name of Kūkai 空海, the Buddhist monk and founder of the Shingon 真言 sect in Japan, he has, as Kōbō Daishi, become the focus of numerous folkloric legends and tales of miracles (largely recounted under the rubric of *Kōbō densetsu* 弘法伝説) and, as such, has transcended both sectarian (i.e. Shingon) and Buddhist bounds to become a genuine Japanese folk religious hero. Because he thus has many of the attributes accorded to saints (e.g. the transcendence of worldly death and the performance of miracles) I use the term 'saint' to refer to him, a point I have discussed further in 'Pilgrim, miracle worker and wandering saint: Kōbō Daishi in Japanese popular lore', paper delivered at the Folklore Society conference on 'Saintlore and popular religion', Glasgow, April 1992.

10 I have discussed at some length the issue of professional and cultic pilgrims in *Sendatsu and the development of contemporary Japanese pilgrimage: spiritual guides,*

The Shikoku pilgrimage, like the large majority of Japanese pilgrimages, is voluntary in that, unlike the Muslim pilgrimage to Mecca which is a cardinal obligation of faith for all who profess to be Muslims, no one is obliged to perform it. This voluntary nature is further expressed in the manner in which the pilgrims travel. While the Meccan pilgrimage has a fixed and obligatory ritual format once the pilgrims have arrived within the holy precincts of the pilgrimage area, Shikoku pilgrims are constrained by no such rules. There are no pre-ordained routes or rituals that must be followed: each pilgrim determines his or her own manner of travel, forms of behaviour and styles of prayer and action at the sites. Most nowadays go by bus or car, taking a few days to do the route, but some continue to walk and perform austerities; others still break the route up into convenient sections and do these as and when they have time, and may take a number of years to visit all the sites. The important factor and basic attitude of all those I have spoken to (whether pilgrims or temple priests) is that one should complete the route and visit all the sites in the manner most relevant to the individual's abilities and needs.

If participation and action are thus, as with so much of Japanese religious behaviour, largely self-determined, fluid and even casual, this does not mean that Japanese pilgrimages are devoid of intense spiritual meaning. In a pattern familiar to many other pilgrimages in which the physical journey may symbolise a spiritual movement from one state of being to another, the Shikoku pilgrimage is suffused with the symbols of a spiritual journey to enlightenment and with signs and signals of rebirth and salvation. In performing the pilgrimage the pilgrim, according to popularly held beliefs, walks in the footsteps of Kōbō Daishi and metaphorically follows his journey to enlightenment and salvation.

This symbolism is transposed onto the geographical and political landscape of Shikoku, with the four prefectures of Shikoku through which the pilgrimage passes (Tokushima, Kōchi, Ehime and Kagawa, formerly the four han 藩 of Awa, Tosa, Iyo and Sanuki) serving as metaphors for four stages on the path to ultimate enlightenment. In this symbolism Awa stands for *hosshin* 発心 (awakening of the Buddha mind), Tosa for *shugyō* 修行 (the practice of the austerities required to attain awareness), Iyo for *bodai* 菩提 (opening of enlightenment) and Sanuki for *nehan* 涅槃 (full, absolute enlightenment). This symbolism that sets the pilgrim apart from the everyday world and on a journey to the other is further affirmed through the traditional clothing and accoutrements worn and carried by pilgrims, all of which signify that the pilgrim is dead to the mundane world. The white pilgrim's shirt

narrators of miracles, travel agents and professional pilgrims, Nissan Occasional Papers 17 (Oxford: Nissan Institute, 1993)

(*hakui* 白衣), which is tied in the manner normally only used for the clothing of the dead, symbolises a burial shroud; its colour also stands for purity and denotes that the pilgrim is untouched by the impurities of the everyday world for the duration of the pilgrimage. Other elements of the pilgrim's garb, such as the bamboo hat (*kasa* 笠) upon which a funeral inscription has been written, and which symbolises the pilgrim's coffin, and the *tsue* 杖 or pilgrim's staff, which represents the pilgrim's gravestone, further underline the images of death that surround the pilgrimage. In this imagery of death there is also a latent sign of rebirth, for returning from the pilgrimage (and hence from the symbolic realms of death) represents a sense of renewal and rebirth that is vitally important to pilgrims.

If the images of death and the symbolic preparedness for death that the pilgrims carry with them appear stark, they are tempered by the protective aid of the saint. The *hakui* and other accoutrements also bear the ideograms *dōgyō ninin* 同行二人 (two people, one practice) to denote that Kōbō Daishi is symbolically travelling with each pilgrim, while the staff is considered to represent the body of Kōbō Daishi and the saint's immanent presence. Consequently the pilgrim is never alone but always in the company of the saint, and always protected by him.

Through these images and symbols of separation, rebirth and salvation the pilgrimage has come to be regarded not just as a metaphorical journey to enlightenment but as a practical means of ensuring salvation after death and of rebirth in the Pure Land. Many pilgrims perform the route as a memorial (*kuyō* 供養) for their deceased kin to enable them to attain peace after death; others still do it because of the popular belief that a completed *nōkyōchō* 納経帳, the book pilgrims carry with them and in which each temple stamps its seal to signify that the pilgrim has worshipped at the site, serves as a passport to the Pure Land. The custom of placing the completed *nōkyōchō* in the casket at death for this purpose is followed by many pilgrims..[11]

However, while these aspects of pilgrimage are important on a symbolic level to most pilgrims, it would be inaccurate to interpret pilgrimage only within this framework of metaphorical journeys to enlightenment and of spiritual salvation in life or after death. Pilgrims, as Morinis has remarked in his study of Hindu pilgrimage, have a marked tendency to juxtapose such

11 This is a popular belief common in pilgrimage lore: Maeda Takashi 前田卓, *Junrei no shakaigaku* 巡礼の社会学 (Kyoto: Minerva, 1971), p. 56. I have encountered it not only among the pilgrims I have met, but also among my Japanese friends, one of whom informed me that his father-in-law, at death, was placed in his casket dressed as if on a pilgrimage to another land, in full pilgrim's regalia with a *nōkyōchō* at his side to serve as his passport to the next world.

aspirations to salvation and spiritual experiences with quite worldly and material, here-and-now wishes and requests for benefits.[12] Similar themes are found elsewhere among pilgrims; 'Umar al-Naqar comments, in his study of pilgrims to Mecca, that besides any salvationist and spiritually rewarding dimensions that it might contain, Muslims believe that the pilgrimage provides an opportune setting for seeking personal gain, for asking Allah for the fulfilment of ambitions while on the pilgrimage is believed to be extremely efficacious.[13]

Very similar themes can be seen in the attitudes of Japanese pilgrims in Shikoku, where pilgrims, even while clad in the clothing and symbols of enlightenment and salvation, seek earthly and pragmatic wishes and help from the holy figure they venerate during their pilgrimages. Praying for various forms of here-and-now benefits (*genze riyaku*), which is one of the major (if least widely analysed) themes within Japanese religion, is a practice wholeheartedly endorsed by Shikoku pilgrims. The vast majority of pilgrims whom I have met or travelled with have frequently prayed at the sites or have requested temple priests to perform prayer services on their behalf, during which they have expressed a litany of requests, ranging from general safety in travel and in the home for all members, to individual requests for business success or the success of offspring or grandchildren in their examinations, and directed them to Kōbō Daishi and the various Buddhas and Bodhisattvas enshrined at the sites.

Most pilgrims carry with them slips of paper known as *osamefuda* 納札, which bear an image of, and invocation to, Kōbō Daishi, as well as space for the pilgrims to write in their names and their requests to Kōbō Daishi; usually, also they have one or more standard prayers or requests such as *kanai anzen* 家内安全 (family safety and welfare) printed on them. The *osamefuda* are used as a form of name card and are handed to fellow pilgrims met along the way and to those who proffer them alms, and also, perhaps more commonly still, as a means of communicating the pilgrim's presence to the various entities enshrined at the sites. As such they are are deposited in special boxes set out for the purpose at each pilgrimage site, as a gesture of veneration and as a means of transmitting the pilgrims' requests to Kōbō Daishi and the Buddhas.

The requests made are multiple, covering the whole range of requests and needs that the Japanese people feel it is legitimate to seek from their figures of worship. In February 1991 I was able to sort through and investigate

12 Morinis, *Pilgrimage in the Hindu tradition*, pp. 249–55.
13 'Umar al-Naqar, *The pilgrimage tradition in West Africa* (Khartoum: Khartoum University Press, 1972), p. 135.

over 3,000 *osamefuda* left during the previous four months at one of the Shikoku pilgrimage temples, Gokurakuji 極楽寺, near Tokushima.[14] Many of them did not have specific requests written in by hand by the pilgrims, probably because all *osamefuda* have, as I have indicated, some standard prayer requests for commonly sought benefits already printed on them. Nevertheless, many pilgrims see fit or are sufficiently motivated to write particular wishes, sometimes even reiterating the ones already printed on them, and, of the 3,164 *osamefuda* I examined, just under 20 per cent, 569 in all, had specific requests inscribed on them. Breaking these down into a number of general categories, these were as follows (listed in order of numbers):

Good health	179
For the ancestors	92
Family safety/welfare	70
Healing of illness	58
Travel safety	47
Help in studying/success in education	47
Finding a spouse/having children	27
Business prosperity	15
Good luck/attainment of wishes	15
Memorials for dead babies	11
Prevention of danger	8
Others (various uncategorisable requests)	(12)
Total	569

These requests show a particular and prevalent concern for help and benefits in this world, *genze riyaku*, such as safety, protection, good health, worldly success in business and education, and for the veneration and memorialisation of the dead (in which category I include both ancestors and *mizuko* 水子), in other words for benefits in the other world (*kōsei* 後世 or *raise* 来世 *riyaku*).

This brief survey tends to reinforce the findings of recent research into the nature of requests made by Japanese people at shrines and temples through

14 It is common practice for the temples to burn the *osamefuda* every few months. This has a dual function of symbolically sending the messages to the deities, a symbolism found also in the fire ritual known as *goma* 護摩 in Buddhist settings and *hitakisai* 火焚祭 in Shintō ones, and of clearing out the offertory boxes where they are deposited. I would like to thank Revd Aki Hiroshi 安芸博 of Gokurakuji for the kindness he showed to me, permitting me to stay at the temple, allowing me to go systematically through the *osamefuda* there, and placing a room at my disposal in the temple so that I could do this undisturbed.

the medium of votive tablets (*ema* 絵馬) and, as such, presents, I would suggest, a fairly clear statement of one cardinal dimension to Japanese religious concerns: the direct concern with direct benefits both to oneself in this world, and to one's kin in the other.[15] The consistency with which pilgrims in Shikoku seek such benefits affirms the relevance and importance of praying for amelioration of one's personal and immediate situation as a core theme and practice in Japanese religion in general.

What comes out of any such examination of pilgrims' requests is the extent to which they are personalised, either directed to the welfare of the individual who wrote the *osamefuda* or to his or her family. One could, of course, class memorial requests for the ancestors within this category as well, for in praying for the ancestors, people are in effect seeking the family prosperity and tranquillity that contented ancestors are believed to bring. Only a very few *osamefuda* sought help for someone else (usually a family member), and only one that I came across (for *sekai heiwa* 世界平和, world peace) made any broader or less personally directed request.

The seeking of benefits displays a strongly personal and individualistic motivation that transcends the underlying group dynamics of contemporary pilgrimage.[16] Even when groups of people travel together with a clear group focus, such as a family group, their motivations may vary and express highly individualised needs. Often while sorting through the Gokurakuji *osamefuda* I have come across several stapled together, all bearing either the same family name, address and date, or the title of a particular pilgrimage organisation with which all are travelling, yet with very different requests on each, with particular variations depending on the ages of the pilgrims.[17]

Despite its apparent group orientations in terms of organisation and performance, then, for Japanese pilgrims the relationship that they seek with the focus of their pilgrimage, and the results they hope to receive from it, are personal and individual. Thus the individual focus that is symbolically

15 See Reader, 'Letters to the gods: the form and meaning of *ema*', *Japanese Journal of Religious Studies* 18 (1991): 40–3; Shūkyō Shakaigaku no Kai 宗教社会学の会, eds., *Ikoma no kamigami: gendai toshi no minzoku shūkyō* 生駒の神々 現代都市の民族宗教 (Osaka: Sōgensha, 1985), pp. 58–60, 92, 126.

16 The groups pattern of pilgrimage has been especially prominent in Shikoku since the early 1950s, with the majority of pilgrims travelling in organised tour groups. Maeda's (1971) research in *Junrei no shakaigaku* suggested that over 70% of pilgrims went in large groups, while my own investigations in Shikoku over the past few years, but most recently in 1990–1, tend to suggest that this pattern persists.

17 This current discussion is only preliminary as I am in the process of analysing a further collection of *osamefuda*, after which a more detailed study of the results will be published.

expressed through the pilgrims' garments and their personal, one to one, relationship with the holy figure at the heart of the pilgrimage is further substantiated by, and reiterated through, the prayers and requests for benefits that the pilgrims make.

MIRACULOUS EVENTS AND PERSONAL EXPERIENCE

This direct, unmediated and therefore personally verified relationship with Kōbō Daishi which is untrammelled by any intervening religious forces or structures, further illustrates how the gap between the spiritual and physical worlds is narrowed through pilgrimage. This, too, is epitomised by the corpus of stories and legends of miraculous happenings (*reigen* 霊験), spiritual cures and incidents of salvation from imminent danger that have developed around the pilgrimage and that, in the eyes of the pilgrims, act as examples of the intervention and manifestation of the spiritual realm in the present, material world.

Miraculous events are closely associated with pilgrimage, and although not absolutely necessary for the development or continuation of pilgrimages, they have generally played a vital role in promoting the cults of devotion at the heart of many pilgrimages, in firing the enthusiasm of pilgrims and encouraging them to set out for distant sites in pursuit of the miraculous, and in offering them the hope of a direct and personally meaningful experience.[18] Much the same is true of Japanese pilgrimages such as Shikoku, around which large numbers of tales faithfully reported by pilgrims and then often embellished and dramatised through oral traditions, have grown up. Many have been published over the centuries, ranging from the earliest published collection of Shikoku miracle tales told by seventeenth-century pilgrims and

18 The relationship between miracles (and the *rumours* of miracles) and the development of pilgrimage sites has been widely discussed in the general and comparative literature on pilgrimage. Good examples of this material are Ronald Finucane's *Miracles and pilgrims: popular beliefs in medieval England* (London: J. M. Dent, 1977), a study of medieval English pilgrimage centres which shows how the reporting of miracle stories helped create a growth in the numbers of pilgrims visiting such sites; Benedicta Ward's *Miracles and the medieval mind: theory, record and event 1000–1215* (London: Scholar Press, 1982), a comprehensive study of the idea of miracles in medieval Europe which details the close relationship existing between them and pilgrimage centres (pp. 110–26); and Candace Slater's analysis of pilgrimage culture in Brazil through the medium of miracle tales, in *Trail of miracles: stories from a pilgrimage in northeast Brazil* (Berkeley: University of California Press, 1986).

276

recorded by the ascetic Shinnen 真念 in his *Shikoku henro kudokuki* 四国遍路功徳記 of 1689, through the various pilgrims' diaries and accounts of pilgrimage that record miracle stories heard along the way, such as the numerous stories told Nishibata by pilgrims and temple priests, to more recent collections such as the *Shikoku hachijūhakkasho reigenki* 四国八十八ケ所霊験記録, which contains 30 contemporary tales of pilgrimage experience framed by a sense of the miraculous and the *Nihon junreikishūsei*, which contains 84 contemporary miracle stories. In all of these collections and narrations, there are stories of Kōbō Daishi intervening to cure illness or acting in ways that contain a special significance for the pilgrim.[19]

To give a flavour of the types of event experienced by pilgrims as interpreted through the lens of the miraculous, I shall report two such stories. The first mentioned here was narrated to me in December 1990 by an ardent pilgrim in his eighties named Tsujita Shōyū 辻田昌祐. His story started with being brought up in a family which was devoted to the worship of Kōbō Daishi and told of how his blind great-grandfather had gained his sight by fasting and praying to Kōbō Daishi for 21 days. Tsujita recounts that, in 1937, he had fallen seriously ill and was at death's door with beriberi, kidney disease and tuberculosis, having been told by his doctors that they could do no more for him. According to Tsujita, he was lying in his room, his life ebbing away, when Kōbō Daishi in the guise of a wandering priest appeared before him to cure him miraculously and to encourage him to go off on pilgrimage to Shikoku. In gratitude Tsujita did so, walking the pilgrimage and, along the way, encountering Kōbō Daishi again. These experiences have framed the rest of his life, for since then, he believes fervently, Kōbō Daishi has guided his life, every moment of which has been lived in a special, personal relationship with the saint. As a result, too, he has performed the pilgrimage a number of times and has led parties of pilgrims, inspiring them with his tales of miracles and the benefits bestowed by Kōbō Daishi.[20]

For Tsujita the miracle (as he regards it) served as a point of departure, and his pilgrimages are acts of faith in gratitude for the benefits he has

19 For the text of *Shikoku henro kudokuki*, see Iyoshi Dankai 伊予史談会, ed., *Shikoku henro kishū* 四国遍路記集 (Matsuyama: Ehimeken Kyōka Tosho, 1981), pp. 209–32; Nishibata Sakae 西端さかえ, *Shikoku hachijūhachifudasho henroki* 四国八十八札所遍路記 (Daihōrinkaku, 1964); Shikoku Hachijūhakkasho Reijōkai 四国八十八ケ所霊場会, ed., *Shikoku hachijūhakkasho reigenki* (Sakaide:1984); Kōbō Daishi Kūkai kankōkai 弘法大師空海刊行会, eds, *Nihon junrei kishūsei* 日本巡礼記集成 (Takamatsu: 1985).

20 A short account of Tsujita's experiences is given in *Nihon junrei kishūsei*, pp. 218–20.

received. For others, miraculous happenings have occurred not as sources of inspiration that set them on the road to Shikoku, but as incidents that happened because they were already there. One story of this ilk is told by Ogasawara Umaichi 小笠原馬市 in the aforementioned *Shikoku hachijūhakkasho reigenki*. The story is interesting because it shows that miracles can be discerned, by the pilgrims, within the modern world and that they need not be inseparable from the machine age. According to his story Ogasawara was on his fourth pilgrimage around Shikoku, riding his motorbike and wearing the pilgrim's bamboo hat and white shroud, when, going round a bend by a precipice on a narrow mountain road, he met and was struck by a bus. He flew off down the steep precipice, bouncing three times before his body was stopped from falling further to what he felt would have been certain death, by the lone pine tree that clung to the hillside. In an instant Ogasawara realised, or decided, that his salvation was due to the benevolent intervention of Kōbō Daishi; that one lone tree was a manifestation of Kōbō Daishi's grace, placed there to save him. Such, indeed, was his gratitude that as he scrambled back unscathed up the bank, he even thanked the rather startled bus driver and passengers and expressed his gratitude to the bus for being the catalyst that enabled him to realise experientially that Kōbō Daishi was indeed with every pilgrim. This experience has also served to strengthen and intensify his devotion to the pilgrimage and its holy figure.[21]

These two stories show how the events that occur to pilgrims assume, through the lens of interpretation that they utilise, a special significance, appearing as miracles and as personal messages from Kōbō Daishi. It is not my intention here to become involved in an analysis of the nature or indeed the very existence of miracles. Clearly, what are reported as miracles by the faithful can be discussed from very different perspectives by sceptics; Ogasawara's view that the tree has been placed there for a purpose and that, therefore, a miracle had occurred, could be seen, by another person, as a case of striking good fortune and pure chance. What lies behind his interpretation is the mind-set of the pilgrim predisposed, by faith and by the symbolism of the pilgrim's clothing, to view events from a perspective that assumes that the psychic will influence the material (a point that is also, of course, emphasised in perhaps less dramatic form by the prayers for benefits cited above).

Not all miracles as they are so viewed by pilgrims need be of such a life-saving dimension: for many pilgrims, their pilgrimages and relationship with Kōbō Daishi are highlighted by smaller, less dramatic events that are pregnant with meaning for them alone. For example, one meets numerous pilgrims who talk of minor aches and pains that have disappeared because of

---

21 *Shikoku hachijūhakkasho reigenki*, pp. 89–95.

their pilgrimage. A good example that illustrates the ways in which seemingly ordinary events may, through the ambience of a pilgrimage and from the pilgrim's mind-set that accompanies it, be transformed into something with spiritual significance, is shown in a story narrated by the priest Shimizutani Kōshō 清水谷孝尚 in one of the many volumes he has written on the history and nature of pilgrimage in Japan. Shimizutani recounts how Honma Kōichirō 本間康一郎, the editor of the well-known Buddhist magazine *Daihōrin* 大法輪, had while on the Kannon pilgrimage at Chichibu dropped a tiny glass filter lens for his camera in the deep snow somewhere near one of the temples. Although finding such a small transparent object in the snow was virtually impossible, Honma had searched and, (in his words) by the grace of Kannon, had found it; Shimizutani reports this as a miraculous event, the sort of thing that happens when one has a true pilgrimage spirit.[22] Neither he nor Honma seemed to think that the finding of a lost object was a matter of chance or even a result of perseverance (even though he had had some idea of where he had dropped it and where, therefore, to look), so much as a miraculous affair intimately linked to the fact that he was on a pilgrimage.

Here one notes a distinct parallel to the experiences and attitudes of the members and followers of various of the Japanese new religious movements that have a powerful orientation towards miraculous explanations and events, and towards deities that intervene to bring about some benefit in the lives of their followers. As Winston Davis' study of miracles in Mahikari has so amply shown, miracles may be, in the eyes of the believer, small ones such as catching buses that one thought one was bound to miss, just as much as large ones such as cures for cancer.[23] This matrix, in which events are interpreted in terms of the intervention of spiritual and psychic forces and causes in the physical world, and in which such intervention is expressed as a miracle, is central not just to pilgrimage but, as the case of the new religions shows, to Japanese religion in general. It illustrates the extent to which – despite the apparently rationalising forces of scientific enquiry – Japanese religious perceptions of the external world revolve around an underlying and active relationship between the psychic and physical, and to which the material world cannot be divorced from, or treated separately from, the spiritual. Further, the notion that miracles can and do happen points to an understanding that the spiritual world cares for and is involved in the human world and that there is an accessible, direct and affirmative relationship between the two.

22 Shimizutani Kōshō, *Junrei no kokoro* 巡礼の心 (Daizō shuppan, 1986), pp. 161–2.
23 W. Davis, *Dojo: magic and exorcism in modern Japan* (Stanford: Stanford University Press, 1980), pp. 201–22.

FOUNDERS AND FIGURES OF POWER: NAITŌ KINPŌ 内藤欣法 AND THE SHIGA SHINGYŌKAI 滋賀信行会

The miracles experienced by Shikoku pilgrims come about because of the pilgrim's relationship with Kōbō Daishi, who acts as a mediating agent bringing the world of the holy closer to the human domain. He is also very much a *living* saint, and as such is a transcendent figure, standing above and beyond the normal boundaries of death, even though the name Kōbō Daishi is in fact a posthumous one, bestowed on Kūkai some decades after his apparent demise. In this transcendent guise of living sainthood Kōbō Daishi exhibits many traits and strands important to the fabric of Japanese religion: the individual who, through personal asceticism and religious practice attains awakening, transcends the normal human condition and becomes a holy figure who mediates between the human and spiritual worlds, and the wanderer who moves on the margins of society and of the everyday world, gleaning from those margins the power that may be mediated to the human world to alleviate the sufferings of others. As such he has served as a role model and ideal image for those who wish to follow in his path and attain the enlightened states and powers he has. The very development of the pilgrimage, which has evolved over centuries, has its roots and inspiration in the travels and practices of ascetic practitioners who sought out sites in Shikoku connected with the life of Kūkai (Kōbō Daishi), such as his birthplace Zentsūji 善通寺, and places where he had performed austerities, such as Muroto 室戸. If such ascetics modelled themselves on the image of Kōbō Daishi as a wanderer, they also became the guides, and thus the role models, for others who followed in their footsteps, who were led by them and whose experiences of the performance of pilgrimage were thus mediated by them.[24]

This pattern, which was prominent in the earlier formation of the pilgrimage cult in the Muromachi and earlier parts of the Tokugawa, has not entirely died out. Over the centuries many such figures have not only led pilgrims to Shikoku but have established their own pilgrimage societies in their home towns or villages, through which they have promoted the veneration of Kōbō Daishi and the pilgrimage cult, and through which they have

---

24 The development of the Shikoku pilgrimage, and reference to these ascetic origins, has been described in numerous works. Probably the most comprehensive in historical terms are Kondō Yoshirō 近藤善博, *Shikoku henro kenkyū* 四国遍路研究 (Sanmii shoten, 1982), and Shinjō, *Shaji sankei*, pp. 479–92, while Gorai Shigeru 五来重, *Yugyō to junrei* 遊行と巡礼 (Kadokawa sensho, 1989), pp. 105–54, and Shinno Toshikazu 真野俊和, *Tabi no naka no shūkyō* 旅のなかの宗教 (NHK, 1980), pp. 71–83, both provide accessible if rather general accounts of the same process.

themselves often become revered figures in their own right. In the contemporary world of the Shikoku pilgrimage, too, the *sendatsu* 先達, or pilgrimage guide, who leads other pilgrims, organises pilgrimage parties and regales those he leads with stories of Kōbō Daishi's grace, remains an important figure; even if many *sendatsu* nowadays are little more than commercial agents, some still function as inspirational religious leaders and become the focus of veneration by other pilgrims.[25]

A good example of this process can be seen in the formation and activities of the Shiga Shingyōkai, a pilgrimage association based in Nagahama 長浜, Shiga prefecture.[26] Its founder, Naitō Kinpō, had been sick with tuberculosis and, despairing of a cure that medicine had failed to provide, had in 1923 aged 28, decided to go to Shikoku to seek Kōbō Daishi's grace. While walking the pilgrimage his illness disappeared, and he returned home a fervent believer in the saint and in the efficacy of the pilgrimage. This led him to walk the route several more times, either alone or with family members such as his wife, with whom he first did the pilgrimage in 1927 soon after their marriage, and, some years later, with his nine-year-old son. He also began to preach about Kōbō Daishi to those around him, gathering a small but growing number of disciples around him devoted to the cult and encouraging them to go on the pilgrimage. He also commenced the construction of a small hall of worship (Daishidō) to Kōbō Daishi in his home town of Nagahama, and this has subsequently become the headquarters of the Shiga Shingyōkai, the association that Naitō established in order to promote the worship of Kōbō Daishi and the Shikoku pilgrimage. The society has since developed branches throughout the prefecture and now has a membership of around 1,000 people.

Naitō led the association until his death in 1978, since when the tradition has been carried on by the current leader, his son Naitō Hirozō 内藤弘三. The small construction established by Naitō has grown into a small complex with two halls of worship, and several other rooms. The association remains, as it was founded, entirely a lay organisation; there are no priests, and the daily services held there are led by lay members. Members of the association

25 See my *Sendatsu and the development of contemporary Japanese pilgrimage*.
26 The information in this section is based on the following: interviews with members of the Shiga Shingyōkai, including the widow, son (Naitō Hirozō) and grandson of Naitō Kinpō, conducted at Nagahama on 16 March 1991; an interview with Revd Hatada Shoyū, assistant priest of the temple Anrakuji 安楽寺 in Shikoku (which has a close relationship with the Shiga Shingyōkai) on 2 February 1991; correspondence with Revd Hatada and with Naitō Hirozō, current head of the society; and a volume published by the organisation outlining its history and the life of Naitō Kinpō, and generously given to me by Naitō Hirozō: Shingyōkai Honbu 信行会本部, ed., *Henro* (Nagahama: 1981).

are, for the most part, by sect, members of the Ōtani 大谷 branch of the Jōdo Shin sect which is particularly strong in the region. None of the members I have talked to felt that this official religious orientation and sectarian affiliation was particularly important or relevant in comparison with what they saw as their real faith and involvement in the activities at the Daishidō. To them the difference was that the Shingyōkai, as its name implies, represented their faith (*shin* 信) and practice (*gyō* 行), while their relationship to their Jōdo Shin temple was merely 'religion' (*shūkyō* 宗教) in a social milieu that had little direct personal validity. In making what is a common Japanese distinction between official religion and personal faith, they inclined to the dynamism of the latter rather than the formalised structures of the former, a point that is of course emphasised in the importance placed on miracles and personally valid experiences.

Not only did Naitō organise parties of pilgrims to Shikoku and persuade many people to walk the pilgrimage; from being the leader and organiser of the group he seems to have become transformed into a spiritual leader giving members and followers advice on how to cure illnesses and how to lead their lives, and ultimately, after his death, into a focus of veneration in his own right. Several elderly members narrated to me stories of how Naitō-sensei, as they called him, gave advice that helped them towards a cure or a solution of their problems. One elderly man, for instance, told of how his wife was crippled by various ailments that made her hardly able to walk. On a friend's advice they went to see Naitō, who told them that she would be cured if they had faith enough. He told them to come to the Daishidō for the morning prayers each day at 6 a.m. To their protests that she could not possibly walk the three kilometres this entailed, Naitō replied that, with faith, she could and that Kōbō Daishi would guide her. Thus inspired, they began to walk this distance there and back every morning, and this led to a general recovery. In gratitude they then decided to go to Shikoku, to perform a pilgrimage there and give thanks to Kōbō Daishi. If the cure was, as the man implied, due to Kōbō Daishi's grace, it was also, as his narrative implied, closely connected with the spiritual guidance given by Naitō: it was, for instance, Naitō's ability to convince them of Kōbō Daishi's salvific powers, and hence his power to engender their faith, that persuaded them that the wife could do something they previously considered impossible. In line with the miracle narrations that have previously been discussed, the potential physical reasons for the woman's recovery, (i.e. the regimen of exercise) seemed to have been regarded as less important than the spiritual dimensions of faith and the beneficial powers of Kōbō Daishi and of their association with Naitō.

Naitō, as the founder and spiritual motivator of the Kōbō Daishi cult in Nagahama, has become, as such stories show, a figure of worship to the Shingyōkai. In the courtyard before the hall there are two statues of equal size and prominence: Kōbō Daishi and Naitō Kinpō, both depicted as pilgrims. In both halls of worship at the Daishidō, Naitō's photograph occupies a prominent position on the altar, in the newer one being so large as to virtually obscure its main image of worship, Dainichi Nyorai (the chief image of the Shingon sect of Buddhism most closely associated with Kōbō Daishi), to whom the hall is dedicated. Kōbō Daishi by contrast seems almost marginal.

Just as Kōbō Daishi is a figure who is closer to human beings, and hence is that much more accessible than, say, Dainichi Nyorai or other Buddhas, so, too, is Naitō, who was personally known to most of the older members, and whose influence led them and subsequent members towards faith in Kōbō Daishi, even closer and more accessible still. As one might also expect from such a Japanese religious cult, a concomitant element in its development has been its hereditary nature. Naitō's son Hirozō, who first walked the pilgrimage with his father as a young boy in the 1930s, is the current head of the association, while the continuation of the dynasty seems assured in that Hirozō's son, who is the head of the young people's section of the Shingyōkai, is scheduled to be the next leader.

One can discern a familiar Japanese religious pattern here, in which the founders of religious movements (although they may be intended to venerate someone or something else) themselves become objects of worship. The veneration of, and faith in the powers of, founders (*kyōso shinkō* 教祖信仰, *kyōso sūhai* 崇拝), which can be linked to the basic Japanese tendency to venerate ancestors (founders are, of course, within the framework of the cults they establish, exalted ancestors), is most commonly seen nowadays in the new religions. Many of the new religions base their claims to truth on the experiences of founders who have, through a process of vision and revelation brought about or reinforced by ascetic practice, opened up paths to new truths and new deities. Yet, as these religions have developed, it is generally the founders, rather than the revelatory deities themselves, that have assumed centrality and become the objects of worship, displacing, as it were, the very figures whose truths they extolled. Visitors to Tenri, for instance, or those reading Tenrikyō writings, are liable to come away with the impression that Nakayama Miki 中山ミキ, rather than God the Parent, is the major focus of worship, and the source of Tenrikyō's spiritual power. Much the same is true of the sects of established Buddhism, all of which place great emphasis, both canonically and in terms of rituals, statues and halls of worship, on their founders. Again, as with the new religions, an outsider might be forgiven for

283

wondering whether it is Shinran 親鸞 (whose statues and halls of worship are often more prominent than those of Amida) in the Jōdo Shin sects, Nichiren 日蓮 in the Nichiren sects, or Kūkai (Kōbō Daishi) in Shingon, who is the main focus of veneration, rather than the official main images of these sects.

None of these entirely displaces the official and theoretical main images of worship: just as Tenrikyō members do offer thanks to God the Parent and Jōdo Shin followers pray to Amida, so do members of the Shingyōkai continue to pray to Kōbō Daishi and Dainichi Nyorai. Nevertheless, each has secured a focal place in the religions they have founded. This is partially because of the Japanese predilection for ancestors and powerful charismatic figures, but also because of a very basic tendency of Japanese popular religion, to move the centre of veneration ever closer to the human world both in space and time.

The importance of Naitō Kinpō in Nagahama, which has grown out of the Shikoku pilgrimage and the Kōbō Daishi cult, shows precisely this tendency towards proximation (i.e. moving the focus of worship closer to the realms of human experience, and making it more concrete). Just as the figure of Kōbō Daishi, the venerated ancestor of Shingon and intercessory miracle worker and folk hero, was more realisable than spiritual entities such as Dainichi, for the ascetics who first opened up the Shikoku route and for the ordinary people amongst whom they preached his cult, so it would appear that later charismatic figures who have preached his cult have also, being closer to the human realm even than he, partially displaced him and usurped some of his powers. Certainly the prominent mementoes and statues of Naitō at the Shingyōkai headquarters in Nagahama, and the stories that his followers tell about him, illustrate the extent to which the cult's members find it easier and more culturally amenable to concentrate on a religious figure who is comparatively close in time and space to themselves.

CONCLUDING REMARKS

I have pointed, in this paper, to a number of themes common to the Shikoku pilgrimage and to Japanese religion in general. Amongst these are the entreaties for personal graces and benefits that are significant to people in their present life, the memorialisation of the ancestors, the continuing validity of miraculous events which speak directly to the individual, and the importance of powerful religious figures who act as guides for others and who, because of their inherent proximity, along with the benefits they appear to give to those around them, may become objects of veneration in their own right. Yet, interwoven within these themes is the strong underpinning of spiritual salvation, and of the potentiality of the pilgrimage – and hence, one would suggest, of folk and popular religion – to offer a path to spiritual liberation. This theme is not just found in such metaphorical respects as the four-stage journey to enlightenment or the symbolically ascetic meanings of death to the mundane, and of regeneration and rebirth, shown in the pilgrims' clothing. While it is true there are many pilgrims – probably, indeed, the vast majority – for whom these metaphors are a lot less important than the more direct issues of ancestral memorialisation and this-worldly benefits, and for whom these symbols and clothes are little more than a convenient and conventional form to assume while doing the pilgrimage, there are others who find, in the pilgrimage, a very clear and real pathway to liberation and salvation, and indeed, to a form of religious inspiration and leadership in their own right.

All these common themes in the Japanese religious context suggest that, above and beyond any religious divisions marked by different traditions and doctrines, there exists a common core of practice, behaviour and popular faith. This is much the same point as was made by Carmen Blacker in her seminal study of shamanistic practices in Japan, in which she demonstrated how these formed a coherent unity that cut across any specific religious (e.g. Buddhist, Shintō, new religions) boundaries. In the context of her studies of shamanism she wrote:

> The area in which our investigation will take place makes nonsense of that conventional distinction hitherto observed by most western writers on Japanese religion, the separation of Shinto from Buddhism. Shinto, with its liturgies, rituals and myths, has been usually treated in isolated purity, unadulterated by Buddhist elements. The Buddhist sects have likewise been described according to doctrines respectably based on scriptures with their proper place in the Buddhist canon. The large area of religious practice common to the two, in which the worshipper is scarcely aware whether the deity he is addressing is a Shinto kami or a bodhisattva, has been either ignored or relegated to various snail patches with pejorative labels such as superstition, syncretism or magic.[27]

27 Carmen Blacker, *The catalpa bow: a study of shamanistic practices in Japan* (London: George Allen and Unwin, 1975), p. 33.

In the years since those words were written many welcome advances have appeared in the study of Japanese religions in the West, and such narrow modes of definition have been largely set aside in favour of more inclusive approaches. What Blacker said then, and what others have tried to emphasise since, is that, despite all the specific religions and their doctrines and philosophies that exist in Japan, it is those areas of common religious practice (the snail patches, as it were) that are the most vital, alive and dynamic elements within the Japanese religious tradition, and that it is these that have to be studied, instead of being condescendingly written off as superstitions unworthy of consideration. Blacker's treatment of shamanism and its concomitant elements, such as asceticism, views of the spirits of the dead and of spirit possession and exorcism, showed that shamanism could be viewed as a religious tradition in its own right, cutting across formal traditions yet manifesting and providing a clear picture of the common ground of Japanese religion.

The study of Japanese pilgrimage, I would suggest, indicates something similar. The pilgrimage is a cult or religion in its own right, displaying many of the attributes – for instance, focuses of worship; a particular set of religious rituals, signs and symbols; avenues for the expression of personal prayers, requests and wishes; the potential for salvation or enlightenment; an arena for religious practice on a number of levels from the ascetic to the devotional; and a corpus of myths, legends and miracle stories that formulate a structure of underlying assumptions and beliefs that in turn generate faith and devotion and indicate a religious world view in which the influence of the spiritual domain in the physical world is powerfully affirmed – that are normally ascribed to religions. All are intrinsic themes in Japanese religion, as also are the charismatic religious figures who, being close at hand, provide accessible and alternative focuses of worship, and provide fresh stimulus for the formation of new cults that, in turn, add to the continuing vitality of the religious tradition. Thus, to return to the comments of Sumption and Morinis cited at the beginning of this paper, whatever Japanese pilgrimage may have to say about pilgrimage in universal terms (and it certainly does have much to say here as well), it can also be seen as a specifically Japanese religious phenomenon, presenting not only an excellent lens through which to view and study Japanese religion, but also a detailed picture image of Japanese religion at every stage of its own complicated development.

13

The sacred power of wrapping

Joy Hendry

> si je dis que là-bas la politesse est une religion, je fais entendre qu'il
> y a en elle quelque-chose de sacré, l'expression doit être dévoyée de
> façon a suggérer que la religion n'est la-bas qu'une politesse, ou
> mieux encore, que la religion a été remplacée par la politesse.[1]

Barthes may have gone a little too far when he suggested that religion in
Japan had been replaced by politeness, but he was, as usual, perceptive in
noticing a connection between the two. Politeness is taken very seriously in
Japan, and aspects of etiquette are often virtually indistinguishable from
aspects of ritual which may be described as religious. This essay will attempt
to draw out the connection between politeness and religion by focusing on
one pervasive element of polite behaviour and examining the degree to which
it could be described as having sacred qualities. This endeavour has grown
out of an interest in the field of polite language, an interest which gradually
broadened into a concern with other aspects of polite behaviour, and which
eventually alighted for particular attention on an apparently highly pervasive
cultural concern, with wrapping. This includes wrapping observed in various
manifestations, the wrapping of objects, the wrapping of the body, the wrapping
of space, and, to return to my original interest, language as a form of wrapping.
Although this subject has now been examined from various points of view,
the role of wrapping in a religious context has only been touched on
tangentially.[2]

---

1 Roland Barthes, *L'empire des signes* (Paris: Flammarion, 1970), p. 88.

2 Arguments presented below about wrapping in general are not always supported
with documentary references since they have mostly been developed in more detail in
Joy Hendry, *Wrapping culture: politeness, presentation and power in Japan and
other societies* (Oxford: Clarendon Press, 1993). Further information should therefore
be sought there or in other works such as Joy Hendry, 'Sutorenja to shite no minzokushi-
gakusha – Nihon no tsutsumi bunka o megutte' ストレンジャーとしての民族誌学
者 – 日本の「包文化」をめぐって, in Yoshida Teigo 吉田禎吾 and Miyake Hitoshi
宮家準, eds., *Kosumosu to shakai* コスモスと社会 (Keiō tsūshin, 1988); 'To wrap
or not to wrap: politeness and penetration in ethnographic inquiry', *Man* (N.S) 24
(1990): 620–35; and 'Humidity, hygiene, or ritual care: some thoughts on wrapping
as a social phenomenon', in Eyal Ben-Ari, Brian Moeran and James Valentine, eds.,
Unwrapping Japan (Manchester: Manchester University Press, 1990). Sources by

The cultural form of wrapping appears very widespread in Japanese thinking, as will be shown, and parallels have been found between all the different arenas in which the notion of wrapping may be applied. Each has also been found to have a religious dimension, and this paper attempts an examination of the relationship between the religious phenomena identified and principles associated with wrapping elsewhere. This is a line of inquiry which has been greatly aided by Carmen Blacker's work, and it may, in return, make a small contribution to her study of elements of the ritual surrounding the enthronement and consecration of the Japanese emperor.[3]

Wrapping clearly has high aesthetic value in Japan, and this characteristic constitutes the substance of depictions of Japanese forms of wrapping made available to the wider world through exhibitions, and in several beautifully illustrated books which have appeared in Western languages.[4] Japanese authors who have introduced the subject, however, also often emphasise that wrapping has qualities which may be described as 'sacred' or 'spiritual'. According to Ekiguchi Kunio, for example, 'It [wrapping] plays a central role in a wide variety of spiritual and cultural aspects of Japanese life'.[5] This view is reiterated in publications about wrapping in Japanese too, as will be seen below.[6]

By turning in this paper to examine in more detail some of these sacred aspects of Japanese wrapping, I hope to shed some new light on the relationship between religion and politeness, and to see whether these religious elements of wrapping may help to explain why this particular cultural form should be so highly valued in a Japanese view. On the other hand, as this approach

---

Japanese commentators include Nukada Iwao 額田巌, *Tsutsumi* 包み (Hōsei daigaku shuppansha, 1977), and Oka Hideyuki, *How to wrap five eggs: Japanese design in traditional packaging* (Meguro Museum of Art, 1988 [reprint of Weatherhill edition]) and 'The embodiment of spirit: reflections on Japanese packaging traditions', introduction to *The art of Japanese packages*, catalogue for the Canadian tour of an exhibition of the same name (Quebec: Musée de la Civilisation, 1988).

3 Carmen Blacker, 'The *Shinza* or god-seat in the Daijōsai – throne, bed, or incubation couch?', *Japanese Journal of Religious Studies* 17.2–3 (1990): 179–97.

4 An exhibition of Japanese wrapping, many of the objects of which appear in Oka, *How to wrap five eggs*, has toured no fewer than 30 countries across three different continents. See also Oka, 'The embodiment of spirit'; Ekiguchi Kunio, *Gift wrapping: creative ideas from Japan* (Kōdansha International, 1986); and *Package design in Japan* (Köln: Taschen, 1989).

5 Ekiguchi, *Gift wrapping*, p. 6; *cf.* Oka, 'The embodiment', p. 15

6 Araki Makio 荒木真喜雄, *Tezukuri no kurashi: orikata – tsutsumu kokoro* 手作りの暮し – 折形 – 包む心 (Bunka shuppankyoku, 1978), pp. 19, 22; Nukada, *Tsutsumi*; Ogasawara Tadamune 小笠原忠統, *Zukai Ogasawararyū reihō nyūmon* 図解小笠原流礼法入門 (Chūō Bungeisha, 1985), p. 42.

provides some indication of the detail of attention paid generally to wrapping in Japan, and some interpretation of the level of communication it offers, I hope it may also make a small contribution to the rethinking of the subject of Japanese religion, the aim of the original conference to which the paper was submitted. At times, for example, it seems as if the wrapping is more important than whatever may be enclosed inside it, and I suggest that a Western inclination to uncover the perceived 'essence' of a wrapped object may be locking foreign observers of things Japanese into an ethnocentric trap. As we cast aside the wrapping in our efforts to reveal, we may be casting aside the meaning of the interaction, concealed within the wrapping rather than inside it. In the next few pages, then, we will turn to examine the wrapping itself, and try to decipher its meaning in a variety of different contexts.

THE SPIRITUAL VALUE OF WRAPPED OBJECTS

It is usual in Japan for gifts presented in a polite and formal fashion to be carefully enclosed, very often with several layers of wrapping. It is thought to be rude and inappropriate to open such a gift in front of the donor, indeed many people put the gifts they receive aside, perhaps to pass on when they themselves must make a presentation. The meaning of the exchange is clear from the outward appearance of the object, a precise indication of the occasion often even being inscribed on the outside of the package, along with the name of the donor. The value of the contents is more important than its nature, and for this reason many presentations simply take the form of bank notes, suitably wrapped, with a space for their value to be written on the outside of the packet.

Religious objects, such as amulets and talismans, known as *ofuda* お札 or *omamori* お守り, are also very often wrapped. Indeed, they may consist of little more than wrapping. They may be made of wood, wrapped in paper; or paper, wrapped in cloth; or layers of one enclosed in layers of the other so that it is sometimes hard to distinguish between the wrapping and the wrapped. They also usually carry some words, such as the name of the temple or shrine where they were purchased, the particular aspect of life they are designed to protect – road safety, good health, luck with examinations – perhaps part of a sūtra, and sometimes also the name of their owner painted in at the point of purchase.

Some such objects are even thought to lose their power if they become unwrapped.[7] In any case, they are thought to be efficacious for only a

7   Brian McVeigh, 'Gratitude, obedience and humility of heart: the cultural construction of belief in a Japanese new religion', unpub. PhD diss. (Princeton

limited period of time, after which they should be destroyed. The objects receive the power to bring benefits to human beings by being presented before the shrine or altar of the place where they are sold. The power of the divinity is thus chanelled into protection or aid in everyday life. Swanger describes *omamori* 'essentially as conduits through which sacred power ... flows'.[8] Their power thus lies less in the object itself than in ideas about its power to transmit divine assistance, the precise nature of which is depicted on the wrapping of the object.

Gifts, too, are sometimes considered to be the vehicles of spiritual power.[9] In an interesting discussion, though unfortunately unpublished, about the origins of the Japanese gift known as *omiyage* お土産, the French ethnographer Joseph Kyburz emphasised the way an exchange of gifts, a parting one and a return present from afar, could be seen as representing a magical link between people temporarily separated.[10] In pre-modern Japan, many travellers were pilgrims, very often representing a group which had saved together to send one of their members away, and the *omiyage* they brought back were also *engimono* 縁起物, carrying back to those who had stayed behind something of the religious benefits the travellers had received.

Objects presented as gifts of course always carry some form of symbolic meaning. Even if there is no relation with the spiritual world, a gift is evidently a link between two human beings, possibly also between organisations they represent, and it may well carry a very specific message. It may represent gratitude for some past favour, good wishes for the future, or a request for some fairly immediate benefit. The transfer of a gift may be thought to have the power to bring about a desired effect, but the effect will be related to its movement rather than to the object itself, and further information about its importance and meaning will very often be depicted in its packaging. The writing on the packaging is fairly explicit, but the wrapping itself may carry more subtle messages.

The choice of material for enclosing an object may be related to the nature of the object in that sometimes the contents need to be preserved, or protected from damage. Layers of careful packaging may thus serve a functional

University, 1991), pp. 151–6.

8 E. Swanger, 'A preliminary examination of the *omamori* phenomenon', *Asian Folklore Studies* 40.2 (1981): 237.

9 Marcel Mauss, *The gift* (Glencoe: Free Press, 1954).

10 'Engimono, miyage, omocha – three material manifestations of the notion of *en*', unpublished paper presented at the 5th Triennial Conference of the European Association for Japanese Studies (Durham, 1988). For part of the text, see Joseph Kyburz, 'Des liens et des choses: engimono et omocha', *L'Homme: Revue française d'anthropologie*, 117 (1991): 96–121.

purpose of this kind, and the same principle of care is also invoked in explaining that care for an object to be presented also represents care and respect for the person to receive the object. Since the word *teinei* 丁寧 has connotations both of 'care' and 'politeness', it is quite understandable that a gift with many layers of wrapping is a gift regarded as being presented in a polite and respectful way, especially if it is not particularly fragile. It is also polite to demonstrate care in the way the packaging is made, perhaps in the precision of the folds, or the intricacy of its construction.

Plain white *washi* 和紙, literally 'Japanese paper', is regarded as a particularly valued type of wrapping. This paper has also been described as having sacred connotations because of the Shintō association of white with purity. Wrapping something in white paper separates it from the dirt and pollution of the outside world, and, according to Araki Makio, purges the heart of the presenter from sin, so that no bad feeling will be transferred to the recipient.[11] When this paper is folded, the mark is indelible, so that it is clear that new paper has been used. This kind of concern Araki relates to the importance attached to the spiritual purity of human relationships in Japan, an interesting religious aspect which may be applied to even the most mundane activity.[12]

There would also seem to be sacred associations attached to the folding itself. In an explanation about the etiquette of folding paper, Ogasawara traces back the now widespread practice of *origami* 折り紙 in Japanese culture to ancient customs of creating objects to be used as *yorishiro* 依代, vehicles for making contact with the deities, and articles for purification and exorcism.[13] A remaining link with this early association is perhaps to be found in the way friends and relatives will make one thousand paper cranes to hang up as a magical force for the recovery of a sick person.

Nukada Iwao argues that the sacred value of paper in an indigenous Japanese view is related to the fact that the words for 'paper' (*kami* 紙) and for 'deity' (*kami* 神) are homophonous, although of course written differently.[14] He traces the value of folding and wrapping with paper back to the ritual role of a daughter of the emperor, known as Itsukinomiya 斎宮, a role which was practised at the Ise shrine from the Yayoi to the Kamakura periods.[15] The assiduous practice of folding, wrapping, and tying was, he reports, a means

11 Araki, *Tezukuri no kurashi*, p. 19.

12 *Ibid.*, p. 22.

13 Ogasawara, *Zukai Ogasawararyū*, p. 42.

14 Nukada, *Tsutsumi*, p. 139.

15 *Ibid..*, p. 135.

to know and understand the will of the gods.[16] For this reason, perhaps, the *omamori* need consist of little more than folded, wrapped, or tied-up paper.

Paper still features in several other parts of Shintō ritual. Before a ceremony, for example, when a priest prepares the various utensils required, he is very often seen carefully cutting and folding paper into appropriate shapes. Sacred space is marked off with rope and paper streamers, and branches of the *sakaki* 榊 shrub are decorated with paper to be offered to the altar by the participants. A ritual staff, known as a *gohei* 御弊, used to purify everything and everyone involved, is made almost entirely out of paper streamers, attached for manipulation to a stick. According to Yanagita's investigation of the development of this implement, it can also be interpreted as a *yorishiro*, a place to receive the divine, and therefore again a vehicle of spiritual power.[17]

In this respect, the *gohei* resembles the Ainu *inau*, or prayer stick, very often created from natural wood, shaved in such a way that long curls hang, like the paper streamers from the *gohei*. Again it is highly valued as a vehicle of spiritual power.[18] Wood is, of course, another substance used for enclosing precious objects, and again, a beautiful box adds a layer of politeness and formality to a presentation, even if only of foodstuffs such as cake or beanpaste. Such wood may also be examined for its own quality, sought in the colour, texture, and grain. Precious goods, like scrolls and ceramics, may be kept wrapped in cloth, and enclosed in more than one box, each stamped with the seal of their artistic creator. They are even thought to lose much of their value if the containers should be lost.

Another important traditional wrapping substance is straw, useful for its preservative qualities as well as for protection, and particularly amenable to elaboration into attractive designs.[19] Straw is also used in a religious way to mark off sacred space and objects and, indeed, as a base to create ritual objects. At the entrance to shrines, for example, there is often a huge plaited straw rope called a *shimenawa* 標縄 (or 注連縄 or 七五三縄) hanging across the archway, and thinner straw rope may be tied round bamboo branches to create a temporary altar, or around houses during a festival to mark out the area involved. Elaborate straw knots may decorate fish for ritual offerings, and objects made of straw are hung up over rivers after rice-planting as a ritual expression of the crops' need for water.

16 *Ibid.*, pp. 134–8.

17 Yanagita Kunio 柳田国男, 'Gohei' and 'Yorishiro', in Otsuka Minzokugakkai 大塚民俗学会, ed., *Nihon minzoku jiten* 日本民俗学事典 (Kōbundō, 1971), pp. 263, 789.

18 Neil Gordon Munro, *Ainu creed and cult* (Westport, Connecticut: Greenwood Press, 1962), pp. 28–9.

19 For some examples, see Oka, *How to wrap five eggs.*

It seems, then, that we can identify an association between materials used for wrapping objects and materials used to attach a sacred value to something. The form of wrapping may also be reminiscent of the use of the same material in a clearly religious context. Even if the item in question is not always regarded as sacred, there would certainly seem to be a parallel in the potential power of a form of wrapping to carry meaning about the relationship it depicts. The argument can be developed by examining other forms of wrapping outlined above, though interestingly sometimes with the same materials. Let us turn, then, to another example of the genre.

WRAPPING OF THE BODY

There are clear parallels between the wrapping of objects and the wrapping of the body in the Japanese context. Traditional Japanese garments are, first of all, literally wrapped around the body, and tied up, much in the same way that parcels are wrapped and tied up. Indeed, in a book of etiquette, explanation about tying the strings used for presents is given in the same section as explanation about tying the elaborate sashes worn with kimono.[20] Garments worn for formal occasions may also have multiple layers, each visible at the neck and cuffs, with suitably contrasting colours. The type of garment, its material, colour, design, and style, will also provide information about the occasion for which it is to be worn, and the role of its wearer on that occasion.

A particularly good example of the multiplicity of layers in the wrapping of the body is the *jūnihitoe* 十二単, literally a twelve-layered garment, although the number could go even higher than this, worn by ladies of the court during the Heian period. Nowadays, such garments are seen only in museums, or at an Imperial wedding, and the most recent example was the wedding in 1993 of Prince Hiro, the Crown Prince, when the Crown Princess was attired in precisely this way. Ordinary brides also very often wear layers of kimono, the outside layer being a very heavy, luxuriant garment in bright colours appropriate for a celebration, such as red, orange, or deep purple. A bride's head-dress is also a special feature of her attire, and depicts a type of symbolic submission to the husband.[21]

The kimono worn underneath this outer layer is more directly comparable with sacred garments, however, for a wedding may be an apparently secular

20 Ogasawara, *Zukai Ogasawararyū*, p. 7.
21 Joy Hendry, *Marriage in changing Japan* (London: Croom-Helm, 1987), p. 170.

affair.[22] The undergarment is supposed to be pure white, like the garments of pilgrims, babies, and the dead, and in all cases we can identify a parallel with the pure whiteness of *washi* as a symbol of purity or purification. The white garments also represent a *tabula rasa*, a clean slate, for a new life. The bride is supposed to put behind her all her sins and previous traits and be prepared to colour herself in the way that her husband and his family desire. The white also symbolises a bride's death to her old house and her rebirth to a new one, a classic element of a rite of passage.[23]

The pilgrim's white attire, like that of garments donned by youths carrying a portable shrine at a festival, identifies the wearer as somebody involved in a religious activity, separated from everyday life. A pilgrimage is a kind of rite of passage, too, where participants seek to break with the deficiencies of their past lives, ready to begin anew, and in this the white garment depicts the same symbolism as the wedding robe. In reference to medieval pilgrimage, Grapard writes about the experience as follows: 'the processes involved ... were complex and had to become the basis for a complete change in the pilgrim's consciousness and perspective on the universe.'[24]

Some other aspects of pilgrimage, discussed by Grapard, are useful in making comparisons between types of wrapping. There is, for example, a parallel with the white fronds of the *gohei*, and the curly wood shavings of the *inau*, for pilgrims in their white garb travel to sacred sites and return with some of the sacredness attached to them. From the point of view of others who remain behind, pilgrims bring some of the spiritual power back with them, and for this reason people salute them, make them offerings, perhaps even reach out to touch them.[25] While the pilgrim is away, removed from the

common world, he or she is also described as residing nowhere, a 'walker ...

---

22 A Japanese wedding can easily incorporate a religious element if desired, however. It is not a vital part of the proceedings, but most wedding halls in Japan offer the possibility of a Shintō ceremony, and some couples insist on holding their nuptials in a Christian church, though they may otherwise have no Christian convictions. There are even Buddhist equivalents, developed for followers of the Sōka Gakkai 創価学会 sect: see Hendry, *Marriage*, pp. 171–85.

23 *Ibid.*, p. 170; Arnold van Gennep, *Rites of passage* (London: Routledge and Kegan Paul, 1960).

24 Allan G. Grapard, 'Flying mountains and walkers of emptiness: toward a definition of sacred space in Japanese religions', *History of Religions* 20 (1982): 206.

25 *Ibid.*, p. 207; *cf.* Carmen Blacker, *The catalpa bow* (London: Allen & Unwin, 1975), p. 100.

who abides in emptiness'.[26] This is a point to which we will return.

THE WRAPPING OF SPACE

Grapard's paper is actually about sacred space, a subject which brings us into the next realm of wrapping, namely the wrapping of space. He is talking about 'sacred sites' as points of contact between a divinity and the earth. They are thus further examples of *yorishiro*, though this time more permanent and sedentary than the *gohei*. Such sites may be located at a tree, or a stone, very often marked (or 'wrapped') by a plaited straw rope, and usually enclosed within a Shintō shrine. They are like the *shintai* 神体, or divine body, kept, usually well wrapped, at the heart of the shrine, and also a point of contact with the divine.

Shrines are an excellent example of the wrapping of space, since they are generally composed of a series of layers of gradually decreasing sacred space, moving out from the *shintai* through the inner and outer buildings, down the path through the surrounding land, sometimes marked by one or more fences, out through the *torii* 鳥居 arch or arches, the number of these depending on the size of the establishment. Entry may also involve rites of purification as one approaches the central area. Inside the first *torii*, there is often a source of water to rinse one's hands and mouth; to enter the buildings, one must remove shoes, and to proceed even further into the sacred area, one must be purified by a Shintō priest who himself observes austerities of purification.

The *shimenawa* at the *torii* thus marks a point of separation of the sacred from the profane outside world, and other boundaries – gardens, stones, fences, cloth or paper wrappings – mark further layers of wrapping as one approaches the supposed point of contact with spiritual power. However, the *shintai* itself is rarely regarded as the target of the visitor to a Shintō shrine, and rites may be held, calling on the power of the deity, at various points in the spatial wrapping, typically just outside the building. Even the imperial family worships at the gate of one of the four fences of the Ise shrine.[27] In the village shrine in Kyūshū where I worked, the children's swings were located in the outer areas of the compound since it was thought the children might there benefit from the protective powers of the deity.

The Hungarian architect, Botond Bognar, noted the decentralised aspect

26 *Ibid.*, p. 206.

27 Inoue Mitsuo, *Space in Japanese architecture*, trans. Watanabe Hiroshi (New York & Tokyo: Weatherhill, 1985), pp. 43–4.

of Japanese religious edifices when he wrote:

> The Ise shrine stands as a huge symbolic object rather than a building with interior space, and as such its exterior space-organizing role increases in importance. Shrine buildings, starting with Ise, are in effect not meant to be spaces to enter, but rather remote places to approach and arrive at.[28]

Thus, although the *shintai* may be the focal point of the shrine, the sacred power is actually accessed at a suitable point in the spatial wrapping which surrounds it, and it is by observing this wrapping that the sacred site is identified. The word *kamigaki* 神垣, literally, 'god fence', is used for the fence which surrounds a shrine and also sometimes to denote the shrine itself, so that it provides an interesting form of metonymy where the wrapping is actually standing for the wrapped.[29] In the case of *shintai* enclosed within the inner sanctum of the shrine buildings, it is also interesting that the object inside the wrapping may very well be a mirror, which would, if revealed, reflect the viewer's attention back to the surrounding area.

The notion of wrapping space is by no means confined to religious areas, and various authors have discussed the layered nature of Japanese cities and houses too.[30] In the case of houses, the use of paper would again seem to be a persistent trait, so that even where glass windows have been installed, paper *shōji* 障子 may well be found inside them. A concern with the quality and grain of the wood used in house construction is another aspect of Japanese architecture which demonstrates a concern with the value of spatial wrapping. Domestic space, too, may be penetrated to different degrees and, again, various small rites are required to cross the different boundaries. 'Coming up' from the porch is the most evident, since shoes must be removed and left in the doorway, but entry to a *tatami* room, or to more intimate parts such as the kitchen or bathroom may also require further attention to footwear and general demeanour. The type and quality of interaction with members of the house will also depend on where it is carried out, and the most formal behaviour, with the most formal language and bodily wrappings, will of course be found

28 Botond Bognar, *Contemporary Japanese architecture* (New York: Van Nostrand Reinhold Company, 1985), p. 44.

29 *Nihon kokugo daijiten* 日本国語大辞典 (Shōgakkan, 1973), vol. 5, 122.

30 Bognar, *Contemporary Japanese architecture*; Maki Fumihiko 槙文彦, 'Nihon no toshi kūkan to "oku"' 日本の都市空間と「奥」, *Sekai* 世界 (December 1978): 146–62; Yoshida Tetsurō, *The Japanese house and garden*, trans. Marcus G. Sims (London: The Architectural Press, 1955).

in the most formally wrapped room.[31] This is usually the *zashiki* 座敷, marked by the presence of the *tokonoma* 床の間, which the architect Yoshida Tetsurō describes as being at the centre of 'the grouping of rooms'. This space, which Yoshida further notes has 'throughout the ages ... been honoured as the sacred place in the house', should be uncluttered, if not empty, although usually decorated with a scroll.[32] On a formal occasion, it is polite for the person being granted the highest status to be allocated the seat in front of the main post supporting the *tokonoma*, and others should be able to measure their status according to their relationship to that top position. Thus, the wrapping, again, plays a role in helping to bring about a desired effect, this time in human interaction, rather than in supplications to the divine. The formal arrangements of space offer a way for human beings to show respect for one another, just as was the case in the presentation of gifts. To receive a visitor in another part of the house would be to express something else, perhaps intimacy, in the case of allowing a guest access to family rooms, or a different sort of distance. A brief business transaction, such as the paying of an account, may for example be carried out in the front porch, a more lengthy one in the entrance hall. In front of the Buddhist altar, the space again takes on sacred qualities, and this would be the place to invoke relations with the ancestors of the home. These are remembered daily in many homes, when the first of the day's rice is offered to them, and more formally on certain days relating to the death of particular individuals. Appeals to them may also be made at any time for help and encouragement with human endeavour. This communication with the spiritual world is also made through a series of 'wrappings', the tablets which stand for the ancestors enclosed first in a box, itself enshrined in a larger altar with doors, often enclosed again in a cupboard protecting it from the outside world.

WORDS OF POWER

An approach to the spiritual world is also very often made in special language appropriate for the particular occasion, and it would seem reasonable to regard this formal language as a further example of wrapping. Special language is also used on ritual occasions of a secular nature, such as weddings or other

31 A demonstration of the different types of interaction associated with the intimate side of the house, as opposed to the formal side, is to be found in Jane M. Bachnik, 'Time, space and person in Japanese relationships', in Joy Hendry and Jonathan Webber, eds., *Interpreting Japanese society*, Journal of the Anthropological Society of Oxford, Occasional Paper No. 5 (1986), pp. 49–75.

32 Yoshida Tetsurō, *The Japanese house*, pp. 10, 98.

celebrations, and politeness in Japanese involves a whole range of special linguistic forms known as *keigo* 敬語. Uno Yoshikata 宇野義方 makes an explicit connection between language and material wrapping when he points out that the use of *keigo*, like the multiple wrapping of objects, may be seen as an expression of care and respect.[33] In using polite forms of speech, a speaker wraps up the communication in a form suitable to the occasion, and to the recipient of the information.

In the context of this so-called 'honorific' language of *keigo* we find another good example of value and power being ascribed to the forms of expression, the wrapping, rather than to the literal meaning of the words. Particularly when it is used to formalise an occasion, it is much less the content of the words spoken than their register and their style, which creates the appropriate effect. Moreover, the fixed words used in ritual are seen as an important part of bringing about a desired transformation. For some, the use of *keigo* is enough to instil in others a fear or just a willingness to comply with directives; for others its use has the power of a passport into desired company.

Keigo is not itself regarded as particularly religious, although it has been described as having magical (*miryoku* 魅力) qualities, and as being the 'essence' (*sui* 粋) of the Japanese language, but a glance at the work of Carmen Blacker soon provides a religious analogue of the way the power of words may lie rather in their form – their wrapping value – than in their content or their literal meaning. In *The catalpa bow* there is a detailed analysis of the religious or magical power of words, to 'cure sickness, overcome demons, vanquish enemies, cause rain to fall and children to be conceived'.[34] Blacker notes that the sounds themselves may have two kinds of power, first to bring about the desired effect in the world, and secondly, under certain conditions, to create power in those who recite them. Some sounds have power because of their literal meaning, but for others the power lies entirely in their form, since very few people understand their meaning. These include the *mantras* and *dhāraṇī* of esoteric Buddhism, originally written in Sanskrit, but with pronunciation now so distorted that only a scholar of the language shifts involved is likely to be able to extract any meaning.[35] The power, then, lies not in the meaning of the words but in the way they are chanted, and this also applies to the chanting of the ancient language of Shintō prayer.

33 Uno Yoshikata, *Keigo o dono yō ni kangaeru ka* 敬語をどのように考えるか (Nan'undo, 1985), pp. 118–19.
34 Bunkachō 文化庁, ed., *Kotoba shiriizu: keigo* ことばシリーズ: 敬語 (Bunkachō, 1974), p. 10; Kusakabe Enta 草壁焰太, *Keigo de haji o kakenai hon* 敬語で恥をかけない本 (Nihon bungeisha, 1983), p. 5; Blacker, *The catalpa bow*, p. 93.
35 Blacker, *The catalpa bow*, p. 95.

Another religious example which actually seems to cross rather easily into the secular world is the power attributed to words by followers of the Mahikari 真光 sect. The idea is that 'clearly articulate chanting, loud energetic greetings, and addressing others (and things) in a warm, friendly manner has a beneficial effect'.[36] All these forms of speech are referred to as *kotodama* 言霊 ('a spiritual power of words') and doses of this can apparently help alleviate family discord, educational problems, or work-related stress, as well as encouraging the growth of plants.[37]

It is not an alien idea to Japanese speakers, then, that language may have power over and above the words articulated, and the case of *keigo* is clearly comparable with the religious ideas. Apart from the examples mentioned above, the use of *keigo* also plays an important part in creating the harmonious, aesthetically pleasing atmosphere so highly valued for formal social interaction in Japan. In this aspect, it may be seen alongside the white paper and unpainted wood of a formal room, the rich silk and brocade of kimono and men's formal Japanese dress, and the intricate rules of movement which characterise the polite exchanges of ritual events.

THE POWER OF SECLUSION

It is in religious ideas, too, that we may seek an answer to the question of why wrapping should be such a valued, and indeed powerful, cultural form. In Buddhism, for example, there is a good deal of power attached to figures and images, known as *hibutsu* 秘仏, literally secret Buddhas, which are kept hidden away. These are revealed only on certain special days which, during the Tokugawa period, became lively festival occasions.[38] Some images are revealed as often as once a month, on a day associated with the particular figure; others are kept hidden for years at a time, and the power they bestow on revealment may well be related to the length of time they have been shut away. Some such figures offer tens of thousands of times the normal benefits of devotional practice when they are opened up.

In *The catalpa bow*, Carmen Blacker discusses the power associated with the ascetic practice of *komori* 籠り, or seclusion, in the darkness of a cave, in a temple or shrine, or even in a specially prepared room of one's own house.[39] She points out that the power-giving qualities of an enclosed

---

36 McVeigh, 'Gratitude', p. 133.

37 *Ibid.*

38 See P. F. Kornicki, 'Public display and changing values: early Meiji exhibitions and their precursors', *Monumenta Nipponica* 49 (1994): 174–9.

39 Blacker, *The catalpa bow*, p. 98.

vessel have much wider application, as discussed by Origuchi Shinobu 折口
信夫 in his analysis of the concept of *utsubo* うつぼ. This is a word which
has several applications, and several possible *kanji* renderings, but which,
according to Origuchi, invariably refers to the notion of being wrapped up.[40]
The idea is that the wrapping is like a sealed vessel, which encourages the
gestation of sacred power growing within it until it eventually bursts forth
into the world. As Blacker notes, this type of power is well illustrated in
Japanese stories about supernatural children, such as Momotarō, who was
born from a peach, and Kaguyahime, who emerged from a segment of
bamboo.[41] A particularly interesting aspect of *utsubo* in this context is its
basic meaning, discussed by Ouwehand, using several references to the work
of Origuchi and Yanagita, which is in his view 'the empty', in the sense of
empty wrapping into which something may be put.[42] At the same time it is
'the empty in which, invisibly and supernaturally, a divine principle resides
or can reside'.[43]

We have here the components of several ideas related to 'the point' of
wrapping. First, the wrapping itself may actually create a kind of power,
preserved especially if the wrapping is kept intact, but accessible on certain
limited occasions.[44] Secondly, there is nothing particularly strange about the
idea that the inside of the wrapping may be physically 'empty', and thirdly, it
is perfectly reasonable to suppose that there may be some kind of spiritual or
animistic content within this emptiness. Indeed, according to Japanese folklore,
this may be precisely the purpose of creating this 'empty' wrapped space.

These ideas in fact fit rather neatly with some of the examples of wrapping
we have described, such as empty paper transmitting divine intervention,
white garments creating a symbolic *tabula rasa* for the walkers in emptiness,
an uncluttered space at the centre of the house, and powerful words without
any very clear meaning. They also tally, at least at a conceptual level, with
the Shingon 真言 Buddhist idea that the abode of the Buddha is one's own
heart or mind, whose fundamental residence, according to Kūkai 空海, is
emptiness.[45] They even appear to make some sense out of the depiction of
Tōkyō by Barthes and Bognar as a city with an 'empty centre', especially

40 Origuchi Shinobu, 'Reikon no hanashi' 霊魂の話, in *Origuchi Shinobu zenshū*
(Chūō kōronsha, 1945), vol. 3, p. 267.

41 Blacker, *The catalpa bow*, p. 98.

42 Cornelius Ouwehand, *Namazue and their themes* (Leiden: E. J. Brill, 1964), pp.
122–4.

43 Ibid., p. 123.

44 *Cf.* McVeigh, 'Gratitude', pp. 156–8.

45 Grapard, 'Flying mountains', p. 208.

since the 'forbidden forest' where the emperor lives cannot help but radiate some kind of power since the land has such staggering monetary value.[46]

The emperor who lives away behind the trees has very little direct political power, but he can command a great deal of wrapping for ceremonial occasions, in terms of language and as well as of garments, and in his spatial surroundings. The emperor's power again resides not in his person, but in his social wrapping. He used to be another example of a *yorishiro*, a point of contact with the divine, which his person represented, as the *shintai* represents the deity associated with a particular shrine. Now he represents the nation and people of Japan, and the economic power they have achieved was reflected in the sumptuous ceremonial wrapping of the occasion of the funeral of the emperor Shōwa 昭和 in 1989, the enthronement of the present emperor in 1990, and the wedding of the crown prince in 1993.

CONCLUSION

All the ceremony surrounding the death of an emperor and the enthronement of a successor of course involves a great deal of 'tradition', passed down through the generations or of more recent origin. At the funeral of emperor Shōwa there was a delicate balance to be achieved between the religious meaning of the existing Shintō ritual and the new status of the emperor in post-war Japan. These ritual occasions thus provided some good examples of the overlap between religion and etiquette in Japanese ceremony, especially during the occasions which were attended by an international audience of a more political nature. In fact, I would argue that it is perhaps precisely because of the lack of a clear dividing line between religious and secular ritual in a Japanese view that potential problems were avoided. The same ceremony can have religious content for some, and be regarded as a purely secular occasion by others. It can even be described in religious terms in some contexts and secular terms in others. A ceremony which may well have been seen as religious by members of the Shintō establishment, and visiting religious specialists, could thus be presented to the outside world, if necessary, as purely ceremonial in a secular sense. The importance of wrapping in either case is an example of a cultural form which is not dependent on categories of classification introduced from another system of thought, which has in this

46 Augustin Berque, 'The rituals of urbanity: temporal forms and spatial forms in Japanese and French cities', unpublished paper pressented at the Japan Anthropology Workshop, Leiden (1990). See also Maki, *Nihon no toshi kūkan*, where the 'inner space-envelopment' of Japanese cities is contrasted with the 'centre-demarcation' of European cities.

case for long distinguished between the religious and the secular. This is, however, by no means a universal dichotomy, as critics of Durkheim's attempt to define 'religion' were quick to point out.[47] Japan is a good example of a place where the distinction is unclear and, indeed, unnecessary. The notion of wrapping and its power may be invoked to describe and analyse events which, from an outside point of view, fall into several categories, including religion, etiquette, and politeness.

Finally, then, to illustrate the potential such a cultural form may have for interpretation, I would like to turn to a recent publication of Carmen Blacker's about the role of the *shinza* 神座 or 'god-seat' in the Daijōsai 大嘗祭, 'the oldest and most mysterious ceremony in the ritual sequence which marks the consecration of the Japanese emperor'.[48] Of the various theories put forward to explain the unused bed-seat which forms part of the ceremony, the one which Blacker describes as 'overwhelmingly prominent' and 'extraordinarily influential' is that of Origuchi Shinobu. Origuchi used the idea discussed above of *utsubo*, attributing the power of gestation and growth to an enclosed state, to suggest that originally the emperor, who has received nascent divine power during another part of the ceremony, would have lain in this bed, 'wrapped like a cocoon in the coverlet', to allow the spiritual power to grow and mature before emerging fully empowered to take on the role of the new emperor. Although this theory has been taken up and developed by other writers, it has also been criticised, since there is apparently no evidence at all that the emperor ever did lie down on the *shinza* and wrap himself in the *ofusuma* 御衾 which lies at its side.[49]

Blacker somewhat diffidently offers an alternative explanation of the 'incubation couch' which she argues could have originally been there so that the emperor could lie down and dream, apparently a chief way of communicating with the spiritual world during pre-Buddhist times, in order to receive blessings and advice for his coming reign.[50] This explanation too suffers from a lack of evidence, given that it is not clear that the emperor ever lay down during the course of the ceremony, but a glance back at some of the wrapping material could offer a new way of looking at both of these theories.

47 Émile Durkheim, *The elementary forms of religious life* (London: Allen and Unwin, 1915), p. 47; E. E. Evans-Pritchard, *Theories of primitive religions* (Oxford: Clarendon Press, 1965), pp. 64–5.

48 Blacker, 'The *Shinza*', p. 179.

49 *Ibid.*, pp. 191, 193.

50 *Ibid.*, p. 194.

Given the importance of the wrapping, rather than the wrapped, in most cases, and the frequency of the idea of emptiness, so that significance is sought in what the wrapping represents, as much as what it is, or what it wraps, could we not see the bed and the *fusuma* cloth in a similar way? In other words, could not either of the theories, that of the power of gestation associated with an enclosed state, or that of an incubation couch for receiving a dream, stand up as an idea represented by the couch and the *fusuma*, perhaps never actually involving the person of the emperor at all?

Just as the unopened gift represents a relationship, and the *shintai* represents a deity whose power is accessed elsewhere, I suggest that the bed and its coverlet could well represent the gestation, or incubation, of the power that the emperor is receiving throughout the ceremony. The mysterious bed could thus always have been empty, like the uncluttered *tokonoma*, the destination of the pilgrims, and the heart of the Shingon believer. It is perhaps not the rite itself which has been forgotten, but an important aspect of its interpretation.

INDEX

University of Cambridge
Oriental publications published for the
Faculty of Oriental Studies

314